William W. Bennet

A Narrative of the Great Revival

which prevailed in the southern armies during the late civil war between the states

of the federal union

William W. Bennet

A Narrative of the Great Revival
which prevailed in the southern armies during the late civil war between the states of the federal union

ISBN/EAN: 9783337222406

Printed in Europe, USA, Canada, Australia, Japan

Cover: Foto ©ninafisch / pixelio.de

More available books at **www.hansebooks.com**

A NARRATIVE

OF

THE GREAT REVIVAL

WHICH PREVAILED

IN THE SOUTHERN ARMIES

DURING THE LATE CIVIL WAR BETWEEN THE STATES OF
THE FEDERAL UNION.

BY

WILLIAM W. BENNETT, D.D.,

SUPERINTENDENT OF "THE SOLDIERS' TRACT ASSOCIATION," AND CHAPLAIN IN
THE CONFEDERATE ARMY.

Pres. Randolph Macon College.

PHILADELPHIA:
CLAXTON, REMSEN & HAFFELFINGER,
Nos. 624, 626 & 628 Market Street.
1877.

Entered, according to Act of Congress, in the year 1876, by
WILLIAM W. BENNETT,
in the Office of the Librarian of Congress, at Washington.

PREFACE.

THE author of this book has but few words to write in presenting it to the public.

Twelve years have passed away since the close of our civil war. The passions of men have had time to cool, and their prejudices time to abate. We may, therefore, view the contest as we could not when we stood nearer to it.

Reared under almost directly opposite interpretations of the Federal Constitution, the people of the North and of the South fought with equal earnestness for principles regarded by each as essential to the well-being of the American people and to the perpetuity of a republican form of government.

What is to be the ultimate results of the contest cannot yet be clearly determined. But may we not hope that a country which endured four years of civil war unequalled in the history of the world, and has since endured twelve years of sectional strife, and still lives in freshness and vigor, is destined by a favoring Providence to bear the blessings of Christian civilization onward to the remotest ages, and to stand as a beacon to other peoples as they pass through those stormy periods which are bound up in the bundle of every nation's life. If such shall be the lessons of our civil war, it will not be without its value to the world.

Essentially a religious people, it was to be expected that the faith in which they had been trained should assert itself even amid the strife of arms. And it was so. To what extent the religious element prevailed among the soldiers of the North, they can best tell us who labored among them in word and doctrine. To what extent it prevailed among the soldiers of the South, the following pages tell in part, for so abundant are the records of the revival, that our book might have been twofold larger had all the material been used.

Of one thing the reader may be certain — this work is authentic. The facts of the army revival are stated by those who witnessed them. As Superintendent of one of the Tract Associations during several years of the war, and near its close as an army chaplain, the author, by correspondence and by personal labors and observation, has had ample opportunity to collect materials for his work. Besides, he has been favored with private letters from many of the most faithful and laborious chaplains and army missionaries, and from officers and private soldiers, giving their recollections of the revival in every part of the wide field of strife.

There has been no attempt to write a book on the war, but still, in following the armies and tracing the revival, the successive campaigns have been outlined so that the reader might see the conditions under which the work of grace progressed.

To thousands in the South this book will recall scenes dark and sad in many features, but over them is shed the light of hope, and from them the prayers and songs of war days and nights come floating down to mingle with the joys of the present; and if not to mingle with present joys, to give assurance that He who spread a shield over their heads in the day of battle, is still nigh at hand to guide, to cheer, and to deliver all who put their trust in Him.

To thousands in the North this book will be an enigma. That God should appear in the midst of men, to bless and save them, who, as they believe, rushed to arms without just cause, may be almost beyond belief. To all such persons we can only say, read the narrative, weigh the facts, and then make up your verdict.

RICHMOND, VA., *May*, 1877.

CONTENTS.

CHAPTER I.
Religion Among Soldiers, ... 7

CHAPTER II.
Subjects of the Revival, ... 17

CHAPTER III.
Hindrances to the Revival, ... 31

CHAPTER IV.
Helps to the Revival, ... 46

CHAPTER V.
Helps to the Revival—Colportage, ... 71

CHAPTER VI.
First Fruits—Summer and Autumn of 1861, . . 86

CHAPTER VII.
Winter of 1861–62, ... 120

CHAPTER VIII.
Spring of 1862, ... 137

CHAPTER IX.
Summer of 1862, ... 156

CHAPTER X.
Summer of 1862, ... 172

CHAPTER XI.
Summer of 1862, ... 184

CHAPTER XII.
Autumn of 1862, ... 194

CHAPTER XIII.
Autumn of 1862, ... 204

CHAPTER XIV.
Autumn of 1862, ... 222

CHAPTER XV.
Winter of 1862-63, ... 231

CHAPTER XVI.
Spring of 1863, ... 251

CHAPTER XVII.
Spring of 1863, ... 265

CHAPTER XVIII.
Spring of 1863, ... 285

CHAPTER XIX.
Summer of 1863, ... 308

CHAPTER XX.
Autumn of 1863, ... 321

CHAPTER XXI.
Winter of 1863-64, ... 343

CHAPTER XXII.
Spring of 1864, ... 363

CHAPTER XXIII.
Summer of 1864, ... 380

CHAPTER XXIV.
Autumn and Winter of 1864-65, ... 401

CHAPTER XXV.
Last Days — Spring of 1865, ... 415

THE GREAT REVIVAL.

CHAPTER I.

RELIGION AMONG SOLDIERS.

The late American war has no parallel in history.

When we consider the area of the contest, its gigantic proportions, the number of men under arms, the magazines of warlike stores, the sieges, the marches, the battles, the enthusiasm of the people, the discipline and valor of the soldiers, the wretchedness and desolation which followed the contending hosts,—we may in vain search the annals of the world for the record of a struggle approaching it in all the dreadful elements of war.

The American may now add to his boasts, that his country claims pre-eminence in the greatest of all national calamities—a civil war.

We have read, but now we know by experience, that war, more than all things else, reveals the angel and the demon in man.

Our composite race evinced on both sides in the struggle the special traits of its near and remote ancestors. The good and bad were strangely mingled. So it has ever been in wars, especially in wars between people of the same race. Ours gave a powerful emphasis to this sad truth.

Sincere piety, brazen wickedness; pure public virtue, sordid baseness; lofty patriotism, despicable time-serving; consecration to a sacred cause and shameless abandonment of principle, appeared in every section of the country

To the people of the Old World the war must have been a subject of interest and wonder.

The rapid transformation of peaceful citizens into excellent soldiers must have created among them surprise, if not alarm; the ingenuity and skill displayed in the preparation of war material revealed a progress in this direction which they hardly dreamed that we had made; the steady valor of many battlefields assured them that the American veteran of twenty months was not inferior to the European veteran of twenty years.

The atrocities of the war must have shaken their faith in the sincerity of a people who subscribed the code of nations, and professed to regard the Bible as a revelation from Heaven. On the other hand, the patient endurance of hardships, toil, and all manner of privation by a people whom they had been educated to look upon as voluptuous, tyrannical, and effeminate, by reason of their peculiar institutions, must have filled them with astonishment, if not with admiration. The leading public journal of the world thus described the impression made on the European mind by the attitude of the Southern people:

"The people of the Confederate States have made themselves famous. If the renown of brilliant courage, stern devotion to a cause, and military achievements almost without a parallel, can compensate men for the toil and privations of the hour, then the countrymen of Lee and Jackson may be consoled amid their sufferings. From all parts of Europe, from their enemies as well as from their friends, from those who condemn their acts as well as those who sympathize with them, comes the tribute of admiration.

"When the history of this war is written the admiration will doubtless become deeper and stronger, for the veil which has covered the South will be drawn away, and disclose a picture of patriotism, of unanimous self-sacrifice, of wise and firm administration, which we can now only see indistinctly.

"The details of that extraordinary national effort, which has led to the repulsion and almost to the destruction of an invading force of more than half a million of men will then become known to the world; and whatever may be the fate of the new nationality, or its subsequent claims to the respect of mankind, it will assuredly begin its career with a reputation for genius and valor which the most famous nations might envy."

Such were the compliments which the South wrung from reluctant and opposing nationalities by the genius and ability she displayed in her struggle for independence.

But there is one aspect of the war, on the Southern side, which has been almost wholly overlooked by statesmen and politicians. We mean its religious aspect. Whatever may be the judgment of the world as to the principles on which the Southern people entered into the strife, it must be admitted that they brought with them into it, and carried with them through it, a deep and strong religious element. Their convictions of right in what they did were second only to their convictions of the truth of the Christian religion. Nor has the stern logic of events eradicated this conviction from the Southern mind. The cause is lost, but its principles still live, and must continue to live so long as there remains in human nature any perception and appreciation of justice, truth, and virtue.

The great moral phenomenon of the war was the influence and power of religion among the Southern soldiers. War is a dreadful trade, and the camp has always been regarded as the best appointed school of vice; the more wonderful then is it to see the richest fruits of grace growing and flourishing in such a soil.

Christianity visits and reforms every grade of human society; and some of its greatest miracles of grace are wrought upon the most wicked subjects, and in the worst localities. "The Gospel is the power of God unto salvation to every one that believeth;" and this blessed truth has been as fully tested amid the horrors of war as in the sweet days of peace. We do not usually consider how important a part military characters have borne in the history of our religion. True, it is not to be propagated by means of the sword; and yet many who have borne the sword have been its bright ornaments, and sometimes its most successful preachers.

The soldiers mentioned in the New Testament have great interest connected with their brief history, and some of them are models of faith and piety.

Among the anxious multitudes that flocked to the preaching of John the Baptist, there were soldiers who put in their question as well as others, "saying, and what shall we do?" To whom the Baptist replied, "Do violence to no man, neither accuse any falsely; and be content with your wages." Thus from the beginning did the "men of war" receive the truth.

Was it not a Centurion, a Roman captain of a hundred men, that gave that simple and beautiful illustration of his faith as he kneeled before the Saviour praying for his servant? How pure must have been his life, and how clear and strong his faith, to bring from our Lord that high commendation, "Verily, I say unto you, I have not found so great faith, no, not in Israel."

We cannot forget that amidst the darkness and horror of the crucifixion conviction seized the heart of another Roman soldier, and while the Jews derided the suffering Christ, he exclaimed, "Truly, this man was the Son of God."

It was in the house of Cornelius of the Italian band, "a devout man, that feared God with all his house, who gave much alms to the people, and prayed to God always," that the gospel message was opened to the heathen world. To this godly soldier an angel was sent to assure him that his "prayers and his alms had come up for a memorial before God." On him, his family, and his "devout soldiers," the Holy Ghost fell while Peter preached, and like as it was on the day of Pentecost, they "spake with tongues and magnified God." Thus, at the headquarters of the "Italian band" at Cæsarea was the first Church of Gentile converts established.

Centurion Julius, of "Augustus' band," under whose charge Paul was sent to Rome, was a kind-hearted, gallant soldier, if not a Christian; for he "entreated the Apostle courteously," and gave him liberty, when they touched at Sidon, "to go unto his friends and refresh himself." And when Paul and his companions were shipwrecked on the island of Malta, another soldier, "whose name was Publius," "the chief man," or governor, "received them and lodged them three days courteously." It was doubtless under a deep sense of this man's kindness that St. Paul prayed for his sick father, "and laid his hands on him and healed him."

In every age of the Church since, soldiers have been found among the most zealous and devoted followers of the Redeemer.

When Christianity was made popular by the example and patronage of Roman Emperors, of course thousands of all classes flocked to her standard; but history also shows that every rise of the pure faith in ages of superstition and ignorance, every genuine revival, has been sustained and helped forward by military men. Among the Reformers in Germany, in France, and in England, there were "devout soldiers," who wielded the sword of the Spirit as valiantly against the enemies of the Lord as they did the sword of war against the enemies of their country.

Whatever some may think of Oliver Cromwell, there is no doubt that he was a devout and earnest Christian, and that there was much sound religion among his invincible "Ironsides." He talks of experimental religion as no man could who had not felt its inward and renewing power. After a number of fruitless efforts against the Royalists, he determined to rally "men of religion" to his cause, convinced that "with a set of poor tapsters and town apprentice people" he could never overcome the forces of the King. With these "men of religion" he always conquered. They marched into battle singing psalms and shouting such watchwords as, "The Lord of Hosts!" How far their invincibility was grounded in their religion, Cromwell shall judge for us: "Truly I think he that prays and preaches best will fight best. I know nothing that will give like courage and confidence as the knowledge of God in Christ will; and I bless God to see any in this army able and willing to impart the knowledge they have for the good of others." From this unfailing source he drew the strength and wisdom so conspicuous in his own deeds. "He seldom fought without some text of Scripture to support him."

In his reverses and victories he saw the hand of God. When his cause looked gloomy he urged his soldiers "to see if any iniquity could be found in them," and to put away "the accursed thing." When victory crowned his arms, he would exclaim, "This is nothing but the hand of God." He taught his soldiers to regard themselves as the "instruments of God's glory and their country's good."

In the great revival which prevailed in England under the preaching of Whitefield, the Wesleys, and their associates, godly soldiers bore a conspicuous part. And in America, no lay preacher was more zealous and successful than Captain Thomas Webb, of the British army. Converted under the preaching of John Wesley at Bristol, England, he soon began to recommend in public the grace which had renewed his own heart. Afterwards in America he preached with great fervor, and as he always appeared before the people in his military dress, he attracted large crowds, and many of his hearers felt the power of the gospel proclaimed by this soldier of the Cross.

The name of Col. Gardiner is "like ointment poured forth." Wild and profligate in early life, he strove, after his conversion, to make some amends for his sinful career by his zeal and devotion in the cause of Christ. His full influence for good only the final day will reveal. By the highborn, and the lowly, his religious power was felt and confessed. He found the army an inviting field for Christian effort, and his earnest toil was repaid with richest fruits. One of his dying dragoons said "he should have everlasting reason to bless God on Colonel Gardiner's account, for he had been a father to him in all his interests, both temporal and spiritual."

Such he was to all the men under his command. He fought against every form of vice. "He often declared his sentiments with respect to profanity at the head of his regiment; and urged his captains and their subalterns to take the greatest care that they did not give the sanction of their example to it."

For every oath a fine was imposed, and the money used to provide comforts for the sick men. Of this plan he says: "I have reformed six or seven field officers of swearing. I dine with them, and have entered them into a voluntary contract to pay a shilling to the poor for every oath; and it is wonderful to observe the effect it has had already. One of them told me this day at dinner that it had really such an influence upon him, that being at cards last night, when another officer fell a swearing, he was not able to hear it, but rose up and left the company. So, you see, restraints at first arising from a low principle, may improve into something better."

The renown of Havelock is immortal. But not as a warrior only is he remembered. The odor of his piety and the fruits of his faith will survive the imposing monuments raised in memory of his devotion and valor. He was a brilliant light in the midst of thick darkness. His life was great in deeds of piety; his death was glorious. On a litter, in a soldier's little tent, the stricken warrior lay. "He would allow of no attendance but that of his wounded, gallant boy. On this, the last day of his life, General Outram came to see him. The two friends had often faced death together, and passed through trying scenes side by side, and a warm affection had sprung up between them. Outram approached the side of the dying hero and inquired how he was. Havelock replied that he never should be any better, "but," he added, "for more than forty years I have so ruled my life that when death came I might face it without fear. I am not in the least afraid. I die happy and contented; to die is gain." Finding himself rapidly failing, he left messages for his wife and children far away on the Rhine, and "then told his son to come and see how a Christian could die." "He sleeps on the field of his fame, and his lonely tomb, beneath the tropical grove, is hung round with unfading laurels, and never will the Christian traveller or soldier pass it without dropping one tear to him who sleeps beneath."

Hedley Vicars was an excellent Christian soldier. In the midst of the dangers attending the hard service in the Crimea he was as peaceful and happy as if reposing quietly with his friends at home. In one of his letters from Sebastopol he says to his sister: "It is six months since I have been in reach of a house of prayer, or have had an opportunity of receiving the sacrament; yet never have I enjoyed more frequent or precious communion with my Saviour than I have found in the trenches, or in the tent. When, I should like to know, could we find the Saviour more precious than when the bullets are falling around like hail?" Again he writes: "I have often heard it said, 'the worse man, the better soldier.' Facts contradict this untruth. Were I ever, as the leader of a forlorn hope, allowed to select my men, it would most certainly be from among the soldiers of Christ, for who should fight so fearlessly and bravely as those to whom death presents no after terrors?"

"You should be braver than the rest of us," said some of his brother officers to Dabney Carr Harrison, one of the heroes of the South in the late war, after witnessing some exhibition of his serene fearlessness in danger. "Why so?" said he, pleasantly. "Because," said they, "you have everything settled for eternity. You have nothing to fear after death." "Well, gentlemen," he said, solemnly, after a moment's pause, "you are right. Everything is settled for eternity; and I have nothing to fear."

General Joseph Warren, the first eminent sacrifice in the Revolutionary war, spent two full hours in prayer the night before the battle of Bunker Hill. "When he rose from his knees, there was no anxiety on his face; all was peace and joyful trust in God. He gave a few simple directions, took a cup of coffee and a light breakfast, and left for the lines on Bunker Hill, where his life was given up, as he had prayed, a cheerful sacrifice for his country."

The bravery of Christian soldiers in battle has been well attested. Some rigid, irreligious disciplinarians are often annoyed by the zeal of godly men in an army, but great commanders like Cromwell and Washington know how to turn this zeal to good account.

An officer once complained to General Andrew Jackson that some soldiers were making a noise in their tent. "What are they doing?" asked the General. "They are praying now, but they have been singing," was the reply. "And is that a crime?" the General demanded. "The articles of war order punishment for any unusual noise," was the reply. "God forbid that prayer should be an unusual noise in my camp," said Jackson, and advised the officer to join the praying band.

In a desperate battle a pious cavalryman had his horse killed under him by a cannon ball. "Where is your God now?" exclaimed an ungodly officer near him. He replied, "Sir, he is here with me, and he will bring me out of this battle." The next moment the officer's head was taken off by a cannon ball. Faith in God gives true courage. A line of battle was formed, and waiting for the word to move on. "I stepped out of the line," says a Christian soldier, "and threw myself on the ground, and prayed that God would deliver me from all fear and enable me to behave as a Christian and good soldier. Glory be to God, he heard my cry and took away all my fear. I came into the ranks again, and had both peace and joy in the Holy Ghost." Another, as he marched to battle, exclaimed, in the fullness of hope, "I am going to rest in the bosom of Jesus!" When the day closed he was in heaven.

Such honor God puts upon his faithful servants, even amidst the sins of the camp and the horrors of the battle-field. In the Southern armies the moral miracles were as great as ever appeared among armed men since the dawn of Christianity. And among the sad memories of our struggle, the recollection of the great and blessed work of grace that swept through all military grades, from the General to the drummer-boy, is "the silver lining" to the dark and heavy cloud of war that shook its terrors on our land.

CHAPTER II.

SUBJECTS OF THE REVIVAL.

THERE is a strongly marked difference between armies of invasion and armies of defence. The former are often mere bands of butchers following at the heels of some ambitious leader. But when men fight for country, kindred, and home, they bear a moral character that lifts them above mercenary motives.

Soldiers may fight bravely for glory, or for gain. We should not underrate the valor of the men that bore the standards of Alexander, Cæsar, and Napoleon, to so many victories; but take from such soldiers the *esprit du corps*, and you have left no pure and high inspiration which makes it "sweet to die for one's country."

In our war the Northern people fought, as they declared, to maintain the Union as it came from the hands of the fathers; the Southern people fought for the right of self-government. The war was brought to our doors, and was waged against us with the most determined and relentless spirit. Our people were thoroughly aroused, and rushed into the army from all ranks of society. They bore with them the convictions, thoughts, and habits they had been accustomed to in peaceful life. They were citizen soldiers; and though they shook off to some extent, in the early part of the war, the influences of education and religion; yet, when dangers thickened, and disease and death thinned their ranks, these returned upon them with increasing power.

The feelings of true patriotism lie next to the higher sentiments of religion in the heart, and the man that cheerfully bears the yoke for the sake of his oppressed country will not stubbornly refuse to bear the yoke of

Christ. Therefore, the patriotic fervor which prevailed among the Southern soldiers superinduced a state of mind highly favorable to the work of religion.

In most nations the privates of an army are "raked up from the lowest tier of human society." Their officers look upon them as so much bone and muscle, to be wrought, by iron discipline, into a huge engine of destruction called an army.

If war is a necessary evil, why should we strip those who engage in it of the common attributes of humanity? Soldiers are more than "food for cannon." They have like passions with other men, and may be reached by the same means that have been proved to be efficient in the salvation of other men.

Never were these divinely appointed means more fully tested than during the late civil war; and surely never were they found more effectual in turning men "from darkness to light, and from the power of Satan unto God." In the midst of all the privations and horrors of war "the grace of God appeared" unto thousands and tens of thousands in the camp and in the hospital, "teaching them that, denying ungodliness and worldly lusts, they should live soberly, righteously, and godly in this present world." The subjects of this revival were found among all classes in the army. Generals in high command, and officers of all lower grades, as well as private soldiers, bowed before the Lord of Hosts, and with deep penitence and earnest prayer sought the pardon of sins through the atoning blood of Christ.

Speaking of those who obeyed the call of mercy in the ranks of the army, a writer in the midst of the war exclaims: "We cannot express our feelings while we think of them. Glorious fruits of the grace of God are these men that have been 'born again' on fields of blood. They left their homes for battle with a desperate foe— they entered into associations and upon scenes, by universal consent, the most unfavorable to piety; but the ever-blessed Saviour went with them; listening to ten thousand fervent prayers, he revived his work and made the *still, small voice* to be heard amid the thunder of war. It is a sublime expression of mercy."

In contemplating such a revival, we naturally look at its subjects with deep interest. Who were they? What were they? What characteristics did those men present, who were lions in the day of battle, and yet wept and beat their breasts in great sorrow when they thought of their sins?

Is there not something peculiar in these men who are converted while they stand guard, or lie in their rifle-pits, or sit by their camp-fires, through the dismal, rainy nights? These men that walk their beats filled with the love of God, and shout his praises in the thunder of battle?

We have already referred to the patriotic fervor that pervaded the Southern armies. In addition to this, our camps were blessed from the outbreak of the strife with moral and religious men who never forgot their obligations to God. The army had in it every class of believers, from the bishop to the neophyte. Preachers, students of divinity, Sunday-school teachers and scholars, elders, deacons, vestrymen, class-leaders, stewards, exhorters—men from all the official grades of all the denominations of Christians took up arms and swelled the ranks of the army.

Some of these, alas! cast away the "pearl of great price," others suffered its lustre to be dimmed, but the majority kept it bright and untarnished throughout the dreadful ordeal. The influence of such men in the worst of armies would be powerful for good; how great it must have been among such soldiers as marched under the Southern banner! It has been well observed that "no Christian soldier can pass through a campaign, and exemplify the Christian tempers and qualities looked for in a follower of Christ, without dropping seeds of saving grace into some minds and hearts that will culminate in everlasting life."

The irreligious men who were blessed with these godly examples were not strangers to their pious comrades. They were often from the same town, county, or district, and at home had felt the same religious power that was brought to bear upon them in the army. The gospel preached in the camp was not a new sound to them, nor were the words of prayer a strange language. It was home-like to meet for the worship of God, and not unfrequently the same minister whom they had known in their distant homes lifted up his voice among them "in the wilderness," and called them to repentance. How often were scenes like the following witnessed among the rough-looking men in "gray jackets," who crowded the "log chapels" to hear the glad tidings of salvation. Rev. Dr. Sehon, writing of his labors among the soldiers in General Lee's army, says:

"A most interesting incident occurred during the exercises of the evening:

"A request was made for a Bible for the stand. Several were ready to respond. The book was received from a tall and interesting looking young man. I noticed his large blue eyes and attractive face as he came forward and placed the holy book before me. Instantly his home rose before me. I fancied how father, mother, brothers, sisters, felt when he left, and how they thought of and prayed for him. While lining the hymn I turned to the title page of the Bible and then my eyes were filled with tears. On the blank leaves were written the parting words of love and affection of the dear ones at home, with the kind advice and earnest prayers for the safety and happiness of the owner of the book. I closed the book with feelings of most sacred character, and was far better prepared, by this simple incident, for the solemn services of the hour. In the course of the sermon, I remarked that they were now peculiarly the subjects of earnest prayer and anxious solicitude. That for them, at this very hour, prayer from many a heart and home-altar was ascending to God—that as in the volume I then held in my hand, which had been laid on the table by my unknown young friend, so each had with him a similar silent, yet painful witness of the anxiety, devotion and prayers, as pledged in these sacred gifts of their loved ones at home—that they should now pray themselves to their heavenly Father and engage earnestly in his service.

"There was a low and gentle wail which came up from that weeping crowd like the mournful sounds of the passing breeze through the lofty pines of the distant forest."

The intelligence and social position of the Confederate soldiers were higher than we usually find in large bodies of troops. The private at home was often equal, and sometimes superior in social status to the officer that led him, and did not forget the claims of good breeding after he entered the army. "I am proud to say it for Confederate soldiers," said the venerable Dr. Lovick Pierce, of Georgia, "that for a long time while travelling with hundreds and thousands of them on all the railroads used for transportation, I have heard less profane language issuing from them than I have ever heard from any promiscuous crowd of travellers in all my journeyings. It is a well-earned fame, and deserves an imperishable record. Most of them seem to belong to the gentleman stock."

Said the Rev. J. M. Atkinson: "The talent, the energy, patriotism—and now, it would seem, the piety of the country is, for the most part, to be found in the army. One of the most remarkable manifestations of this time, and of the war, is the *character* of our armies. It is unlike that of any soldiers known in history. In religious fervor, in intelligent patriotism, they resemble the best troops of the English Commonwealth, when least infected with fanatical rancor and selfish ambition. But in refinement, in urbanity, in education, in simplicity of purpose, in intelligent appreciation of the questions involved and the interests at stake, and above all, in Christian sensibility, at once kindly and fervent, catholic and deep, it is incomparably superior to the best soldiers of Cromwell's army. The reciprocal feeling which binds our armies to our people, and our people to our armies, is another peculiarity of this time and this contest. Our soldiers are not foreign mercenaries, fighting for plunder or pay; not worthless adventurers, fighting for fame or power; not religious fanatics or partisan warriors, battling for a name or a man. But their hearts are still in their homes. The cherished images of their dear parents, their wives and children, are still before them. They are fighting with resolute and tenacious power, with generous and self-sacrificing valor."

On the souls of such men the truths of the gospel rested with saving power. And even the most wicked and reckless among them were often readily impressed and easily led into the ways of virtue and religion.

"At the commencement of the war," wrote an officer, "I organized a company of cavalry. My men were taken from all grades of society; the very great majority, however, were wicked and profane. I soon found that it would require very prompt action on my part if I wished to wield a moral influence over them. I had told them from the first that I should not permit gambling in their tents, and I would require them, when off duty on the Sabbath, to observe it as the Lord's day. When we had been out but a few months, one night, after I had gone to rest, I was aroused by one of my faithful boys (poor fellow, he afterwards fell a victim to the Yankees' bullet), who informed me that a number of my men, with others from another company, were gambling in one of the tents. At once I repaired to the place and caught them in the very act. I told them with some warmth that they knew I was opposed to gambling, and that I was sorry to find so many of them doing that which I had forbidden; that I would not consent to command a set of blacklegs and blackguards; that they must look about for some other person to take charge of them, unless they would consent to burn those cards and promise me never again to engage in the game whilst members of my company. The leader, who was dealing the cards at the time, threw them down, remarking, 'We want no other captain.' The others assented. The cards were destroyed, their visitors left, and I never after caught them at cards or heard of their joining in this wicked practice."

The armies of the South were homogeneous. There were but a few thousand foreigners at any time in the Confederate ranks. Hence, there was but little of that beastliness and brutality displayed which marked the foreign mercenaries in the opposing armies. Our forces were strictly native American, of the Southern type, and while they exhibited to a mournful extent the peculiar vices of their race, they also manifested the respect and reverence of their race for all the ordinances and institutions of religion. For, whatever may be thought or said of the Southern people through ignorance or prejudice, one thing is certainly true, that their religious sentiments are deep and strong. And another thing is equally true, that among them there have been fewer departures from the great cardinal doctrines of the Scriptures than among any other people in Christendom. The four or five leading Christian denominations which occupy the South have never been seriously disturbed by any of those false theories which, among other people, have drawn away thousands from the true faith.

Itinerant venders of the various *isms* of the age have found a poor market for their wares among the people of the South. Hence, among the subjects of the army revival there was not found a strange jumble of opinions which had to be cleared from the mind before the simple truths of the gospel could have their full effect.

The heroic men on whom God shed forth his Holy Spirit so abundantly and gloriously are well described in the following extracts:

The Rev. James A. Duncan, D. D., draws this striking picture of the private soldier in the Confederate army:

"If the private soldier be a true man, there is something of moral sublimity in his conduct that attracts our highest admiration. And yet how apt some people are to forget him. There is no star on his collar, no glittering ornament on his arm; but his plain gray jacket may enclose as noble a heart as ever throbbed in a human breast, or thrilled with patriotic devotion on the day of battle. In sleepless vigilance he paces his sentinel watch during the long hours and gloom of night, while the quiet stars shed their soft light on his musket, or the storm and rain beat pitilessly down on his shivering body and weary head. Look at him in battle at his gun, begrimed with powder, weary, hungry, almost exhausted, yet the fire gleams in his fearless eye as he rams home the charge, or sights his piece at the foe. 'Forward' is the command along the line, and you can see him as he brings his musket to a charge and dashes on to the very muzzles of the death-dealing guns to win the day or die in the attempt.

"Kneel down by him, when, wounded and dying, he lies there on the field of victory while the life-blood flows from his heart. He speaks to you—but not a murmur, not a complaint escapes his lips—taking the locket from his neck and the Bible from his bosom, he tells you to give them to some dear one at home, and say that he died bravely for his country. Or, if he be not mortally wounded, accompany him to the hospital, and watch his fortitude and patience while in the hands of the surgeon. See how he suffers, and yet a General could not bear it better.

"The private soldier! His is the coarse fare, hard march, weary fight—the drudgery and the hardships are his!

"There is something as inspiriting in his cheerfulness in the camp as there is grand in his heroism on the field. Now he is a house carpenter building him a shanty, then a dirt-dauber constructing a mud chimney. Now he is a cook frying "middling" on the coals and baking bread on a piece of bark set up before the fire. Now he is washer-*man*, and has stripped off his only shirt to have it done up, that he may enjoy a clean garment. In a word, he is a wonderful creature, that PRIVATE SOLDIER —he is cook, washer-*woman*, (?) carpenter, tent-maker, wagoner, pedestrian, clerk, butcher, baker, market huckster, groom, stable-boy, blacksmith, scout, anything and everything a man can or must be in camp, and then he wins a battle and gives the glory to his officer. We like him. His rich, ringing shout, and his merry, loud laugh, make music of a manly, stirring sort. His wit is as original as it is amusing. It is amusing to hear him, as his regiment passes through a town where hundreds of well-grown exempts stand on the side-walk, 'Fall in, boys! now is your time—ain't going to fight soon?' Or to hear the mock sympathy with which he exclaims, 'Boys, ain't you almost big enough yet? Never mind, if you ain't but *twenty-five* years old, come along with big brother, he will take care of you.' On seeing a fellow dressed up in fine clothes, he cries out, 'Come out of them clothes; I see you, conscript; tain't worth while abiding in them clothes.' Another will exclaim, 'Here's your musket; I brought it 'specially' for you; beautiful thing to tote; just fit your shoulder!'

"He moves our sympathies perhaps yet more while we look at him alone in his tent, or by the camp-fire, holding in his hand the letter from home. We cannot decipher the sacred contents, but we are at no loss to know its effect upon the soldier as he folds up the precious letter which the hand of affection has traced with words of love, fond remembrance, and anxious hopes, and brushes away the tear that has unbidden come in testimony of the memories that have been awakened."

And the following from the pen of Rev. R. H. Rivers, D. D., is not less eloquent and truthful:

"The model Confederate soldier is a patriot. He loves his country with a deep and all-absorbing passion. He sees its broad acres desolated, its towns and cities sacked and burned, its noble women insulted and exiled, its venerable men driven from happy homes to pine in penury, its priests torn down from their pulpits and altars to languish in criminals' cells, its churches desecrated, and the very graves of his sires disturbed.

* * * * * * * * * * *

"Yes, the Confederate soldier is a patriot; it is for this he wields the sword and shoulders the musket; it is for this he surrenders home, bids adieu to all its hallowed associations, and undergoes the hardships of the camp, the fatigues of the march, the privations of the soldier, and the perils of battle.

"He is brave. He marches without fear to the brink of death. The booming of cannon, the shrill sound of rifle and musketry, the clash of arms, the smoke of battle, the groans of the wounded, and the fallen corpses of the dead, inspire him with no terror. Brave, but not reckless, he would stand, if need be, in the very front of the battle, facing danger and braving death. Such is true courage, and it is possessed in all its plenitude by the model soldier.

"He is obedient to his superiors. Obedience is a high duty of the soldier. Accustomed almost from infancy to command, and altogether unused to much of the hard and servile labor which devolves upon him in the army, he feels that it is a high virtue now to obey. Disobedience would be ruinous to the cause; insubordination must bring defeat to our arms, and subjugation or extermination. This he sees, and however hard the labor, however humiliating the work, however severe the task, however perilous the undertaking, he goes forward doing his duty, obeying orders, and exerting an influence as extensive as our armies and as potent, though quiet as 'Heaven's first law.' A private in the ranks—his name unheralded, and his deeds, his noble deeds, unsung—he exerts an influence, by his cheerful obedience, as gentle as the dews of heaven, as pure as the alembic from which they are distilled, and as fragrant as the flowers on which they fall."

These are portraits from friendly hands. Let us look at two others drawn by those who were then ranked among our enemies.

The first is a picture by a Federal soldier of the "Pennsylvania Reserves," who since the war has published a book entitled, "Our Boys." He is describing the conversations that often took place between the Northern and Southern soldiers during a brief armistice:

"In one of those conversations that the soldiers of both armies so frequently took with the Potomac rolling between them, the following occurred:

"May we ask," inquired the Federal soldier, "to what regiment you belong?"

"Thirteenth Virginia Cavalry."

"You are one of its officers?"

"Yes; I am Captain of Company C. My name is Andrew L. Pitzer."

"To repeat all the conversation that followed would be a task indeed. The war was talked of—the soldier's life was discussed. Jokes were perpetrated freely; but one little circumstance occurred during the conversation which made an impression on my mind that time can never efface. It was as follows:

"One of our boys held up a pack of cards, and called out:

"Do you know what this is?"

"Several other rebels had by this time joined the officer, who acted as spokesman, and continued to carry on the conversation.

"I cannot see what it is at this distance,' he replied.

"I'll tell you," said the owner.

"What?"

"The history of the *Four Kings*," was the significant reply.

"Oh! yes—that's—yes—I understand now. Cards, I believe."

"Yes."

"May I show you the history I read?" asked the rebel.

"Yes, sir, if you please."

"Placing his hand to his breast, the rebel officer drew from a side-pocket the most blessed of all books, a small Bible. Ah! what a reproach! Not that it was meant as a reproach, for it was done with the innocence and simplicity of a child; but to witness such an exhibition of surperior morals in one upon whom we looked as being a rebel—an insurgent—was truly abasing. How I should like to know whether he is yet living. Many on our side, who came to the rocky brink and conversed with him on that day of armistice, have passed away forever.

"I do not remember who the soldier was that exhibited the pack of cards to the rebel officer; but there is one thing I do remember, and that is, that he felt the reproof so sensibly, that, after standing for a moment gazing vacantly upon the cards as he held them in his hand, and listlessly twisting the corners, he threw them over the brink, and away they went sailing and fluttering as they slowly descended to the green waters many a fathom below."

The second picture is from Rev. Dr. Bellows, and was drawn by him at the Unitarian Convention which met in the city of New York in the midst of the war. He gave his views of "Southern social life," and the influences proceeding from it, thus:

"No candid mind will deny the peculiar charm of Southern young men at College, or Southern young women in society. How far race and climate, independent of servile institutions, may have produced the Southern chivalric spirit and manner, I will not here consider. But one may as well deny the small feet and hands of that people, as deny a certain inbred habit of command; a contempt of life in defence of honor or class; a talent for political life, and an easy control of inferiors. Nor is this merely an external and flashy heroism. It is real. It showed itself in Congress early, and always by the courage, eloquence, skill and success with which it controlled majorities. It showed itself in the social life of Washington, by the grace, fascination and ease, the free and charming hospitality by which it governed society. It now shows itself in England and France, by the success with which it manages the courts and the circles of literature and fashion in both countries. It shows itself in this war, in the orders and proclamations of its generals, in the messages of the rebel Congress, and the essential good breeding and humanity (contrary to a diligently encouraged public impression) with which it not seldom divides its medical stores, and gives our sick and wounded as favorable care as it is able to extend to its own. It exceeds us at this moment in the possession of ambulance corps.

"I think the war must have increased the respect felt by the North for the South. Its miraculous resources, the bravery of its troops, their patience under hardships, their unshrinking firmness in the desperate position they have assumed, the wonderful success with which they have extemporized manufactures and munitions of war, and kept themselves in relation with the world in spite of our magnificent blockade; the elasticity with which they have risen from defeat, and the courage they have shown in threatening again and again our capital, and even our interior, cannot fail to extort an unwilling admiration and respect. Well is Gen. McClellan reported to have said (privately), as he watched their obstinate fighting at Antietam, and saw them retiring in perfect order in the midst of the most frightful carnage: 'What terrible neighbors these would be! We must conquer them, or they will conquer us!'"

CHAPTER III.

HINDRANCES TO THE REVIVAL.

Our soldiers, though worthy of the eulogies we have recorded, did not escape the vices of a military life. In the first months of the strife the call of the war trumpet was heard above all other sounds. The young men rushed to the camps of instruction; and, freed from the restraints of home, and the influence of pious relatives, thousands of them gave way to the seductive influences of sin.

Legions of devils infest a camp. Vice grows in it like plants in a hot bed, and yields abundant and bitter fruits. "In the Old Testament it is said, 'One sinner destroyeth much good.' If so, what destruction of good must be effected by a large body of ungodly soldiers in close and constant contact, where one may, without extravagance, consider them as innoculating each other daily with the new infection of every debauch through which they pass."

The "strong man armed" keeps watch and ward over a camp of soldiers, and is not overcome and cast out without a tremendous struggle.

All that can hinder a work of grace confronted the revival in our army. Before the "soldiers of Christ" addressed themselves in earnest to the work, gambling, profanity, drunkenness, and other kindred vices, prevailed to an alarming extent.

The temptation to recklessness is strong among all soldiers. Religion is supposed to be well suited to the pursuits of peaceful life, but not to rough, uncertain army life.

"We are led by custom," says the celebrated Adam

Smith, "to annex the character of gaiety, levity, and sprightly freedom, as well as of some degree of dissipation, to the military profession. Yet, if we were to consider what mood or tone of temper would be most suitable to this situation, we should be apt to determine, perhaps, that the most serious and thoughtful turn of mind would best become those whose lives are continually exposed to uncommon danger, and who should, therefore, be more constantly occupied with the thoughts of death and its consequences than other men. It is this very circumstance, however, which is not improbably the occasion why the contrary turn of mind prevails so much among men of this profession. It requires so great an effort to conquer the fear of death, when we survey it with steadiness and attention, that those who are constantly exposed to it find it easier to turn away their thoughts from it altogether, to wrap themselves up in careless security and indifference, and to plunge themselves, for this purpose, into every sort of amusement and dissipation. A camp is not the element of a thoughtful or melancholy man; persons of that cast, indeed, are often abundantly determined, and are capable, by a great effort, of going on with inflexible resolution to the most unavoidable death. But to be exposed to continual, though less imminent danger, to be obliged to exert, for a long time, a degree of this effort exhausts and depresses the mind and renders it incapable of all happiness and enjoyment.

"The gay and careless, who have occasion to make no effort at all, who fairly resolve never to look before them, but to lose in continual pleasure and amusement all anxiety about their situation, more easily support such circumstances."

This is the language of a very eminent philosopher. There is truth and error in it. This effort on the part of the soldier to turn away his thoughts from death is only the more open manifestation of his former indifference to the truth. It is sad, indeed, to think that great dangers are often made the occasion and excuse for great neglect of our highest interests. The philosopher overlooks the great means of overcoming the fear of death—"Repentance towards God and faith towards our Lord Jesus Christ." This sustains the soul with the strength of God, and gives the assurance of eternal happiness.

This reckless spirit, we must admit, greatly prevailed, and was much encouraged by many who had been long in the military profession, and brought with them into our armies the vicious habits of many years of sin.

The general demoralization which spread over the country was a great barrier to the progress of the truth. War brings all evils in its train; and though founded in justice and right, and conducted on the highest principles of civilization, will leave its frightful marks on every feature of society. In the Revolutionary War good men shuddered at the evils which overspread the land.

"Ignorance of God and divine things greatly prevails. Unbelief, hardness of heart, worldly-mindedness, covetousness, hypocrisy, a loathing of the heavenly manna, almost universally prevail. Many count gain to be godliness, and the most part are seeking each one his gain from his quarter.

"There is a grievous inattention to religion and virtue among our civil rulers, which, nevertheless, are the only permanent foundation of good order in civil society; while a gospel ministry is neglected by those who ought immediately to support it.

"Whoredom, adultery, and all the lusts of the flesh, defile our country. Horrid profanation of the sacred word of God, perjury, violation of the holy Sabbath, neglect of secret and family religion, and of relative duties, pride, hatred, malice, envy, revenge, fraud, injustice, gaming, wantonness, extortion, and dissipation, have come in like a flood—and all this while we are under the chastening hand of God."

Such was the work of sin during one of the holy wars of the world.

In some sections of the South during the late war the state of morals was almost as bad—nay, we might say, fully as bad. "Many churches," writes one, "are vacant, their ministers having gone to the war. Most of our Sunday-schools are disorganized, and but few, I fear, will be revived until the war closes. Intemperance and profanity abound, and are fearfully on the increase. Religion is at the lowest ebb. Such a thing as the conversion of souls seems scarcely to enter into the mind of either clergy or laity."

Some may think this picture overdrawn, but there are thousands of living witnesses who can attest its correctness.

Among the soldiers the great, overshadowing evils were lewdness, profanity, and drunkenness; among the people at home, the "greed of gain" was the "accursed thing."

It was a melancholy fact that many men entered the army the avowed enemies of all intoxicating drinks who alas! very soon fell victims to the demon of the bottle. With many there seemed to be a conviction that the fatigue and exposure of their new mode of life could not be endured without the artificial stimulant of ardent spirits. This was a great and fatal error. The soldier does not need, even in the worst climates, and in the hardest service, his rations of rum.

Carefully collected and arranged statistics, prepared by the sanitary officers of the British Army, through a space of thirty years, establish the following facts:

"1. That the total abstinence regiments can endure more labor, more cold, more heat, more exposure, and more privations, than those who have their regular grog rations.

"2. That they are less liable to fevers, fluxes, pleurisies, colds, chills, rheumatisms, jaundice, and cholera, than other regiments.

"3. That when attacked by any of these diseases their recovery is much more certain and speedy.

"4. That they are much more readily aroused from the effects of concussions and severe wounds, and are far less liable to lockjaw, or mortifiation after wounds.

"5. That only about six in the temperance regiments die, from all causes, to ten of the other regiments."

These facts were collected from various fields of observation: Africa, Canada, Greenland, the East Indies, West Indies, and the Crimea.

Robert Southey wrote the following to a kinsman, a lieutenant in the British Army:

"General Peche, an East Indian officer here, told me that in India the officers who were looking out for preferment, and who kept lists of all above them, always marked those who drank any spirits on a morning with an X, and reckoned them for nothing. 'One day,' said he, 'when we were about to march at day-break, I and Captain —— were in my tent, and we saw a German of our regiment. So I said we'd try him; we called to him, said it was a cold morning, and asked him if he would take a glass to warm him. I got him a full beaker of brandy and water, and he drank it off. When he was gone, I said, 'Well, what do you think? we may cross him, mayn't we?' 'Oh, yes,' said he, 'cross him by all means.' And the German did not live twelve months.'"

It is related of the Duke of Wellington, that during the Peninsular war he heard that a large magazine of wine lay in his line of march. He feared more for his men from barrels of wine than from batteries of cannon, and instantly dispatched a body of troops to knock every wine-cask on the head.

General Havelock, in speaking of the forbearance of his troops after storming the city of Ghuznee in Affganistan, says: "The self-denial, mercy, and generosity of the hour were, in a great degree, to be attributed to the fact that the European soldiers had not received spirit rations for several weeks, and that they found no intoxicating liquors among the plunder of the city. Since, then, it has been proved that troops can make forced marches of forty miles, and storm a fortress in twenty-five minutes without the aid of rum, let it not henceforth be argued that distilled liquors are an indispensable portion of a soldier's ration."

The cause of Christ was hindered, and that of Satan promoted in the Southern armies by the influence and example of wicked and licentious officers and men.

One who had observed the course of intemperance in the army wrote:

"The prevalence of vice,—drunkenness and profanity in our camps—is attributable to the officers themselves. By far the larger number of the officers of our Southern army are both profane and hard drinkers, where they are not drunkards."

Another says: "There is an appalling amount of drunkenness in our army. More among the officers than the men. This evil is now on the increase."

A surgeon writing from the army says: "I was greatly astonished to find soldiers in Virginia whom I had known in Georgia as sober, discreet citizens—members of the different churches—some deacons, and official members—even preachers, in the daily and constant habit of drinking whiskey for their health."

An officer who had visited many portions of the army gave it as his opinion that with the exception of the reverse at Fort Donelson, we were defeated not by the Federals but by whiskey.

A distinguished General is said to have remarked that "if the South is overthrown, the epitaph should be '*Died of Whiskey.*'"

This was one of the giant evils. Hundreds all over the land, moved by an unholy desire for gain, engaged in the manufacture of ardent spirits. It was estimated that in one county in Virginia, and that not one of the largest, the distillers, in one year, consumed 31,000 bushels of grain, enough to furnish 600 families with food for the same period. While the commissioners, appointed by the court of that county to procure grain to feed the families of soldiers, could not purchase enough for that purpose, the smoke of fifty distilleries darkened the air; meanwhile, the cries of the poor mothers and helpless children went up in vain for bread.

The same was the case in other States. In one District in South Carolina 150 distilleries were in operation. A gentleman in North Carolina said he could count from one hill-top the smoke of 14 distilleries. One of the Richmond papers declared that a single distiller in that city made at one period of the war a profit of $4,000 a day.

In Augusta county, Va., it was estimated that 50,000 bushels of grain were consumed monthly by the distilleries in operation there.

A writer on this subject estimated that in the second year of the war 1,600 barrels, or 64,000 gallons of ardent spirits, of the worst sort, were daily manufactured in the Confederate States.

Men who flourish and grow rich in such business forget the counsel of Lord Bacon, to "seek only such gains as they can get justly, use soberly, distribute cheerfully, and leave contentedly."

The temptation to drink in the army was very strong; men were cast down in spirit, away from home, wife, children, mothers and sisters, all that makes life dear. Many that ventured to drink at all under such circumstances found it hard to avoid excesses.

But this evil was not confined to the soldiers. In the councils of the General government and State governments its baleful influence was felt. And some bold, stupid men declared that "they had never heard of anything great being accomplished in war without the aid of whiskey."

Such a remark could not have been made in seriousness; it was the senseless babbling of some wretched votary of Bacchus.

The best and ablest officers of the army sought by example and by precept to suppress this vice; and the following noble language from General Bragg is a sample of the general orders issued from time to time against the evils which infested our armies:

"Commanders of all grades are earnestly called upon to suppress drunkenness by every means in their power. It is the cause of nearly every evil from which we suffer; the largest portion of our sickness and mortality results from it; our guard-houses are filled by it; officers are constantly called from their duties to form court-martials in consequence of it; inefficiency in our troops, and consequent danger to our cause, is the inevitable result. No one is benefitted but the miserable wretch who is too cowardly to defend a country he is willing to sell, by destroying those noble faculties *he* has never possessed. Gallant soldiers should scorn to yield to such temptations—and intelligent and honorable officers should set them an example. They should be encouraged to send to their families at home the pay they receive for their services, instead of wasting it in their own destruction, and at the risk of the holy cause in which they are engaged. Small as the amount is, it will cause many a dear one to rise up and call them blessed.

"'Give strong drink unto him that is ready to perish, and wine to those that be of heavy hearts,'—but for us, the glorious cause in which we are engaged should furnish all the excitement and enthusiasm necessary for our success."

When ardent spirits were offered to our great warrior Jackson, in his last illness, as a medicine, he exclaimed, "Give me pure water and milk." And among the soldiers there were many that followed the example of this great leader.

An occasional instance of moral heroism appeared amidst the wreck and ruin wrought by indulgence in strong drink:

"A little drummer-boy in one of our regiments," says an army correspondent, "who had become a great favorite with many of the officers by his unremitting good nature, happened on one occasion to be in the officers' tent, when the bane of the soldiers' life passed around. A captain handed a glass to the little fellow, but he refused it, saying, 'I am a cadet of temperance, and do not taste strong drink.' 'But you must take some now—I insist on it. You belong to our mess to-day, and cannot refuse.' Still the boy stood firm on the rock of total abstinence, and held fast to his integrity. The Captain, turning to the Major, said, 'H— is afraid to drink; and he will never make a soldier.' 'How is this?' said the Major, playfully; and then assuming another tone, added—'I command you to take a drink, and you know it is death to disobey orders.' The little hero, raising his young form to its full height, and fixing his clear blue eyes, lit up with unusual brilliancy, on the face of the officer, said, 'Sir, my father died a drunkard; and when I entered the army I promised my dear mother on my bended knees that, by the help of God, I would not taste a drop of rum, and I mean to keep my promise. I am sorry to disobey orders, sir, but I would rather suffer than disgrace my mother and break my temperance pledge.'"

This boy hero, and thousands of others, have had reason to make the following thrilling lines the expression of their abhorrence of drunkenness:

"A young lady who was in the habit of writing considerably and in stirring tones on the subject of temperance, was in her writings so full of pathos, and evinced such deep emotion of soul, that a friend accused her of being a maniac on the subject of temperance, whereupon she wrote the following:

> "Go feel what I have felt,
>   Go bear what I have borne—
> Sink 'neath a blow a father dealt,
>   And the cold world's proud scorn;
>   Then suffer on, from year to year,
>   Thy sole relief, the scalding tear.
> Go kneel as I have knelt,
>   Implore, beseech, and pray—
> Strive the besotted heart to melt,
>   The downward course to stay,
>   Be dashed with bitter curse aside,
>   Your prayers burlesqued, your tears defied.
>
> "Go weep as I have wept,
>   O'er a loved father's fall;
> See every promised blessing swept—
>   Youth's sweetness turned to gall—
>   Life's fading flowers strewed all the way
>   That brought me up to woman's day.
> Go see what I have seen,
>   Behold the strong man bow,
> With gnashing teeth, lips bathed in blood,
>   And cold and livid brow;
>   Go catch his withering glance, and see
>   There pictured his soul's misery.
>
> "Go to thy mother's side,
>   And her crushed bosom cheer;
> Thine own deep anguish hide,
>   Wipe from her cheek the bitter tear;
> Mark her worn frame and withering brow;
> The gray that streaks her dark hair now—
> With fading frame and trembling limb;
> And trace the ruin back to him,
> Whose plighted faith in early youth
> Promised eternal love and truth,
> But who, foresworn, hath yielded up,
> That promise to the cursed cup;
> That led her down through love and light,
> And all that made her prospects bright,

And chained her there, 'mid want and strife,
That lowly thing, a drunkard's wife—
And stamped on childhood's brow so mild,
That withering blight, the drunkard's child.

" Go bear, and see, and know,
　　All that my soul hath felt and known,
　Then look upon the wine-cup's glow,
　　　See if its beauty can atone—
　　　　Think if its flavor you will try:
　　　　When all proclaim, 'tis drink and die !
Tell me I HATE the bowl—
　Hate is a feeble word,
I loathe—ABHOR—my very soul
　With strong disgust is stirred
When I see, or hear, or tell,
　Of the dark BEVERAGE OF HELL !"

But the revival had other foes to fight besides the beastly devil of intemperance.

History teaches that periods of great national calamity are marked by great public demoralization. Our war gave powerful witness to this sad truth. Worldly-mindedness, a vaunting pride, relaxation of morals, self-seeking, desperate gambling, hard-heartedness, and a host of other evils flourished amidst the woes and wants and consuming sorrows of the war.

But perhaps the most prominent, and in view of the condition of the country, the most appalling evil was the eager greed of gain which fostered a wide-spread and cruel spirit of extortion.

If there ever was a time when the apostolic warning, that "the love of money is the root of all evil," received a full confirmation among any people, it was in those mournful days of the Confederacy when, in all the avenues of trade, and even close on the rear of our war-stricken, but unfaltering army, like a dreadful portent, the extortioners sat, croaking day and night their horseleech cry, Give ! Give !

All classes, all trades, all professions, and both sexes

alas! seemed infected by the foul contagion. So universal was the practice of cutting out the "pound of flesh." that whenever an exception occurred it was thought worthy of special notice in all the public prints, and was referred to in the pulpits as an instance of one, at least, in Israel who had not bowed the knee to Baal.

This cursed lust of gain, this Shylock exaction, more than all things else, embarrassed the Government, impaired public credit, depreciated the currency, caused great distress among the poorer classes, sowed the seeds of disaffection broadcast over the land, and finally broke the spirit of the people and the army.

The pitiful fallacy about the inexorable "laws of trade," which some, retaining a slight degree of sensitiveness, plead as an apology for extortion, the merest tyro in political economy would hardly think of applying to a besieged city, or a country closed by blockade against the commerce of the world.

The evils which hung like an incubus on the South, and finally, with the help of heavy Northern legions, laid her banners in the dust, and her hopes in the grave, were faithfully portrayed by many patriotic citizens who watched the progress of events.

The following extract from a discourse delivered in the city of Richmond during the war by Rev. Dr. Moore, of the Presbyterian Church, gives a dark but truthful picture of the times:

"There are evils inevitable to war from which we cannot expect to escape. We must expect to find personal ambition in the guise of patriotism; itch for office, with its horse-leech cry of "give, give;" favoritism and nepotism, by which the sons, relations and friends of those in office will be placed over the heads of better and older men, who are unable to command this kind of patronage, and must, therefore, drudge in humbler and harder positions; wastefulness in the use of public funds and the granting of public contracts; blunders in movements, both civil and military, that are hard to explain; provoking circumstances and red-tape delays in the transaction of public business; insolence and petty tyranny in men raised from obscurity, and dressed in a little brief authority, who lord it with arrogance and sometimes with cruelty over braver and better men placed under their command; heartless brutality in drunken surgeons and drunken nurses allowing sick men to pine and suffer, and even to die from sheer and inexcusable neglect; drunkenness in the ranks, as well as among the officers, preparing many a gallant man for disgrace and defeat in battle, and a drunkard's grave when the war is ended; profanity, gambling, pillage and speculation at least in small matters. All these evils are well-nigh inevitable in a time of war, with our poor fallen nature as it is, and can only be diminished by looking to that God before whom we bow this day in reverent supplication."

Sins so enormous and prevalent, spreading like dark clouds over all the land, and casting their deep shadows on our brightest hopes, aroused the faithful in all the Churches to the most earnest efforts against the rising tide of iniquity. The pulpits, and the religious and secular press, warned the people of the rocks on which the ship of State was fast drifting. In the general assemblies of all the evangelical Churches, the most decisive measures were adopted, with a view to bring about a thorough reformation among our people.

At the Bible Convention in the city of Augusta, Ga., composed of the leading ministers and laymen of the different Christian denominations, Bishop Pierce, of that State, in an able discourse, depicted the condition of public morals in the following language:

"The history of the world confirms the testimony of the Bible as to the moral dangers of accumulated treasure. Wealth is favorable to every species of wickedness. Luxury, licentiousness of manners, selfishness, indifference to the distresses of others, presumptuous confidence in our own resources—these are the accompaniments of affluence, whenever the safeguards of the Divine word, both as to the mode of increase and proper use, are disregarded. As to the higher forms of character and civilization, unless regulated and sanctified by Scripture truth and principle, *opulence* has always been one of the most active causes of individual degeneracy and of national corruption. Under the influence of its subtle poison, moral principle decays; Patriotism puts off its nobility and works for hire; Bribery corrupts the judgment-seat, and Justice is blinded by gifts; Benevolence suppresses its generous impulses, and counts its contributions by fractions; Religion, forgetting the example of its Author and the charity of its mission, pleads penury, and chafes at every opportunity for work or distribution; Covetousness devours widows' houses and grows sleek on the bread of orphans; Usury speculates on Providence and claims its premium, alike from suffering poverty and selfish extravagance; Extortion riots upon the surplus of the rich and the scrapings of the poor, enlarges its demand as necessity increases, and, amid impoverishment, want, and public distress, whets its appetite for keener rapine, and, with unsated desire, laps the last drop from its victim and remorselessly sighs for more. The world counts gain as godliness, prosperity as virtue, fraud as talent; and *money*, MONEY, MONEY, is the god of the land, with every house for a temple, every field for an altar, and every man for a worshipper. The Church, infected by popular example, adopts the maxims of men, grades the wages of her servants by the minimum standard, pays slowly and gives grudgingly, and stands guard over her treasures, as if Providence were a robber, and they who press the claims of Heaven came to cheat and steal.

"Whenever the conservative laws of accumulation and distribution, as prescribed in the Bible, are ignored, then not only does the love of money stimulate our native depravity, but the hoarded gain furnishes facilities for uncommon wickedness. The attendant evils are uniform. They have never failed in the history of the past. When commerce, manufactures, and agriculture, pour in their treasures, then, without the counteracting power of Scripture truth and Gospel grace, they infallibly breed the sins which have been, under God, the executioners of nations. Such is the suicidal influence of unsanctified wealth, that the greater the prosperity of a people the shorter the duration. The virulence of the maladies superinduced destroy suddenly, and that without remedy. Now, mark how apposite, how prophetic, how descriptive, the word of the Lord: 'They that will be rich fall into temptation and a snare, and into many foolish and hurtful lusts.' 'He that maketh haste to be rich shall not be innocent.' 'He that hasteth to be rich hath an evil eye.' How these passages rebuke the spirit of speculation, the greedy desires, the equivocal expedients, the high-pressure schemes of the people! 'Lay not up for yourselves treasures upon earth.' 'Charge them that are rich in this world, that they be not high-minded nor trust in uncertain riches.' O, ye who make, and save, and hide, and hoard, hear ye the word of the Lord: 'Your riches are corrupted, and your garments are moth eaten; your gold and silver is cankered, and the *rust* of them shall be a witness against you and shall eat your flesh as it were fire.' O, ye who strut and shine in plumage plucked from the poor and needy, 'ye have received your consolation;' 'weep and howl for the miseries that shall come upon you.'"

CHAPTER IV.

HELPS TO THE REVIVAL.

The circulation of the Word of God, and the faithful preaching of the gospel by Chaplains, and other ministers sent forth by the Churches, and the distribution of select religious literature by the hands of pious colporteurs, were the chief means of bringing about the greatest revival, in the midst of the greatest war, of modern times. There were other instrumentalities, subordinate and collateral in their relations to these, which were often successful in giving the thoughts of the soldiers a serious turn.

The loudest calls were for the Holy Scriptures, and the most earnest efforts were made to meet the demand. But owing to the stringency of the blockade, and the poor facilities in the South for printing the Bible, we were never able to put a copy into every hand that was stretched out for one. The Bible Society of the Confederate States, organized at Augusta, Ga., in March, 1862, and the State Bible Societies already in existence, labored nobly to provide for the wants of the country.

Finding that for the main supply they must rely on importations from abroad, the Confederate Bible Society directed its Corresponding Secretary, Rev. Dr. E. H. Myers, to communicate with the British and Foreign Bible Society, with the view of securing such occasional supplies as might be lucky enough to escape the dangers of the blockade and reach our ports.

Dr. Myers, after detailing the operations of the Society, said: "The proposition is simply that we be allowed a credit with your Society for the Scriptures we need—say to the value of about £1,000,—until such time as sterling exchange is reduced to about its usual cost—we paying *interest* on our purchase until the debt is liquidated."

To this letter the following noble response was sent, granting the Society three times the amount they asked, free of interest:

LONDON, 10 Earl Street Blackfriars,
October 10, 1862.

THE REV. DR. MYERS:

Dear Sir,—I beg leave to acknowledge the receipt of your letter of the 19th of August, which did not, however, reach us until the 3d of this month. The request which it contains was immediately submitted to our Committee for their consideration and decision, and, I have much pleasure in informing you that it was unanimously agreed that your request should be complied with, and that the Scriptures should be sent as directed, to Messrs. Fraser, Trenholm & Co. The only portion of your letter to which the Committee demurred was that in which you proposed that interest should be paid upon the debt until it was liquidated. We could not, for a moment, entertain such a proposition. We are only too thankful that God has in his providence put in our hands the means of supplying your wants. Into the political question which now agitates the States of America, it is not our province to enter. We hear of multitudes wounded and bleeding, and we cannot pass by on the other side, when it is in our power to do something towards staunching the wounds and to pour into them some few drops of the Balm of Gilead. May He who sitteth above the water-floods speedily command peace, and as Jesus in the days of his flesh trod the boisterous waves of the Sea of Galilee into stillness, so may he walk upon the rough waters of political strife and fierce contention, which now desolate your country, with such majesty and mercy that immediately there may be a great calm.

"You will then understand, my dear sir, that a credit has been granted by our Society to the Bible Society of the Confederate States to the amount of £3,000 free of interest, and that the books will be forwarded as directed to Messrs. Fraser, Trenholm & Co. The first order, which has already reached us, will be executed with as little delay as possible. It will be gratifying to our Committee to receive any account of the work of God within the District which your Society embraces with which you may be pleased to favor us.

I am, my dear sir,
Yours very sincerely,
CHARLES JACKSON,
Secretary.

This venerable institution gave another illustration of the principles on which it is founded by granting to Rev. Dr. Hoge, of Virginia, who went abroad during the war to procure religious reading matter for our soldiers, 10,000 Bibles, 50,000 New Testaments, and 250,000 portions of the Scriptures, "mainly for distribution among the soldiers of the Confederate Army."

With the portion of these grants that passed in to us through the blockade, the New Testaments printed within our limits, and, we are happy to say, several donations from the American Bible Society—one of 20,000 Testaments to the Baptist Sunday School Board, and others through the Bible Society of the city of Memphis—our camps were kept partially supplied with the Divine Word. We say partially, for often the distribution would be limited to a single copy of the Bible or Testament for a mess of five or six men.

So urgent was the appeal from all portions of the army for more Bibles, that the people at home were called upon to send to the various depositories all the spare copies about their houses. In this way many a precious heirloom copy of the Word went forth on its mission of mercy. One lady sent a beautiful pocket-Bible, with the following note:

"This Bible was the property of my dear son H——, who died three years ago; it was given him by his only sister, about the time he was taken sick. For this reason I have kept it back, but seeing the earnest request in the papers, and as I can no longer read its sacred pages, after dropping a tear at parting with it, I send it for the use of the soldiers. I had given away long since all I could find about the house, and now send you this, hoping that, with God's blessing, it may save some soul."

Before the fall of Nashville, arrangements had been perfected there for printing the entire Bible. The Western Publishing House of the Baptist Church issued an edition in the first year of the war, and a copy was sent to President Davis, who acknowledged it in the following terms: "The Bible is a beautiful specimen of Southern workmanship, and if I live to be inaugurated the first President of the Confederacy, on the 22d of February, my lips shall press the sacred volume which your kindness has bestowed upon me."

In all his career, as the beloved and honored President of the Confederacy, and as the victim of a long and cruel imprisonment, has this eminent Christian Statesman shown that he has been guided in his actions by the principles, and comforted in his sorrows by the promises of this blessed Book of Life.

The eager desire of our soldiers to possess the Bible is worthy of permanent record, and the war abounded with the most touching incidents illustrative of their appreciation of the holy volume.

During a skirmish some of our men were ordered to the front as sharpshooters, and directed to lie on the ground and load and fire as rapidly as possible. After a short time the ammunition of one of these men was expended, and though his position was very dangerous as it was, it would have been certain death to procure a fresh supply. "In this condition," says an eye witness, "this soldier drew from his pocket his Bible, and while the balls were whizzing about him, and cutting the grass at his side, quietly read its precious pages for a few moments, and then closed his eyes as if engaged in prayer." This was not unlike the case of the poor little collier boy, the only son of his mother, and she a widow. A mine had fallen in, and buried a number of men with this poor youth; after several days the mine was opened and the bodies recovered. By the side of the boy was found an old tin box, on which he had scratched these words: "Dear mother, don't cry. We are singing and praying to the last, and God is down here with us."

"We were present not long since," wrote an army correspondent, "when a chaplain, at the close of public service, announced that he had a prospect of being able to get a supply of Testaments for the portion of the men still destitute, and that those who wished a copy could give him their names after the benediction. Scarcely had the last words of blessing died on the minister's lips before the war-worn heroes charged on him almost as furiously as if storming the enemy's breast-works."

Another narrates the following: "As some of the Confederate troops were marching through Fredericksburg, Va., with bristling bayonets and rumbling artillery, a fair lady appeared on the steps of a dark brown mansion, her arms filled with Testaments, which, with gracious kindness and gentle courtesy, she distributed to the passing soldiers. The eagerness with which they were received, the pressing throng, the outstretched hands, the earnest thanks, the unspoken blessings upon the giver, thus dispensing the word of Life to the armed multitude, to whom death might come at any moment— all made up a picture as beautiful as any that ever shone out amid the dark relatives of war. As a rough Texan said, 'If it was not for the ladies, God bless them, there would be no use fighting this war.'"

A chaplain in the army said, that during the battle of Fredericksburg, he saw many soldiers reading their Testaments with the deepest attention while lying in the trenches awaiting orders.

Such scenes were of almost daily occurrence during the progress of the war.

The amount of ministerial labor performed in the Confederate army the final day only can reveal. Many of the best ministers of the various Churches went out as chaplains, and "endured hardness as good soldiers" for the sake of immortal souls. They were instant in season and out of season; some of them fell on the battle-fields by the bullet, and not a few in the hospitals by disease, while ministering to the spiritual wants of the men who bravely fought and died. And many still survive who bear the scars of wounds, and, what is yet more honorable and comforting, the recollection of duties well performed.

But the work became too great for the regular chaplains. A great demand arose for ministerial reinforcements. Pious officers and private soldiers earnestly appealed to the Churches to send their ablest preachers "to the help of the Lord against the mighty." That great and good man, General Jackson, in a letter to the Presbyterian General Assembly, gave the following opinion on the subject of providing adequate religious instruction for the army:

"My views are summed up in few words.

"Each branch of the Christian Church should send into the army some of its most prominent ministers who are distinguished for their piety, talents, and zeal, and such ministers should labor to produce concert of action among chaplains and Christians in the army. These ministers should give special attention to preaching to regiments which are without chaplains, and induce them to take steps to get chaplains, to let the regiments name the denominations from which they desire chaplains selected, and then to see that suitable chaplains are secured. A bad selection of a chaplain may prove a curse instead of a blessing. If the few prominent ministers thus connected with each army would cordially co-operate, I believe that glorious fruits would be the result. Denominational distinctions should be kept out of view, and not touched upon. And, as a general rule, I do not think that a chaplain who would preach denominational sermons should be in the army. His congregation is his regiment, and it is composed of various denominations. I would like to see no question asked in the army what denomination a chaplain belongs to, but let the question be, Does he preach the gospel? The neglect of the spiritual interests of the army may be seen from the fact that not one-half of my regiments have chaplains.

* * * * * * * * *

"Among the wants of the Church in the army are some ministers of such acknowledged superiority and zeal as, under God, to be the means of giving concert of action. Our chaplains, at least in the same military organization encamped in the same neighborhood, should have their meetings, and through God's blessing devise successful plans for spiritual conquests. All the other departments of the army have system, and such system exists in any other department of the service that no one of its officers can neglect his duty without diminishing the efficiency of his branch of the service. And it appears to me that when men see what attention is bestowed secularly in comparison with what is religiously, they naturally under-estimate the importance of religion. From what I have said, you may think I am despondent; but thanks to an ever kind Providence, such is not the case. I do not know when so many men, brought together without any religious test, exhibit so much religious feeling.

"The striking feature is that so much that is hopeful should exist, when so little human instrumentality has been employed for its accomplishment. In civil life, ministers have regular meetings to devise means for coöperation in advancing the interests of the Church. This can be done in the army, and I am persuaded it should be. * * * * * * * *

"Some ministers ask for leave of absence for such trivial objects, in comparison with the salvation of the soul, that I fear they give occasion to others to think that such ministers do not believe that the salvation of the soul is as important as they preach. It is the special province of the chaplains to look after the spiritual interests of the army, and I greatly desire to see them evincing a rational zeal proportional to the importance of their mission. Do not believe that I think the chaplains are the only delinquents. I do not believe, but know, that I am a great delinquent, and I design saying what I have said respecting the laxness of chaplains to apply to all of them. I would like to see each Christian denomination send one of its great lights into the army. By this arrangement I trust that if any one should have denominational feelings, that they will not be in the way of advancing a common and glorious cause."

In response to this and similar appeals, the Churches renewed their efforts on behalf of the soldiers. The army became a home mission field of the greatest fruitfulness. Evangelists, missionaries, and regular pastors whenever they could leave their charges, joined in the noble task of preaching Christ to the struggling sons of the South. The religious wants of the army, and the best methods for supplying them, were among the chief topics of discussion in all the large Church assemblies. There were but few, if any indeed, that drew back from this hard but blessed toil. When we remember, then, that no Christian Church in the South failed to do its part in the great work of army evangelization, we may form some adequate estimate of the amount of moral influence brought to bear on the soldiers by means of the preached Word. And these good men endured cheerfully all the hardships of the soldier's life. In all seasons they toiled for souls; and glorious was their reward. By thousands the men of war rushed to the standard of the Cross, and joyfully embraced the hope of salvation. He who did his work in the army faithfully found the position of an evangelist, a missionary, or a chaplain, no sinecure. There was ample work for all in this grand mission field.

Rev. Dr. Stiles, of the Presbyterian Church, one of the most eloquent and able ministers in America, who gave himself when above seventy years of age as an Evangelist to the army work with an apostolic fervor and zeal, gives us the following sketch of the work of a faithful chaplain:

"These men not only give themselves laboriously to the ordinary duties of the Christian ministry in their peculiar position, but their earnest love of Christ, and the soldiers' life prompts them to a course of extraordinary self-denying service, admirably adapted to revive and extend the interests of the Christian Church in the army.

"They form camp churches of all the Christians of every denomination in their regiments. The members are expected to practice all the duties of brotherly love, Christian watchfulness, and Christian discipline. Indeed, they are taught to feel themselves under every obligation of strict membership. The chaplain writes to every minister or church, with which the member may have been connected, or the young convert desires to be united, and, giving the name of the person, solicits the prayers of the said church, both for the individual and the whole camp church, and by correspondence keeps them apprised of the walk and history of the party.

These chaplains keep a minute record, not only of the names of the whole regiment, but of all that may assist them either to save the sinner or sanctify the believer. Some of them have ten or twelve columns opposite the names of the different companies of the regiment, so headed as to supply all that personal knowledge of the party which might be serviceable in promoting their spiritual welfare. These columns they fill up gradually with such intelligence as they may be able to obtain in their pastoral visitations—when sick, wounded, or slain; when awakened, convicted, converted—all important information is conveyed by the chaplain to the family and the church. These things must necessarily follow—the work of the faithful chaplain is most laborious; he is held in the very highest and warmest estimation by every man in the regiment, saint and sinner. He possesses a power to sanctify and save them which nothing but earnest and hard-working devotion could finally secure."

Working in harmony with these grand instrumentalities, there were other subordinate influences which are well worthy of notice.

The part borne by the noble and pious women of the South in our war is eminently worthy of permanent record. They were the angels of mercy that moved among the sick and dying and turned their thoughts to God and heaven. In the early part of the conflict, before the government had fully organized the Commissariat of the Army, their nimble fingers made up the clothing for nearly all our soldiers. All over the South, matron and maid vied with each other in these glad toils. And with clothing they sent every article that could contribute to the comfort of the troops. Their beds were stripped of blankets and quilts, their pianos of india-rubber covers, their floors of carpets, to shelter their brave defenders from the rigors of winter. Often the costliest jewelry and plate were sold to buy supplies for the army,—and nothing was deemed too valuable to be devoted to the cause which was freighted with all their hopes. Their children were given as freely as their money. A more than Spartan, a Christian heroism glowed in their hearts and brightened all their deeds. Without repining, even with cheerfulness, they bore all the hardships of the war, and amid want and woe, doubt and disaster, cheered on their husbands, sons and fathers in the path of duty.

When in the progress of the war those places of rest and refreshment for the weary and hungry soldier sprang up, the wayside hospitals, the wives and daughters of the South were their presiding geniuses. The white, smooth pillow, the clean bed, the well-swept floor, the tempting food to suit the sick soldier's appetite, were all their handy-work. They met him at the door, and often with their own hands relieved him of the heavy knapsack and the soiled white cotton haversack in which he carried his cold corn dodger and uncooked pork, and sent him to some quiet bed where he lay down thanking God for the angels that had met him in his journey.

These welcome resting-places, and the scenes that daily occurred in them, are thus described by a lady, one of the most gifted women of the South, who soothed the sorrows of many a sick and wounded soldier:

"These wayside hospitals are located, generally, at the depot of some railroad, where the sick and wounded soldier immediately as he leaves the cars, exhausted, weary and faint, finds a grateful shelter, where surgical aid, refreshments and attention, are immediately tendered him. These institutions are generally supported entirely by voluntary contributions, and refreshing and delightful is it to see the unstinted supplies coming daily in and always equalling the demand. Much faith and prayer have been put in exercise for these tarrying-places for the war-worn soldier, so that their 'bread and water' has never yet failed; nor do we believe they ever shall, while the people of a covenant-keeping God claim his exceeding great and precious promises.

"There are many cases of pathetic interest to be met with at these hospitals. One I will relate, as an incitement to early piety, and as another testimony to the power of our holy religion:

"After I had ministered to several of the wounded, I drew near the couch of one whose case was considered one of the worst there, but who appeared, since his wounds had been dressed and refreshments administered to him, much relieved. After conversing some time with him, he asked my name. I told him, and that I was the wife of the gentleman who had just been giving him his breakfast—(for he had to be fed as an infant). I told him, moreover, that the gentleman was a preacher—a Methodist preacher. 'I am a member of the Methodist Church,' said he, 'and would he be kind enough to pray for me now, for I have not heard the voice of prayer for many months.'

"After the prayer was ended, the subject of religion continued to be our theme. He said he was quite resigned to God's will concerning him, and that he was not afraid to die; and while dwelling on the goodness of God, his countenance assumed that serene and beautiful expression, indicative of peace within and joy in the Holy Ghost. Well was it for him that he had strength from on high, and that the everlasting arms of God's love were his support, for in a few hours from the time we conversed together it was found amputation of his arm would be necessary, from which he suffered excruciatingly until death came to his relief. But all the time of his mortal agony his faith remained firm and unshaken, and he pillowed his sinking head on the bosom of Jesus, and 'breathed his life out sweetly there,' while to all around, witnessing a good confession of Christ's power to save, to the uttermost, all those that put their trust in him."

Not only in these, but in the regular hospitals our women showed themselves the dearest earthly friends of the soldier. Some of the best appointed hospitals were under their charge, and the success which attended their efforts to heal the sick drew unwilling praises from those officials who regarded such work as beyond the sphere of womanly duties.

It is a pleasing task to present the reader with a view of Southern women among the sick, wounded and dying, ministering at the same time to the body and the soul. Scenes like the following were witnessed all over the South:

At Richmond, Va., there was a little model hospital known as "The Samaritan," presided over by a lady who gave it her undivided attention, and greatly endeared herself to the soldiers who were fortunate enough to be sent there. "Through my son, a young soldier of eighteen," writes a father, "I have become acquainted with this lady superintendent, whose memory will live in many hearts when our present struggle shall have ended. But for her motherly care and skillful attention, my son, and many others, must have died. One case of her attention deserves special notice: A young man, who had been previously with her, was taken sick in camp near Richmond. The surgeon being absent, he lay for two weeks in his tent without medical attention. She sent several requests to his Captain to send him to her, but he would not in the absence of the surgeon. She then hired a wagon, and went for him herself; the Captain allowed her to take him away, and he was soon convalescent. She says she feels that not their bodies only, but their souls, are committed to her charge. Thus, as soon as they are comfortably fixed in a good, clean bed, she inquires of every one if he has chosen the good part; and through her instruction and prayers several have been converted.

"Her house can easily accommodate twenty, all in one

room, which is made comfortable in winter with carpet and stove, and adorned with wreaths of evergreen paper flowers; and in summer well-ventilated, and the windows and yard filled with greenhouse plants. A library of religious books is in the room, and pictures are hung all round the walls. Attached is a dining-room for the convalescent patients, supplied by private families, except the tea and coffee, which are made in the room; and there is also a dressing-room where they keep their knapsacks, &c. The rooms are kept in order by the convalescents, who serve under her direction, and learn to love their respective duties. The sick are supplied with every thing that can make them comfortable. Morning and evening services are held, consisting of reading the Scriptures, singing and prayer; and she is her own chaplain, except when she can procure a substitute. Thus has she been engaged since April 1861, with uninterrupted health and unparalleled success, making soldiers, and mothers, and wives glad, and heaven rejoice over repenting sinners."

Here is another sketch of a soldier's friend, who labored in some of our largest hospitals:

"She is a character"—writes a soldier—"a Napoleon of her department; with the firmness and courage of Andrew, she possesses all the energy and independence of Stonewall Jackson. The officials hate her; the soldiers adore her. The former name her 'The Great Eastern,' and steer wide of her track; the latter go to her in all their wants and troubles, and know her by the name of 'Miss Sally.' She joined the army in one of the regiments from Alabama, about the time of the battle of Manassas, and never shrunk from the stern privations of the soldier's life from the moment of leaving camp to follow her wounded and sick Alabamians to the hospitals of Richmond. Her services are not confined, however, to the sick and wounded from Alabama. Every sick soldier has now a claim on her sympathy. While but yesterday, my system having succumbed to the prevailing malaria of the hospital, she came to my room, though a stranger, with my ward nurse, and in the kindest manner offered me her services, and soon after leaving returned to present me a pillow of feathers, with case as tidy as the driven snow. The very light of it was soothing to an aching brow, and I blessed her from my heart and lips as well. I must not omit to tell why 'Miss Sally' is so disliked by many of the officials. Like all women of energy, she has eyes whose penetration few things escape, and a sagacity fearful or admirable, as the case may be, to all interested. If any abuse is pending, or in progress in the hospital, she is quickly on the track, and if not abated, off 'The Great Eastern' sails to headquarters. A few days ago, one of the officials of this division sent a soldier to inform her that she must vacate her room instantly. 'Who sent you with that message to me?' she asked him, turning suddenly around. 'Dr. ———,' the soldier answered. 'Pish!' she replied, and swept on in ineffable contempt to the bedside perhaps of some sick soldier.

"She always has plenty of money to expend in her charitable enterprises, and when not attending in the wards, or at the cooking stove, dresses with care in the neatest black silk. Such a woman merits an honorable fame."

A lady, writing from the hospital at Culpeper Courthouse, says: "I have lost four of my patients. Three of them died rejoicing in Jesus. They were intelligent, noble, godly young men. One from Virginia said to me as he was dying, 'Sing me a hymn.' I repeated, 'Jesus, lover of my soul.' He remarked, 'Where else but in Jesus can a poor sinner trust?' Just as he passed away, he looked up and said, 'Heaven is so sweet to me;' and to the presence of Jesus he went.

"Another from South Carolina seemed very happy, and sung with great delight, 'Happy day, when Jesus washed my sins away.' Young B., of Virginia, was resigned, and even rejoiced at the near prospect of death. He repeated the line, 'How firm a foundation, ye saints of the Lord.' His end was peace.

"One of these young men had determined to enter the Christian ministry."

While many engaged in these works of mercy in the hospitals, others toiled at home as earnestly for the benefit of the soldiers, who were supplied with socks and gloves almost wholly by the busy fingers of their sisters, wives and mothers. And when these welcome contributions arrived in camp, what blessings were invoked on our fair benefactors!

The scene described by Rev. Mr. Crumley, as he distributed among the soldiers, after one of the Maryland campaigns, the supplies sent forward by the Georgia Relief Association, one of the noblest institutions of the war, is truthful and touching:

"After leaving Warrenton, I visited the wounded in private houses around the battle-field, where I very narrowly escaped being taken prisoner by the Yankees. In Winchester I found thousands of the wounded from Maryland crowding into churches, hotels, private houses, and tents, in every imaginable state of suffering and destitution. Though kind words and prayers are good and cheering to the suffering, they could not relieve the terrible destitution. At length my anxious suspense was relieved by the coming of Mr. Selkirk, Dr. Camak, and Rev. Mr. Potter, bringing supplies from the Georgia Relief and Hospital Association, which were in advance of anything from the Government. Their coming was clothing to the naked, medicine to the sick, and life to the dying.

"Could that little girl have been with us as we distributed the gifts of the Association, and have seen the pleasure with which the heroic youth, who had made the Maryland campaign barefooted, drew on his rough and bruised feet the soft socks which she knit, no doubt she would knit another pair. Could that young lady have seen the grateful expression upon the face of that noble warrior, as, with lips parched with fever, he sipped the wine, or tasted the pickles her hands had prepared, whispering, 'God bless the ladies of Georgia;' or that other, as he exchanged his soiled and blood-stained garments for those sent by the Association, ejaculating, 'Yes, we will suffer and die, if need be, in defence of such noble women'—fresh vigor would have been added to her zeal in providing comforts for our suffering 'braves.' How much more comfortable and sweet would have been the slumber of that mother could she have seen her 'patriot boy,' who had lain upon the bare ground, warmly wrapped in the coverlet or carpet blanket she had sent for the suffering soldiers."

It is a well-known fact that the wife of our illustrious leader, Robert Edward Lee, though a cripple, unable to walk by reason of disease, constantly employed her time during a great part of the war in making gloves and knitting socks for our soldiers.

Imagine the scene when they were distributed among her husband's veterans.

Our women never grew weary in well-doing. How often were they seen passing along the lines as the troops waited at some railroad station, superintending the servants who had been sent by them loaded with good things for "our dear soldiers." And when trains filled with men paused but a few moments, they were often found ready with refreshments.

The following scene at a village in Georgia was repeated daily along the lines of railroad throughout the South:

"At Greensboro there were no 'little fellows' or 'aunties' popping into the cars or crying at the windows 'wish to buy some fruit, etc.; but there were ladies—old and young—standing in the hot sun, little boys, servants and gentlemen—young and old, many of them with baskets, pitchers, etc. You would think that this was a regular vending shop, but not so; the cars stop; you hear some soft voice from without, saying, 'Any soldiers aboard?' another (bless these young ladies), 'Any sick soldiers aboard?' Some one answers affirmatively, probably a soldier with his head out at some window, moved by the inquiry for soldiers. 'Will you have some milk, some fruit, some bread, some meat?' In comes a servant with a pitcher of nice, fresh milk, and another with bread and meats, and a little boy with fruit. Thus all the time the cars are stopped at Greensboro the soldiers are helped bountifully. Ever and anon you can hear one of them exclaim, 'These are the cleverest people I have met with in a long time.' I have been told that this is an every day business with the good citizens of Greensboro. The writer has passed there four times recently, and found it so every time. These people feel for their soldiers."

There is something in the following scene to touch the heart and moisten the eye:

"After the battle of Sharpsburg we passed over a line of railroad in Central Georgia. The disabled soldiers from Gen. Lee's army were returning to their homes. At every station the wives and daughters of the farmers came on the cars and distributed food and wines and bandages among the sick and wounded. We shall never forget how very like an angel was a little girl; how blushingly and modestly she went to a great rude bearded soldier, who had carved a crutch from a rough plank to replace a lost leg; how this little girl asked him if he was hungry, and how he ate like a famished wolf. She asked if his wound was painful, and in a voice of soft, mellow accents, 'Can I do nothing more for you? I am sorry that you are so badly hurt; have you a little daughter, and won't she cry when she sees you?' The rude soldier's heart was touched, and tears of love and gratitude filled his eyes. He only answered, 'I have three little children. God grant they may be such angels as you.' With an evident effort he repressed a desire to kiss the fair brow of the pretty little girl. He took her little hand between both his own and bade her 'good-bye, God bless you.' The child will always be a better woman because of these lessons of practical charity stamped ineffaceably upon her young heart."

There was a moral grandeur in the following scene that might well stir the heart of a true soldier to its utmost depths:

"As we were on our way to Manassas on the 19th of July, 1861," said an officer of the Virginia troops, "on a crowded train of flats, the people along the route of the Manassas Gap railroad turned out in large bodies, bringing baskets full of provisions and luxuries for the soldiers. Everybody was full of joy, and we rushed on to the battle with railroad speed, amid the waving of handkerchiefs and the loud huzzahs of a loyal people—little thinking that many of the hearts that beat high for praise would 'soon feel that pulse no more.' Not far from one of the depots, which we had just left in great glee, on an eminence near by the road, there stood a lady of more than womanly stature, but of womanly face, with hands uplifted and eyes upturned to heaven in reverential prayer for us and our country. And there she stood with outstretched arms until the train carried us out of sight. I thought of Miriam the prophetess—only the hands of the one were lifted in praise, of the other in prayer to God. I never shall forget that scene, and the deep impression it made upon all. The shout of reckless joy was turned into serious thought, and blessed, I believe, was the influence of that sight on many a brave heart."

The women of the South were faithful and eminently successful co-laborers in the army revival.

There was another instrumentality worthy of our notice. This was the influence of letters from home on the minds of the soldiers. In camp or bivouac, on the march or in battle, the thoughts of the soldier wandered back to his home. It seemed doubly dear to him when absent, and every line sent by the loved ones there was read over and over, often with tear-dimmed eyes, and then carefully put away as a precious treasure. These secret and powerful appeals turned the feet of many a wanderer into the way of life, recalled many a backslider to his duty, and stimulated many a wavering believer to endure "hardness as a good soldier of Jesus Christ."

This home correspondence was as successful in leading thousands to the Lamb of God as it was in the case of the noble soldier who said in a letter to his honored Christian mother:

"I will here state to you what I never have written home to E——, of the thoughts that have most affected my mind, and I hope and trust in God that the same thoughts and reflections have changed my manner of life. E—— has doubtless shown you what I call my farewell letters to my children, as well as the one to her. The letters were written to my children while I was at Richmond, Va. The advice I thought and still think was good, but alas, where does that advice come from. It is from the best friend my children have upon earth, *a father*; *yes, a father*, who says: 'My children, read your Bibles, abstain from bad company and bad habits, the lusts of the flesh and vanities of a wicked world,' but who says at the same time by *his own conduct and example, Come along* children—taking them, as it were, by the hand—I will lead you down to hell; yes, I was leading them by my example as directly to hell as I possibly could. Oh, the horrible thought of being the means of damning the souls of my children! Conviction seized upon me, and *then and there*, on the —th of June, I resolved, if God would spare my life, that I would reform my habits of life; or if he would permit me to return home, that I would set a different example before my children. I have prayed that he would, and that I might keep my resolution to the day of my death. I wrote you a letter on the same day, while my eyes were still wet with tears. I asked your prayers in my behalf; I know you have prayed for me. Can God in justice forgive me? I pray he may, I know my children will; may God bless them and help them to do so, and save them from following my bad example, at the same time to take my good advice and carry it out, that they may be saved from that awful hell to which I was leading them."

Letters from the camp were regarded as precious treasures by the fathers and mothers of the brave boys who had gone to the war. The scene so graphically described below was almost daily repeated throughout the Confederacy:

"I went to a neighbor's some time ago to buy chickens and meat, for I am a new comer in the settlement, and didn't fill my smokehouse at the right time. The man was making a split basket before the door, and his wife was spinning, as nearly every wife in the country is. They were old people, except a hireling boy, alone on their farm. Their three sons went to war last spring. I had not been long in the house before the old lady brought out the last letter from the son before Richmond and put it into my hand, just as you would offer the morning paper to a guest at your office or house. I was at another house where a neighbor called in, and without preliminary said: 'Fetch that letter here you got from the post-office Thursday.' The letter was brought and read to us all, from beginning to end. Every letter, after being opened and read by those to whom it is addressed, seems to be common property. Though roughly written and spelled, some of them are vastly entertaining and informing, and there are touches of the heart toward the close, at which the mother or wife of the writer, who listens for the twentieth time to the reading with unabated interest, will bring the corner of her apron to her eyes."

The influence of devout Christian officers was powerful for good in our armies. We had, it is true, many reckless, unprincipled, and abandoned men, who were leaders in sin. But there were others, and not a few, who combined an humble piety with the most exalted patriotism. Many of these brought their religion with them into the army, and many others were the happy subjects of the great revival. General Lee attached his men to him not less by his goodness of heart and his deep-toned, unobtrusive piety, than by his skill and courage as a warrior—he was to them the model of a Christian soldier. Can the influence of General Jackson over his men ever be fully estimated? And was not this in a great measure owing to the depth and power of his religion? Said a soldier after the battle of Cross Keys: "I saw something to-day which affected me more than anything I ever saw or read on religion. While the battle was raging and the bullets were flying, Jackson rode by, calm as if he were at home, but his head was raised toward heaven, and his lips were moving evidently in prayer." Meeting a chaplain near the front in the heat of a battle, the General said to him, "The rear is your place, sir, now, and prayer your business." He said to a Colonel who wanted worship, "All right, Colonel, but don't forget to drill."

An incident of Jackson is related by one of his staff. Entering the General's room at midnight, Major ———— found him at prayer. After half an hour the Major stepped to the door and asked of the Aid if he did not think the General had fallen asleep on his knees from excessive fatigue. "O no, you know the General is an Old Presbyterian, and they all make long prayers." The Major returned, and after waiting an hour the General rose from his knees.

A writer says: "General Jackson never enters a battle without invoking God's blessing and protection. The dependence of this strange man upon the Deity seems never to be absent from his mind, and whatever he says or does, it is always prefaced 'by God's blessing.' 'By God's blessing we have defeated the enemy,' is his laconic and pious announcement of a victory. One of his officers said to him, 'Well, General, another candidate is awaiting your attention.' 'So I observe,' was the quiet reply, 'and by God's blessing he shall receive it to his full satisfaction.'

"After a battle has been fought the same rigid remembrance of divine power is observed. The army is drawn up in line, the General dismounts his horse, and then, in the presence of his rough, bronzed-faced troops, with heads uncovered and bent awe-stricken to the ground, the voice of the good man, which but a few hours before was ringing out in quick and fiery intonations, is now heard subdued and calm, as if overcome by the presence of the Supreme Being, in holy appeal to the 'sapphire throne.'

"Few such spectacles have been witnessed in modern times, and it is needless to add that few such examples have ever told with more wondrous power upon the hearts of men. Is it surprising that Stonewall Jackson is invincible, and that he can lead his army to certain victory, whenever God's blessing precedes the act?"

All the armies of the Confederacy were more or less blessed with pious Generals, who strove to lead their soldiers to the cross of Christ. General Gordon, writing from the Army in Virginia, urged the ministers of the Churches to come out into the camps. "The few missionaries we have," he says, "are not preaching, it is true, in magnificent temples, or from gorgeous pulpits, on Sabbath days to empty benches, but daily, in the great temple of nature, and at night by heaven's chandeliers, to audiences of from 1,000 to 2,000 men anxious to hear of the way of life."

A writer, speaking of the religious influence in the Army of Tennessee, says: "General Cleburne, the hero of many battle-fields, had a place prepared for preaching in the centre of his Division, where himself and most of his officers were present, and where I was assisted by General Lowry, who sat in the pulpit with me and closed the services of the hour with prayer. He is a Baptist preacher, and, like the commander of the Division, is a hero of many well-fought battle-fields. He takes great interest in the soldiers' religious welfare, often preaches to them, and feels that the ministry is still his high and holy calling."

Generals Findly, Bickler, Stewart, with others of the same army, were pious and devoted Christian officers, and gave much assistance to the chaplains and missionaries in the revival that swept so gloriously through the armies in the West. They recommended religion to their soldiers by precept and example.

But these men were Generals, and their contact with the soldiers was not so close as that of inferior officers. In the companies and regiments the work of pious officers was most effectually done. We select a few out of the many illustrative incidents that crowd upon us:

"In General Lee's army there was a captain who made a profession of religion. As soon as he found peace, he called his company together and told them that they had always followed where he had led them, that he wished to know whether they were willing to follow him to the feet of Jesus and walk with him in the paths of righteousness. All, without a single exception, manifested a desire to follow the example of their leader."

"There was another company whose captain was a wicked man. He exerted a bad influence over his men. He was openly profane, and never attended religious services. In these days the company was known as one of the most wicked in the regiment. Months rolled away, and another man was appointed to the command.

He was a consistent Christian, and a man of earnest, deep-toned piety. He sought to carry his men to church, and in the prayer-meeting strove to lead them to the throne of grace. He showed that he cared for their spiritual as well as their physical interests. Now, mark the change. In that company, once noted for wickedness, prayer-meetings were held every night. Among its members are some active, energetic Christians, and some happy converts have been made there. How responsible the position of an officer!"

Thousands of such men, quiet, unobtrusive, devout, happy Christians, labored with a success in winning souls to the Saviour which eternity alone can reveal. Many of them sleep in their lonely graves on the fields where they prayed and fought and fell; others survive, and, among their comrades in arms and their brethren in Christ, are still fighting for the victory that shall give them the crown of life and an abundant entrance into the heavenly Jerusalem.

CHAPTER V.

HELPS TO THE REVIVAL—COLPORTAGE.

So IMPORTANT was the work of Colportage in promoting religion among the soldiers that we feel constrained to devote to it a separate chapter. And the pious laborers in this department are eminently worthy of a place by the side of the most devoted chaplains and missionaries that toiled in the army revival. Receiving but a pittance from the societies that employed them, subsisting on the coarse and scanty fare of the soldiers, often sleeping on the wet ground, following the march of the armies through cold or heat, through dust or mud, everywhere were these devoted men to be seen scattering the leaves of the Tree of Life. Among the sick, the wounded, and the dying, on the battle-fields and in the hospitals, they moved, consoling them with tender words, and pointing their drooping spirits to the hopes of the gospel. The record of their labors is the record of the army revival; they fanned its flame and spread it on every side by their prayers, their conversations, their books, and their preaching. They went out from all the Churches, and labored together in a spirit worthy of the purest days of our holy religion. The aim of them all was to turn the thoughts of the soldiers not to a sect, but to Christ, to bring them into the great spiritual temple, and to show them the wonders of salvation. If any man among us can look back with pleasure on his labors in the army, it is the Christian colporteur

The number of religious tracts and books distributed by the colporteurs, chaplains, and missionaries in the army, we can never know. But as all the Churches were engaged in the work of printing and circulating, it is not an over-estimate to say that hundreds of millions of pages were sent out by the different societies. And, considering the facilities for printing in the South during the war, we may safely assert that never were the soldiers of a Christian nation better supplied with such reading as maketh wise unto salvation; and certainly, never amidst circumstances so unpropitious to human view, did fruits so ripe, so rich, so abundant, spring up so quickly from the labors of God's servants.

Earliest in the important work of colportage was the Baptist Church, one of the most powerful denominations in the South. In May, 1861, at the General Association of the Baptist churches in Virginia, vigorous measures were adopted for supplying the religious wants of the army.

The Sunday School and Publication Board, in their report on colportage, said: "The presence of large armies in our State affords a fine opportunity for colportage effort among the soldiers. These are exposed to peculiar temptations, and in no way can we better aid them in resisting these than by affording them good books. To this department of our operations we ask the special, earnest attention of the General Association. Shall we enter this wide and inviting field, place good books in the hands of our soldiers, and surround them by pious influences? or shall we remain indifferent to the spiritual dangers and temptations of those who are flocking hither to defend all we hold dear?"

The Association cordially responded, and "recommended to the Board to appoint at once, if practicable, a sufficient number of colporteurs to occupy all the important points of rendezvous, and promptly to reach all the soldiers in service in the State; that during the war as many colporteurs as could be profitably employed, and as the means of the Board would admit, be kept in service; that special contributions to colportage should be raised from the Baptist churches, from the community, and even from such persons in other of the Confederate States as may feel interested in the welfare of the soldiers who are gathered from various Southern States to fight their common battles on the soil of Virginia; that steps should be taken to secure the issue of a tract or tracts specially adapted to general circulation among the soldiers."

The work was put in charge of Rev. A. E. Dickinson, who had already acquired a valuable experience and a high reputation as the Superintendent of Colportage under the direction of the General Association. He sent forth his well trained band of colporteurs into this new field, which they cultivated with the happiest results, and with a zeal and self-denial worthy of the cause of Christ.

One year after these labors were commenced, Mr. Dickinson said in his annual report:

"We have collected $24,000, with which 40 tracts have been published, 6,187,000 pages of which have been distributed, besides 6,095 Testaments, 13,845 copies of the little volume called Camp Hymns, and a large number of religious books. Our policy has been to seek the co-operation of chaplains and other pious men in the army, and, as far as possible, to work through them. How pleasant to think of the thousands who, far from their loved ones, are, every hour in the day, in the loneliness and gloom of the hospital, and in the bustle and mirth of the camp, reading some of these millions of pages which have been distributed, and thus been led to turn unto the Lord."

In his report for 1863, in the midst of the war, he says: "Modern history presents no example of armies so nearly converted into Churches as the armies of Southern defence. On the crest of this flood of war, which threatens to engulf our freedom, rides a pure Christianity; the gospel of the grace of God shines through the smoke of battle with the light that leads to heaven; and the camp becomes a school of Christ. From the very first day of the unhappy contest to the present time, religious influences have been spreading among the soldiers, until now, in camp and hospital, throughout every portion of the army, revivals display their precious, saving power. In one of these revivals over three hundred are known as having professed conversion, while, doubtless, there are hundereds of others equally blessed, whose names, unrecorded here, find a place in the 'Lamb's book of life.'"

And in 1865, in reviewing the blessed work of saving souls amid the bloody scenes of four gloomy years, the Board said:

"Millions of pages of tracts have been put in circulation, and thousands of sermons delivered by the sixty missionaries whom we have sent to our brave armies. If it could be known by us here and now how many souls have been saved by this agency, doubtless the announcement would fill us with surprise and rejoicing. Hundreds and thousands, we verily believe, have in this way obtained the Christian's hope, and are now occupying some place in the great vineyard of the Lord, or have gone up from the strife and sorrow of earth to the peaceful enjoyments of the heavenly home."

The Evangelical Tract Society, organized in the city of Petersburg, Va., in July, 1861, by Christians of the different denominations, was a most efficient auxiliary in the great work of saving souls. It was ably officered, and worked with great success in the publication and circulation of some of the best tract reading that appeared during the war. More than a hundred different tracts were issued; and in less than one year after the organization of the Society, it had sent among the soldiers more than a million pages of these little messengers of truth. The Army and Navy *Messenger*, a most excellent religious paper, was also published by this Society, and circulated widely and with the best results among the soldiers. Holding a position similar to that of the American Tract Society, this association was liberally sustained by all denominations, and had ample means for supplying the armies with every form of religious reading, from the Holy Scriptures to the smallest one-page tract. Its officers, editors, agents, and colporteurs, were among the most faithful, zealous and successful laborers in all departments of the army. During the period of its operations, it has been estimated that 50,000,000 pages of tracts were put in circulation by it.

The Presbyterian Board of Publication, under the direction of Rev. Dr. Leyburn and other ministers of that Church, entered the field and did faithful service in the good cause. The regular journals of that denomination, a monthly paper—"The Soldier's Visitor," specially adapted to the wants of the army, Bibles, Testaments, and most excellent tracts in vast numbers, were freely sent forth to all the camps and hospitals from their centre of operations.

The Virginia Episcopal Mission Committee heartily united in the work, and spent thousands of dollars per annum in sending missionaries to the army, and in printing and circulating tracts. Rev. Messrs. Gatewood and Kepler, of the Protestant Episcopal Church, were the zealous directors of operations in Virginia, while in other States such men as Bishop Elliott, of Georgia, Doctor, now Bishop, Quintard, of Tennessee, and the lamented General Polk, gave the weight of their influence and the power of their eloquence, written and oral, to promote the cause of religion among our soldiers.

At Raleigh, N. C., early in the war, Rev. W. J. W. Crowder commenced the publication of tracts, encouraged and assisted by contributions from all classes of persons. In less than a year he reported: "We have published, of thirty different tracts, over 5,000,000 pages, more than half of which we have given away, and the other half we have sold at about the cost of publication— 1,500 pages for one dollar." This gentleman continued his labors in this good work throughout the war, and furnished millions of pages of the best tracts for army circulation.

"The Soldiers' Tract Association," of the Methodist Episcopal Church, South, was organized and went into operation in March, 1862, and became a valuable auxiliary in the work of colportage and tract distribution. By midsummer it had put in circulation nearly 800,000 pages of tracts, and had ten efficient colporteurs in the field. Its operations steadily increased to the close of the war; and besides the dissemination of millions of pages of excellent religious reading, with thousands of Bibles and Testaments, two semi-monthly papers were issued, "The Soldiers' Paper," at Richmond, Va., and "The Army and Navy Herald," at Macon, Ga., 40,000 copies of which were circulated every month throughout the armies.

In addition to these, there were other associations of a like character successfully at work in this wide and inviting field.

The Georgia Bible and Colportage Society, Rev. F. M. Haygood, Agent, was actively engaged in the work of printing and circulating tracts in the armies of the Southwest.

The South Carolina Tract Society was an earnest ally in the holy cause, and sent out its share of tracts to swell the vast number scattered like leaves of the tree of life all over the land.

The presses in every great commercial centre were busy in throwing off religious reading of every description, and yet so great was the demand that the supply was unequal to it during the whole of the war. At Richmond, Raleigh, Columbia, Charleston, Augusta, Mobile, Macon, Atlanta, and other cities, good men labored day and night to give our gallant soldiers the bread of life; and still the cry from the army was, Send us more good books. At one period of the war the Baptist Board alone circulated 200,000 pages of tracts weekly, besides Testaments and hymn-books; and with the joint labors of other societies, we may estimate that when the work was at its height not less than 1,000,000 pages a week were put into the hands of our soldiers.

Our readers will be pleased, we doubt not, to learn from the colporteurs themselves what they saw of the work of the Lord.

Rev. Dr. Ryland, of the Baptist Church, writing of his labors in Richmond, says: "Many cases of deep and thrilling interest have come under my observation. Some were fervent disciples of Jesus, who, during the war, having maintained their integrity, gave me a cordial welcome to their bedside. Others were .rejoicing in recent hope of eternal life; and many others exhibited marked anxiety about their salvation. Since the battle of Seven Pines, I have conversed with probably five hundred who, having passed through the recent bloody scenes, have told me with different degrees of emphasis that they had resolved to lead a better life. All these battles [the seven days' fighting around Richmond], with their hair-breadth escapes and their terrible sufferings, have produced a softened state of mind, which harmonizes well with our efforts to evangelize. I have almost from the beginning of the war been laboring as a colporteur in the hospitals of Richmond; and my impression is, that the results of this work are infinitely greater and more glorious than many believe."

Rev. W. M. Young gave a like testimony: "I have seen scores of instances in which the reading of tracts had been instrumental in the conversion of souls. Yesterday, going up Main street, I was hailed by a soldier sitting on the pavement, 'Parson, don't you know me? Under God I owe everything to you. While languishing in the hospital you gave me a tract, 'Christ found at the lamp post,' which has brought joy and peace to my soul. If God spare me to go home, I expect to devote my life to the public proclamation of the gospel.'"

Rev. Joseph H. Martin wrote from Knoxville: "While

I was opening a box of tracts a soldier said, 'Some of those tracts were given to our regiment at Chattanooga, and never before in my life have I seen such an effect on men. Many have given up swearing, and I among the number, through the influence of these silent but powerful preachers.'"

Rev. M. D. Anderson says: "I met a young man wounded, and began to talk with him on religion. He said, 'O sir, don't you remember that at the camp-meeting at ——— you spoke to me on the subject? Do get down and pray for me.' He has since been converted, and is an active co-laborer with me. An old marine who had weathered many a storm, and was lying sick in the hospital, seemed astonished that I should urge upon his attention the claims of the gospel. 'How is it that you, a young man, should be so concerned about me, a poor old sailor?' He said that rarely, if ever before in his life, had any one spoken to him about his soul. His interest in divine things increased until, I think, he became a true Christian. He died a most happy death."

Rev. B. B. Ross, of Alabama, writing to Rev. A. E. Dickinson, says: "I am just from a pleasant tour among the hospitals in Mississippi, where I found 3,000 sick. They are greedy, yea ravenous, in their appetite for something to read. Under the labors of your colporteurs there has been a revival of religion at Quitman, and there is also a revival in progress at Lauderdale Springs. The surgeons have been especially kind to me—at times calling my attention to certain cases of the sick, at others making appointments for me to preach."

Rev. S. A. Creath, Army of Tennessee: "I am still following up the army, trying to be of service to them. At Atlanta I saw 3,000 sick men. Started to work this morning before sun up, and by 9 A. M. had distributed 20,000 pages of tracts. Several have professed religion, and the Lord's blessing seems to be on us."

"I have been a month," wrote a colporteur from Richmond, "laboring in this city, during which time I have distributed 41,000 pages of tracts. I preach almost daily in the hospitals; and a notice of a few minutes will give me a large congregation. Never in my life have I witnessed such solemn attention to the preached word. Oftentimes I meet with soldiers who tell me that they have become Christians since they entered the army, and not unfrequently I am asked by anxious inquirers, what they must do to be saved. 'O, how encouraging to a soldier is a word of sympathy,' said one of the sick men to me."

Another from Petersburg writes: "I have been for some weeks devoting my time to the hospitals in this city. The noble men are so fond of having one to talk with them about the Friend of sinners, and the heavenly home, that my heart is made to rejoice with theirs. The other day I was reading a few tracts to a sick soldier, and while reading one on 'The Blood of Christ,' he became so happy that he shouted, 'Glory to God!' Another said, 'When I first came into the hospital I was sad and dissatisfied, but since I have been here I have learned of Jesus, and thank God even for tribulations.'"

A colporteur from the army at Corinth, Miss., writes: "I have distributed 70,000 pages of tracts here, and feel much encouraged. The officers grant me free access to the camps, and commend my work. Oftentimes have I seen the men throw aside their cards to take up the tracts I would place on their table, saying that they played only because they had nothing to read. There are many pious men here, and they warmly co-operate with me."

From Savannah, Ga.: "The Testaments and tracts have effected good—some have made a public profession of religion, whilst others are deeply interested in divine things. We need more tracts and more Bibles."

Rev. J. A. Hughes thus speaks of his labors at Atlanta: "In going among the thousands in the hospitals.

I have met with many things to gladden my heart, and to cause me to love the work. I find a number of Christians; some tell me that camp-life has had a very unfavorable influence on their religious character; others say it has been of great service to them, that it has bound them closer to the Saviour, made them more acquainted with their own weakness and sins, and afforded them a fine field in which to labor for the souls of their fellow-men. Some few hesitate to take a Testament, though they will accept a tract. One man positively refused a Testament but took the tract, 'A Mother's Parting Words to her Soldier Boy,' by the reading of which he was deeply moved and became a true penitent, asked me to pray for him, and finally died in the triumphs of faith. To a young man who felt himself a sinner I gave 'Motives to Early Piety.' He was led to Christ, whom he publicly confessed. A soldier said to me on the street, 'You are the gentleman who gave me a tract the other day. I had read it before, at home, but never has the reading of that book so affected me as of late; away from home and friends, it is doubly sweet.' Three have professed conversion from reading, 'Why will ye die?' several from reading 'A Mother's Parting Words.' A soldier told me 'The Call to Prayer' had roused him to a sense of his duty as a professor of religion."

Rev. Joseph E. Martin, from Chimborazo hospital at Richmond, writes: "We have had lately sixteen conversions. One young man was very anxious to learn to read. I procured him a spelling-book, and in a few days he learned so rapidly as to be able to read the Testament. He has since professed religion. A middle-aged man from Georgia has learned to read since he joined the army, and has committed to memory almost all the New Testament with the book of Job."

Another faithful laborer says: "A young man said to me, 'Parson, you gave me a book, (Baxter's Call,) which I have been reading, and it has made me feel very unhappy. I feel that my condition is awful, and I desire to find peace.' I pointed him to the Lord Jesus. While passing through a hospital with my tracts one poor, afflicted soldier wept piteously and said, 'Sir, I cannot read; will you be good enough to read some of those tracts to me?' I read several, and among them, 'A Mother's Parting Words to her Soldier Boy.' 'Oh,' said he, 'that reminds me so much of my poor old mother, who has faded from earth since I joined the army.' He wept and seemed greatly affected."

Rev. George Pearcy, writing from Lynchburg, Va., says: "I collected from Sunday Schools and individuals above a hundred Testaments, a few Bibles, and some books and tracts—these were placed in three large hospitals for the sick soldiers. There have been as many as 10,000 soldiers in the encampment here, hence it is a most interesting field for usefulness. Many soldiers have the Bible or Testament, and love to read it. A good number are members of Churches. Far away from home and kindred, they are delighted to receive the visits of a brother Christian, and get something to read. All receive the tracts, and read them with delight. The Lord has blessed the work. He has poured out his Spirit upon many. Several have died in the triumphs of faith. It was a great pleasure and privilege to speak to them of the Saviour, and witness their trust in him during the trying hour. One who died a week ago, said, in a whisper, a short time before he breathed his last, when the nurse held up the tract, 'Come to Jesus,' 'I can't see.' He was told it was the tract, 'Come to Jesus,' and that Jesus says, 'Him that cometh unto me I will in no wise cast out.' 'Thank the Lord for that,' he replied. 'Have you come to him? and do you find him precious?' 'Precious, thank the Lord.' 'He has promised never to leave nor forsake his people.' 'Thank the Lord for that;' and so he would say of all the promises quoted. One young man, to whom I gave a tract, told me that at home he was a steady, sober man, never swore; but that becoming a soldier, he did as many others did—threw off restraint, and did wickedly; 'But now,' said he, 'I have done swearing, and will seek the salvation of my soul.'"

"When I joined the army," said a soldier to a colporteur, "I was a member of the Church, and enjoyed religion, but since I came into camp I have been without anything of a religious character to read, and assailed on every side by such temptations as have caused me to dishonor my religious profession. O, sir, if you had been with me, and extended such aid as you now bestow, I might have been kept from all the sin and sorrow which, as a poor backslider, I have known."

One who had visited the hospitals at Richmond wrote: "The field of labor opened here for the accomplishment of good is beyond measure. An angel might covet it. At three o'clock services were held in the main hall of the hospital. It was a most imposing spectacle to see men in all stages of sickness—some sitting upon their beds, while others were lying down listening to the word of God—many of them probably for the last time. I do not think I ever saw a more attentive audience. They seemed to drink in the Word of Life at every breath."

"Some time since," says Rev. A. E. Dickinson, "it was my pleasure to stand up in the presence of a large company of convalescent soldiers in one of our hospitals to proclaim salvation. During the reading of a portion of Scripture tears began to flow. I then announced that dear old hymn,—

".'There is a fountain filled with blood,
Drawn from Immanuel's veins,' &c.,

the reading of which seemed to melt every heart, and the entire audience was in tears before God. Every word in reference to spiritual truth fell with a soft, subduing fervor on their chastened hearts."

Lately a colpoteur at Lauderdale Springs, Miss., was distributing tracts, and a captain approached him and asked for one. "Select for yourself, captain," said he. The captain looked over them, and selected "Don't Swear," and began to read it aloud to the soldiers standing around, pausing occasionally to comment on the points made in the tract. When he had finished, he exclaimed, "I am done swearing. Take this," handing the colporteur a ten-dollar bill, "and send it to aid in bringing out another edition of this tract."

The soldiers themselves were often the most successful tract distributers. A private in a Virginia regiment, all the time that his command was near Richmond, sold the daily papers to his comrades, and with the profits bought tracts which he circulated among them. It was truly a noble sight to see this pious young man, after a long walk to the city, and after having sold his papers, worn down with fatigue, coming with the proceeds to purchase religious reading for his fellow-soldiers.

"When I entered the army," said a soldier, "I was the chief of sinners. I did not love God, nor my soul, but pursued the ways of unrighteousness with ardor, without ever counting the cost. I studiously shunned preaching and our faithful chaplain, lest he should reprove me; and when he was preaching in the camp I would be in my tent gambling with my wicked companions. One day he presented a tract entitled, 'The Wrath to Come,' and so politely requested me to read it that I promised him I would, and immediately went to my tent to give it a hasty perusal. I had not finished it until I felt that I was exposed to that wrath, and that I deserved to be damned. It showed me so plainly where and what I was, that I should have felt lost and without a remedy had it not pointed me to that glorious Refuge which has indeed been a refuge to me from the storm, for I now feel that I can trust in Christ."

The history of this little tract is the history of thousands of like character that preached silently but powerfully and successfully, in camp and hospital, in tent and bivouac. The following incident is a simple, truthful, and touching illustration of the good that may arise from the humble work of a tract distributer:

"Richard Knill did not become a subject of the grace of God until he was twenty-six years of age. A sermon preached by his pastor, in which various extracts were given from 'Buchanan's Christian Researches in the East,' had a powerful effect on the heart of Knill, and he resolved to prepare himself for the work of a missionary.

"While he was considering the question of future duty, opportunities for usefulness, presenting themselves in various directions, he was not backward in improving them. On one occasion he heard that a military company of a thousand men were about to be disbanded and sent to their homes. He resolved to distribute among them the choicest religious tracts, with the hope that they would benefit not only the soldiers themselves, but the families and the homes to which they were about to return. 'I proceeded,' he tells us, 'to the grenadiers, who were all pleased, until I came to one merry-andrew kind of a fellow. He took the tract and held it up, swore at it, and asked, 'Are you going to convert me?''

"I said, 'Don't swear at the tract; you cannot hurt the tract, but swearing will injure your soul.'

"'Who are you?' he exclaimed. 'Form a circle round him,' said he to his comrades, 'and I will swear at him.'

"They did so; he swore fearfully, and I wept. The tears moved the feelings of the other men, and they said, 'Let him go; he means to do us good.'

"So I distributed my thousand tracts, and left them in the care of Him who said, 'My word shall not return unto me void.'

"Many years after I had taken leave of these soldiers, I returned from India to my native country and visited

Ilfracombe. There I was invited to preach in the open air, a few miles distant. Preparations were made for my visit, and during the time that I was preaching, I saw a tall, gray-headed man in the crowd, weeping, and a tall young man, who looked like his son, standing by his side, and weeping also. At the conclusion of the service they both came up to me, and the father said:

"'Do you recollect giving tracts to the local militia at Barnstable, some years ago?'

"'Yes.'

"'Do you recollect anything particular of that distribution?'

"'Yes, I recollect one of the grenadiers swore at me till he made me weep.'

"'Stop,' said he, 'Oh, sir, I am the man! I never forgave myself for that wicked act. But I hope it has led me to repentance, and that God has forgiven me. And now, let me ask, will you forgive me?'

"It quite overcame me for the moment, and we parted with a prayer that we might meet in heaven. Is not this encouragement? May we not well say, *one tract may save a soul.*"

CHAPTER VI.

FIRST FRUITS.

SUMMER AND AUTUMN OF 1861.

The Southern people entered upon the dreadful ordeal of war with extreme reluctance.

History will attest that in every honorable way they strove to avert the threatened danger.

Regarding the political tenets which culminated in the elevation of Abraham Lincoln to the presidency of the United States as fraught with evil to the South, they resolved to assert those rights of Sovereign States which they had learned from the fathers of the Republic; and to attempt the establishment of a government free from those disturbing causes which had for many years threatened the peace of the Union. The South was not alone in its apprehensions of danger from the triumph of a sectional party. Wise and moderate men at the North felt and expressed their fears for the safety of the country. A prominent divine, in a funeral discourse on the eminent Judge McLean, of the Supreme Court of the United States, who was taken away just as the dark shadows began to fall on the land, says:

"He told me that he had marked the downward progress of our nation and of our government for many years; that he knew that, as a people, we had become corrupt to the very core; that politics had degenerated into a mere trade, or rather a mere gambling speculation; and he added, with emphatic solemnity, and, as there is too much reason to fear, with prophetic sagacity, 'I do not believe there is virtue enough in the nation to sustain such a government as ours much longer. In one of the last letters I received from him, he repeated with great confidence the remark that our national corruption had destroyed us."

The attempt to coerce the South into submission, after the right of self-government had been asserted in the most solemn and authoritative forms, was felt to be a war of invasion, and the determination to resist was deep and almost universal. The strong feelings of religion and patriotism were evoked at the same moment, and by the same act, and men entered the ranks under the conviction that in so doing they were faithful alike to God and their country. This we must bear in mind, or we shall not be prepared for that pervasive spiritual influence which so eminently marked the Southern armies. That these convictions were well founded, the revival which moved with the war, and deepened as it deepened, was the great attestation. The revival in our armies, tried by all the tests known to men, was a genuine revival; its fruits were rich, abundant, and permanent. It was carried forward by the means which have been employed for the salvation of men in all ages; and to-day there are thousands in heaven, and tens of thousands on earth, who enjoy the blessedness of that spiritual baptism which fell upon them amidst the strife, and anguish, and bloodshed of war.

The best index to the state of mind and heart with which the Southern people entered upon the war may be found in the religious papers of that period.

The secular papers were employed in discussing the great political doctrines involved; it is in the religious press that we are to find those views of religious duty which the soldiers took with them into the army.

The honored President of the Confederacy struck the key-note of national feeling in the following extract from one of his earliest messages:

"We feel that our cause is just and holy; we profess solemnly in the face of mankind that we desire peace at any sacrifice, save that of honor and independence; we seek no conquest, no aggrandizement, no concession of any kind from the States with which we were lately confederated; all we ask is to be let alone; that those who never held power over us shall not now attempt our subjugation by arms. This we will, this we must resist to the direst extremity. The moment that this pretension is abandoned the sword will drop from our grasp, and we shall be ready to enter into treaties of amity and commerce that cannot but be mutually beneficial."

The religion of the people, no less than their patriotism, fully responded to these sentiments. One thing, indeed, the world must understand, that while the Christian people of the Southern States engaged in the war, they did so under the full sense of what behooved them as members of the Church of Christ.

In the early part of the war, in an "Address to Christians Throughout the World," signed by one hundred of the prominent ministers of the various denominations in the South, the following language was held:

"The war is forced upon us. We have always desired peace. After a conflict of opinions between the North and the South, in Church and State, of more than thirty years, growing more bitter and painful daily, we withdraw from them to secure peace—they send troops to compel us into re-union! Our proposition was peaceable separation, saying, 'We are *actually* divided, our *nominal* union is only a platform of strife.' The answer is a call for troops to force submission to a government whose character, in the judgment of the South, has been sacrificed to sectionalism."

The Southern people did not shrink from, indeed they courted, an investigation into the moral and religious condition of the slaves, that unfortunate race, concerning whom they have been so thoroughly misunderstood and abused.

In the same address, it was said:

"We are aware that in respect to the moral aspects of

the question of slavery, we differ from those who conceive of emancipation as a measure of benevolence, and on that account we suffer much reproach which we are conscious of not deserving.

"With all the facts of the system of slavery before us, 'as eye witnesses and ministers of the word, having had perfect understanding of all things' on this subject of which we speak, we may surely claim respect for our opinions and statements.

"Most of us have grown up from childhood among the slaves; all of us have preached to and taught them the word of life; have administered to them the ordinances of the Christian Church: sincerely love them as souls for whom Christ died; we go among them freely and know them in health and sickness, in labor and rest, from infancy to old age. We are familiar with their physical and moral condition, and alive to all their interests, and we testify in the sight of God, that the relation of master and slave among us, however we may deplore abuses in this, as in other relations of mankind, is not incompatible with our holy Christianity, and that the presence of the African in our land is an occasion of gratitude on their behalf, before God; seeing that thereby Divine Providence has brought them where missionaries of the Cross may freely proclaim to them the word of salvation, and the work is not interrupted by agitating fanaticism. The South has done more than any people on earth for the Christianization of the African race. The condition of slaves here is not wretched, as Northern fictions would have men believe, but prosperous and happy, and would have been yet more so but for the mistaken zeal of abolitionists. Can emancipation obtain for them a better portion? The practicable plan for benefitting the African race must be the providential plan—the scriptural plan. We adopt that plan in the South, and while the State should seek by wholesome legislation to regard the interests of master and slave, we as ministers would preach the word to both as we are commanded of God. This war has not benefitted the slaves. Those that have been encouraged or compelled to leave their masters have gone, and we aver can go, to no state of society that offers them any better things than they have at home, either in respect to their temporal or eternal welfare.

"We regard abolitionism as an interference with the plans of Divine Providence. It has not the sign of the Lord's blessing. It is a fanaticism which puts forth no good fruit; instead of blessing, it has brought forth cursing; instead of love, hatred; instead of life, death—bitterness and sorrow and pain and infidelity and moral degeneracy follow its labors. We remember how the Apostle has taught the minister of Jesus upon this subject, saying, 'Let as many servants as are under the yoke count their own masters worthy of all honor, that the name of God and his doctrine be not blasphemed. And they that have believing masters, let them not despise them, because they are brethren; but rather do them service, because they are faithful and beloved, partakers of the benefit. These things teach and exhort. If any man teach otherwise, and consent not to wholesome words, even the words of our Lord Jesus Christ, and to the doctrine which is according to godliness, he is proud, knowing nothing, but doting about questions and strifes of words, whereof cometh envy, strife, railings, evil surmisings, heresies, disputings of men of corrupt minds and destitute of the truth, supposing that gain is godliness: from such withdraw thyself.' This is what we teach."

Speaking of the religious work of the South, they say:

"The Christians of the South, we claim, are pious, intelligent, and liberal. Their pastoral and missionary work have claims of peculiar interest. There are hundreds of thousands here, both white and colored, who are not strangers to the blood that bought them. We rejoice that the great Head of the Church has not despised us. We desire as much as in us lieth to live peaceably with all men, and though reviled, to revile not again.

"Our soldiers were before the war our fellow-citizens, and many of them are of the household of faith, who have carried to the camp so much of the leaven of Christianity that amid all the demoralizing influences of army life the good work of salvation has gone forward there.

"Our President, some of our most influential statesmen, our Commanding General, and an unusual proportion of the principal Generals, as well as scores of other officers, are prominent, and we believe consistent members of the Church. Thousands of our soldiers are men of prayer."

"In conclusion," said these representatives of the religious sentiments of the South, "we ask for ourselves, our churches, our country, the devout prayers of all God's people—'the will of the Lord be done.'"

The spirit which marked the Churches in the North and in the South was widely different. Referring to this, a leading Southern religious paper said:

"They of the Northern Church say that they 'glory in this war.' We of the South glory in no such thing. Forced to defend ourselves, we shall certainly meet our enemies without an iota of fear, and hope to drive them back to a glory they will not be proud of in history ; but we will warn them, in the name of truth and God, to pause before they put foot on Southern soil. Every man in the South who is strong enough to pull a trigger is ready to do it, and here we stand to defend ourselves while a man, woman or child of the South is alive. While the Northern Christians are so piously trusting in superior numbers, we arm, and fast, and pray, and our cry is, O, Lord of Hosts. we trust in thee ! While they are making every effort to get up and keep at fever heat the Northern war spirit, we need no appeals beyond their own ferocious and boastful cries to keep us ready for their coming. And while they claim to have God's blessing, we are content.—if God bless them with success, be it so,—he is the Lord, let him do what he will. We know 'in whom' we 'have believed.' We seek no man's blood, and we are not afraid while the Lord reigneth."

Another thus expressed the belief of almost the entire population of the Southern States:

"In this unhappy war we find, on our side, no compromise of Christian principle. The South has accepted it as a last necessity—an alternative in which there was no choice but submission to a dynasty considered oppressive, and in its very principles antagonistic to her rights and subversive of her existence.

"Hence her sons, who are true Christians, have no compunctions of conscience when they go forth in her armies. They find, on the contrary, an approbation of conscience in their decision to fight for their homes and altars. 'In the name of our God we set up our banners.' We go to meet the invaders 'in the name of the Lord of hosts.'

"We speak the common sentiment of Southern Christians when we say that we are willing for Him to decide this contest on its merits. We protest, in the face of Heaven, we want nothing but our rights, we demand nothing but our rights. We have wronged no man, no State, no government. What is our own, and nothing more, do we claim.

"It is this view of the case that has caused so large a representation from the domain of the Church in the army of the Confederate States. The very love for justice and righteousness—the intense sympathy with equity, for its own sake—engendered in the heart by the Spirit of truth, have influenced the hundreds of Israel to gird on the sword."

While the war was accepted as a dire necessity, our

people were urged to draw from its calamities the most salutary lessons. Another journal exhorted us to remember that "He who rules and overrules all things after the counsels of His own will, suffers no wind to rise that does not blow good to somebody. To His people, especially, every wind, from the gentle breeze to the terrible hurricane, bears seeds of blessing on its wings. Full often, too, it is the violent wind that scatters these seeds most widely and abundantly—converting the scene of its devastation into the richest harvest-field of happiness for those who exercise the husbandry of faith and patience. May we not make this our experience, as respects the storm of war which beats on the land, threatening to rain tears and blood through all our borders? May we not gather from it lessons of highest value, on the insecurity of earthly things, the folly of idolatrous attachment to the possessions of the present life, and the necessity of a better and an enduring substance in heaven? May it not awaken us to the blessedness of sacrifice and suffering for a great and worthy cause? May it not enforce the wisdom of constant readiness for eternity, and lead to a closer walk with God and a more unwavering trust in him? May it not deepen the sense of personal guiltiness and strip the mask more and more from the deformity of sin, as shadowed forth in the selfishness and the desolation of war? May it not render increasingly precious the privilege of intercession, which casts all our care for those we love upon One who loves them far more? May it not lead us to recognize, with profounder gratitude, the hand of God in all that is left to us of temporal blessing? Oh! these, and many other teachings of like sort, Eternal Wisdom reads to us out of the volume of war. Be it our purpose and prayer, to hearken with obedient ear to the stern but salutary instruction."

Even when our people were wild with excitement, and the cry, "To arms! To arms!" resounded through the land, they were counselled to moderation, and to a cultivation of charitable feelings towards those who opposed them:

"Men's heads," said a prominent journalist, "may be wrong when their hearts are right. This we must bear in mind; for it will not do to discredit the whole Christianity of the North. A deep and prevalent political heresy, an overwhelming outside pressure, a misapprehension of the principles and purpose of those against whom they war, local prejudices, social atmosphere, a mental bias and ignorance that is not wholly voluntary—these all must be taken into the account in our moral estimate of many of our enemies, even those proposing, for their good and our own, to subjugate or exterminate us. And we must consider these things if we would fulfill the commandment, 'Love your enemies.'

"Love is the royal law, and its dues are not intermitted even in war. It is never superseded by martial law, or any other law. Always difficult of exercise, 'Love your enemies, bless them that curse you,' is now the severe test of Christian character on a national scale.

"'If it be possible, as much as lieth in you live peaceably with all men.' It may not always be possible. In our case it is clearly impossible unless we sacrifice *rights*, in the defence and preservation of which the highest duties to God and man are involved. But even in this case we must, and by grace we can, keep the heart free from malice, hatred, revenge."

Another, in the following earnest strain, begged the people not to forget God, and their duties to him, while they buckled on the weapons of carnal warfare:

"Do not, my brother, let your mind run too exclusively upon our political condition—do not think too constantly about the war. There is something of more moment to us than what is involved in these questions which are shaking our social fabric to its foundations. The Christian is interested in a greater contest than that which founds or upturns empires. Momentous as our present revolution is, it is but one of the passing incidents of the world's long history, and to be classed only as an important one among the many contingencies of a life-time—none of which should ever rise between our faith and the view of things eternal. No Christian duty or work should be intermitted, because greater events than we have yet known are passing in review and obtruding upon our anxious minds. Great as they are, the work of a Christian is greater still. Our duty may be fully done to our country, but we are undone if it be not discharged toward God. Our country may be saved and ourselves lost. Peace may come to the land, while war springs up between our hearts and God. A worldly inheritance may be gained, and yet its cost may be the sacrifice of a heavenly. A great republic may rise out of the chaos around us, while the kingdom of heaven, which should be our first love and our constant care, may become secondary in our affections."

The felt dependence of the people on God in their momentous struggle expressed itself in the calls that were made for earnest and importunate prayer. It was widely proposed through the religious papers of the South, "that at *precisely* ONE O'CLOCK, every day, until these calamities be overpast, a few minutes be set apart for prayer by each individual in the Confederate States, or in States which sympathize with the Southern Confederacy. There may be no meeting for prayer at any particular place, but let each one for himself, wherever he may be, at one o'clock, spend a little while in devout supplication to the Almighty. Let the merchant retire for a moment from his counting-room, or if this be not possible, let him lift up his heart to God in pious ejaculation; let the farmer stop his plough in the furrow; let the mechanic stay his hand from labor; let the physician pause for a moment on his mission of mercy; let the lawyer lay aside his brief; let the student rest from his toil; let the mother lay her babe in the cradle; let the busy housewife suspend her domestic cares; let every man, whatever his calling or pursuits, suspend them; let all business halt, and the whole land BE STILL. In that moment of quiet, in very mid-day, when stillness is so unusual, when it will be then all the more impressive, let every praying soul remember his country and its defenders before God. It would be best, if possible, to retire for the moment to some private place, and on bended knees give oral utterance to the desire of the heart. But if this cannot be done, the silent prayer may be sent up to God as we walk the street or pursue our journey, or even in the midst of all the whirl and din of business life. Thus shall every heart be engaged, and every soul come to the rescue; thus shall all the devout of the land be brought nigh to each other, for

> "Though sundered far, by faith they meet,
> Around one common mercy-seat."

In midsummer of 1861, the President, in accordance with the recommendation of the Confederate Congress, called the people to fasting, humiliation, and prayer, declaring in his proclamation, that "it becomes us to recognize God's righteous government, to supplicate his merciful protection, and to implore the Lord of Hosts to guide and direct our policy in the paths of right, justice, and mercy." In response, the Christian people of the South bowed, fasting and praying, before the Throne of Grace, supplicating the guidance and protection of the God of their fathers.

A leading journal, in urging the people to a higher national morality, said, in view of the general observance of this day:

"Two weeks ago hundreds of thousands of them were assembled in our churches, fasting and praying. Confession was made of sins, thanks were rendered for mercies, and our defensive struggle was commended unto God."

The following description of the manner in which the day was observed at Galveston, Texas, will give an idea of the unanimity and fervor of the people all over the South:

"In this city the day was observed with unparalleled unanimity. All places of business were closed; a Sabbath stillness reigned in the streets; and our places of prayer were filled several successive times with solemn and devout worshippers. At five o'clock morning prayer meeting the Methodist church was crowded; and so of the Presbyterian church at the nine o'clock prayer-meeting, and the Baptist church at the prayer-meeting which closed with the setting of the sun. Sermons appropriate to the occasion were preached in several of the churches at eleven o'clock. The Presbyterian, Baptist, and Methodist denominations united their arrangements, by special agreement. It is a day long to be remembered in Galveston; and will, we feel confident, leave a lasting impression for good. The prayers were fervent for the prosperity of the Confederate States; for the success of their cause; for those in authority; for our generals and armies; for our enemies, that God would give them a better mind; for a speedy and honorable peace, or for the victory of our armies in the war of independence, if it must be waged."

Those who entered the army went with the most ardent prayers and the most fervent exhortations to be good patriots and good Christians. In the midst of every company, just before it started for the camp, might be heard the voice of the minister humbly invoking the blessing of God on those who were going forth to the strife of war. And after they reached the army they were not forgotten; prayer went up hourly for the gallant men who stood in battle array, and by private letters and the public press they were exhorted to bear themselves like men that feared God.

The venerable Bishop Andrew, of the M. E. Church,

South, in writing to the ministers and members of his Church in the army, said:

"Remember, brethren, wherever you are, that you are ministers of the Lord Jesus; never let the Christian minister be merged in the soldier. You will, doubtless, in camp, be surrounded by those who will have little sympathy with your religious views and feelings, and who will closely and constantly scrutinize your whole conduct. Oh, do not, by any inadvertence of act or speech, give occasion for the enemies of Christ to blaspheme; but let your walk be such as to constrain them to glorify your Father in heaven. Oh, be witnesses for Jesus!

"There is no position in which a Christian can be placed in which he may not exert much influence for good. It will be necessary to reprove those who sin, and it is an important lesson to learn how to give reproof in love and gentleness, and yet with faithfulness, and a proper measure of Christian dignity. Many opportunities will be afforded you of strengthening the weak, and recovering those who are just on the verge of falling. And should you so deport yourselves as to command the confidence and respect of your companions in arms, you will find many unexpected calls for advice. Strive to prepare yourself to give it. In a word, be a thorough and consistent Christian yourself, and you will be always prepared to help others. Yet once more, the voice of affliction will frequently greet your ears: a brother soldier, sick and dying far from home and loved ones, is struggling with disease and death among those who are comparatively strangers; no wife's or mother's or sister's soft hand chafes his fevered brow, or with woman's sweet and gentle voice, speaking words of kindness, points the dying man to Him of Calvary,—how sweet, under these circumstances, will be the words of kindness from your lips, and how grateful to his ears the voice of prayer and praise, as you kneel beside him and wrestle with God in his behalf, and talk sweetly to him of Jesus and his salvation! But, oh! who can describe the blighting influence of one ungodly minister in a company or regiment! May God preserve our armies from all such!"

These extracts, which might be indefinitely multiplied, will show the religious *animus* of the Southern people when they entered upon the war.

We have now reached a point from which we may cast our eyes over the assembled hosts of the South, and mark the buddings of that glorious work of grace which is the great moral phenomenon of the present age.

There have been revivals in the midst of wars in other countries, and in other times; but history records none so deep, so pervasive, so well marked by all the characteristics of a divine work as that which shed its blessed light on the armies of the South in their struggle for independence.

So vast were the proportions of the revival in the second, third and fourth years of the war, that we are apt to overlook the first fruits in the opening of the conflict. In the spring of 1861 the troops were gathered at the important points of defence. The chief interest centred on Virginia, as it was felt that, after the affair of Fort Sumter, the storm would burst upon her soil.

In the armies stationed at Manassas, Winchester, Norfolk, Aquia Creek, and other places, the most cheering signs appeared.

Rev. C. F. Fry, of the Baptist Colportage Board, wrote from the Army in the Valley of Virginia:

"I have visited most of the encampments in the Valley, and could have sold more than $100 worth of books a month if my assortment had been larger—especially if I could have had a good supply of Testaments. A captain said to me, 'I am a sinner, and wish you to select some books to suit my case.' I did so; and at night he called his men into line and asked me to pray for them. Another captain seemed much interested on the subject of religion. I tried to explain to him the way to be saved, and in a few days I heard of his fighting bravely at Manassas. I have prayer and exhortation meetings frequently, which are well attended, and often tears flow from eyes unused to weep, while I point them to the Lamb of God."

Rev. R. W. Cridlin wrote of his labors at Norfolk and the vicinity:

"I visited Craney Island last Saturday. Col. Smith, who has charge of the forces there, is a pious man, and has prayers with his men every night. He seemed glad to have me labor among his command, and will doubtless render me any aid I may need."

Mr. J. C. Clopton wrote from among the sick and wounded at Charlottesville:

"This is a most inviting field, as hundreds are here on beds of suffering, and consequently disposed to consider things that make for their peace. The deepest feeling is often manifested; they listen to what I say, and read with great eagerness the tracts and books I give them."

Another faithful colporteur, Mr. M. D. Anderson, said of the scenes he witnessed at Fredericksburg and Aquia Creek:

"I have gone nearly through the regiments stationed between Fredericksburg and the Creek. The soldiers are eager for religious reading; and frequently, when they have seen me coming, they have even run to meet me, exclaiming, 'Have you any Testaments?' Much of my time has been spent with the sick in the hospitals, where, oftentimes, my heart was made to rejoice at witnessing the sustaining power of Christianity in those who were struggling with the last enemy. One, with whom I had often conversed on personal religion, was sick—nigh unto death; I stood by him, but doubted the propriety of speaking; at last, he fixed his eyes upon me and said: 'Talk to me about Jesus.' I asked if the Lord was with him, and he replied, 'Yes, with me, and that to bless. I know that my Redeemer liveth,' &c.

Another remarked to me that at home he had been a prominent member of the Church; but that since he had been in camp he had wandered off and brought reproach upon his profession, but that this sickness, from which he was then suffering, had been blessed to his soul, and that he should, with divine help, live a new life and consecrate himself to the cause of God. I have been able to supply many with the Bible, especially as the President of the Christian Association in Fredericksburg had given me a fine lot of Bibles."

A writer, speaking of the religious services in the Fourth North Carolina regiment, says:

"There are four ministers of the gospel attached to this regiment. Sabbath before last a most solemn service was held at Garysburg. The sacrament of the Lord's Supper was administered to the Christian professors of the regiment. The services were conducted by Rev. Captain Miller, aided by several other clergymen. The thought that it would probably be the last time in which some would participate in the ordinance, and that before another opportunity occurs they might be on the field of battle, affected every mind, and gave great tenderness to the meeting."

"I have spent," says Rev. W. J. W. Crowder, "most of the time for several weeks among the soldiers, to whom I gave about 200,000 pages of tracts, and had conversations on personal religion with over 2,300 in their camps and hospitals. I find many of them pious, daily reading the Bible and praying to God. But, by far, the largest portion of them are irreligious. In three companies, of about three hundred men, only seven were professors of religion, and there were but few Bibles and Testaments among them. A lady requested me to give for her all I had of the excellent tract, 'Come to Jesus,' $10.76 worth; a copy of which I gave to a soldier one Sunday morning, on which I marked the 91st Psalm. The Sunday following he wished me to sit with him in his tent. He stated that the tract caused him to get his Bible and read the Psalm. On opening to it he was surprised to find a piece of paper pinned to this Psalm, upon which was written in a beautiful hand by his sister Emma these lines:

> "When from home receding,
>   And from hearts that ache to bleeding,
> Think of those behind who love thee;
>   Think how long the night will be
> To the eyes that weep for thee."
>   "God bless thee and keep thee."

"The melting tenderness before God in that tent cannot be expressed. Some of his mates were religious and ready to encourage him in seeking salvation."

The same useful man says that when he handed his tracts to the soldiers they would say, "This is the kind of reading we want, to help us fulfill the promises we made to our wives, parents, sisters, ministers, and loved ones on leaving home, that we would seek God to be our guide and refuge."

"Such expressions," he says, "I have frequently heard from a great many of the more than 7,000 soldiers with whom I have talked on personal religion."

A prominent officer came to Mr. C. and said: "I feel it my duty to say that the good influence exerted upon the minds and actions of our men by the Bibles, books, and tracts you have sent us, is incalculable; and, to my knowledge, they have been blessed of God in producing a spirit of religious inquiry with many of a most encouraging character. I trust you and Christian friends at home will continue to supply all our soldiers with this means of grace, which is so well adapted to our spiritual wants, and can be diffused among us as perhaps no other can so effectually."

"A soldier," he says, "came to express his thanks for the saving influence of the tracts he had received since being in camp. He believes they were sent to him in answer to a pious mother's prayers. He stated that before leaving home he felt but little interest in religion, but now it is his delight and comfort.

"Another soldier, in a Mississippi regiment, writes that the tract, 'Come to Jesus,' has been the means of leading him to Christ since being in Virginia."

"Many persons," says a writer from the 19th Virginia regiment, "having relatives and friends in the army, are concerned about the religious privileges which we enjoy. A brief sketch of this feature of camp life in the 19th regiment will doubtless be gratifying to them. Every night the voice of prayer and praise is heard in one or more of the tents, and on the Sabbath mornings and evenings and on Wednesday nights, sermons are preached in a church in the immediate vicinity of the camp by the chaplain, the Rev. P. Slaughter, assisted by the Rev. Mr. Griffin. The interest of these services was much enhanced on last Sunday by the celebration of the sacraments of baptism and the Lord's Supper, and by the admission of three officers to their first communion. Many hearty prayers were offered that they may manfully fight under the banner of the Cross, and continue Christ's faithful soldiers until their lives end. It is encouraging to see the disposition of those in command to furnish facilities for public worship, and the alacrity of the men in responding to every call, marching to church sometimes in double quick time, lest they should fail to get seats. Let those who remain in their pleasant homes remember the soldier in the tented field. He needs the grace of God to enable him to bear patiently the toils and sufferings of the campaign, even more than to face the enemy in the field."

Good tidings came from many other portions of the army. Scenes like the following became more frequent every week:

"For more than a week a revival has been in progress among the soldiers stationed at Ashland. Services are held every night in the Baptist church, and the seats set apart for the anxious are frequently well nigh filled by the soldiers, who are asking for the prayers of God's people. Rev. W. E. Hatcher, of Manchester, preaches every night. At Aquia Creek thirty have professed conversion within a few weeks, a number of whom were baptized in the Potomac by Rev. Geo. F. Bagby, a chaplain. The entire regiment with which the converts were connected turned out to witness the ceremony. Our informant says he has never looked upon a more lovely and impressive scene. We understand that a protracted meeting is in progress in Col. Cary's regiment, and that Rev. Andrew Broaddus, of Caroline, is officiating. We hear of another revival in which twelve soldiers professed conversion, five of whom united with the Methodists, four with the Baptists, and the remainder with the Presbyterians. The religious community of the Confederate States ought to feel encouraged, by these tokens of the Divine power, to put forth still greater efforts in behalf of the spiritual welfare of our army. Fully *one-third* of the soldiers are destitute of a copy of the New Testament, and of all other religious reading."

From Fairfax Court-house Rev. J. M. Carlisle wrote to a religious paper at Richmond:

"As chaplain of the 7th regiment, South Carolina Volunteers, I desire to return thanks to certain unknown parties, in your city, for a donation of religious books and tracts, forwarded to me for distribution among the soldiers. They were gladly received, and are being generally read, and I trust will be a positive good. May the blessing of God be upon those whose gift they are."

These brief records reveal a deep sense of religious obligation, and much zeal and prayer among our soldiers, even at this early period of the war.

The battles which occurred during the time of which we write showed the purity and power of religion in the face of danger and death. Shortly after the battle of Great Bethel, in Virginia, a writer, speaking of the religious influence among the soldiers, said:

"There is reason to hope that the scene of the late glorious battle below Yorktown was, indeed, a 'Bethel,' the 'house of God,' the very gate of heaven, to some of the brave, but previously irreligious, young men engaged in it. It is certainly a delightful thought, and one full of encouragement for the future of our country, that God is with us, not only in the sense of giving victory to our arms, but also, *present by his Holy Spirit*, impressing the hearts of our soldiers, and turning their thoughts to himself in grateful recognition of his merciful dealings with them."

During this battle an incident occurred of a deeply interesting character. Captain John Stewart Walker, of the company known as the "Virginia Life Guard," was ordered by the Commanding General to take his men from the front, where they were doing good service, to the flank to hold in check a heavy force of the enemy supposed to be moving in that direction. On reaching his new post of danger, Captain Walker drew up his company and addressed them in a few stirring words. He reminded them that God had mercifully preserved them in the heat of battle, and that they were now called to face the enemy in greater numbers; that, as Christians and patriots, they should resolve to do their whole duty to their country; then, kneeling down, he called upon a minister, who was a private in the ranks, to offer prayer. When they arose, nearly every eye was suffused with tears, and God was felt to be present. During that day of battle it is said that three of this company sought and obtained the pardon of their sins.

The religious services were well attended by the troops stationed at Yorktown, and were not without spiritual fruits. The Colonel Hill referred to in the following extract from the letter of a soldier was afterwards General

D. H. Hill, a soldier of the Cross, as valiant for Christ as he was for his country:

"We had two sermons yesterday; one last night by Mr. Page. It is quite romantic to see four or five hundred soldiers gathered under trees; some sitting on camp stools or the ground, others standing, while the moon comes peeping through the leaves, shedding light and beauty on all around. Then, when the hymn is given out, to hear so many manly voices join in praise to the God of the universe, renders the service very solemn and impressive. This is truly a time and place to cause man to reflect on his latter end—not knowing at what moment he may be hurried into eternity. I have heard much less profane swearing since Colonel Hill gave us a lecture a short time ago. I have not seen a man, no matter how wicked, but acknowledged that the God of battles was with us and shielded us in the hour of danger."

This lecture of Col. Hill is more fully described by an officer writing to a religious paper from Yorktown; he says:

"Yesterday was emphatically a day of rest to us all. We had only to undergo an inspection of arms and attend dress parade in the evening, which was a light day's work. At night we had a good sermon from Mr. Yates, our chaplain, and a plenty of good singing. After Mr. Yates had finished, Col. Hill gave us a fine address, full of good advice and counsel, *every word* of which was exactly fitted to his hearers. He has cut off all spirits of every kind, and not a drop is to be had in camp; he is down on profanity; told us last night that he knew many regarded swearing as a sort of necessity attaching to a soldier; that it gave emphasis and eclat to the speech, but he said no greater mistake could be made; that, for his part, he would be afraid to trust to the courage of the man who had to bolster it up with whiskey and profanity. The God-fearing, moral soldier was the man to depend on. He spoke of Washington, Cromwell, and others of like caste; said they are the men to be successful; that the enemy seldom *saw the backs* of such men. He told us that three times since we had been in this camp, the long role had sounded, and we had promptly answered, expecting in a few hours to meet the enemy and risk our chances of success. He said he would, however, venture to say, that under these circumstances many of us had called upon God for help, who had *neglected* to do so while *they felt secure*. He appealed to them to know if, as soldiers and fair men, this was reasonable and proper. He appealed to the moral men in camp to let their influence be felt; said that a few might deride them at first, but they would be few, and if these men did their duty in all the varied scenes of camp life, these scoffers would see it, and soon hang their heads in shame. Thus he went on for half an hour; not a man left his place, not a word was said, and save the constant coughing of the sick, we had perfect silence. I confess this will give you but a poor idea of the best speech I ever heard, taking the time, place, and circumstances, into consideration."

The battle of Manassas, on the 21st, and the preliminary fight at Blackburn's Ford, on the 18th of July, were both marked by striking instances of Christian heroism and devotion. The peaceful and often triumphant deaths of pious officers and men had a powerful influence for good on the hearts of careless and irreligious persons. "I have known many noble specimens of the Christian soldier," said Rev. Dr. John C. Granbery, then chaplain of the 11th Virginia regiment, afterwards Superintenent of Methodist missionaries in Gen. Lee's army, whom the soldiers will never forget on account of his zeal and faithfulness; "I shall never cease to remember with admiration one of the earliest victims of this war, Major Carter Harrison, of the 11th Virginia. He was an earnest servant of Christ; modest, firm, unostentatious, zealous. He seized at once the hearts of the regiment by his many virtues, by his courtesy to all and his kind visits to the sick, to whom he bore a word not only of sympathy, but also of pious exhortation. On the lovely morning of July 18th, as we awaited the advance of the enemy and the opening of our first battle, our conversation was on sacred things. In a few hours he was mortally wounded, and until midnight endured untold agony; but in his soul was the peace of God, and all was patiently borne for the sake of God and country. He was ready to be offered up, and to leave even his loved family, at the call of duty. I had a conversation with him; he spoke of his faith in Providence, and the answers to prayer which he daily received. I questioned him concerning the state of his mind at the time. He replied that it did not rest on any subject, but now thought of a military order, and then of a Scriptural promise; now of his country, and then of his family; and often arose in a holy ejaculation to God. His flesh rests in hope; his spirit rose to God."

"I recall," says Dr. Granbury, "an interview with the sweet-spirited and gallant Captain James K. Lee, of Richmond, Va. 'How glad I am,' said he as he gave me a cordial grasp, 'to shake the hand of a brother in Christ!' I referred with sympathy to his intense sufferings. With emphasis he answered, 'Oh, they are nothing to the sufferings which Jesus bore for me!' In a few days he too was in the bosom of his Father."

On Sunday, July 21, 1861, was fought the first battle of Manassas. "As the first gun was fired," says the same writer, "a few minutes after 7 A. M., I mounted my horse and hastened from the Junction to our regiment, still stationed at Blackburn's Ford. On my way I met several regiments, some of them Mississippians, moving from that Ford to some other part of the line of action. I hailed them as they passed: 'Virginia's salutation to her sister Mississippi! Let each State of the

Southern Confederacy cover herself with glory, and pour a common glory on the cause of the united South to-day. God bless you, friends. Commit your souls and the righteous cause you uphold to him.' Rev. Dr. Bocock was with me, and addressed them in a similar strain. I cannot tell much of this day's work. The hard fighting was on our left, and we had nothing to do but to take quietly the cannonading of the enemy. Being a non-combatant, I was not exposed, but I sat beneath a hill by a wounded soldier and read to him the 13th and 14th chapters of John." Of his feelings in this first battle he says:

"I sat down by Captain Rev. F. J. Boggs, and we conversed about the strange manner in which we were spending the Sabbath. He wore a determined but anxious face. His company had been in the hottest of the fight on Thursday, and acted nobly. He spoke of the souls now being sent into eternity, and of the hard conflict raging above us, whose guns were incessantly roaring in our ears, whose issue was so doubtful. We watched the bombs as they exploded in quick succession over the spot which his regiment had left a few minutes before. So moved on the hours. Our men had eaten not a mouthful all day. At length our suspense is broken by a loud cheering. Down, down the Run, from left to right, flew the shouting, taken up by successive regiments. Here comes Gen. M., with an intensely excited countenance. 'What means that shouting?' he asks. 'The enemy flee, and the day is ours,' we replied, for so we interpreted. 'Are you sure that the cheers are on our side?' 'I will run to the South Carolinians and enquire,' I replied. So off I hasted, and got to them just in time to see the two last companies form and march in pursuit of the routed foe. Then we took up the cheering, and fell in the pursuit. I trust that many hearts went up that hour in gratitude to the God of battles."

Many noble sacrifices were laid on the altar in this

battle. Generals Bee and Bartow, Col. Egbert Jones, of the 4th Alabama, Col. Johnson, of South Carolina, and a host of other noble patriots, laid down their lives for the cause of the South. A young Georgian of Bartow's brigade said, as he lay dying on this bloody field: "I will go up and make my report to the Almighty as to the Commander-in-Chief of all. I will tell him I have been a faithful soldier and a dutiful son, though an unfaithful servant of God; nevertheless, my fearless trust is in Jesus Christ, the Saviour of men." Rev. C. W. Howard, who commanded a company in the famous 8th Georgia, here fell a martyr to the cause. He was killed in the grove where the 8th Georgia was first engaged. "He stepped in front of his company, and was in the act of dressing his line, which threw his back to the enemy, when a ball entered his head, rather in the rear, passing through his brain and out near the temple on the opposite side. He fell dead instantly." And thus hundreds of Christian men gladly yielded up their lives, cheered and sustained by the glorious hope of a better life in heaven.

While this battle was raging the earnest prayers of the Southern people were ascending to God for his protection to our soldiers and his blessing on their arms. A remarkable answer to prayer is recorded in reference to a company from Georgia. "A prayer-meeting was held at Atkinson's church, in Oglethorpe county, in that State, to pray for the safety of the Oglethorpe Rifles, who went from that neighborhood. The prayers were ascending in their behalf while the battle was raging, and they were mingling in the tornado of shells and bullets which mowed the gallant 8th Georgia regiment, of which they composed a part; and yet, of all the companies engaged, this alone showed from the record, '*none killed.*'"

Those who recall the prevailing sentiments of our people at this period will recognize the following language of two leading religious journals as expressing their firm trust in God and their deep gratitude for his great mercies:

"The Southern people are humble in their joy, and yet are not ashamed of their sorrows over the noble dead. We do not tremble at our loss, though in undisguised grief we weep by the graves of the brave soldiers who fell in the fight. The sacrifices which we have laid on the altar of our country are not the *blemished* of the flock. The Lord has asked of us the young, the brave, and the lovely; and the fathers and mothers of Israel have brought forth the first born and said, with unwavering faith in God, as the young men went to the field, 'Let the will of the Lord be done!' Though 'we sing the songs of woe, let the right prevail.' But the grief of noble, Christian suffering is not without its hallowing influence, and 'behold, we count them happy which endure.'"

From the "Old North State," whose sons nobly bore their part in this battle, came these fervent utterances:

"It is with deep emotion that we refer to the news from the seat of war in Virginia. God has favored our cause. The skill of our commanders and the bravery of our soldiers have been crowned with splendid success. Let the nation bow before God in humble acknowledgment of his mercy. Let the hearts of the people be filled with his praise.

"But our joy must be mingled with grief. Hundreds, it may be thousands, of our noble soldiers have fallen in these terrible conflicts. The homes left by them so lately are desolate; and the wail of the widow and the orphan is heard through the land. God comfort and sustain them under their sore bereavements. The sympathy and gratitude of their country will never cease to attend them."

Among the gallant men from that State who fell was young Lieutenant Mangum, the only son of his honored father. Fighting in the 6th regiment of North Carolina, he was mortally wounded near the close of the struggle. "When he was dying," said a friend, "he reposed a beautiful trust in his Saviour and spoke sentences whose echoes would awake the melody of thanksgiving and gladness in the harps of earth and the harps of glory. Between these hallowed utterances he asked a friend, 'Do you think I have accomplished anything for my country? As I only had my sword instead of a musket, I fear I did but little in the fight.' Instead of remorse for having defended an unrighteous cause, he only bewailed the conviction that, falling in the first conflict, he had done so little for a cause that he honestly esteemed worthy of the sacrifice of life itself. It was a matter of high, patriotic principle with him, and he was so just in it as to be unshaken and complacent in the tremendous entrance into the presence of Almighty God."

The feeling of dependence on God pervaded all classes. When the great victory was announced in the Confederate Congress, a Christian statesman from South Carolina arose in his place and offered the following:

"1. Resolved, That we recognize the hand of the Most High God, the King of kings, and Lord of lords, in the glorious victory with which he hath crowned our arms at Manassas, and that the people of these Confederate States are invited by appropriate services on the ensuing Sabbath to offer up their united thanksgiving and praise for the mighty deliverance.

"2. Resolved, That, deeply deploring the necessity which has washed the soil of our country with the blood of so many of her noblest sons, we offer to their respective families and friends our warmest and most cordial sympathy, assuring them that the sacrifice made will be concentrated in the hearts of our people, and will there enshrine the names of the gallant dead as the champions of free and constitutional government."

By all the day was felt to be one of "prayer, of praise,

of action, of heroism," and the richest offerings were freely laid on the altars of the South. The desire for liberty had not then yielded to the desire for gain; and the patriotic fervor of the people had not yet felt the benumbing touch of Mammon. Worldly men and Christian men alike acknowledged the hand Divine, and the season was well adapted to the scattering of the "precious seed" of life.

Many incidents of the battle were fraught with solemn lessons, and deep and lasting were the impressions made amidst the ghastly sights of war. Just after the battle a soldier wrote:

"I can't realize myself in 'the pomp and circumstance of war.' But, great God, what have I seen—the wounded, the dead, and the dying. You can possibly imagine my first feelings, though they were Yankees, when I looked upon them—some shot through the head, some with legs and arms broken, some through the stomach, and, in fact, all over; and to hear their moaning and their groanings, and I thought, 'Is this war!'"

A gentleman from the far South, who came, like scores of others, to look after "the dear boys," describes the following touching scene:

"We were straggling over the battle-field, examining the ground upon which we had such a bloody conflict and won such a glorious victory two days before. We came unexpectedly into the Centreville road, and seeing a house upon our left with the usual signs betokening a hospital, one of our party being a physician, expressed a wish to get down and examine the wounded. Upon inquiry we learned that a stable just below the house contained thirteen wounded Yankees; we forthwith proceeded to the stable, and upon entering found a Washington Artilleryman seated by the side of a wounded soldier, evidently ministering to him with great care and tenderness. I introduced myself to him, and asked if he aided in working the battery which fought with the 1st Virginia brigade.

He told me he did not—he had fought in a battery lower down, and then remarked 'that it was very hard to fight as he had fought, and turn and find *his own brother* fighting against him,' at the same time pointing to the wounded soldier from whose side he had just arisen. I asked if it was possible that was his brother. 'Yes, sir, he is my brother Henry. The same mother bore us—the same mother nursed us. We meet the first time for seven years. I belong to the Washington Artillery, from New Orleans—he to the 1st Minnesota Infantry. By the merest chance I learned he was here wounded, and sought him out to nurse and attend him.' Thus they met—one from the far North, the other from the extreme South—on a bloody field in Virginia—in a miserable stable, far away from their mother, home, and friends—both wounded—the infantryman by a musket ball in the right shoulder, the artilleryman by the wheel of a caisson over his left hand. Thus they met after an absence of seven years. Their names are Frederick Hubbard, Washington Artillery, and Henry Hubbard, 1st Minnesota Infantry. We met a surgeon of one of the Alabama regiments and related the case to him, and requested, for the sake of the artilleryman, that his brother might be cared for. He immediately examined and dressed his wounds, and sent off in haste for an ambulance to take the wounded 'Yankee' to his own regimental hospital."

Alas! that our country should ever have been visited by a war in which brother was often thus arrayed against brother. Another sad incident of the same kind was related by the Hon. Lewis D. Campbell, of Ohio:

"I had two brothers in the war; one in the Confederate army in Texas, and the other in the Union army. They were sons of one who, at the age of seventeen, fought at the battle of Eutaw Springs. One of my brothers, at the head of a regiment of Texans, fell in Louisiana, and the other, at the head of a Union regiment, fell at the battle of Chancellorsville. And the news of the death of both of these—one on the one side and the other—reached their afflicted mother on the same day."

This peculiar horror of civil war a poet has pictured but too truly in the following lines from an English periodical:

BELLUM CIVILE.

"Rifleman, shoot me a fancy shot
    Straight at the heart of yon prowling vidette;
Ring me a ball in the glittering spot
    That shines on his breast like an amulet!"

"Ay, Captain! here goes for a fine drawn bead,
    There's music around when my barrel's in tune!"
Crack! went the rifle, the messenger sped
    And dead from his horse fell the ringing dragoon.

"Now, rifleman, steal through the bushes and snatch
    From your victim some trinket to hansel first blood;
A button, or loop, or that luminous patch
    That gleams in the moon like a diamond stud!"

"Oh, Captain, I staggered and sunk in my track,
    When I gazed on the face of the fallen vidette;
For he looked so like you, as he lay on his back,
    That my heart rose upon me, and masters me yet.

"But I snatched off the trinket—this locket of gold,
    An inch from the centre my lead broke its way,
Scarce grazing the picture, so fair to behold,
    Of a beautiful lady in bridal array."

"Ha! rifleman, fling me the locket!—'tis she,
    My brother's young bride—and the fallen dragoon
Was her husband—Hush! soldier, 'twas heaven's decree;
    We must bury him, there, by the light of the moon.

"But, hark! the bugles their warnings unite;
    War is a virtue—weakness a sin;
There's lurking and looping around us to-night;
    Load again, rifleman, keep your hand in!"

During the autumn of this year (1861) the religious influence among the soldiers gradually increased. The appeals from the army for tracts, books, and for more preachers, were earnest and importunate. Even the secular papers were urged to lend their aid to the work by calling the attention of the Churches to the moral wants of the soldiers.

A soldier wrote from the army to the Richmond *Examiner* in the following strain :

" There are at present in your noble State about three hundred thousand men ' armed in the holy cause of liberty.' These men are far from their homes and the sweet influences which are there brought to bear upon them to restrain them from sin. Many of these men, however, are more serious and solemn, and inclined to seek to know their Saviour, than at any other time. The thoughts of their happy homes and dear friends far away, both in this State and the far sunny South, will often act as a check to any vicious course to which their inclinations may lead them. What I propose, sir, is that you write one of your very powerful articles, urging ministers of the gospel and chaplains in the army to put forth their utmost strength for the conversion of soldiers. What a grand moral spectacle would be presented to the world, of any army being converted ? What grandeur would it not lend to our cause ? With how much more courage will truly brave men go into danger, when they know that the messenger of death is but God's angel to call them home. And then, when this 'grand army' disbands, and the various regiments return to their several States, how much will it tend to unite us more and more in the bonds of unselfish love for the rising and brave generation that will soon turn from the field of strife to the arena of the political world, to go there with hearts full of love to God, and with the highest and most religious sense of honor towards their fellow-men."

Every new regiment that went to the army had some token of the deep concern felt by the "home folks" for its religious welfare. When the 7th regiment of South Carolina was about to leave home for the seat of war, the colored members of the Methodist Church in the town of Aiken presented to the chaplain, Rev. J. M. Carlisle, 'a magnificent copy of the Word of God for the use of the regiment.' After reaching Virginia, the chaplain wrote: "Our regiment is doing well. I try to preach on the Sabbath—usually twice. We have also a regimental prayer-meeting every evening at twilight. Upon these services there is usually a good attendance, and a serious attention that is very gratifying. Ask for us the prayers of all."

Among the troops that were stationed in the vicinity of Leesburg, Va., there was a fine state of religious feeling. In the 17th Mississippi regiment, one of the most gallant in the army, there was a deep concern. Prayer-meetings were held in their camp every evening, a number professed conversion, and the good work increased in depth and power. The Christians in the vicinity of the camp were urged to join the soldiers in their meetings. Many did so, and the people learned that the Lord of Hosts was in the midst of their brave defenders.

A true moral courage was requisite, in this early period of the war, for every old believer and every new convert. The camps, it is true, were almost filled with vice; swearing, gambling, and drunkenness, abounded, and one might have supposed that all were leagued against religion; but in the midst of all this many were found earnestly seeking light from God's Holy Word.

That high moral courage that resolves to do right in the very midst of wrong tells powerfully on young men at College, and on soldiers in an army. In that charming book for boys, "Tom Brown at Rugby," there is a fine illustration of moral courage. A large number of boys slept in the same room, and Tom Brown, though brought up to pray, was afraid to kneel down before his schoolmates, and went to bed every night without prayer. But a timid little fellow came to the school, whom everybody was disposed to call a "milk sop," and on the very first night, while all others were laughing and talking about him, he fell on his knees devoutly to pray. His bold example soon had many imitators.

"The religious soldiers at a military station in India," says an English missionary, "greatly enjoyed themselves at the union prayer-meetings, but none of them at first had courage to kneel down and pray in the presence of their wicked comrades before going to bed. One man told me that he was in the habit of waiting until all the lamps were put out, and then kneeling down in the dark. But after a while, he said, his comrades began to suspect him. So they challenged him one night, and a number gathering round, swore they would not go to bed nor put out the light until he did. He told them he was a praying man, and that he would pray whether they put out the light or not. This, he said, was the signal for a general hurrah, and storm of oaths; and that when he knelt down they kept up a bellowing and mocking, throwing their boots at him, and hitting him with balls of dough, until he had finished. He continued, however, night after night, and at last they ceased to scoff and left him in peace."

Such scenes were seldom, if ever, witnessed in our armies; but still there were many occasions on which a soldier's religion was put to as severe a test. Scenes like the following are much more interesting to contemplate:

"Many a time," says a pious colporteur, "officers and privates, who make no profession of religion, have gathered around me at night, listened with undisguised pleasure to the reading of God's Word, and joined in the sweet songs of Zion, until the forests rang again with their grateful pæans. I have never once been unkindly turned away by soldiers, but their universal politeness and gratitude have removed any fear of intrusion when I would approach. Parties playing cards have frequently broken off their games, and scattered to read my good tracts, while others engaged in rude jesting or relating wicked anecdotes have thanked me cordially for the interest I took in them, and the good reading I troubled myself to bring them. I have had officers and men to hail me, and run from a distance, to get as many of the 'silent preachers' as I could spare, pressing me to visit their regiments."

CHAPTER VII.

WINTER OF 1861-'62.

The stationary condition of the armies during most of the winter gave the chaplains, and other pious laborers, fine opportunities for pressing religion on the attention of the soldiers.

Along the Potomac, where the Army of Northern Virginia lay for the autumn and early part of the winter, religious services were held with encouraging signs. Rev. Joseph Cross, D. D., chaplain of the Walker Legion from Tennessee, writing of his labors, says:

"It is interesting to see how they flock to our nightly prayer-meetings, frequently in greater numbers than your Sabbath congregations in some of your city churches. I preach to them twice on the Lord's day, seated around me on the ground, officers and men, in the most primitive order you can imagine. But the most interesting, probably the most useful, part of my work is the visitation of the sick. Every morning I go to the hospital, visiting the several apartments successively; in each of which I talk privately with the men, then read a passage of Holy Scripture, make some remarks upon it, and finish with prayer. However wicked and thoughtless they are in camp, they are all glad to see the chaplain when they are sick; and I have yet to meet with the first instance of any other than the most respectful and reverent attention. I think I never occupied a field that afforded an equal opportunity for usefulness."

The soldiers eagerly read everything that was put in their hands in the camp; and often sent appeals like the following, accompanied with a donation taken out of their scanty pay:

"The soldiers here (in Western Virginia) are *starving* for reading matter. They will read anything. I frequently see a piece of newspaper, no larger than my hand, going the rounds among them. If the bread of life were now offered them through the printed page, how readily they might be led to Christ." From Culpeper Court-house a pious lady wrote of her labors among the sick and wounded: "The poor soldiers here are really begging for something to read. This is true especially of the wounded. Pray that the divine blessing may be bestowed on these afflicted ones, and that I may be a blessing to them. There is nothing I desire so much as by nursing to do good to those who have given up all for their country. There is great room for usefulness opened to pious friends now in ministering to the wants of our sick soldiers." And never did Christian women more nobly discharge their duties to the suffering. Our war brought out from the sweet retirement of home, and into the midst of agony and death, not one, but a thousand Florence Nightingales.

"It is truly gratifying," wrote a chaplain, "to see the eagerness manifested by the soldiers to get a Testament. While we are in camp, we are deprived, to a great degree, of the comforts of home and the advantages of the family library; and while we earnestly seek for a book to read, what a blessing that the Bible can be obtained, which is a library in itself!

"May God bless all who aid in any way to send the Bible or other religious books to the soldiers. To one outside of the army there can be no proper estimate of the value placed upon the Word of God by the soldiers. In perusing it, his thoughts go back to the kind instruction received around the paternal hearthstone. We had the pleasure of knowing that in one instance, at least, these books were instrumental of good. A young man of our regiment, when told that he must die, and who had carefully attended to the reading of his Testament, said, 'I had thought until this morning that I would again be permitted to see my dear mother, but I know I shall never see her in the flesh; tell her I cannot go to her, but she can come to me; I am dying in the arms of Jesus, my Redeemer, and will welcome her on the shores of a better land.'"

Another chaplain wrote from Evansport on the Potomac:

"I spent all Christmas with our men, and I am sure I never spent it more agreeably. Some of our men wished to visit their old friends in a neighboring regiment, but would not do so on account of the drunkenness and profanity going on in their midst. I know the mother of one of the young men, and I hope to return to Georgia when the war is over and tell her how Charlie looked as I met him returning to his camp, unwilling to risk himself among them. We are considered the most moral, best behaved regiment connected with this part of the army.

"'This, of course, speaks louder and longer than victories on the battle-field, and is owing greatly, I must add, to our regimental officers, who enjoin such conduct by precept and encourage it by example. No embargo is laid upon our religious operations. The soldiers are accessible, and the officers co-operate with the chaplain. It is not unusual for the chaplain to receive several visits during the day from men desirous of having religious services in their tents at night. How gratifying that the rose of Sharon blooms under the war-cloud that overhangs us and scatters its fragrance through our encampment!"

Scarcely anything is more pleasing than to note the influence of religion on the hearts of our soldiers in prompting them to every good work. Though in the army toiling, fighting, suffering, their hearts were responsive to all the calls of the Church of God. How noble are the following words from one of them:

"It has been many a day since I have had the pleasure of looking in upon my pleasant home, and seeing for myself the 'first fruits of the harvest'—nor have I heard whether the ingathering from my wheat, oats, and rye patches has been abundant or meager. But God has been good to me in the camp in shielding me against disease, and preserving my health unimpaired, and in taking care of my family, and I desire to make a thank-offering and contribute my mite towards paying the Missionary Debt and relieving the Treasury. The paymaster is now in camp, paying us the first installments for services rendered. Of *these* 'first fruits,' earned in the service of the Confederate States, I enclose $10 for the Missionary Debt, and the balance for the *Advocate*, which you will please forward to me here."

Here are the genuine fruits of the Spirit; he sends his means to help give the gospel to the destitute, and calls for his pleasant home companion, the religious family paper, to follow him into the camp.

Another, sending a contribution for any charitable pupose to which it might be thought best to devote it, says: "I am afraid that in the army my feeling has been that a 'poor private' could hardly be expected, out of his scanty means, to contribute to the world's great needs. God forgive me, and make me more sensible of my accountability to him for the smallest talents entrusted to my care."

As we advance in the narrative, we shall meet with repeated instances of the noblest self-denial and generosity on the part of our soldiers.

A little after mid-winter this year, a series of disasters occurred to our arms, which chilled the hearts of the people, and cast a gloom over the fair prospects with which the first year of the war had just closed. First came the disaster at Fishing Creek, in Kentucky; then at Roanoke Island, in North Carolina; Fort Henry, and Fort Donelson, which guarded the Cumberland and

Tennessee rivers, fell in quick succession before the overwhelming forces of the Federals; Columbus, in Kentucky, was given up, Nashville was evacuated in the midst of dismay and confusion, and the remains of the Southern army retired southward.

In all these battles there were instances of that high Christian courage which became the leading characteristic of the Southern soldiers. The capture of Roanoke Island was made by General Burnside with an immense force compared with the handful of men that defended it. Here many valuable lives were lost. Among the killed was Captain O. Jennings Wise, son of Hon. Henry A. Wise. He commanded the Richmond Virginia Blues, and fell in the thickest of the fight. Speaking of the battle and fall of his son, in reply to a letter of condolence from a friend, General Wise said:

"Ah! the report of the *military murders* of Roanoke Island reached you!

"The enemy came in mist and storm, and I sent my men, only seventeen companies of infantry, to meet 15,000 of the best appointed troops. I, prostrated by pleurisy the most excruciating. When I ordered the meanest man of my command, I was obliged to order *that son*, to be an example of devoted service and of sacrifice. O, God! Thou gavest him and thou took him away. What a son, what a sacrifice! I parted from him saying, 'My son, fight the enemy close.' He replied, 'I think I will,' with a smile. He fought and watched and led, and led again, into action—was marked, fell with four balls piercing his precious form—cheered on to action as they bore him off, and died smiling, calm, composed, and grandly."

Captain Coles, of Charlottesville, Va., a noble young soldier, was also among the killed. In the midst of the fight, it is said that a gallant officer rode up to his superior and asked for reinforcements, who, in reply, assured him that it was madness to contend with a mere handful of men against such numbers. On receiving this answer, he sat down for a moment and cried bitterly, then taking his sword, he broke it in pieces, mounted his horse, and rode off.

The struggle at Fort Donelson was one of the most terrific in the annals of war. "The snow," says an eye-witness, "lay upon the ground to the depth of three inches—soon to be the pall of the bridegroom death to many a brave fellow—and a cold, blinding sleet came slanting down like a shower of lances. Four days in such weather our soldiers continued the fight, without time to eat or sleep—tired, hungry, and cold, and all the while fresh troops pouring against them, making another army greater than their own."

A Northern account of the battle said: "Never, perhaps, on the American continent has a more bloody battle been fought. An officer, who participated and was wounded in the fight, says the scene beggars description. So thickly was the battle-field strewn with dead and wounded that he could have traversed acres of it, stepping at most every step upon a prostrate body. The rebels fought with desperation, their artillerists using their pieces with most fearful effect. On either side could be heard the voices of those in command cheering on the men."

Among the many Christian soldiers who fought and fell on this bloody field, not one has a brighter record than the Rev. Dabney Carr Harrison, who was mortally wounded while bravely leading on his company amid a storm of bullets. The following notice of him was written when the memory of his deeds and his death was fresh in the hearts of his countrymen:

"When the sun rose on the morning of that bloody Saturday, it saw him already in the thickest of the battle. Through seven hours of mortal peril he wrestled with the foe; with dauntless heart he cheered on his men; they loved him as a father, and eagerly followed wherever he led. Their testimony is, that he never said 'go on,' but 'come on,' while ever before them flashed his waving sword. At length, they saw with fear and pain that his firm step faltered, that his erect form wavered and was sinking. They sprang forward and bore him from the field to die. He had 'warred a good warfare, ever holding faith and a good conscience.'"

"With reverence I have taken in my hand the hat he wore in the battle—with tears and swelling heart have I gazed on it. It is pierced by four balls. Three whistled partly through and did no harm. The fourth, partly spent, marred that beautiful brow. But these were as nothing. He calmly fought on. A more fatal aim sent a ball into his left breast, above his heart, quite through his body. His men did not know it. He still cheered them on. Another deadly aim drove a ball through his right lung; just where, cannot be told. His face was to the foe and his step onward even when, from loss of blood and exhaustion, he began to sink. Yet he did not die till next day. Like his brother, seven months before; like his sister, seven days after; like the little one to whom he had given his name, he was to die on the Sabbath, with the calm of the eternal Sabbath filling his breast. He was carried to Nashville and tenderly nursed by faithful men. Only two incidents of his dying hours have reached us. Calling for one of his manuscript books, he took his pencil and, with a trembling hand, feebly wrote these words, 'Feb. 16, 1862, Sunday. I die content and happy, trusting in the merits of my Saviour, Jesus, committing my wife and children to their Father and mine.—Dabney Carr Harrison.' Precious legacy of love and prayer! Precious testimony of faith and blessedness!

"When he felt that death was just upon him, he gathered up his remaining strength for one more effort. Resting in the arms of one of his men, and speaking as if the company, for which he had toiled, and suffered, and prayed, so much, was before him, he exclaimed, 'Company K, you have no Captain now; but never give up; never surrender.'

"Thus was his last breath for his country, for the young Confederacy, whose liberty, honor, and righteousness, were inexpressibly dear to him; for which he wept, and prayed, and made supplication in secret; for which he was content to endure hardness as a good soldier, and then cheerfully to die.

"These dying words beautifully connect themselves with those of his brother Peyton on the field of Manassas, and, taken together, they have a special fitness to our country's present need.

"When the second Virginia regiment, fighting on our left at Manassas, was broken by a sudden and destructive flank fire of the enemy, and by the unfortunate command of its Colonel, Peyton, and a few officers of like spirit, rallied a portion of the men and led them in a perilous but splendid and victorious charge. In the midst of it, however, he fell, shot like his brother, in the breast. Two of his men bore him from the field. His face was radiant with heavenly peace. He spent a few moments in dictating messages of love, and in prayer for himself, his family, and his country. 'What more can we do for you?' asked the affectionate men who supported him. 'Lay me down,' was his answer, 'I am ready to die; you can do no more for me; rally to the charge!'"

These reverses, following each other so quickly, deeply affected the people, and produced a feeling of profound humiliation before God. The shortest month of the year carried the record of nearly all our disasters, and in the same month the Provisional Government expired, and the Permanent Government was established. The President deemed this a fitting occasion for us "again to present ourselves in humiliation, prayer, and thanksgiving before God," and accordingly issued a proclamation, in which he said:

"A tone of earnest piety has pervaded our people, and the hundred victories which we have obtained over our enemies have been justly ascribed to Him who ruleth the universe.

"We had hoped that the year would have closed upon a scene of continued prosperity, but it has pleased the Supreme Disposer of Events to order it otherwise. We are not permitted to furnish an exception to the rule in divine government which has prescribed affliction as the discipline of nations, as well as of individuals. Our faith and perseverance must be tested, and the chastening which seemeth grievous will, if rightfully received, bring forth its appropriate fruits.

"It is meet and right, therefore, that we should repair to the only Giver of all victory, and humbling ourselves before him, should pray that he may strengthen our confidence in his mighty power and righteous judgment. Then may we surely trust in him, that he will perform his promise, and encompass us as with a shield in this trust."

The day following, 22d of February, Jefferson Davis was inaugurated, and closed his address in the following words:

"With confidence in the wisdom and virtue of those who will share with me the responsibility, and aid me in the conduct of public affairs, securely relying upon the patriotism and courage of the people, of which the present war has furnished so many examples, I deeply feel the weight of the responsibilities I now, with unaffected diffidence, am about to assume; and fully realizing the inadequacy of human power to guide and to sustain, my hope is reverently fixed on Him whose favor is ever vouchsafed to the cause which is just. With humble gratitude and adoration, acknowledging the Providence which has so visibly protected the Confederacy during its brief but eventful career, to thee, oh God! I trustingly commit myself, and prayerfully invoke thy blessing on my country and its cause."

When the President "reached the concluding lines, the manuscript dropped upon the table, and raising his hands to heaven, he exclaimed : "'To thee, oh God! I trustingly commit myself, and prayerfully invoke thy blessing on my country and its cause.'

"The effect was thrilling. An electric flame ran through the multitude. The prayer of the President, thus made in open day before the people, found an echo in a thousand hearts."

In response to the pious sentiments of the President, the people were urged by the pulpit, and by the religious, and, indeed, by the secular press, to give themselves to fasting, prayer, humiliation, and self-examination in earnest.

"We call upon the ministry to stand up bravely in their place and to rebuke every form of sin. God, whose messengers they are, adds the solemn and terrible sanctions of his judgments to the word of his inspiration with which they are commissioned to arouse the dormant consciences of the people. When these thunders of the pulpit and of Providence combine, the deafest ear must hear, the most stupefied soul must arouse from its slumbers.

"Tell the people of their sins. Lift up the voice and spare not. Let Jeremiah teach the prophet of the Most High how to denounce sin, and Isaiah how to promise good to the repentant sinner. Give no place to worldliness in the Church. Teach the profane swearer, the Sabbath-breaker, the licentious, the intemperate, that they are the real enemies of their country, because they have made God angry with us. Tell the same thing to the worldly-minded, luxurious, penurious professor of religion, who sees souls die by whole generations for want of that gospel which he might carry or send to them.

"But the work to be done must not stop here. Men's lives must be reformed. Those who are living in disregard of the laws of God are public enemies—more to be dreaded than our foe. The drunkard, the debauchee, the extortioner, the man who grows rich upon the vices of others, the profane swearer, the Sabbath-breaker, the adulterer, the liar, the brawler, the man-slayer, the thief, are all to be classed together as sinners against God, as those who help to make up this aggregate of national sin, of which our rulers call upon us to repent—and only the guilty sinners themselves can so repent as to make sure of the Divine favor."

Such were the truthful and stirring appeals that sounded from pulpit and press before and upon the day of fasting and prayer. We have taken the pains to record them in order to show that deep and earnest religious spirit which pervaded the South at every period of our struggle.

Among the cheering signs of good among the soldiers was their earnest desire to procure Bibles and Testaments, or any part, indeed, of the Word of God. In the close of the winter, Rev. E. A. Bolles, General Agent of the Bible Societies in South Carolina, said, in speaking of his work:

"Three months ago I commenced the work of distribution among the soldiers on our coast under the auspices of the Executive Committee of the South Carolina Bible Convention. During this time several thousand copies of the Scriptures have been given away to needy and grateful soldiers, and thousands of copies are yet needed to meet the demand. I may safely say that twenty thousand copies are needed for distribution among the soldiers on the coast. I therefore earnestly appeal to the benevolent for funds to procure the Scriptures, so that the good work so successfully begun may be continued until every destitute soldier is supplied with the Word of Life."

To this gentleman the chaplain of the 15th South Carolina regiment sent an encouraging report of the state of religion in his regiment:

"The Testaments you sent to me were eagerly sought after by the men, many coming to me long after they were all distributed, and were much disappointed at not receiving one. Could you send us some more they would be thankfully received and faithfully distributed. As almost all the men lost their Bibles on Hilton Head, our regiment is perhaps the most destitute on the coast. I am happy to say there is much religious feeling pervading our regiment, and our nightly prayer-meetings are well attended, and I hope ere long the Lord will bless us with an outpouring of his Holy Spirit."

To the same the Lieutenant-Colonel of the 10th South Carolina regiment wrote:

"I would be glad if you will supply the regiment to which I am attached with the Scriptures, as I see by the papers that you are engaged in the work of distribution among the soldiers. We prefer Testaments, as they would be much easier for soldiers to carry in their knapsacks. I have made this application to you because of finding that all our men have not Bibles or Testaments, and I consider a *soldier poorly equipped without one or the other*."

While it is a pleasing task to mark the progress of religion among the soldiers comprising the main armies of the Confederacy, it is scarcely less interesting to look at its influence upon the native Indians, thousands of whom espoused the cause of the South. The following statement of the religious condition of our Indian soldiers appears in the report on Missions made to the General Assembly of the Presbyterian Church in the spring of 1862:

"It is well known that all the Indians in the Southwest, with the exception of a portion of the Creeks and a few straggling bands of Cherokees and Seminoles, espoused the cause of the South with much heartiness from the very commencement of our troubles, and not a few of them have given proof of their sincerity on more than one battle-field. The first call for volunteers aroused much of the old war spirit among them. War songs, scalp dances, painted faces, and feathered heads—sights and scenes that were scarcely known to the present generation—were revived in many parts of the country, and, for a time, it looked as if the people were about to relapse into their former savage condition. But these things had but a short and transient existence, and in the course of a few months no traces of them whatever could be found. Many have entered the army, no doubt, from mere excitement and the love of warfare, but the great body of them, and especially the members of the Church, it is believed, have been actuated purely by motives of duty and patriotism. Mr. Stark visited the Choctaw regiments at their encampments in the Cherokee country the latter part of January, and gives a good account of their general deportment, especially of that of the members of the Church. He supposes there were 1,600 Choctaws in the encampment—about one-sixth of these were professing Christians, some of whom were the best and most prominent men of the nation. He writes: 'Prayer and praise went up every evening from around many of the camp-fires.' And he adds that the captain of the company with whom he lodged allowed no drinking, swearing, gambling, or Sabbath-breaking among his men; and indeed he had seen and heard of very little of these vices among any of the soldiers."

Thus it will be seen that among all classes in the armies of the South the element of true piety was found. The white man and the red man felt alike, that the cause in which they struggled was just and right, and that upon it they could invoke the blessing of God without doing violence to their conscience or their faith.

The early part of the war, without the blessing of

deep and general revivals, was not barren of the fruits of righteousness in the lives, and the peace and glory of religion in the deaths of our soldiers. The scenes often witnessed by the humble cot of the dying patriot were abundant in proof that the gospel is the power of God unto salvation to every one that believeth.

The Rev. Dr. James A. Duncan thus describes a soldier's death:

"During the first year of the war we were called up at midnight to visit a dying soldier. He was at the Columbian hotel, in Richmond. As we entered the room, we saw the sufferer lying upon his bed, pale and emaciated: the signs of death in his face. At the foot of his bed stood the Adjutant of his regiment; on one side sat a kind old lady, a nurse from one of the hospitals, and who, from the familiar and tender way in which she spoke to him, had evidently known the young soldier well at his own home in Savannah, Ga. We sat down on the edge of the bed and began a conversation with the three.

"Whitfield Stevens belonged to Bartow's regiment; had fought through several battles, and was now dying from fever occasioned by the exposure and hardships incident to the soldier's life. He was the son of Methodist parents, but was himself not a member of the Church. He had, however, spoken in a way that greatly encouraged the attendants around his bed to cherish the hope that he was truly concerned about his spiritual condition, and had asked that a minister of the gospel might be sent for to converse and pray with him. Such was the information we obtained in the course of conversation. He was a tall, manly fellow, and in spite of the ravages of disease his fine face, clear, bright eye, and expressive mouth, revealed at a glance that he was a young man of decided character.

"'I sent for you, sir, to talk with and pray for me,' with a calmness and directness that interested, and at the same time made us feel that we could approach him freely upon the subject of religion.

"'Whitefield, are you a member of the Church, or professor of religion?' 'No,' he replied, 'but I'll tell you how far I have committed myself to religion. After the battle of Manassas—and you know that Bartow's regiment suffered a great deal—I felt that the Almighty had been very merciful to protect my unworthy life; and late in the evening, just a little after sunset, I went off by myself amid some pines, kneeled down upon the green grass and thanked God for sparing me to my mother, and I gave him my word that I would try and serve him as long as I lived.' Pausing a moment to gather strength, he continued slowly, distinctly, and with an emphasis that we rarely ever hear except from the lips of the dying: 'Father came on soon after that battle to see me. When he was about to return, and had said good-bye, I noticed that he still lingered, looked anxious, came back, and seemed loath to leave. I said to him, 'Father, I know what is the matter with you; you think I am not a Christian, and you don't like to leave me in my present perilous position without being able to think of me as ready to die.' He said that was exactly what made him linger and hesitate. I told him then about my praying on the evening of the Manassas fight. He seemed greatly comforted by it, and said he could return home with a more cheerful heart.'

"We said: 'Then, Whitefield, you are not afraid to die?' 'No, sir,' he answered, 'I shall go up and make my report to the Almighty as the Commander-in-Chief of all things. I'll tell him I have been a *faithful* soldier and a *dutiful* son—' Here the nurse interrupted him, and seeming to think he was trusting to his own goodness, said: 'Whitefield, my son, you know all that won't save you—' 'Stop! stop! wait till I get through,' said he; 'I'll tell him I've been a *faithful* soldier and a *duti-*

ful son, but an *unfaithful* servant of God; nevertheless, *my trust* is in Jesus Christ, the Saviour of men.' As he finished the sentence, he turned and looked upon the kind nurse, as though to ask, 'Is my faith right?' The good old lady burst into tears. We all kneeled down in prayer around his bed; fervently we commended the dying soldier to his Saviour, and arose feeling that, truly, God was in that place.

"'Sing to me,' said he, 'some of those good old hymns I used to hear at home.' We sang—

"'Father, I stretch my hands to thee,' &c.,
"'Amazing grace, how sweet the sound,' &c.

"He seemed to appreciate the sentiments of the hymn, and tried, now and then, to join in the singing. Finding that he enjoyed these hymns so much, we commenced and sung the beautiful words—

"'Jesus, lover of my soul,
Let me to thy bosom fly,' &c.

"He became very happy. It was an impressive scene—between midnight and daybreak—every sound hushed on the street—silence reigned in that crowded hotel—the light in the room threw fitful flashes upon the quiet, pale face of the young hero—the Adjutant leaned upon the foot of the bed, weeping—the generous Christian nurse, amid her tears, joined in the hymn—we felt,

"'Angels now are hovering round us.'

As we sang the lines—

"'Cover my defenceless head
With the shadow of thy wing,'

"Whitefield exclaimed, 'Adjutant! Adjutant! is not that grand? Ah! you don't know what that means! I will tell you what it means. At Manassas, when the bullets were whistling around us like hail, and our boys were dropping in the ranks, and poor Bartow fell, then the Almighty 'covered *my* defenceless head with the shadow of *his* wing!' With a deeper emphasis than we had employed, he repeated—

"'Cover MY defenceless head
With the shadow of THY wing.'

"It was the crowning triumph. The noble boy, weaker, sank back on his pillow. We said, 'You had better now rest.' 'No,' said he, 'let me talk. I have but a little while to live; let me talk. I wish one thing could be.' 'What,' asked we, 'do you wish?' 'I would like,' he replied, 'that my dear mother could come and sit down right here on the bed by me, and I could kiss her once; then I would lie down and die, and they would carry me away to Georgia, and bury me by the side of my sweet little sister—nurse, you knew my sister; she was a good child—and then—ah! then I would go up to heaven, and wait till the rest all came. Oh! would not that be grand! I hoped to live long enough to see father. He will be here to-morrow morning. But never mind, God knows best—it is all right. Adjutant, you know ——, of my company? Well, give my love to him. In the battle, as he was marching by my side, 'Whitefield,' said he, 'I'll stand by you to the death.' Noble fellow! Tell him I'll think of him in eternity.'

"The dying soldier grew weaker, his bright eyes closed, and the morning sun threw his golden splendors upon the brow of the sleeping hero. His father arrived by the early train, but too late to see his son alive. We told him the story of his son's death, and recounted more fully than in these pages the touching scene of that memorable night. The old man smiled through his tears, and grew happy with hope in the midst of his grief. 'I am satisfied,' said he. 'Whitefield died as I would have him die—died for his country; died honorably; and, above all, died in the faith of the gospel. It will comfort his mother. I shall return to my home and praise God for his goodness in the midst of our sorrows.'"

CHAPTER VIII.

SPRING OF 1862.

The military movements of this season alternately elevated and depressed the public mind. The memorable naval victory in Hampton Roads, the evacuation of Manassas, the great battle of Shiloh, and the fall of New Orleans—all occurred within two months. But the people and the soldiers kept up their courage, and while they lamented over reverses, rejoiced humbly in our successes.

The march from Manassas to the Peninsula was attended with great suffering on the part of the soldiers. "You would pity our hungry patriots," wrote a chaplain, "if you could see them toasting the middling bacon on long sticks, and consigning their dough to the ashes for want of an oven. We have had no tents either, and a great many drenching showers. How would you enjoy sleeping, if it had to be effected out in the woods, in a driving rain, with a sobby, spongy soil for a bed, and no covering but a blanket? I have waked up at midnight under such circumstances, and found half the regiment standing silently and gloomily around the camp-fires, while now and then the barking, Lectic cough of some afflicted soldier preached a sermon on death."

Another, who moved from a different part of the line, says, in a rather more cheerful strain:

"We experienced mingled emotions of joy and sadness on the morning of our departure from our old camp at Evansport. Our men had grown tired of the winds, rains, mud, sleet, and snow, on the border, and were ready to rejoice at the prospect of any change of position.

"Some things pained us. I shall never forget the parting glance at our regimental graveyard. Some were leaving brothers on that lonely hill; some, near and dear relations; *all*, gallant comrades.

"Our second day's march was on the Sabbath. About noon I ascertained that by getting permission to leave ranks I could attend Methodist Circuit preaching in the afternoon. A walk of three miles brought me up, about 3 o'clock, to a little schoolhouse, where I was affectingly reminded of my dear old Circuits in Georgia.

"We had a good meeting. It was Bro. McSparran's first appointment at that place, and when he announced his next appointment for them, an old brother spoke up somewhat amusingly and not very encouragingly to the preacher: 'The Yankees will have us all before then.'

"Feeling very much fatigued, I spent that night with the young itinerant in the rear of our regiment, and had he called upon me to select for him a text to correspond with what I conceived his feelings to be, I would have fixed upon 'A prudent man foreseeth the evil and hideth himself.' We have had some happy times on this side of the Rappahannock since.

"Let me tell you something about that Methodist woman whose hospitalities we so abundantly shared that Sabbath evening. Her husband was a poor man, but a *brave Virginian*. He spoke of enlisting for the defence of the soil with which mingled the dust of a noble ancestry.

"'Go,' said that Christian woman; and looking around upon a large group of little bright-eyed boys, she added, 'You can defend us best in the ranks. *I* will remain and defend our home and these children. Oh, for an army of such heroines! I felt like giving three cheers for her patriotism, and did not object in the least to that sort of *Methodism*."

The desolation that follows war is well depicted by another writer:

"Whole square miles of woods have been shaved off close to the ground. The whole country is, I might say, one great road; at least, it is impossible to travel one mile from our old camp without crossing from ten to twenty highways. We never saw a child or lady, hardly ever a citizen. One could hardly move about for the dead horses that lay in multitudes around. Every old field is marked with tent-drains, rotten beef and other provisions, with a wilderness of rude chimneys, and all manner of camp trash. The mud and filth are so great that it is a feat to walk a hundred yards, and every mile of road has its wreck of a wagon. These are the Elysian fields which General Johnston has deserted."

About the same time General Jackson was compelled to move his forces up the Valley of Virginia, and leave Winchester and other places exposed to the incursions of the Federals. When asked by a citizen of the Valley whether he would really fall back and desert them, he replied, "By the help of God, I will be with you again soon."

These movements, while they interrupted the pious labors of chaplains and colporteurs, did not divert the minds of the soldiers from the great truths of religion. No sooner was the main army in position near Williamsburg, on the Peninsula, than the work was resumed, and the fruits of righteousness began to appear. The following interesting reports were sent to Rev. A. E. Dickinson, Superintendent of Colportage for the Baptist Church: "I have known twelve men in my regiment," wrote a chaplain from Williamsburg, "who have professed conversion from reading your tracts. One came to me with a tract in his hand, and the tears flowing down his cheeks, and said, 'I would not take thousands for this tract. My parents have prayed for me, and wept over me; but it was left for this tract to bring me, a poor convicted sinner, to the feet of Jesus. Oh, sir, I feel to-day that I am a new man, and have set out for heaven.'" Another wrote from Yorktown: "For three months I have not preached a sermon. We have no preaching place, and I do not know when we shall have one. The most that can be done is by colportage work, from camp to camp, distributing the pages of divine truth. The soldiers are anxious for Testaments and tracts, and read them most eagerly."

The scenes in the hospitals were very touching. "As I would go from cot to cot," says a colporteur writing from Winchester, Va., "leaving a tract or a Testament, and speaking of Jesus, it was not uncommon for some sufferer in another part of the room to call out, 'Bring me one.' I shall never forget my first visit to one of the hospitals. There, stretched out before me, on coarse, hard beds, lay perhaps a hundred sick soldiers, most of them young men, some of them the flower of the land. They were far from happy homes, lonely, despairing, sick—some of them sick unto death. How cheering the sight of any friend! What an opportunity for the child of God!"

General Jackson gave every encouragement to religion among his soldiers; he was the model Christian officer in our armies, "active, humble, consistent—restraining profanity and Sabbath-breaking—welcoming colporteurs, distributing tracts, and anxious to have every regiment in his army supplied with a chaplain." Indeed, even the most irreligious officers gladly welcomed these tract distributors to their camps. "Sir," said a notoriously cross and profane General to a colporteur, "you have come, I hope, to do all the good you can;" and he showed his sincerity by inviting him to mess at his table and share his blankets.

It is sadly pleasing to follow these good men in their walks through the hospitals, and listen to their talks with the sick men. "I was once tempted to be ashamed of the work," says one of them, "and was about to pass by a group of soldiers without giving them any tracts, but it appeared to me that this might be a temptation of the evil one, and I determined to overlook no one. Going up to a soldier, I asked if he was a Christian. He was deeply moved, and said, 'I wish to have some conversation with you; can you sit down with me awhile?' He then told me that he had been a professor of religion; had enjoyed the smile of God on his soul; but that temptation and vice had led him astray, until now he was almost ready to despair. Weeping and sobbing, he confessed his sin. I urged him again to seek the favor of God. A very sick man said to me, 'Oh, sir, I would give worlds for an interest in the blood of Jesus and the pardon of sin.' He has since passed away."

Another writes: "The saddest, the happiest deaths I have ever known have been in the army. Soldiers jolting along in the wagons, which bore them to the hospitals, have died in the triumphs of faith. And in the hospitals, without a pallet or a pillow, without an acquaintance to cheer or comfort or alleviate, what scenes have I witnessed! It has been my privilege to read, sing, and pray with these pallid, dying men, and to see in their moist eyes the evidence of feeling hearts—to hear from whispering lips the most exultant expressions of trust in the Saviour. Called up some cold night to stand by a death bed, I've had the soldier to clasp my hand in his, and, with heavenly joy, point up to the shining home of a dear brother gone before. The blessings often invoked on my head by these devoted men have filled me with humble joy, and urged me to redouble my feeble efforts for the defenders of our once happy land. I would not part with these pleasing recollections of my work for all the honor a soldier can gain from a grateful country.'

"A few days ago," wrote another, "a soldier said to me, 'On going into my tent, I found lying on my table the tract, 'Why will ye die?' I read it and became alarmed in regard to my spiritual state, and re-read it until I became perfectly miserable. In this state of mind, I went off into the woods to pray that I might be delivered from this awful condition. While wrestling in prayer before God, I was enabled to lay hold of Jesus as one mighty to save, and since have had peace and joy in believing, and now I wish to make this contribution to aid in sending the same tract to my comrades, that they too may be warned to flee from the wrath to come;' so saying, he handed me five dollars."

"I found a young soldier," says another, "sinking in death. On asking him how he was, he said, 'I know in whom I have believed, and am persuaded that he is able to keep that which I have committed unto him.' At my next visit he was unable to speak save in a whisper. I put my lips to his ear and asked how it was with him? He replied, 'I had rather depart and be with Christ, which is far better.' In this frame of mind he passed away to his heavenly home."

"Some of the cases," said Rev. James B. Taylor, Sr., writing of his visits to the hospitals at Staunton, Va., "were peculiarly touching. One man from Southwestern Georgia told me, with deep feeling, that out of 98 composing his company 24 were buried in Western Virginia. I pressed upon him the claims of the gospel, and he seemed thankful and penitent. Another, far from home, seemed near the grave. The tears flowed from his languid eyes when I asked him about his spiritual condition, and with trembling lips he replied, 'No hope.' He gazed at me wistfully, as I pointed him to the 'Lamb of God that taketh away the sin of the world.' "I was specially affected by the remarks of a soldier who said, 'O, sir, you know not how difficult it is to stem the tide of corruption in the army. Many of our officers drink and swear, and discourage all manifestations of religious feeling.'"

Such scenes were witnessed every day and night, and every hour of every day and night, from the first battle of the war to its disastrous close. The batte-fields, as well as the hospitals, have their records of unselfish devotion and Christian heroism; and the deeper the struggle the brighter shone those elements of character that truly ennoble our nature.

The battle of Shiloh, fought this spring, was made illustrious, both by the prowess of our arms, and by the costly sacrifices there laid upon the altar of the South. On this bloody field, that accomplished soldier and noble gentleman, Albert Sidney Johnston, offered up his life. "While leading a successful charge, turning the enemy's right, and gaining a brilliant victory, a minnie ball cut the artery of his leg, but he rode on till from loss of blood he fell exhausted, and died without pain in a few moments." Such were the brief words in which his fellow-warriors told of his death.

The President, in communicating this sad intelligence to Congress, after announcing the victory, said:

"But an allwise Creator has been pleased, while vouchsafing to us his countenance in battle, to afflict us with a severe dispensation, to which we must bow in humble submission. The last lingering hope has disappeared, and it is but too true that Gen. Albert Sidney Johnston is no more.

"My long and close friendship with this departed chieftain and patriot forbids me to trust myself in giving vent to the feelings which this sad intelligence has evoked. Without doing injustice to the living, it may be safely asserted that our loss is irreparable, and that among the shining hosts of the great and the good who now cluster around the banner of our country, there exists no purer spirit, no more heroic soul, than that of the illustrious man whose death I join you in lamenting.

"In his death he has illustrated the character for which through life he was conspicuous—that of singleness of purpose and devotion to duty. With his whole energies bent on attaining the victory which he deemed essential to his country's cause, he rode on to the accomplishment of his object, forgetful of self, while his very life-blood was fast ebbing away. His last breath cheered his comrades to victory. The last sound which he heard was their shout of triumph. His last thought was his country's, and long and deeply will his country mourn his loss."

The case of General Johnston was particularly sad. After the disasters in the West, and the retreat of his army to Corinth, he was under a cloud, censures were heaped upon him, and there were loud clamors for his removal. It was said, at the time, that men high in position urged the President to displace him, but he was inflexible, and only replied, "If Albert Sidney Johnston is not a General, then I have no General."

His military movements in Kentucky, and his march Southward, were freely and severely criticised in the Confederate Congress by men who "never set a squadron in the field," but the noble General bore it all in silence.

After his lamented death, and while the glory of his great victory was still shining on the country, a letter was read in this same Congress which he wrote to the President explaining all his movements, and giving the reasons for them. The writer was present in the hall of Congress when this letter was read, and never can he forget the profound impression it made on the entire audience.

Abundant tears, and a silence more eloquent than the words of the greatest orator, were the tribute paid to the memory of the departed patriot.

Our space will not permit us to lay the whole of this noble letter before the reader, but we cannot deny him the gratification of seeing its closing sentences.

After alluding to the fall of Fort Donelson, he says:

"The blow was most disastrous, and almost without a remedy. I, therefore, in my first report remained silent. This silence you were kind enough to attribute to my generosity. I will not lay claim to the motive to excuse my course. I observed silence, as it seemed to be the best way to serve the cause and the country. The facts were not fully known—discontent prevailed, and criticism or condemnation were more likely to augment than to cure the evil. I refrained, well knowing that heavy censures would fall upon me, but convinced that it was better to endure them for the present, and defer to a more propitious time an investigation of the conduct of the Generals, for in the meantime their services were required and their influence useful—for these reasons, Generals Floyd and Pillow were assigned to duty, as I still felt confidence in their gallantry, their energy, and their devotion to the Confederacy.

"Thus I have recurred to the motives by which I have been governed, from a deep personal sense of the friendship and confidence you have always shown me, and from the conviction that they have not been withdrawn from me in adversity.

"The test of merit in my profession, with the people, is *success*. It is a hard rule, but I think it right."

At the reading of the last sentence, the recollection of the injustice done to the hero rushed upon the minds of the hearers, and the scene was morally sublime. Albert Sidney Johnston was dead, but he was enshrined in the hearts of his countrymen.

The instances of heroic valor in the battle of Shiloh are abundant. A chaplain, Rev. I. T. Tichnor, of the 17th Alabama regiment, in a letter to Governor Watts, of that State, who at one time commanded the regiment, says:

"During this engagement we were under a cross fire on the left wing from three directions. Under it the boys wavered. I had been wearied, and was sitting down, but seeing them waver, I sprang to my feet, took off my hat, waved it over my head, walked up and down the line, and, as they say, 'preached them a sermon.' I reminded them that it was Sunday. That at that hour (11½ o'clock) all their home folks were praying for them, that Tom Watts (excuse the familiar way in which I employed so distinguished a name) had told us he would listen with an eager ear to hear from the 17th; and shouting your name loud over the roar of battle, I called upon them to stand there and die, if need be, for their country. The effect was evident. Every man stood to his post, every eye flashed, and every heart beat high with desperate resolve to conquer or die. The regiment lost one-third of the number carried into the field."

Among the Christian soldiers that fell was Lieutenant-Colonel Holbrook, of a Kentucky regiment. He was mortally wounded, and fell at the head of his regiment in a victorious charge. After the battle, several of his officers came to see him in the hospital. He was dying fast, but desired to be propped up in bed, and then he talked with them like a Christian soldier: "Gentlemen, in the course of my official duties with you I have had little or no occasion to speak to you upon the subject of religion, but this is a time when, as fellow-men, we may commune frankly together. And I desire to bear witness to the fact that I am at the present moment deriving all my strength and consolation from the firm reliance which I have upon the blessings of religion. I know I am not prepared for death, as I ought to have been, and as I hope you may be, but I feel safe in reposing upon the strong arm of God, and trusting to him for my future happiness. Before this war is closed, some of you may be brought upon the threshold of the eternal world, as I have been, and my earnest prayer is that the messenger of death may find you waiting. Throughout my existence, I have found nothing in my experience that has afforded me more substantial happiness than Christianity, and I now, as I lie here conscious that life is waning, desire to bear testimony of a peaceful mind, of a firm faith in the grand scheme of salvation.

Farewell, my comrades, may we all meet in a better world."

One of the rarest instances of youthful heroism that ever occurred is recorded in connection with this battle. Charlie Jackson, whose brief career as a soldier, and whose happy death we place here upon permanent record, was worthy of the great name he bore:

"Some months ago," says a writer, "Charlie's father raised a company of soldiers, in which he was permitted to drill with the privates, and finally became so expert in the manual of arms that, young as he was, he was chosen the drill-master. In due time, marching orders were received. Then the father, consulting the age of his boy, and probably his own paternal feelings, gave him to understand that it was his wish he should remain at home. To this Charlie strenuously demurred, and plainly told his parent that if he could not go with him he would join another company. Yielding to his obstinacy, a sort of silent consent was given, and the lad left Memphis with his comrades. The regiment to which they belonged was detached to Burnsville, several miles distant from Corinth, and here it remained until the Friday or Saturday preceding the battle. Orders were then received that it should repair at once to the field and take its position. Charlie was asleep at the time of the departure, and the father, unwilling that one so young should undergo the fatigue of the long march of twenty miles and the dangers of the coming fight, gave orders that he should not be disturbed. Several hours after, the boy awoke of his own accord.

"At a glance, his eye took in the condition of affairs, and his knowledge of coming events satisfied him of the cause. With him, to think was to act. He seized his little gun, a miniature musket which his father had made for him, and alone started on the trail of his absent regiment. Hour after hour he trudged along, and finally, just as they were about halting preparatory to going into battle, he succeeded in joining his company. He had travelled more than fifteen miles. His father chided him, but how could he do otherwise than admire the indomitable spirit of his boy? The battle commenced. Charlie took his place by his father's side, and was soon in the thickest of the fight. A bullet struck him in the body and tore an ugly wound. Still he pressed on, firing, cheering, and charging with the remainder of his regiment. He seemed not to know the sensation of fear, and his youthful example on more than one occasion was the rallying point from which the men took fresh spirit. Suddenly, at a late hour in the day, the little fellow fell shot through the leg a few inches below the hip. He gave a cheer and told his father to go on. 'Don't mind me,' said he, 'but keep on; I'll lay here till you come back.' This of course the feelings of the parent would not permit him to do, and picking him up in his arms, he carried him to the nearest hospital. Within a day or two Charlie was brought to his home in Memphis, feeble, yet full of hope and courage.

"Dr. Keller was called upon to examine the wound and, if necessary, to perform amputation; but at a glance his experienced eye saw that the poor boy was beyond the hope of recovery. Mortification had set in, and an operation would only increase his sufferings without prolonging life. The lad noticed the sober countenance of the physician as he turned away and went to an adjoining room to break the mournful intelligence to the weeping father and mother. Nothing could be done but to relieve him of pain by means of opiates.

"A few moments afterwards he returned to the bedside of the sufferer, when the young hero abruptly met him with the question—

"'Doctor, will you answer me a straightforward question, and tell me the truth?'

"The physician paused a moment, and then said:

"'Yes, Charlie, I will; but you must prepare for bad news.'

"'Can I live?' was the response.

"'No! Nothing can save you now but a miracle from Heaven.'

"'Well, I have thought so myself. I have felt as if I was going to die. Do father and mother know this?'

"'Yes,' replied the surgeon. 'I have just told them.'

"'Please ask them to come in here.'

"When the parents had done so, and taken their places on either side of the bed, Charlie reached out, grasped their hands in his, and said:

"'Dear father and mother, Dr. Kellar says that I can't live. And now I want to ask your forgiveness for all wrong I have done. I have tried to be a good boy in every way but one, and that was when I disobeyed you both and joined the army. I couldn't help that, for I felt as if I ought to be right where you were, father, and to fight as long as I was able. I'm only sorry that I can't fight through the war. If I have said anything wrong or done anything wrong, won't you forgive me?'

"The afflicted parents could only weep their assent.

"'Now, father,' continued the boy, 'one thing more. Don't stay here with me, but go back to camp. Mother will take care of me, and your services are more necessary in your company than they are at home. I am not afraid to die, and I wish I had a thousand lives to lose in the same way. And, father, tell the boys when you get back how I died—just as a soldier ought to. Tell them to fight the Yankees as long as there is one left in the country, and *never give up!* Whenever you fill up the company with new men, let them know that besides their country there's a little boy in heaven who will watch them and pray for them as they go into battle.'

"And so is dying one of the bravest spirits that was ever breathed into the human body by its Divine Master. The scene I have described is one of which we sometimes read, but rarely behold, and the surgeon told me that, inured as he was to spectacles of suffering and woe, as he stood by this, a silent spectator, his heart overflowed in tears and he knelt down and sobbed like a child.

"How true are the lines of the poet—

"The good die first,
And they whose hearts are dry as Summer's dust,
Burn to the socket."

From this, and other battles, the hospitals were filled with thousands of sick and wounded men, among whom there were the most cheering evidences of true religious feeling. Rev. B. B. Ross, of Alabama, who gladly gave himself to the work of colportage, says of his labors:

"I visited Corinth, the hospitals, and some of the camps, and am glad to report that the soldiers are very greedy for all kinds of religious reading—take the tracts from the agent with delight, and read them with avidity; and, whenever he sees proper to drop a word of admonition or warning, listen to it with patience and respect. But this is especially so in the hospitals."

From Okolona, Miss., Rev. J. T. C. Collins wrote to Mr. Ross:

"The soldiers received the books with great eagerness. I never in all my life saw such a desire to get Bibles. Every ward I went into they would beg me for *Bibles and Testaments*. While they gladly received the other books, they wanted *Bibles*. I have been to every man's cot and left either a book or a tract. And when I re-visited them, and asked how they liked the books, my heart was greatly cheered by the accounts they gave me. One said he had been improving ever since he had gotten something to interest his mind. Another said, while a friend was reading for him the 14th chapter of John (a chapter to which I had called his attention), he was blessed and made very happy. He is now dead—went safely home."

This eager desire for religious reading was as manifest

in the camp as in the hospital. A chaplain gave this pleasing testimony :

"Religious reading is highly appreciated by the soldiers; and what few tracts we can get are carefully read, and many tears have been seen to run down the soldier's face while reading these friendly visitors. They do not wait for me to go out to distribute them, but come to my tent inquiring, 'Have you any more tracts to spare?' There have been two conversions in the regiment. The soldiers were sick at the time, and one of them has since 'gone to his long home,' but felt before he died it was much the best for him to go, that 'he would be in a better world,' where wars and rumors of wars would no more mar his peace."

The evacuation of the Peninsula, and the falling back of our army from Yorktown to the vicinity of Richmond, crowded the hospitals with thousands of sick and wounded men. No person who was in Richmond in the spring of 1862 can forget the painful scenes as the long trains of sick and wounded moved into the city day and night, and emptied out their loads of human wretchedness. The hospitals were poorly supplied with beds, medicines, provisions, physicians, and nurses, and but for the supplies of all kinds carried to them by the citizens, who also gladly volunteered to nurse the helpless sufferers, the mortality would have been a hundred fold greater than it was. This state of things, however, was but temporary; as soon as the hospital accommodations were enlarged, and the corps of surgeons and nurses increased, the condition of the wounded and sick was much improved. But still, with all that the government could do, assisted by the people, who cheerfully opened their houses to their suffering countrymen, the amount of misery was appalling.

The writer almost shudders now at the bare recollection of what he witnessed in the hospitals, and especially in the sick camps in the open country. Within and without the scanty tents were hundreds of wretched, woe-begone, sick soldiers, from the tender boy of sixteen to the man of fifty; some lay on the outside of the tents muttering in the delirium of fever, of friends and home; others within, lay shaking with ague, under filthy rags and blankets; some with pale faces, and sunken eyes and cheeks, sat against trees or stumps, the very pictures of despair; others lay perfectly still on the bare ground, too weak to move, wasted literally to skeletons by dysentery. Thus on every side the eye fell upon the forms of human beings bruised, broken, slain by cruel war; and when we remember that in most of these sick camps garbage and filth of all kinds lay reeking in every direction, we have a picture of horrors that can find no counterpart except in the midst of such a war.

These unfortunate creatures claimed and received the careful attention of the noble men and women who gave their days and nights to hospital work, and their best earthly reward was the word or, perhaps, look of gratitude from the sick and dying soldier.

Rev. Dr. Ryland, speaking of his labors this Spring in the Richmond camps and hospitals, says:

"I have conversed with, addressed, and prayed for, many hundreds of invalid soldiers during the month, and given to each a tract, or a religious newspaper, or a New Testament, and have received from *all* great respect, and from *many* the most tender expressions of gratitude. I have found about forty-five men who could not read; to these I have given such books as McGuffey's First Reader, after demanding and obtaining promises that they would try to learn. The work is full of encouragement and delight, and worthy of far more piety, learning and talents than I possess."

Many of the hospital scenes touchingly illustrated the value of religion to the poor sufferers. A dying soldier said to the kind physician who had administered medicine to body and soul:

"Doctor, I bless God that you ever taught me the way of life and salvation. I have been a poor blind sinner all my life; but now I feel an assurance of happiness in heaven through Christ my Redeemer. Oh, I hope to meet you in heaven, and bless you there for the interest you have taken in my soul's salvation."

This physician said that he accepted the appointment of army surgeon that he might enjoy the privilege of preaching Christ to the soldiers; a rare exception—he found his reward in the success of his pious labors.

From the hospital, the fire of holy love was often carried by some happy soldier to the camp, and gloriously re-kindled there among his comrades. One who was converted while in the hospital, on returning to his regiment made known the blessed change in his life. He invited such as desired a similar one to join him in a prayer-meeting. Five met with him; they prayed together, and the interest extended until scores became anxious on the subject of salvation. They had no minister with them, but one came from another regiment and preached to them;—as the result of this effort, no bigger than a man's hand at first, more than one hundred professed faith in Christ.

As the revival progressed, there was scarcely any situation in which our soldiers could be placed where they did not find God ready and willing to pour out his Spirit in answer to earnest prayer. An awakened soldier was converted on a march,—when a minister inquired whether he had yet given himself to Christ, he said, "Yes, I have found him! Why, sir, when we set off on that march I felt such a weight on my soul that I could scarcely drag myself along, but after a while God heard my prayers, and then the burden was gone, and I felt as if marching was no trouble at all."

In the midst of the battle of Williamsburg, while the conflict was raging, and a chaplain was encouraging the men of his regiment to do their duty, a soldier passed, and, taking the hand of the chaplain, he said, "It is a glorious thing to be a Christian." His face was radiant with divine peace in the midst of a storm of bullets. How clearly this incident illustrates the power of grace as expressed in that comforting passage, "Thou wilt keep him in perfect peace whose mind is stayed on thee, because he trusteth in thee."

Among the noble men who fell during this period were two faithful chaplains, Rev. J. W. Timberlake of Florida, attached to the 2d Florida regiment, and Rev. W. H. C. Cone of Georgia, chaplain of the 19th Georgia regiment.

Mr. Timberlake came to Virginia in feeble health, but was indefatigable in his exertions to promote the temporal and spiritual welfare of his regiment. One who knew him as an intimate friend says:

"Mr. Timberlake was certainly a model man, and one whose untiring zeal and energy in the cause of his country is worthy of emulation, and whose self-sacrificing observance of duty has placed him in a premature grave. His devotion to our sick soldiers while in the city of Richmond left a remembrance which time will not soon efface from the hearts of his many friends there."

He died of consumption at West Point, on York river, and quietly sleeps beneath the soil which he gladly came to defend.

Rev. Mr. Cone was exhausted and broken down by long marches and exposure in the Peninsula. "Becoming very warm after a march, he imprudently bathed in a stream near the roadside, which produced a check of perspiration, terminating in typhoid fever. The regiment being on the retreat, and doing picket duty, there was but little accommodation for the sick. He fell behind, and a Presbyterian clergyman said he saw him lying by the road on the wet ground, where the mud was splashed on him by the passing army. He was taken up and sent to Richmond in a delirious state. Not being able to express his desires, he was not sent to the Georgia hospital."

"He was calm, patient, and resigned," says Rev. Mr. Crumley, who was with him in his last hours, "and expressed himself as having given all up into the hands of God, and could say, 'Thy will be done.' When a little dreamy, he would say, 'My dear Jane, don't grieve after me—all is for the best.' Then he would call, 'Jessie, come Jessie, and let me kiss you—be a good child.'

"On Sabbath morning, having lain some time quiet, facing my window that commands a beautiful landscape on the James river full of fishing smacks, and beyond, the green wheat fields, with the darker shades of clover fields further on, and the distant woods all lit up with a bright May morning's sun, he asked me to turn him over and straighten him on the bed. Fixing his eyes, as though he saw heaven opened, he, with a smile, said, 'Come. Lord Jesus, come quickly;' and folding his arms on his bosom, he fell asleep in Jesus, calm as an infant slumbers.

"We buried him at the head of the still increasing host of our noble soldiers who have fallen. There are officers, surgeons, and soldiers. He is the only chaplain among the fifteen hundred that forms that pale and quiet congregation."

CHAPTER IX.

SUMMER OF 1862.

The Spring closed brightly on the Confederate cause. The successful evacuation of Corinth was a strategic victory. The campaign of Jackson in the Valley of Virginia was as brilliant and rapid as that of Napoleon in Italy. In little more than twenty days, he marched over two hundred miles through a mountainous region, fought four battles and a number of skirmishes, killed and wounded great numbers of the enemy, took 3,000 prisoners and millions of dollars' worth of stores of all kinds, besides destroying vast quantities, chased Gen. Banks out of Virginia and across the Potomac river; and all this with a loss of less than two hundred of his own army. When we add to this his subsequent march up the Valley, his strategy against Gen. Fremont, and his decisive victory over Gen. Shields, the severest military critics must admit that the game of war was never more successful in the hands of any of the great masters of that dreadful art.

The Christian hero of this victorious army did not forget the hand that led him to conquest. Though compelled to spend a Sabbath in chasing the Federals out of the Valley, he rested the next day, and devoted a portion of it to religious services. The following is an extract from his General Order to the troops:

"The General Commanding would warmly express to the officers and men under his command his joy in their achievements, and his thanks for their brilliant gallantry in action, and their patient obedience under the hardships of forced marches, often more painful to the brave soldier than the dangers of battle. The explanation of the severe exertions to which the Commanding General called the army, which were endured by them with such cheerful confidence in him, is now given in the victory of yesterday. He receives this proof of their confidence in the past with pride and gratitude, and asks only a similar confidence in the future. But his chief duty to-day, and that of the army, is to recognize devoutly the hand of a protecting Providence in the brilliant successes of the last three days, which have given us the result of a great victory without great losses, and to make the oblation of our thanks to God for his mercies to us and our country in heartfelt acts of religious worship. For this purpose the troops will remain in camp to-day, suspending, as far as practicable, all military exercises, and the chaplains of regiments will hold divine service in their several charges at 4 o'clock P. M. to-day."

The victories of Jackson in the Valley were speedily followed by the hard-fought battle of Seven Pines. In the evening of the first day of this battle, Gen. Joseph E. Johnston was severely wounded, and Gen. R. E. Lee was placed in command of the army. Nearly the whole month of June was spent in active preparations for the great struggle which was to decide the fate of Richmond. Gen. McClellan's immense army, with every appliance of modern warfare, lay below the city, and gradually approached under cover of immense earthworks and entrenched camps. The Confederate General, having completed his arrangements for the attack on the "grand army," opened the battle on the 26th of June by a spirited assault on the extreme right of the Federal forces. Meanwhile, General Jackson, having been heavily reinforced, came swiftly down from the Valley, and took a position from whence he could fall upon the rear of the enemy. The Confederates were now ready to open the great battle.

On that memorable Thursday afternoon the daily union prayer-meeting of the city was held in the First Baptist church. It began at 4 o'clock, and nearly at the same hour the booming cannon announced the opening of the struggle.

Deeply solemn and earnest were the prayers offered up for the success of our arms, inexpressible were the feelings of the Christians there assembled as they thought of their loved ones just then entering "the perilous edge of battle." After an hour spent in the most devout exercises, the meeting closed; and while some retired to their homes to renew their prayers in secret, many others, with hundreds from every part of the city, repaired to the range of hills in the northern suburbs, from whence the "confused noise of the warriors" could be heard and the smoke of battle seen slowly rising above the dense forests of the Chickahominy.

As darkness gathered, the scene became grander and more impressive. The groups of men, women, and children, crowning the hill-tops, some conversing in undertones, many silent and awe-struck, others with lips moving and eyes upraised to heaven in silent prayer, the smoke of battle settling along the intervening valleys, the strains of martial music floating on the still evening air, as the long lines of soldiers marched out to join their comrades on the field of blood, the bomb-shells from the opposing lines, with their fiery trains, some plunging amid the dark woods, others bursting in their flight and raining deadly fragments on the heads of the struggling combatants, the sharp, rattling volleys of musketry mingled with the roar of cannon, the thought of hundreds an hour before in joyous health now wounded and dying, the fate of the beleaguered city and its helpless thousands suspended on the issues of the fight—all these furnished the elements of a scene truly sublime, and filled the mind with contending emotions of hope and fear.

The contest thus begun raged with varying intensity and results for six days, when it closed with the terrific battle of Malvern Hill. The Federal army was driven from every position with immense loss in men and munitions, and forced to take shelter on the banks of James river, thirty miles from Richmond, under the protection of a fleet of gun-boats.

The splendid achievements of the Confederate army were thus announced by Gen. Lee in an address to his soldiers:

"The General Commanding, profoundly grateful to the 'only Giver of all Victory' for the signal success with which he has blessed our army, tenders his warmest thanks and congratulations to the army, by whose valor such splendid results have been achieved. On Thursday, June 26th, the powerful and thoroughly equipped army of the enemy was entrenched in works vast in extent, and most formidable in character, within sight of our capital. To-day, the remains of that confident and threatening host lie upon the banks of the James river, thirty miles from Richmond, seeking to recover, under protection of his boats, from the effects of a series of disastrous defeats."

After briefly referring to the defeat and pursuit of the enemy, Gen. Lee says:

"The immediate fruits of our success are: The relief of Richmond from a state of siege, the rout of the grand army that so long menaced its safety, thousands of prisoners, including officers of high rank, the capture or destruction of stores to the value of millions, and the acquisition of thousands of arms and 51 pieces of superior artillery.

"The services rendered to the country in this short, but eventful period, can scarcely be estimated; and the General Commanding cannot adequately express his admiration of the courage, and endurance, and soldierly conduct of the officers and men engaged. These brilliant results have cost us many brave men; but while we mourn the loss of our gallant dead, let us never forget that they died nobly in defence of their country's freedom, and have linked their memory with an event that will live forever in the hearts of a grateful people."

This series of battles was illustrated by many instances of the noblest Christian heroism. The model hero, Jackson, was as terrible in the swamps as he had been in the mountains.

Rev. E. W. Yarbrough, a chaplain in the army, gives an interesting notice of this great and honored warrior:

"Before leaving, Colonel Zachry proposed to show me 'Stonewall Jackson,' if I would ride with him a short distance. We found him quartered under an apple tree, and at work of course. My first impressions of this Southern Boanerges will never be forgotten. His form is slender, not very erect, and of medium height. His lion heart is concealed under as pleasant a countenance as I ever saw. Had we met on the road before this war broke out, I would have taken him for a Methodist itinerant preacher on his way to an appointment pondering a most serious discourse. Notwithstanding all the feebleness of form and sweetness of expression, he was the hero of the Valley, having clipped the wings of at least four soaring Federal Generals in a short time, and having thundered upon McClellan's rear simultaneously with the advance of our forces upon his front, completely unearthing him, and then joining with his shouting hosts in the most glorious pursuit of an invading foe ever recorded.

"You are aware that he is a man of God. On that memorable Thursday, in the hottest of the fight, he was seen by his men to fall upon his knees and there remain for several moments, with his right hand raised to heaven in the most earnest supplication. He is almost idolized by his men. One of his Aids lost his right arm some time since in an engagement, and I saw him a few days ago in the saddle, still clinging to his General and acting his full part. He is not the only David in our army. Our chieftain, the noble Lee, communes with God, and

LEE AND JACKSON AT COLD HARBOR.

asks for reinforcements from on High. Bethel Hill is a man of prayer, and a host of others, from our Chief Magistrate down, daily invoke the intervention of Heaven in our behalf."

The expressions that fell from the lips of the Christian soldiers slain during this bloody week are worthy of a permanent place in the annals of their country.

Mr. Yarbrough, speaking of the part the 35th Georgia bore in one of the battles, says:

"Our Adjutant, J. H. Ware, was killed. As Colonel Thomas bent over him, the heroic youth grasped his hand and delivered his dying message: 'My dear Colonel, tell my mother that I fell in the discharge of my duty, and died *happy*.'"

Another gallant soldier received his death-wound, and lay gasping on the ground; as the roar of battle sounded in his ears, he asked a friend near how the fight was going. "Are we whipping them?" said the dying man. "We are," replied his friend. "Then I die satisfied."

"Say to my father," said another, "that all is well between me and my Saviour; tell him to meet me in heaven."

Another, carried from the battle-field with a dreadful wound, said to his sister who sat by him, "Sister, I am going home to heaven—I am so glad it is such a good home."

B. F. Leitner was wounded while bearing the colors of the 2d South Carolina regiment:

"Though shot down, he did not suffer the flag to fall, but kept it upright, floating proudly in the battle-storm, until he transferred the sacred charge to another, saying, 'Bear it forward and never let it fall.' He was afterwards removed to the house of Mr. Perdue, Manchester, where he was kindly cared for till he died. Just before his death, Capt. Leitner writes: 'I asked him what he would have me write to father and mother about his end. 'Write,' said he, 'I die happy. My confidence in God and our Saviour is unshaken. I am going to heaven.' I asked, 'Do you know that you are dying?' 'Yes,' was the answer, 'and I am glad of it; I want to join the army of Jesus Christ.'"

A young soldier, soon after he was shot, said to a comrade:

"My wound is mortal; I shall never see my father and sisters, but tell them I died at my post and in the discharge of my duty. Tell my friends not to grieve for me, but to meet me in heaven."

Another, with that strange presentiment of death which so often with soldiers precedes the fatal event, said to his brother just before a battle:

"I shall be in a battle shortly, and I expect to fall; if I do, tell my parents it will be all well with me."

A soldier, on coming home with a fatal wound, said to his mother as she met him, taking out his Bible:

"Mother, here is the Bible you gave me—I have made good use of it." He died in triumph, exclaiming, "Not my will, but thine, O God, be done."

As a brave young man was being carried from the field dreadfully mangled, he stopped the bearers and told them he was dying; "but," he added, "it is all well with me—I am not afraid to die."

Another wrote to a friend a day or two before the battle in which he fell:

"You inquire in reference to my religious condition. Though I do not live altogether up to my duties, yet I do not fear death; and if it be the will of God to take me, I feel willing to go; yet I would prefer to live. I put my trust in the merits of a crucified Redeemer, and depend on him alone for salvation. I would like to live to see you all again, but if God determines otherwise, I hope we will meet in heaven."

Again this Christian soldier wrote:

"May heaven grant that if I fall a martyr in the cause of my country, my kindred and their posterity may be proud that they had a relative who offered his life upon the altar of liberty. If I fall, I hope you will hear that I died bravely."

"The desire of his heart was gratified," said his brother; "he died as a hero, in front of the foe, on the bloodiest field of the war, and was buried without a coffin near the spot where he fell. We leave him to sleep in his soldier grave, in the sacred soil of distant Virginia; but, in the morning of the resurrection, we shall hope to meet him where the battle's thunder is never heard, and where the smile of God shall fill our hearts with peace forever."

Such was the end of Wateman Glover Bass, a noble Georgia soldier.

Said a young soldier to one of his comrades, as they were standing in line of battle, waiting for the order to advance:

"This is a solemn time, I intend to do my duty, and am willing to spill my blood freely for my country." In his last letter home, he had said to the loved ones: "If I see you no more, I have a good hope of meeting you in heaven." He saw them no more, for as he moved forward in the front rank he was pierced by a ball and fell dead instantly.

Another said, as he moved on: "If I fall in battle, all is well;" and another, to the last question of a friend: "If I fall on the field of battle, I shall be safe, for I know in whom I have believed, and he will keep what I have committed to his charge."

A brave man, writing to his wife after a terrible battle, said of his feelings during the action:

"For my part, fear was dispelled. I felt, though I should fall a victim to the enemy's balls, I had a house in heaven. With such feelings, I endeavored to discharge my duty in the best possible manner." In a subsequent engagement, in which he was killed, he said, on beginning the fight: "If I fall, it shall be well with me."

Another exclaimed just before he died:

"Oh, what joy! What boundless bliss! How my soul exults in the prospect of being so soon released from the sorrows of earth and initiated into the joys of heaven. Tell all my friends to meet me in heaven."

A noble young Virginian said to a comrade, as he lay mortally wounded on the bloody field:

"It is sweet to die for one's country—I would not have it otherwise."

As a captain stood by one of his men who was dying, the soldier said to him:

"Captain, I am going to die—death has no terrors for me—I do not fear to die—there is a beauty in death. Give my love to all at home, and tell them I die in a good cause—fighting for my country, and in Christian faith. Captain, you have been kind to me. Captain, quit swearing and try to meet me in heaven." Then, pressing the hand of his officer, he fell asleep in Jesus.

An officer, passing over the bloody battle-field of Frazier's Farm, saw a soldier kneeling with eyes and hands upraised to heaven; on approaching and touching him, he found him dead.

Among the many Christian soldiers who fell in the seven days' fighting around Richmond, no man has a brighter record for virtue, religion, and patriotism, than Colonel Robert A. Smith, of the 44th Georgia regiment. He was a resident of Macon, Ga., and greatly beloved and honored by his townsmen. In a brief tribute to his memory, they said of him:

"As a lawyer, he attained a high degree of proficiency in his profession, to which he devoted himself with prayerful energy, and in his practice he never swerved from the teachings of his conscience. Day after day he became more and more spiritual, drifting farther and farther from the world and 'nearer, nearer home;' and, turning a deaf ear to the syren tones of ambition, heard but the divine assurance, 'Blessed are the pure in heart, for they shall see God.' And whether weeping o'er the grave of the wife of his early manhood, kneeling by the bedside of the dying Lazarus, pleading with the felon in his cell for mercy from on high, or in the halls of pleasure trying to steer the bark of the giddy and thoughtless toward a better and a brighter world, in the camp or in the bivouac, on the march or in battle, he was always the same good, true, brave, Christian man. He gave generously of his worldly possessions, and the poor and the friendless, the widow and the orphan, weeping around the grave where they buried their benefactor, tell more eloquently than words how he had lived. His life was a living poem.

"'He did noble acts, nor dreamed them all day long,
And made his life, death and that vast forever
One grand, sweet song.'

"And one who knew him long and knew him well says:

"'No man was more severe upon his own faults or more charitable toward those of others.'

"As a Christian, so he was a patriot. At the inception of the war, at the head of his gallant little band, the Macon Volunteers, he tendered his services and was ordered to Norfolk, Va. After giving to his company an enviable reputation and discharging his duties for nearly twelve months, he was elected Colonel of the Forty-fourth Georgia regiment. His exposure and unceasing labors to perfect his regiment produced the disease which, in connection with his wounds, caused his death. In his soldier life, his character was as spotless and consistent as in the peaceful days before. When the day's work was done, he was wont to gather his command around him, and reading a lesson from the Bible, pray the Giver of all good for guidance and protection.

"When his regiment left Goldsboro for Richmond, though having suffered for weeks with sickness, he refused to remain behind. At Petersburg, on account of his serious illness, Gen. Walker deemed it unadvisable to apprise him of the departure of his regiment. He thus wrote to a friend: 'I learned of their departure after they left, and I sat on the railroad side till midnight to come with Gen. Walker, and *came with him notwithstanding his grumbling.*"

"On the day of the battle of Ellyson's Mill he was so feeble and exhausted by long sickness that it was absolutely necessary to assist him on and off his horse. He was so weak that it was with difficulty he could sit upright in his saddle. But his brave spirit and inflexible, iron will refused to succumb. Emaciated and exhausted as he was, he yet unfalteringly led his regiment through that deadly tempest of shot and shell until he fell, three times wounded. After he had fallen, to those who went to assist him he would still cry, 'Charge, men! charge!' It was a Marmion scene. With much reluctance he then consented to be carried off the field of carnage. Two days later the brave soldier and Christian warrior breathed his last, and angel voices in choral strains bade his hero soul welcome to 'home, sweet home.'"

Worthy to stand by the side of Colonel Smith was Major John Stewart Walker, of the 15th Virginia regiment, who closed a useful and holy life on the bloody hill of Malvern. He entered the army from a sense of duty. The pomp and circumstance of war had no charms for him apart from the principles involved. As the captain of a company, he joined the Army of the Peninsula, and nobly shared in that arduous campaign, which, opening with the battle of Bethel, closed with the evacuation of Yorktown. He was a friend and father to the young men whom he led to the war. He watched over their health and their morals, and thus gained their confidence and love. During the dreary days spent in winter quarters, he provided a library of select reading for his men, and thus relieved while he instructed and elevated their minds.

Upon the reorganization of the army, in the spring of 1862, he was elected Major of the 15th Virginia regiment, and by his firmness, valor, and Christian deportment, soon gained the hearts of the regiment. A simple but touching incident will show that the weapons of his warfare were not wholly carnal: After his death there was taken from his pocket a little volume stained on the back and leaves with his heart's blood. It was found to be a sort of Scripture Diary, containing selected passages suitable for each day in the year, with comments selected from the most eminent writers on practical religion. This little book seems to have been the constant companion of his Bible, and many of the most striking passages and comments were marked in pencil. The following are the texts marked from the 25th of June, the day before the series of battles, to the 27th, the day of the fierce conflict at Gaines' Mill. Amidst all the preparations for the death struggle his mind dwelt on spiritual things:

June 25.—"But I would not have you ignorant, brethren, concerning those which are asleep, that ye sorrow not even as others which have no hope; for if we believe that Jesus died and rose again, even so them also that sleep in Jesus will God bring with him."—1 Thess. iv: 13, 14.

"It is the most melancholy circumstance in the funerals of our Christian friends, when we have laid their bodies in the dark and silent grave, to go home and leave them behind; but, alas! it is not *we* that go home and leave *them*—no; it is they that are gone to the better world, and left us behind."

"The angel of the Lord encampeth round about them that fear him."—Psalms xxxiv: 7.

"In sorrow the angels are around us; they came to the Saviour in that garden of agony, where such a cup of sorrow was pressed to his lips as his people never drank, and he was strengthened. So they visit the chamber of sickness, where the good man lies, and minister unto him when all earthly comforters fail. They call the saint to follow them; they take him on their wings and bear his soul to heaven."

"And he went a little further and fell on his face, and prayed, saying: 'Oh, my father, if it be possible, let this cup pass from me; nevertheless, not as I will, but as thou wilt.'"—Matt. xxvi: 39.

"The poorest circumstances in life, with a religious spirit of resignation, are far better than the greatest abundance and highest honors without it; for these can never give that peace of mind which the other can never want."

"But the very hairs of your head are all numbered."—Matt. xvi: 30.

"Let the world imagine to itself a magnificent Deity, whose government is only general: the Christian rejoices in his providential superintendence of the smallest matters."

"And take the helmet of salvation, and the sword of the Spirit, which is the word of God."—Eph. vi: 17.

> It was a two-edged blade,
>   Of heavenly temper keen,
> And double were the wounds it made
>   Where'er it glanced between.
> 'Twas death to sin—'twas life
>   To all who mourned for sin;
> It kindled and it silenced strife—
>   Made war and peace within.

Friday, June 27.—"And whosoever doth not bear his cross and come after me cannot be my disciple."—Luke xvi: 27.

"Every Christian should be a martyr in spirit."

Such were the truths upon which he stayed his soul; and sustained and comforted by them, he went calmly, with God, and had the blessed assurance that he pleased him.

An officer of his regiment, who knew him long and intimately, gave the following testimony to his religion and patriotism:

"Leaving his family and home early in the contest, he was always found at his post. He avoided no danger and shunned no responsibility which demanded his presence. As captain of a company, and commandant of a regiment, he won the love and confidence of his men. They knew that he would never order them where he was not willing to lead the way. When I say that duty was his watchword, I say all. The last word that I heard him utter, far in advance of his regiment, amidst a shower of shot and shell, was *Forward!* and with that glorious utterance for soldier or for saint, he fell pierced by a deadly ball.

"It is impossible to separate his character as a soldier and as a Christian. He was a soldier because he was a Christian; and while he fought manfully against the enemies of his country, his fervent spirit labored and fought earnestly against the enemies of his Lord. The Word of God was his light in camp, and the tumult of war did not disturb his daily devotions. I believe he prayed without ceasing, and that in his last end the arms of the Everlasting One were under him.

"The deadly ball that pierced his body could not pierce the panoply with which God had armed him, but he fell as a Christian should fall, with his harness on at the post of duty. He rests from his warfare."

Amidst the storm of battle this Christian warrior fell. From the field of blood his spirit ascended to heaven. How sudden, how vast, how glorious, the change! From the rush of contending hosts, from the thunder of cannon, and the fierce rattle of musketry, he rose to the joys and songs and beauteous scenes of Paradise.

The death of Lieutenant Virgil P. Shewmake, of the

The death of Lieutenant Virgil P. Shewmake, of the 3d Georgia regiment, was another bright testimonial to the value of our holy religion:

"Though young, having just entered his 21st year when he joined the army, none of the temptations incident to camp-life moved him from his Christian integrity and gentlemanly propriety. Severely wounded, and his right arm amputated, twenty days after the battle of Malvern Hill he breathed his last in the triumphs of Christian faith. Frequent conversations were held between himself and father on the subject of his religious hopes, and he ever concluded with, 'If I die, tell mother and sisters to meet me in heaven.' On the day of his death, he asked his father what he now thought of his case. With aching heart his father replied: 'I think, my son, you will die.' 'How long, then, do you think I will live?' 'Perhaps till night, possibly through the night.' Then, turning his face from his father, he most fervently and pathetically prayed God that, if consistent with his will, he would spare him to reach home, and once more see his dear mother and sisters. If he willed otherwise, then to bless them and his dear father with grace to live so that they might all meet him in heaven. A short time before he expired, he was seen to shudder and slightly struggle. After this, lying quiet a moment, he turned to his father, and with animation said: 'Pa, is this death?' who, with choking utterance, replied: 'Yes, my son, you are dying.' 'Then, Pa, it is easy to die—I thought it would be hard.' Calling his comrades who were present, he with great composure bade them all farewell, then extending his hand to his father, said: 'Good-bye, Pa; meet me in heaven; tell mother and sisters I have gone to heaven and to meet me there.' A few moments after this affecting scene, he calmly, gently fell asleep in Jesus."

It is a sad yet pleasing task to record such instances of religious heroism. It shows how deep and genuine was the piety that not only cheered our soldiers amidst the usual hardships of war, but sustained them in the hour of mortal agony, and opened to the eye of faith the glorious prospect of life eternal. The solemn hour of death fully tests the religious life, strips the soul, and leaves it bare to its own inspection, reveals the true character of our motives, and the real bearings of our actions upon our future destiny.

To such a test thousands in the armies of the South were brought, and clear and happy were their souls in the consciousness of duty well performed. Truly, our Christian soldiers died well.

CHAPTER X.

SUMMER OF 1862.

The moral impressions of the sanguinary battles around Richmond were of the most salutary character. A wounded soldier, referring to them, said: "God preached to us as all the preachers on earth could not do."

All felt that the hand of God was manifest in these tremendous struggles. A pious officer wrote immediately after the close of the battles:

"Never before have I seen so clearly and powerfully intervened in our behalf the right arm of the Lord of hosts.

"The names of Lee, Hill, Jackson, Magruder, and others, have been rendered immortal by their gallantry and skill so strikingly evinced in this series of engagements; but while their names are in our hearts and their praises upon our tongues, let there go up from the Southern Confederacy a warm and a universal shout of "Glory to God in the Highest;" for had not God been with us, we must have been almost annihilated. Such will be the impression upon the minds of all who may hereafter traverse the battle-fields with a correct idea of the positions of the contending parties."

The powerful preaching of "the seven days' fighting" is thus described by an eye-witness:

"Probably at no period of the war has the religious element in the army been more predominant than at present. In many instances, chaplains, army missionaries, colporteurs, and tracts, have accomplished great benefits, but by far the most cogent influences that have operated upon and subdued the reckless spirit of the soldiery are those which are born in the heart itself upon the field of battle. There is something irresistible in the appeal which the Almighty makes when he strikes from your side, in the twinkling of an eye, your friend and comrade, and few natures are so utterly depraved as to entirely disregard the whisperings of the 'still small voice' which make themselves so vividly heard at such a moment. Every man unconsciously asks himself, 'Whose turn will come next?' and when, at the termination of the conflict, he finds himself exempted from the awful fiat that has brought death to his very side, and all around him, his gratitude to his Creator is alloyed, though it may be but dimly, with a holier emotion, which for the time renders him a wiser and a better man. In this respect, the recent battles have done more to make religious converts than all the homilies and exhortations ever uttered from the pulpit. A man who has stood upon the threshold of eternity, while in the din and carnage of a fight, has listened to eloquence more fiery than ever came from mortal lips.

"It is not strange, therefore, as you go through various camps, even on a week-day, that your ears are here and there saluted with the melody of a choir of voices, rich, round, and full, sung with all the seriousness and earnestness of true devotion; or, that before the lights are out in the evening, manly tones are heard in thanksgiving for the blessings of the day; or, that when Sunday arrives, the little stand, from which the chaplain is wont to discourse, is the centre of a cluster of interested and pious listeners.

"In many of the regiments, much of this kindly influence is due to the pure and elevated character of the officers. Wherever these are found, you invariably also find a neat, well-disciplined, orderly, quiet command, as prompt in the camp as they are brave upon the field. Now and then you may hear a taunt about 'our praying chaplain,' or 'colonel,' but even these thoughtless expressions come from men who venerate their officers, and would follow them to the death. Some of our ablest generals are men who have dropped the gown for the apparel of the soldier. Polk was a Bishop, Pendleton a clergyman, D. H. Hill a religious author, Jackson a dignitary of the Church, while scores of others, occupying subordinate positions, are equally well known for their devotion at the shrine of Christianity. All of these gentlemen have been eminently successful in whatever they have undertaken, have passed unharmed through the dangers by which they have been frequently environed, and are living illustrations of the truth that a fighting Christian is as terrible to his enemies as he is gentle to his friends."

The testimony to the blessed fact of God's presence among the soldiers is most abundant. "God is in the army," wrote a pious man; "many in my regiment have passed from death unto life." "One hundred of my regiment," said a chaplain, "have professed conversion since we have been in the service."

The power of grace to sustain and comfort the believer amidst the hardships and dangers of war is richly illustrated in the following experience of a pious Elder of the Presbyterian Church:

"I have been in the active service of my country just four months. I cheerfully sundered the ties that bound me to my little paradise of a home in Mississippi, and came out to the war because I believe the Lord hath called me. I viewed the contest as one of unparalled wrong and oppression against truth and the right. I was persuaded that not only civil liberty but evangelical religion had a large stake at issue in the struggle. My conscience, therefore, was clear, and, in following the convictions of duty, I was made happy. The Lord has been most gracious in according to me daily the rich consolations of faith in the Lord Jesus in buckling on my armor to fight the battles of my country. He has constantly reminded me that I am a soldier of the cross, and that I owe allegiance to *him*. He has favored me with many precious opportunities of doing good, of which, in an humble, unobtrusive way, I have tried to avail myself. His grace has been sufficient for me amidst all my trials and difficulties. In the battle of Seven Pines, in which we lost one-third of our regiment in about twenty minutes, amid the most terrific shower of shot and shell of this whole war, the Lord not only so far sustained me as to enable me to stand up and do my duty to my country, but to do it without the least fear of anything man can do unto me. Nor did I, as many men seem to do, lose sight of my personal danger. My mood was so calm that my calculations were perfectly rational. I felt that the Lord's hand was with me, that his shield was over me, and that whatever befell me would be by his agency or permission, and therefore it would all be well with me. It was a period of positive religious enjoyment, and yet of the most vigorous discharge of my duties as a soldier.

'Again, at the battle of Gaines' Mill, or Cold Harbor, on Friday, June 27th, the most furious of the whole series, and in which one-third of our regiment was reported as killed and wounded, I was visited with the same peace of mind and the same resolute composure. The two battles leave me with nine perforations in my clothing, made by at least six balls, a slight contusion from a piece of bomb, and a severe wound in my left thigh, a large ball passing clear through, ranging between the bone and femoral artery. Upon perceiving it, I looked down and discovered the hemorrhage to be very copious. I supposed at once that the artery was involved, and that I would live but a short time. I was not only not afraid to die, but death seemed to me a welcome messenger. Immediately there came over my soul such a burst of the glories of heaven, such a foretaste of its joys as I have never before experienced. It was rapturous and ecstatic beyond expression. The new

Jerusalem seemed to rise up before me in all its beauty and attractiveness. I could almost hear the songs of the angels. My all-absorbing thought, however, was about the Divine Redeemer, whose arms were stretched out to receive me. So completely overwhelming and exclusive was the thought of heaven, that I was wholly unconscious of any tie that bound me to the earth. I was still standing within a few steps of where I was wounded, and yet I utterly forgot my danger, and thought of no means of preserving my life. There I stood in the midst of men, and where deadly missiles were flying thick and fast, and yet my thoughts were completely abstracted from everything around me. So fully was God's love shed abroad in my heart, and so delightful was the contemplation of the offices of the blessed Saviour, that I could think of nothing else."

Rev. J. M. Stokes, chaplain in Wright's Georgia brigade, says of the religious condition of the troops:

"I am happy to state that the health of our troops seems to be much better than it was a few months since. It will be a source of delight to Christians and all thinking people to know that the religious element among our troops is much greater now than at any time previous since the war began. I believe sincerely that *there is less profanity in a week, now, than there was in a day, six months ago.* And I am quite sure *there are ten who attend religious services now to one who attended six months ago.* I speak principally with reference to our own regiment, but I have been informed by those who have travelled among the different parts of the army in Virginia that such is the case everywhere."

This was the case not only in the army in Virginia, but in almost every other department of the South. Rev. B. H. Perry, writing from Columbus, Miss., of the state of religion in the 37th Alabama regiment, under the command of a sincere Christian, Col. Dowdell, says:

"We set out religiously, by having preaching twice on Sabbath and prayer-meeting twice a week. A good influence prevails, and a high moral tone has characterized our men from the first. The sentiment seems to be rife among us that instead of retrograding, Christians ought to progress decidedly in camp. This is a just opinion, for the frequent and unusual temptations which they meet, the absence of those restraints and associations that ordinarily sustain them, the position of antagonism into which they are placed perforce in the resistance of overt sin, and the simple and direct reference to God to which they are shut in, as it were, all are calculated to *develop* and *strengthen* the *principles* of their religion. We have had a protracted meeting at night for a week. There have been nineteen conversions in the time, two of them professing in their tents while sick. The regiment numbers something over 1,000, and the aggregate of Church-members is 245. Many of those who have died were happy and triumphant.

"Our Colonel cares for his men with a Christian conscience, and the other field and staff officers, as also those of the companies, are for the most part religious men. In the start, the Colonel prescribed the public recognition of God by closing dress parade with prayer, and this order we observe daily. Oh! if our officers did but feel that 'except the Lord build the house, they labor in vain that build it!'"

In the hospitals, among the sick and wounded, the power of grace was gloriously revealed. The soldiers brought with them from the battle-fields the solemn impressions they had received amidst the dreadful scenes of carnage. "Strange as it may appear to some," writes an experienced post chaplain, "scores of men are converted immediately after great battles. This has become so common that I as confidently look for the arrival of such patients as I do for the wounded. It is not very strange, if we remember that before they went into battle they had been serious and thoughtful. Here God covered their heads, and their preservation was a manifestation of his power and goodness that humbled their souls. 'What cause for gratitude to God that I was not cut down when my comrades fell at my side.' 'But for God I would have been slain.' 'I do not see how I escaped. I know that I am under renewed obligations to love him, and am resolved to serve him.' 'After the battle at Malvern Hill, I was enabled to give my soul to Christ—this war has made me a believer in religion, sir,' said a wounded soldier. These and other expressions show how God is working out his purposes of grace and wisdom in these times of darkness and distress."

Among the many thousands of wounded that filled the Richmond hospitals, the work of salvation was deep and general. "The Lord is with us at Seabrooks' hospital," wrote Rev. W. R. Gwaltney; "we have a great revival of religion here. A greater one I scarcely ever witnessed. Rarely a day passes but I find one or more new converts. The number in our hospital is being rapidly reduced, many being transferred to other places, and many having died; but the religious element in our midst is by no means dying out. A large number are yet enquiring, 'What must we do to be saved?' Those who have professed a hope in Christ seem to be in the full enjoyment of faith."

"I am happy," says another minister, "to report the manifest tokens of the presence of the Spirit among us, even in these times of strife and battle. I do believe that these solemn visitations of Providence have been His chosen way of touching many a heart. There are earnest desires awakened in many a bosom, which I trust will lead them to the Cross. I believe there are many of our brave men lying on their hard pallet in the hospitals who are now secretly indulging a hope in Jesus; and I console myself with the sweet thought that others, who have never told it, have died on the battle-field looking to their Saviour. I know there are dreadful exhibitions of deliberate wickedness, but Satan ever delights in placing his abominations in the porch of God's temple. There is great occasion for earnest prayer in our behalf. Brethren, pray for us, that God may sanctify his dealings with us to the conversion of souls."

Ministerial labor in the hospitals was a blessed work, and those who gave themselves to it greatly rejoiced in the success that attended their efforts. That saintly man, Rev. John. W. Miller, who has lately entered into rest, and whom many of our soldiers remember as post chaplain at Summerville, South Carolina, says of his work:

"We have had some to die peacefully and happily. One poor fellow who had long been sick with typhoid fever died last week. When I questioned him about his preparation for death, his answer was scarcely articulate, but in his thick mutterings I could distinguish these blessed words of trust in the Saviour, '*He will not let me perish.*'

"Upon asking another why he was not afraid to die, he said: 'Because I am going home to heaven, through Christ.' Another, a little while before he died, said: 'I love God.'

"I find a number of them are members of the Church. Testaments are greatly coveted, and you can scarcely walk through the wards at any time without seeing some of them engaged in reading the sacred Word. Divine service has been held several times for the convalescents—and we frequently assemble them for evening prayer."

"It was just after a battle, where hundreds of brave men had fallen," writes another chaplain, "and where hundreds more were wounded, that a soldier came to my tent and said: 'Chaplain, one of our boys is badly wounded, and wants to see you right away.' Immediately following the soldier, I was taken to the hospital and led to a bed, where lay a noble young man, pale and blood-stained from a terrible wound above the temple. I saw at a glance that he had but a few hours to live. Taking his hand, I said: 'Well, my brother, what can I do for you?' He looked up in my face, and placing his finger where his hair was stained with blood, he said: 'Chaplain, cut a big lock from here for mother—for *mother*, mind, chaplain.' I hesitated to do it. 'Don't be afraid, chaplain, to disfigure my hair. It's for mother, and nobody will come to see me in the dead-house to-morrow.' I did as he requested me. 'Now, chaplain,' said the dying man, 'I want you to kneel down by me and return thanks to God.' 'For what?' I asked. 'For giving me such a mother. Oh, chaplain, she is a good mother; her teachings comfort and console me now. And, chaplain, thank God that by his grace I am a Christian. Oh, what would I do now if I was not a Christian! I know that my Redeemer liveth. I feel that his finished work has saved me. And, chaplain, thank God for giving me dying grace. He has made my bed feel 'soft as downy pillows are.' Thank him for the promised home in glory. I'll soon be there—there, where there is no more war, nor sorrow, nor desolation, nor death—where I'll see Jesus and be forever with the Lord.' I kneeled by him, and thanked God for the blessings he had bestowed upon him—a good mother, a Christian hope, and dying grace to bear testimony to God's faithfulness. Shortly after the prayer, he said: 'Good-bye, chaplain; if you see mother, tell her it was all well.'"

In the Southern army were many mere youths, and among these there were found not a few rare instances of earnest piety maintained amidst all the evils and temptations of camp life. The following illustrative incident occurred under the ministrations of Rev. Dr. John C. McCabe, one of the post chaplains at Richmond:

"One day, in making his usual visitations, Dr. McCabe called in at the Maryland hospital, Richmond, and in making his rounds, was attracted to the bed of a young and delicate boy, suffering from the effects of protracted fever. The little fellow had seen only fourteen summers, and his thin, pale face bore marks of disease and suffering. The following occurred, as reported by the chaplain:

"'How old are you, my son?' said the reverend gentleman.

"'I was fourteen my last birthday.'

"'Why, that is very young to be in the army?'

"'Yes, sir; but I thought it my duty.'

"'Where are you from?'

"'Mississippi, sir.'

"'What is your name?'

"'Dwight Sherwood.'

"'Why, that is a Northern name.'

"'Yes, sir; my father was a Northern man, but he has lived in the South for many years, and is a good Southern man.'

"'And your mother, where is she?'

"His little thin lip quivered, as he said with an effort to suppress emotion, 'She is dead.'

"'Well, my son, you are very young, and you are very sick. You are not able to endure the fatigues of a campaign, and if you get better, you had better return home, hadn't you?'

"The boy turned his large, eloquent eye upon his interrogator, and firmly, but modestly, replied, as a slight flush passed over his pale, expressive face, '*Not until the war is over.*'

"'Why, what can you do, you are so young and so delicate?'

"'I am a marker, sir, and I hope soon to be up and in the field again. I think it my duty.'

"'Well, you ought to try and be a good boy, to avoid

everything that is wrong, and you ought to pray to God to give you a new heart, and to keep you from falling into bad habits.'

"'I do, sir,' said the little fellow, his eyes half concealed beneath the long, soft lashes. 'My mother taught me to pray. I have kept out of scrapes, and have had no difficulty with any one but once, and I did not seek that one.'

"The reverend gentleman then held further conversation with the brave little fellow, and promised to see him again."

The death scenes among these youthful soldiers often evinced the full power of the gospel in conquering death. The glory and triumph of religion were never more fully manifested than in the following scene:

"A young soldier, while dying very happily, broke out in singing the following stanza:

> 'Great Jehovah, we adore thee,
>   God the Father, God the Son,
> God the Spirit, joined in glory
>   On the same eternal throne:
>   Endless praises
>   To Jehovah, three in one.'

"The chaplain then asked if he had any message to send to his friends. 'Yes,' said he. 'Tell my father that I have tried to eat my meals with thanksgiving.' 'Tell him that I have tried to pray as we used to do at home.' 'Tell him that Christ is now all my hope, all my trust, and that he is precious to my soul.' 'Tell him that I am not afraid to die—all is calm.' 'Tell him that I believe Christ will take me to himself, and to my dear sister who is in heaven.' The voice of the dying boy faltered in the intervals between these precious sentences. When the hymn commencing, 'Nearer, my God, to thee,' was read to him, at the end of each stanza he exclaimed, with striking energy, 'Oh, Lord Jesus, thou art coming *nearer to me.*' Also, at the end of each stanza of the hymn (which was also read to him) commencing,

> ' Just as I am—without one plea,
> But that thy blood was shed for me,
> And that thou bid'st me come to thee,
>   O Lamb of God, I come,'

he exclaimed, '*I come! O Lamb of God, I come!*' Speaking again of his friends, he said, 'Tell my father that I *died happy.*' His last words were, 'Father, I'm coming to thee!' Then the Christian soldier sweetly and calmly 'fell asleep in Jesus.'

"This was witnessed by about twenty fellow-soldiers, and the effect upon the feelings of all was very marked. Said a Roman Catholic who lay near the dying one, with tears in his eyes, and strong emotion, 'I never want to die happier than that man did.' Said another, 'I never prayed until last night; but when I saw that man die so happy, I determined to seek religion too.'"

It was such evidences of the power and value of faith in Christ that made the truth effectual in the salvation of thousands, and that enshrined the cause, for which such Christians fought and fell, so deeply in the hearts of the Southern people.

To the hearts of anxious fathers, mothers, wives, and sisters, what could give greater consolation in the hour of darkness and grief than the letter of the chaplain giving the simple and touching narrative of the death of the dear one on the battle-field, or in the hospital, in the fullness of joy, and sending with the last breath and the last gush of life-blood sweet words of comfort to the loved ones at the old homestead.

In their darkened homes, hundreds praised God that their children had found Christ in the camp.

CHAPTER XI.

SUMMER OF 1862.

The Army of Northern Virginia had scarcely a breathing spell after the terrible battles around Richmond. The concentration of a powerful Federal army under General Pope on the upper Rappahannock, and its reinforcement by the shattered columns of McClellan, indicated a purpose to try again the original Manassas route to the coveted city. General Lee, who seemed to have an intuitive perception of the plans of his adversaries, at once disposed his forces to meet this new emergency. No sooner had McClellan shipped his heavy war material on board a fleet of transports, and commenced his stealthy retreat down the Peninsula with a broken and dispirited army, than Jackson was moving with his veterans to watch the braggart, Pope.

It was a memorable day when his "foot cavalry" filed through the streets of Richmond in the highest spirits, chanting their songs and cracking their rude war jokes. "If the Yankees trouble you again, just send for us to wipe them out," exclaimed a sun-browned, stalwart Georgian in faded butternut clothes, and a slouch hat with the brim half torn off. "*We* can flank 'em, but *they* can outrun us," cries another; "You'll hear from old Jack again soon," breaks out a third; "Marse Robert knows what he's about," exclaims a fourth; and thus the brave fellows trudged on gay and happy, following their great leader.

Having reached a convenient point for observation, Jackson soon divined the purposes of General Pope. This vain man, who had pompously announced to his troops that his headquarters would be in the saddle, felt the power of our great warrior first at the battle of Cedar Mountain. The fight took place on one of the hottest days of summer. The Federal troops were terribly worsted and driven in confusion from the field, leaving their dead and wounded and many prisoners in our hands. The South was called to deplore the loss of many brave men. General Winder, who commanded the "Stonewall Brigade," was killed on the field, and a number of other gallant officers and men here gave their lives to the holy cause.

This blow from Jackson was an earnest of what was soon to follow. Withdrawing from the vicinity of Cedar Mountain, he completely deceived the enemy, and began that famous flank movement which brought him so unexpectedly to the rear of Pope's army. The Federals in great force had spent weeks in and around the town of Warrenton, Fauquier county, Va., and between that place and Culpeper Courthouse. They had plundered the people without mercy, taking food, clothing, servants, horses, cattle, and, in fact, whatever they fancied was freely appropriated. Implements of agriculture were burned or broken to pieces, on the principle of subduing the rebellion by cutting off the means of living from citizens and soldiers. The conduct of many of the Federal soldiers was worthy of the most ferocious savages. They would ride over the graves of Confederates in the burying-ground near the town of Warrenton, and stick bayonets and fire guns into the graves. The church edifices were abused, and the walls defiled with vulgar and licentious scribblings, and in one instance, if not more, the communion table and chairs were stolen from the altar and possibly shipped to the North. A negro brought in from the country a fine piano, which was bought for a trifle by some soldier or sutler, boxed up and sent off as a present to some fair lady in a loyal State.

But the triumph of the wicked is short. In the midst of these outrages the appalling news came that Jackson was in their rear. The mighty host was thrown into confusion; and in vain it labored to check that series of brilliant movements on the part of the Confederates which culminated in the terrific battles of the 28th, 29th, and 30th of August. Jackson's column was followed by that of Longstreet, and General Lee came after his two great Lieutenants with the remainder of the Confederate army. The troops were ordered to relieve themselves of everything except what was actually necessary.

"After marching with the army on foot from Gordonsville to Leesburg," says Rev. J. W. Mills, "sleeping on a single blanket, with heaven's blue vault for a covering, suffering hunger and weariness in common with officers and men, I am convinced that the soldier's life in Virginia is one of fighting and toil, and the chaplaincy is no sinecure. By order of those in command, we carry nothing with us but one blanket, a small haversack, and the clothes we wear. The wagons carry only a half or one-third of a load; every weight thus laid aside, men and teams are put up to their best speed, marching by day and by night—sometimes forty hours together—with now and then short halts for rest and sleep. Thus you may account for our celerity of movement. Our troops are notwithstanding always in fine spirits, having much pleasurable amusement along the way, calling themselves General Lee's foot cavalry, etc."

The same writer, attached to Longstreet's corps, gives a lively account of the march and its incidents:

"Soon after leaving Gordonsville, we commenced shelling the Yankees. First, on Mountain Run creek, we had a pretty sharp artillery duel with them, but with little loss to us, hung a spy, and moved forward. Then, on the Rapidan river, we shelled them again. Next they appeared on the Rappahannock river, and we skirmished again. Here we saw some Yankees two days dead on the battle-field, and buried them. They were horrible to behold. Gen. Jackson had been there before us. We pushed forward, passing through Orleans and Salem; at the latter place we learned the Yankees were only a few hours ahead of us. The young ladies waved their handkerchiefs at us, saying, 'Whip the Yankees; don't let them come here.' One sweet little girl said, in her own winning way, 'Oh, they run, they run.' Our boys declared they felt perfectly rested, and moved forward with eager haste. At Thoroughfare Gap they made a stand, and part of our forces had a sharp battle with them, completely routing them with great slaughter. This took place among the mountains to the right of the Gap. We were not delayed more than three hours by this battle. Night came on, but we pressed forward through the Gap, over the rocks, through the water and mud—one of the darkest nights I ever saw. Early the next morning we passed through Haymarket. The Yankees were two hours ahead of us, double-quicking. At their camp was a hog half consumed in the fire. Near the road was a beef skinned and abandoned. All along the way we found small arms thrown away, wagon-wheels with half the spokes cut out, one wagon on fire, and other evidences of hasty *skedaddling*. Our troops pushed forward, 'faint but pursuing.' Soon we came up with them, and fighting commenced. This was on Tuesday, the beginning of the battle which ended on Saturday so gloriously for our cause. Thursday and Friday were spent in skirmishing. Early Saturday cannonading commenced in earnest, both sides manifesting great spirit; about noon the musketry fighting commenced; at four o'clock P. M., the battle was general and most terrific. For about one hour the Yankees stood and fought heroically. Those who stood and fought thus were nearly annihilated. They were compelled to give way. I could hear the well-known whoop of our troops, as they charged and took battery after battery from the enemy. About sundown the last battery was charged and taken; then followed an ominous silence. The Yankees were fleeing in wild confusion; our artillery moved forward rapidly, and from the higher ground poured shot and shell into their broken and fugitive columns. Nothing could be heard on their side but the roar and rush of getting away over the rocky turnpike. Night closed the scene."

It is well known that at the second battle of Manassas the position of the two armies was exactly reversed. The contest raged over the same ground already made sacred by the memorable victory of the preceding year. Many a brave man marched back to die on the spot where he had first met the storm of battle. The Confederates were stimulated to deeds of true heroism by the memories that clustered around the field of strife—the Federals fought under the depressing recollection of former defeat and disaster. The three days' struggle ended on Saturday evening in the total route of Pope's army. We again quote from Mr. Mills' graphic letter:

"On Sunday morning, I rode along the road by which they fled across Bull Run. That must have been a terrific race for dear life, if broken wagons, capsized ambulances, dismounted cannon, the road for miles paved with scores of boxes and barrels of hard bread, abandoned haversacks and blankets, dead horses and dead men, is any evidence of such a race.

"The battle-field! what a scene! Here death is feasting on his thousands at a meal. The field was red with wounded and dead Zouaves. They were literally cut to pieces by the Texans. In one part of the field I saw an intelligent looking Yankee with his thigh broken. He had lain all night in the rain in that condition. I said to him: 'My dear fellow, you are in great pain; can I do anything for you?' Said he: 'Oh, sir, if I could get some one to amputate my leg, I think I would not suffer so much.' 'Our surgeons are all busy now with our own wounded; when they are through with them, I presume they will attend to you,' I replied. Close by was another, shot through the lungs, breathing his last.

In his mouth was a mass of froth, tinged with blood, almost half as large as his head. Another was shot through the head, his brains scattered upon the ground; yet he had lived all night, and was now groaning in the agonies of death. These are only a few cases out of thousands. I stood there in my place and counted in a small space twenty dead Yankees—five of them shot through the head, blood and brains running out together in a stream of several feet. From all that I could see in the part of the field I visited, there were ten dead Yankees to one of ours. This was the position occupied by Gen. Longstreet's division.

"The field was literally filled with small arms of the best quality. When they broke to run, every one must have thrown away his gun. Some were broken—others were loaded and in good condition. Our men swapped guns, as they found those which suited their fancy better than their own. Having eaten but little for two days and nights, many of them fared sumptuously that night from the well-filled haversacks of their vanquished foe. They also supplied themselves with splendid oil-cloths and blankets. Love-letters and letters from wives, mothers, and sisters, with many likenesses, were picked up from among the slain.

"I heard from the battle-field on Tuesday after the battle, and the dead of the enemy were unburied. The enemy made no halt—were pushing forward to get advantage of us. Our hands were full. Some of their braves, who would have a farm at the South, and wantonly destroyed the property of private citizens under the infamous order of their leader, were there on the field half-eaten up by the hogs."

In the quiet, rural districts in the vicinity of these battle-fields, the same scenes were repeated that had so recently been witnessed in and around Richmond. Gen. Lee, moving rapidly after the retreating foe, was compelled to leave his broken-down, sick, and wounded men behind. Every village, and almost every farm-house, for many miles around, was crowded with sick and wounded Confederates. The condition of our own men was pitiable enough, but the Federal wounded suffered to the last degree of horror. For five or six days hundreds of them lay about in the ravines, and under clumps of shrubbery, and in the open fields, exposed to the pelting rains, without covering, suffering the intolerable pangs of hunger and thirst, superadded to the torture of fly-blown, festering wounds.

The victorious legions of Lee swept on toward Maryland, leaving the discomfited army of Pope huddled around Washington city. As the army approached Leesburg, Va., the Federals who occupied that place precipitately fled across the Potomac.

"They had come over from the Point of Rock," says Mr. Mills in his narrative, "to arrest some offensive citizens, among them some soldiers. They had gone so far in their cowardly work as to leave some of their victims under guard, when our cavalry came to their rescue. An old citizen of Leesburg described the scene to me thus: 'We were like Israel of old—the mountains flanking us, the Red Sea before us, and the Egyptians in our rear. We could see no means of escape, and were trembling with alarm, with a haughty foe dictating to us. I was sitting in the piazza, and saw a little dirty fellow dash into the street on a little gray pony with a double-barrel shot-gun in his hand. Said I to myself, 'That must be one of our boys.' The Yankees were rushing past in wild dismay. I saw him present his gun and fire, and down tumbled a Yankee. He wheeled and fired the other barrel, and another fell. I heard somebody say, 'Two of the rascals are down.' The Yankees retreated a short distance from town and made a stand. Our boys charged them with their swords, and they broke for the Potomac, screaming as they approached, 'Bring over the boat! bring over the boat!' But a ferry-boat was too slow business for them, and they plunged in and swam across.'

"The ladies of Leesburg, regardless of the deadly missiles, rushed into the streets, clapping their hands and shouting, 'Victory! victory!' There is nothing they fear so much now as a return of the Yankees. Thank God! this part of Virginia is now free from their polluting tread. Through the strong arm of Omnipotence we have shelled them out, and wives, mothers, and daughters, breathe freely once more in their dear homes."

The devotion and self-sacrifice which our people manifested in their attentions to the sick and wounded men, who were left along the track of the army, can never be surpassed. Warrenton, a small town of fifteen hundred inhabitants, was crowded with more than two thousand wounded soldiers from the battle-fields, hungry, bleeding, and with no clothes but what they had on, and these cut, and torn, and bloody; and in many instances their gaping wounds were alive with crawling maggots.

Rev. J. W. Talley, of Georgia, who labored in the place as a nurse of the poor, suffering men, and there consigned to the grave his first-born son, pays a feeling tribute to the citizens who opened their hearts and houses to their countrymen:

"The ladies, aided by their husbands, are seen everywhere. They are angels of mercy, not idle lookers-on, but busy, carrying food and helping in every way they can to alleviate and soothe the sufferer. They divided their beds and bed-clothing and fed these hundreds as long as they had wherewith to do it, and until the Government sent aid—for nearly a week—all were supported by the inhabitants. When aid did come from Government, it was inadequate. Every house in the town was appropriated to the wounded and sick, as each family took in as many as it could. Some sixty tents were pitched, and these were filled. Our soldiers, after all the people could do, were to be seen lying on a handful of straw, or on the floor or ground, without a blanket to cover their lacerated and bleeding bodies."

In the midst of these scenes of horror there was many a bright and joyous departure to the world of peace and rest. Speaking of the death of his son, Mr. Talley says:

"My son, after he had lain in a storehouse from Monday to Tuesday evening on a blanket and a handful of straw, was furnished by a kind lady with a straw mattress, on which he is now dying. May God remember her in mercy 'in that day.'

"The night of the 29th was a night of pain, anxiety, deep, unutterable emotion. We sat or kneeled by his couch, and poured out our souls in prayer for the sufferer. He wanted me to pray for him, and almost suffocated with emotion, silent prayer yielded to sobs and prayers. At the close, I asked him if he loved Jesus. He answered 'Yes.' I asked him if he was going to heaven; he said: 'I hope so;' and wanted us all to meet him in heaven. He then threw his arms around his mother's neck, and returned her fond embrace and kisses, sent by her a kiss to each of his sisters, and one by me to his brother Willie, now in Gen. Bragg's army. The struggle lasted until Tuesday, September 30th, at 2 o'clock P. M., when the tranquil, happy spirit was released from its clay prison. The casket was broken and the jewel was gone."

The same triumphant death scenes were witnessed on the battle-field of the Second Manassas that had cast such a radiance over Southern patriotism in the previous battles of the war. "Give my love to parents and friends," said a young soldier, dying of his wounds; "tell them all is well; I am not afraid to die, for I know they are praying for me." Another, the son of a faithful clergyman, fell mortally wounded by a shell. A friend near by gave him water, for which he thanked him, saying, "I am a dying patriot," and then added, "Tell my father I died like a man and a hero." A brave young Christian, when told by the surgeon that he could not live, sent home his last message: "Tell my relations, father and mother, sisters and brothers, that I trust I am prepared to meet my God. Farewell, one and all, I bid you a long farewell, I hope to meet you all in heaven." Another gallant soldier, who was killed as the line of battle was being formed, left a pleasing testimony; just before leaving to join the army, he wrote: "I wish only to know my duty; it then remains for me to perform it. It was a great trial to part with my family; I seemed to realize that the parting was final; but my country calls, and I cheerfully go forward to death." It was soon after that he went from the carnage of battle to the peaceful home of the blessed.

But it is needless to multiply these instances of heroic devotion and pious resignation. In every hospital, and on every field, they appeared, giving sanctity to the cause of the South, and forever enshrining those who laid down their lives for it in the warm affections of a grateful people.

CHAPTER XII.

AUTUMN OF 1862.

The sudden appearance of the Confederate army in Maryland, after the second great victory at Manassas, startled and perplexed the Federal authorities. The unfortunate General Pope was at once displaced from the chief command as unequal to the emergency, and General McClellan again took the direction of military affairs. General Lee moved rapidly into Fredericktown, from which place, on the 8th of September, he issued an address to the people of Maryland. From this point a portion of the Southern army was moved seemingly in the direction of Pennsylvania, but really for important operations in Virginia.

After sending a portion of his force to hold the Maryland Heights, opposite Harper's Ferry, General Jackson was directed by General Lee to recross the Potomac at Williamsport, capture Martinsburg, and, by a rapid movement, completely surround Harper's Ferry.

Jackson marched with his wonted celerity; Martinsburg fell with its garrison and stores, and the investment of the Ferry was effected on the 13th of September. No sooner did McClellan hear of the movements of Jackson than he resolved to make a powerful effort to defeat his plans. Leaving Washington with 80,000 men, on Sunday, near Boonsboro, he threw his whole force against the corps of Gen. D. H. Hill, which was the rear guard of our army, and had been placed at this point by Gen. Lee to impede the reinforcing column. The battle was obstinate and bloody, but General Hill nobly stood his ground, reinforced in the afternoon by Longstreet's corps, and the object of the Federals, the relief of Harper's

Ferry, was defeated. While the battle was raging, the place was surrendered by General Miles, with his entire force of 11,000 men, the same number of small arms, 73 pieces of cannon, 200 wagons, with a vast amount of stores and camp equipage.

General Jackson announced this event in his laconic style : " Yesterday God crowned our arms with another brilliant success in the surrender of Harper's Ferry."

The Federals having gained Crampton's Gap in the rear of Gen. McLaws, who held the Maryland Heights, Gen. Lee retired to Sharpsburg, where he could readily unite his whole army. On Monday our army took position in front of Sharpsburg, and Jackson, leaving Harper's Ferry, rejoined his chief in time to participate in the impending battle.

The fight opened on Tuesday afternoon about six o'clock, and was kept up until nine at night, when it subsided into skirmishes along the lines. It was reopened by Jackson on Wednesday, and soon became general. Both armies fought desperately throughout the whole day. At night the Confederates held nearly the entire field, and the Federals retired to their former position. The next morning our men stood ready to recommence the work of death, but no assault was made by the Northern army. Each army, it seems, expected the other to attack. Late in the evening of the 18th, Gen. Lee issued the order for the return of his army to Virginia. The able correspondent of the Savannah *Republican*, who was on the spot, gives the following account of this masterly movement :

" Whether Gen. Lee took this step from a military necessity, or for some strategic purpose, or because he had accomplished the object of his movement into Maryland—the capture of Harper's Ferry—I am unable to say. The order was issued late last evening, and by the time it was quite dark the wagons, artillery, and troops began to move. All the wounded that were in a condition to be moved had been taken across the river. Those whose wounds were very severe or mortal, unfortunately, had to be left behind, and fell into the hand of the enemy. Some of the wounded had never been removed from the field, having fallen on a part of the ground still held by the enemy. Many of the dead were buried yesterday, and some were transferred to this bank of the river. It was not quite three miles to the Potomac, and our wagon trains extended from Sharpsburg over to the Virginia side. There were only two roads by which we could proceed, one of which was taken by the troops and the other by the artillery and wagons. Our lines came up within a short distance of the enemy's, yet so silently and adroitly was the movement conducted that McClellan was not aware of it until next morning. It had rained in the afternoon, and the roads were muddy below, while the heavens were covered with a light fog above, both of which facilitated the enterprise. We had crossed into Maryland by the bright and early morning sun; we returned in silence and at the dead hour of night. The columns wound their way over the hills and along the valleys like some huge, indistinct monster.

Whatever was the motive to the movement, it must be regarded as one of the most successful and extraordinary exploits in the history of any country, and stamps the man that ordered and executed it as one of the greatest military leaders in our time and generation. With the exception of the wounded and a few wagons that got turned over in the darkness, not a man or wagon nor a single piece of artillery was lost. The crossing was accomplished by half-past six this morning, and soon thereafter the enemy's artillery opened a harmless fire from the opposite heights. The bird had flown, however, and his rage was impotent."

The Federals themselves confessed to the admirable generalship displayed by the great Confederate leader.

The correspondent of the New York *Tribune*, in referring to it, said:

"The whole of the rebel army has got entirely off across the river by this morning with everything—guns, ammunition, provisions—everything, as far as I have seen, worth taking. My fears are thus realized—the enemy has taken the advantage of yesterday's repose and last night's darkness, and has quietly passed over the river and effected a successful retreat. The retreat, so far as the marching part of the army was concerned, was a splendid success. But two disabled guns, one ambulance, five barrels of flour, and two barrels of salt, were all the property they left in our possession. A cleaner, neater retreat, considering all the circumstances, was never made. 'It is,' said a gentleman to me, 'Corinth repeated, only much more neatly.' The enemy outwit us under our very noses."

The battle of Sharpsburg was fought under almost every disadvantage on the part of the Confederates. The men had been marching or fighting nearly every day from the time they left Richmond; the transportation was deficient, food was scarce, thousands were sick, and thousands were straggling along the entire line of march from Richmond to Maryland. The writer just quoted thus speaks of the men who, from early dawn to dewy eve, hurled back the columns of McClellan's immense army on the memorable field of Sharpsburg:

"I can recall no parallel instance in history, except Napoleon's disastrous retreat from Moscow, where an army has ever done more marching and fighting, under such great disadvantages, than General Lee's has done since it left the banks of James river. It proceeded directly to the line of the Rappahannock, and moving out from that river, it fought its way to the Potomac, crossed that stream and moved on to Fredericktown and Hagerstown, had a heavy engagement at Boonsboro Gap, and another at Crampton Gap below, fought the greatest pitched battle of the war at Sharpsburg, and then recrossed the Potomac back into Virginia. During all this time, covering the full space of a month, the troops rested but four days! And let it always be remembered to their honor, that of the men who performed this wonderful feat one-fifth of them were barefooted, one-half of them in rags, and the whole of them half-famished. The country from the Rappahannock to the Potomac had been visited by the enemy with fire and sword, and our transportation was insufficient to keep the army supplied from so distant a base as Gordonsville; and when the provision trains would overtake the army, so pressing were the exigencies of their position the men seldom had time to cook. Their difficulties were increased by the fact that their cooking utensils, in many cases, had been left behind, as well as everything else that would impede their movements. It was not unusual to see a company of starving men have a barrel of flour distributed to them, which it was utterly impossible for them to convert into bread with the means and the time allowed to them. They could not procure even a piece of plank, or a corn or flour sack, upon which to work up their dough.

"No army on this continent has ever accomplished as much, or suffered as much, as the army of Northern Virginia within the last three months. At no period during the first Revolutionary war—not even at Valley Forge—did our forefathers in arms encounter greater hardships, or endure them more uncomplainingly.

"If the Army of Virginia could march through the South just as it is—ragged and almost barefooted and hatless—many of the men limping along and not quite well of their wounds or sickness, yet cheerful and not willing to abandon their places in the ranks—their clothes riddled with balls, and their banners covered with the smoke and dust of battle, and shot into tatters, many of them inscribed 'Williamsburg,' 'Seven Pines,' 'Gaines'

Mill,' 'Garnett's Farm,' 'Front Royal,' 'McDowell,' 'Cedar Run,' and other victorious fields—if this army of veterans, thus clad and shod, with tattered uniforms and banners, could march from Richmond to the Mississippi, it would produce a sensation that has no parallel in history since Peter the Hermit led his swelling hosts across Europe to the rescue of the Holy Sepulchre."

But the highest eulogy on this army came from him who had led it to victory, and under whose eye its heroic deeds were performed. After their return to Virginia, General Lee spoke to his half-famished, half-naked, but invincible legions in this noble strain:

"In reviewing the achievements of the army during the present campaign, the Commanding General cannot withhold the expression of his admiration of the indomitable courage it has displayed in battle, and its cheerful endurance of privation and hardships on the march.

"Since your great victories around Richmond, you have defeated the enemy at Cedar Mountain, expelled him from the Rappahannock, and, after a conflict of three days, utterly repulsed him on the plains of Manassas and forced him to take shelter within the fortifications around his capital.

"Without halting for repose you crossed the Potomac, stormed the heights of Harper's Ferry, made prisoners of more than eleven thousand men, and captured upwards of seventy pieces of artillery, all their small arms, and other munitions of war.

"While one corps of the army was thus engaged, the other insured its success by arresting at Boonsboro the combined armies of the enemy, advancing under their favorite General to the relief of their beleaguered comrades.

"On the field of Sharpsburg, with less than one-third his numbers, you resisted, from daylight until dark, the whole army of the enemy, and repulsed every attack along his entire front of more than four miles in extent.

"The whole of the following day you stood prepared to resume the conflict on the same ground, and retired next morning, without molestation, across the Potomac.

"Two attempts, subsequently made by the enemy, to follow you across the river have resulted in his complete discomfiture and being driven back with loss.

"Achievements such as these demanded much valor and patriotism. History records few examples of greater fortitude and endurance than this army has exhibited; and I am commissioned by the President to thank you, in the name of the Confederate States, for the undying fame you have won for their arms."

The valor and endurance of the Southern troops in this campaign are attested by their faithful ministers who labored day and night for their spiritual good. Rev. J. W. Mills, chaplain of a Florida regiment, gives a graphic picture of the havoc of war:

"Many of our regiment fell in the terrible battle of Sharpsburg. We occupied the centre, where the enemy made his fiercest attack, hoping to break our lines in that vital part of the field, and so win the day. The enemy were formed in a semicircle on the side of a hill. Our brave men marched up to the attack until they could see the heads and shoulders of their adversaries over the summit of the hill, when firing commenced. From the two wings and the centre of this semicircle they poured upon us a murderous fire for about one hour. Five times our colors fell, but as often our men rushed to the spot and raised them to the breeze. Finally, a retreat was ordered—at that moment the colors fell and were left. The enemy had suffered too much, notwithstanding his advantages, to pursue, and our gallant Lieutenant-Colonel, already wounded in the arm, went back and brought them away under a shower of bullets."

In the midst of this carnage many a heart turned to

the God of battles for refuge and comfort. Mr. Mills again writes:

"A young man said to me after the battle: 'When I was going into the battle, I put my trust in God, and he has brought me through untouched, and I am grateful to him.' And the tears stood in his eyes as he spoke. He was an unconverted man when he went into the fight. Last night at preaching, while referring to the incidents of the battle and how God had preserved them, many tears fell, and many countenances spoke louder than words undying gratitude to the God of all grace."

The instances of calm Christian courage exhibited on the field of Sharpsburg have never been surpassed. Here, with thousands of other heroes, Captain James G. Rogers, of Macon, Ga., offered his life on the altar of his country. He was a worthy citizen and a most useful Christian. As a minister and Sabbath School Superintendent, he exerted a happy influence wherever he labored to do good. He entered the service a captain of the Central City Blues, of the renowned 12th Georgia, and endured cheerfully all the hardships of the soldier's life. He passed unharmed through seventeen desperate battles, and fell gloriously on this bloody field. Wearied and almost worn out by the investment of Harper's Ferry and the march to the battle-field, his men lay on their arms awaiting the attack which was to be made at dawn of day. The assault was terrible, and for an hour Captain Rogers, in command of the regiment, passed up and down the line encouraging his men. While thus exposed, all the fingers of his left hand were shot off, and he was severely wounded in the thigh, but he remained with his men until forced to leave by sheer exhaustion. As he was moving off, supported by some of his men, a bullet struck him in the back of the head, killing him instantly. "Thus fell," says the friend from whom we take this account, "one of the purest, bravest men of our immortalized Confederate army." When he bade adieu to his family, he said: "If we meet no more on earth, let us meet in heaven." In his letters home he often said: "I never go into battle without feeling prepared to meet my God." On the morning of his last battle he arranged for the disposal of his effects as if he fully expected to fall. "Blessed are the dead who die in the Lord."

On the same field fell Major James Harvey Dingle, of South Carolina. He was a true Christian soldier. His Colonel said of him: "He was one of the bravest men I ever saw. He did not know what fear was. He was killed near me, and I took the flag from his hand as he was dying; he died without a groan, and looked as if he was sleeping. He was blessed by the men and officers, and was a kind, courteous, efficient, and accomplished officer; his loss to the Legion (Hampton) is great. His name will be cherished by the sons of Carolina so long as the good, patriotic, and brave are appreciated."

Such cases were not isolated ones in the Southern armies; there were hundreds, yea, thousands, of such earnest, faithful, godly men, who endured hardships, poured out their blood, and died in peace amid the rage and carnage of the battle. The dying words of our Christian soldiers, their messages of love, whispered amid the roar of cannon and the rattle of musketry, in the ear of some comrade who bent over them and gave a cooling draught from his canteen, would fill volumes if they could be collected. It is only by fragments, however, that we can gather up their precious sentences that sparkle with a heavenly light in the midst of the gloomy horrors of war. Many of the best and purest were left scattered over the wide, blood-soaked fields, and languished and died from home and friends in hospitals and prisons; and not until the coming of their comrades who survived and returned home did their friends and families receive the sweet messages of love that were laid like healing balm on their bleeding hearts.

Never were stronger proofs given of the sustaining and comforting power of religion than during this terrible war, which stripped our homes of loved ones, our land of plenty, our hearts of joy, and left us nothing to fall back upon in our sufferings and humiliation but the promises of God, who poured out his Spirit so richly upon our soldiers in all the hardships of the march and in all the unutterable anguish that followed our great battles.

CHAPTER XIII.

AUTUMN OF 1862.

The return of the army to Virginia, and the repose absolutely necessary after so arduous a campaign, were highly favorable to the spread of religion in all our camps. The men were deeply impressed by the dangers they had escaped, and their hearts were opened to receive the truth.

"They gladly hear," writes a clergyman, "and with alacrity assist the chaplain in all his work. They gather the congregations for preaching by singing hymns under some spreading tree in the midst of our camp after circulating the appointment among the different companies. These sweet songs of Zion may sometimes be heard in different parts of the camp at the same time, reminding one very forcibly of our camp-meetings at home. I have seen or heard of but little scoffing at religion and religious people in the camps. In this respect I have been very happily disappointed, from what I had been told of camp-life. The most perfect decorum is observed during divine service, and the most perfect respect is manifested for those who serve God."

Early in October, while the army lay near Winchester, there were evident signs of a deep awakening among the troops. Rev. J. W. Mills, in a letter to Bishop Pierce, of Georgia, spoke cheeringly of their religious meetings:

"Since my last," he writes, "the great Head of the Church has wonderfully favored us with a gracious revival of his work in the camp among the soldiers. We had preaching every night for nearly a week. There was an average of about twenty-five anxious seekers, who approached when the invitation was given, and kneeled upon the ground near the spot occupied by the chaplain. It was a solemnly impressive scene. Many manly tears were shed, and many noble hearts throbbed with deep emotion. If there was mocking, we heeded it not; the loud whistling, talking, hallooing, cooking, eating, and constant moving about the camp, disturbed us not; the loud calls of the sentinel close by, 'Sergeant of the guard, post number four,' drew us not off from our purpose. God was in our thoughts and hearts. We were dead to the things of this world. Fifteen joined the Church during this protracted meeting, and we have good hope that many of them have been soundly converted.

"During the meeting a man said to me, 'Sir, I am a renegade from your Church, and am now a skeptic; I want your advice.' Said I, 'If I had been in your present condition when you were in the full enjoyment of religion, and had applied to you for advice, what advice would you have given me?' 'Get back into the Church and the service of God as soon as possible,' said he, quickly. 'That is my advice to you then,' I responded. 'I'll do it,' said he; and so he did the first time the door of the Church was opened.

"Friends and our loved ones at home have not been forgotten by us in our prayers and our rejoicing. One said to me, just before service one night: 'I want you to remember my wife and children in your prayers tonight.' What a privilege! God will hear us and bless them. Many knew not what blessings wife and children, home, and peace were, till this cruel war poured over us its tide of woe and misery. Oh, God! convert the soldier and protect his wife and children during his absence."

The hearty singing in these gatherings in the fields or forests was truly delightful. Hundreds of strong, manly voices poured out a volume of rich melody on the evening air. Among the favorite hymns of the soldiers were—

> "How firm a foundation, ye saints of the Lord,
> Is laid for your faith in his excellent Word!"

And those stirring lines, so applicable to our suffering heroes—

> "Am I a soldier of the Cross,
> A follower of the Lamb,
> And shall I fear to own his cause,
> Or blush to speak his name?"

These scenes were full of the elements that stir the soul in all its noblest feelings. In their tattered garments, some hatless, many shoeless, wrapped in their blankets, sat these Confederate soldiers around their camp-fires, listening to the Word of Truth from the lips of the chaplain or some pious comrade; and, in the absence of preacher and exhorter, joining in the prayer-meeting with hearts full of gratitude to God for his protecting power amidst the dangers of the war.

The following scene, described by Captain Kirkpatrick, of Lynchburg, Va., will give the reader a vivid picture of those blessed seasons of grace among the men of war:

"A few, including seven who were not professors of religion, as they sat around their camp-fire, began to sing hymns in God's praise. I went and joined in the singing. After a little while, I made a few remarks to the little company—no formal address, but as I sat on the ground, and in a conversational way. I said to them that it would be such a blessed thing if those present would agree to consecrate themselves to God from that hour. I pointed them to the blood of Jesus as the only atonement for sin, and to his righteousness as our only ground of acceptance with God the Father. I then asked each man present what he purposed with reference to the salvation of his soul. To my surprise, every man present, except one, declared himself ready then

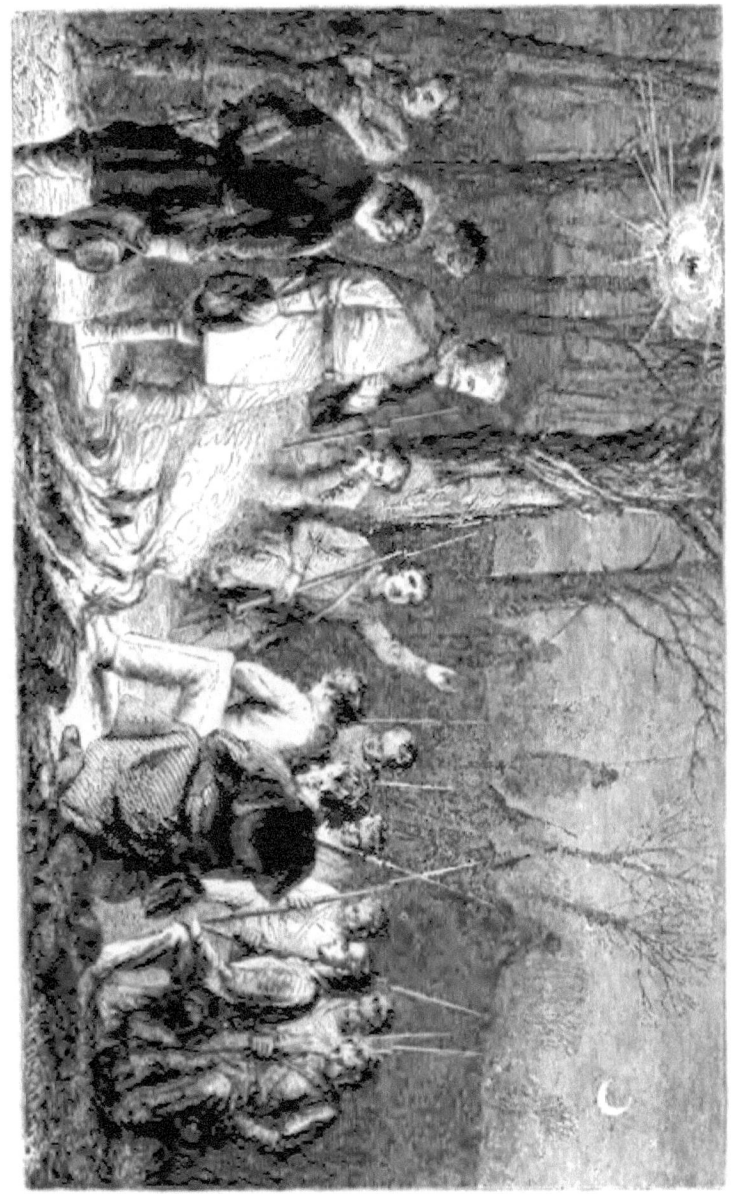

LEE AT THE SOLDIERS' PRAYER MEETING.

and there to give up sin, to turn unto God with a full purpose of new obedience, and, resting on Jesus for salvation and grace, to lead a new life thenceforth. This was the happy beginning of a glorious work. Every night since that it has grown in the depth of its solemn earnestness, until it has in many respects become the most remarkable outpouring of converting grace I ever witnessed. During a part of the time the weather was very threatening and unpleasant, but this did not prevent the gathering of rejoicing saints and anxious inquirers around the bright camp-fire. To them the gospel has been preached most fully and tenderly. Between forty and fifty of my own company have been hopefully converted, and are very happy in hope of a blissful and peaceful immortality. Some of the hardest hearts, long-lived and desperate sinners, have been melted under the power of the truth, and, like little children, have come to Jesus. I am rejoiced to see that the young converts seem to be aiming more at the substantial graces of faith, humility, and love, than to obtain joy, or peace, or comfort. Another good sign is the fact that every one immediately engages in the work, and seems most anxious to do something for perishing souls around him."

Rev. Dr. Stiles, whose eloquent and powerful sermons can never be forgotten by those who heard them in the army or elsewhere, gives a deeply interesting account of his labors while the army lay in the neighborhood of Winchester. In a letter to the *Christian Observer*, he says:

"My object in addressing you a note at this time is to apprise you and all sympathizing Christian brethren and sisters in Richmond of the *happy, religious condition* of that part of the army of the Potomac which lies within the range of my present observation.

"At his earnest request, I preached to General Pryor's brigade last Sabbath. Upon one hour's notice, he marched up twelve or fifteen hundred men, who listened with so much interest to a long sermon, that I was not surprised to hear of such a beginning of religious interest in various regiments of the brigade as issued in a half-way promise on my part to fall in with the proposal of the General to preach very early to his soldiers for a succession of nights. In General Lawton's brigade there is a more decided state of religious excitement. The great body of the soldiers in some of the regiments meet for prayer and exhortation every night, exhibit the deepest solemnity, and present themselves numerously for the prayers of the chaplains and the Church. Quite a pleasant number express hope in Christ. In all other portions of Gen. Early's division (formerly Gen. Ewell's), a similar religious sensibility prevails.

"In Gen. Trimble's, and the immediately neighboring brigades, there is a progress, at this hour, of one of the most glorious revivals I ever witnessed. Some days ago a young chaplain of the Baptist Church—as a representative of three others of the same denomination—took a long ride to solicit my co-operation, stating that a promising seriousness had sprung up within their diocese. I have now been with him three days and nights, preaching and laboring constantly with the soldiers when not on drill. The audiences and the interest have grown to glorious dimensions. It would rejoice you over-deeply to glance for one instant on our night-meeting in the wild woods, under a full moon, aided by the light of our side stands. You would behold a mass of men seated on the earth all around you (I was going to say for the space of half an acre), fringed in all its circumference by a line of standing officers and soldiers—two or three deep—all exhibiting the most solemn and respectful earnestness that a Christian assembly ever displayed. An officer said to me last night on returning from worship, he never had witnessed such a scene, though a Presbyterian Elder, especially such an abiding solemnity and delight in the services as prevented all whispering in the outskirts, leaving of the congregation, or restless change of position. I suppose, at the close of the services, we had some sixty or seventy men and officers come forward and publicly solicit an interest in our prayers, and there may have been as many more who, from the press, could not reach the stand. I have already conversed with quite a number, who seem to give pleasant evidence of return to God, and all things seem to be rapidly developing for the best.

"The officers, especially Generals Jackson and Early, have modified military rules for our accommodation. I have just learned that Gen. A. P. Hill's division enjoys as rich a dispensation of God's Spirit as Gen. Early's. Ask all the brethren and sisters to pray for us and the army at large. I would not be surprised to learn that the condition of things above described prevails extensively in portions of our soldiers at present out of our view.

"P. S.—I have opened this letter the second time to inform you of the wide spread of holy influence. In Gen. Pickett's division, also, there are said to be revivals of religion."

There was scarcely a brigade in the army in which the work of revival did not go forward with deepening power. Some of the far Southern troops were signally blessed with great outpourings of the Spirit. The 60th Georgia regiment was favored with the services of a most excellent chaplain, Rev. Samuel S. Smith, under whose ministry many were brought to Christ. In a letter describing the revival among his men, he says:

"About the first and middle of October, we held a series of meetings in camps, during which time many souls were renewed and encouraged, several were made happy in the love of God, and the altar was crowded from day to day with seekers of religion. The like was hardly ever before witnessed in camps. I was blessed with the assistance of the Rev. Dr. Joseph Stiles, of the

Presbyterian Church, to whom the army owes a debt of gratitude for his arduous labors and efforts to save sinners from the wrath to come."

The revival was not confined to the soldiers in camp; in the towns in Virginia where military hospitals were located, there were gracious displays of the power of God in the salvation of souls. The convalescent soldiers flocked to the churches and crowded the altars as humble penitents. In Farmville, under the ministry of Rev. Nelson Head, there was a most interesting revival, and the greater number of the converts were soldiers from Georgia and Alabama. In Lynchburg, Charlottesville, Petersburg, and Richmond, the work was pervasive and powerful.

A writer in one of the Richmond secular papers, speaking of the work of grace in the hospitals in that city and other places, says:

"At Camp Winder, for some weeks, there has been in progress a revival of religion. Thirty-five soldiers have professed to be converted. Daily meetings are being held, and numbers are manifesting a deep interest in reference to spiritual things. A revival is also in progress at Chimborazo, and frequently from thirty to forty present themselves as 'inquirers.' Many have professed to experience the saving change. One hundred have professed conversion within a comparatively brief period in the hospitals in Petersburg. For more than a month a protracted meeting has been in progress in Lynchburg, at which some twenty soldiers have made the good profession. We learn from the post chaplain in Farmville that there is considerable religious interest among the hospitals there, and that eight have professed conversion. At other points the divine blessing is being richly bestowed upon the pious efforts of chaplains and colporteurs. There can be no more inviting field for Christian enterprise than that presented by the hospitals. In this city alone, over 99,000 sick and wounded soldiers have been in the hospitals. At no time do men feel more grateful to the Giver of all Good, and more like becoming pious, than when recovering from long spells of sickness."

The revival, at this period of the war, was undoubtedly greater and more glorious in the army in Virginia than in other portions of the Confederacy, but there were happy signs of spiritual life among the troops in the far South and West. On Sullivan's Island, near Charleston, S. C., there was a blessed work of grace, which powerfully checked the ordinary vices of the camp and brought many souls into the fold of the Good Shepherd. Speaking of this work, in a letter of October 9th, Rev. E. J Meynardie, chaplain of Col. Keitts' regiment of South Carolina Volunteers, says:

"On Thursday evening, 25th ult., the religious interest, which for some time had been quite apparent, became so deep and manifest that I determined to hold a series of meetings, during which, up to last night, *ninety-three* applied for membership in the various branches of the Church, nearly all of whom profess conversion. Every night the church at which we worship was densely crowded, and obvious seriousness pervaded the congregation. To the invitation to approach the altar for prayer prompt and anxious responses were made; and it was indeed an unusual and impressive spectacle to behold the soldiers of the country, ready for battle, and even for death on the battle-field, bowed in prayer for that blessing which the warrior, of all others, so much needs. God was with us most graciously, and it was a period of profound interest and great joy.

"The influence of this meeting has pervaded the regiment, and is still operating most beneficially. To what extent it has improved the morals of the soldiers it is impossible to estimate. Suffice it to say, that it has struck at the very root of camp vices, and the great crime which is more frequently committed in the army, against God and common decency, than any other, hides its hideous head—I mean profanity. The testimony of a soldier who writes for the *Southern Lutheran* is: 'When we first came into camp, swearing was a common practice; but now, thank God, an oath is seldom heard. Our men seem to feel as if they ought to be more observant of God's law.'

"The Church of Christ is very strongly represented in the regiment. We have many praying men; and indeed a more quiet, orderly, and religiously-disposed body of troops cannot, I presume, be found in the service; and be assured that when the time for fighting comes, beneath the banner of the Cross and our country's flag, we shall present an unflinching front. It was the religious fanaticism of Cromwell's puritanic army which made it invincible. It is the genuine religious tone of Jackson's which, under a pious commander, has thus far rendered it unconquerable, and we trust that the powerful religious element in this command will inspire sentiments of the highest order of patriotism when the occasion comes for every man to stamp himself a hero!"

But while the fruits of these genuine revivals appeared so abundantly in many portions of the various armies of the Confederacy, it is but due to the truth of history to say that in some regiments the godly labors of the chaplains were treated with indifference, and sometimes actually opposed by the officers in command.

A devout and eminent minister, in speaking of the conduct and influence of this class of officers, says:

"In many of the regiments there are no chaplains; perhaps because in some instances the commanding officers of the regiment do not desire one, and none is sought for, although hundreds of the rank and file desire the presence of the minister of God among them.

"Yet, what is the wish of this large majority of the regiment to weigh against the purposes of an ungodly, drunken, swearing Colonel, who thinks himself too great a man to be reproved for his sins in the presence of the men who are the daily witnesses of his transgressions of the laws of God. Pity that any such men should have the control to such a great extent of the souls and bodies of our citizen soldiers; but, unfortunately, there are many such officers in our army. I recollect a case in which one of this class took the chaplain to task for having preached against profanity, and charged him with having taken advantage of his position to lecture him on swearing, and that, consequently, he should hear him preach no more. Was not this very dignified behavior from a man who filled the important and responsible position of Colonel, commanding perhaps a thousand men, who were not only to obey his orders, but also look to him for an example as an officer and a gentlemen? He should have encouraged his men to attend on religious services and should have set them the example, whatever may have been his own personal predilections on the subject of religion. And this man is, I fear, only a type of a large number of men who occupy positions of command in the Confederate army."

Such cases, we are happy to say, were rare exceptions in our army. The great majority of the officers, if not personally pious, were men who had been trained up under moral influences, and they gladly afforded the chaplains every facility for conducting religious services.

Among the episodes of this period of the war, there are few more touching than one that furnished the ground work for a tract written by the Rev. William M. Crumley, of Georgia, and widely circulated among the soldiers with the happiest results. Mr. Crumley was one of the most faithful and untiring chaplains that labored in our armies. Thousands yet living remember with grateful hearts the self-sacrificing devotion of this excellent minister. He was chaplain of the Georgia hospitals at Richmond, but did not confine his labors to the city; on every battle-field where the army of Northern

Virginia fought, and bled, and won, he was found, with other members of the Georgia Relief Association, feeding the hungry, clothing the naked, cheering the wounded, consoling the dying, and revealing, in every form of toil for the good of his fellow-men, the highest type of the Good Samaritan. As the writer often met him in these labors of love, it gives him unusual pleasure to offer this slight tribute to a servant of God, whose faithfulness in answering every call of suffering humanity has never been surpassed, and seldom equalled, even in the midst of a great civil war, that moves to their utmost depths the best and worst passions of human nature.

But we will not longer keep the reader from Mr. Crumley's narrative:

"Among the multiplicity of knapsacks, haversacks, bundles, and old clothes, stored in one of the baggage rooms of a hospital in Richmond, I found a *Soldier's Bible*. It was a neat London edition, with a silver clasp, on which were engraven the initials A. L. C. On the fly-leaf was written, in a neat and delicate hand, 'A present to my dear son on his fifteenth birth-day, from his mother, M. A. C.' Below was written, in the same hand, 'Search the Scriptures; for in them ye think ye have eternal life, and they are they which testify of me.' 'Remember now thy Creator in the days of thy youth.' 'If sinners entice thee, consent thou not.'

"The book had the appearance of having been carefully read, there being many chapters and verses marked with pencil, as though they had strongly impressed themselves on the mind of the young reader. Among them were the chapters which describe the heroic daring of the youthful David, the saintly purity of Joseph, and the unflinching fidelity of the three captive boys at the court of Babylon. The 1st, 23d, and 51st Psalms, bore marks of an interested reader. In the New Testament, such Scriptures as speak of the love of God to sinners were carefully noted: 'God *so* loved the world that he gave his only begotten Son, that *whosoever* believeth in him should not perish, but have everlasting life.'—John iii: 16. 'Though your sins be as scarlet, they shall be as white as snow; though they be red like crimson, they shall be as wool.'—Isaiah i: 18. At this remarkably encouraging promise was a large blood-stain, as though gory fingers had been tracing out every word; also at John xiv: 1, 2—'Let not your heart be troubled: ye believe in God, believe also in me. In my Father's house are many mansions'—were the same stains of still broader and deeper dye.

"Albert was the only son of a pious and wealthy planter of the South. Most of his time during his childhood was spent in the country on his father's plantation. The little white cottage was half-buried in evergreens, and richly festooned with fragrant vines, among which the wild birds nestled, and sang with their sweetest melody. On the hill, at the end of a long avenue, stood the quiet country church, where little Albert, accompanied by his parents, sister, and aged grandmother, met the families of the neighborhood to spend an hour in Sabbath School, and then listen to the reverend man of God, who preached to them the precious word of the Lord. Here, and around the family altar, Albert received that moral training which laid a deep and broad foundation for a character, in many respects, worthy of the imitation of all who may read this simple narrative.

"In the Sabbath School Albert first formed the acquaintance of little Jennie, neatly dressed in a white muslin with a blue sash, who aftewards became the beautiful and accomplished Miss S., whose daguerreotype we found in the soldier's coat-pocket. She was the intimate friend of his sister Hattie, and often his successful competitor for prizes offered by the Superintendent of the Sabbath School.

"In the year 1856 Albert was sent to College to complete his education, and Jennie went to a ladies' College of high grade to complete her studies.

"A few notes that ran the College blockade, and vacation meetings, sufficed to keep up their acquaintance and friendship. In the summer of 1860 they both graduated with honors highly creditable to them and gratifying to their friends. On their return home, early attachments ripened into something more than friendship; but scarcely had the bright vision of hope dawned when it was overcast by the dark cloud of war that suddenly rose upon our horizon. The country called the brave young men from every quarter to rally in Southern prowess, and with battle shock roll back the invading foe. Albert was one of the first to respond. He took his place in the ranks as a common soldier, feeling it was honor enough to be a private, defending his country, his home, and his beloved Jennie; and all the more, as he had her approving smile to encourage him.

"Albert's departure and transfer to Virginia by rail are scenes so common to soldiers that they can be imagined or remembered far better than I could describe them.

"There is one incident, however, which I will mention. Just before he took leave, they were all called around the old family altar. Jennie was there. Maum Patty, the nurse of his childhood, was there, with snow-white kerchief about her ebon brow and silver locks. Many were the bitter sobs, while the deep, earnest voice of the father in solemn prayer, like the patriarch Abraham, bound his son, his only son, a sacrifice on his country's altar. When the amen was pronounced, there was in every heart a feeling too deep for utterance. In this moment of silence, a mother's hand placed the Soldier's Bible in a pocket near his heart. Albert moved slowly down the avenue, the embodiment of youthful chivalry and manly beauty. The spectators stood like breathless statues, fearing most of all that they should see his face no more. Just as he turned the corner at the end of the avenue, he cast one glance back to the scenes of his childhood, which never seemed half so dear.

"After a long and uncomfortable transit by rail and forced marches, with weary limbs and blistered feet, he was thrown into the battle of Manassas, on the 21st of July, 1861, with scarcely time to kneel by an apple-tree in battle line, over which the shells were howling furiously. Here, in prayer, he hastily committed his soul and body to his faithful Keeper, then rose calm and serene, with an assurance that no weapon of the enemy would harm him.

"When the battle was over and victory perched upon our banner, Albert found himself surrounded with the dead and dying, among whom were some of his particular friends. He was strongly and strangely exercised with a mingled feeling of joy and grief, a sort of hysteric paroxysm of laughing and crying, weeping for the slain, and rejoicing that he had escaped unharmed, with a deep consciousness that God had been his shield and hiding-place in the hour of danger. Albert endured all the sufferings of fatigue, cold, and hunger, incident to a winter campaign; none murmured less, none were more faithful in the discharge of duty, than he. The demoralizing effects of the camp, with almost the entire absence of religious privileges, produced a coldness in his state; and although he did not compromise his moral character by profanity, gambling, and drunkenness, as many others did, yet he failed to enjoy the close communion and clear sense of the Divine presence which he had done in former days. In this state of mind, he entered upon the seven days' battles before Richmond. The solemnities of the occasion aroused him to a sense of his danger, causing him to cleave more closely to his Bible and its precious promises. With his hand on this blessed book pressed to his heart, he called on God to be his shield and support in the hour of battle. He passed the terrible ordeal of Gaines' Mill on Friday, and Malvern Hill on Tuesday, where the men fell around him like grain before the reapers, and covered the ground thick as autumn leaves. A degree of joy and gratitude swelled his heart as he surveyed the field of death, in view of his own wonderful escape, but not so deep and warm as on a former occasion, when his faith and piety were more earnest and simple. Albert continued at times to read his Bible; but it was evidently more as a task than a pleasant duty; his keen relish for Divine things had abated very much; the excuses of camp-life, long marches, and the general indifference of officers and men upon the subject of religion, offered his conscience the consolation of a temporary opiate. Sometimes, however, on the reception of letters from home, and sometimes when alone on his midnight round of picket duty, he would shed a penitential tear, and resolve to double his diligence and regain his lost ground as a Christian; but a plant so tender and unprotected by the pale of the Church, unwatered by the dews of the sanctuary, persecuted and scathed by the lightnings of contempt, nipped and browsed upon by every wild beast of the forest, necessarily became greatly dwarfed in life and growth; a feeling of self-security, a trust in fate or chance, impressed him more than a simple faith in the ever-present God. In this spiritually demoralized condition he entered the Sharpsburg fight, without even asking God to protect and save him from danger and death. Soon after the battle opened he was struck by a ball and carried back to the rear a wounded man; from profuse hemorrhage, a sick, dreamy sensation stole over him; the light faded from his eyes, while a thousand mingled sounds filled his ears, and a faint vision of home, friends, green turf, battle-fields, and grave-yards, flitted by like phantoms of the night. With returning consciousness, there came a sense of shame and sorrow for having declined in his religious state, and a conviction that his wound was the chastening of the Lord to rebuke his wanderings and check his self-reliance.

"As soon as he was sufficiently restored, he drew from his pocket his neglected Bible, kissing it many times over, and bathing it in tears as truly penitential as Peter when he wept at the feet of Jesus. His bloody fingers searched out the old-cherished promises of God, leaving many a gory stain on the blessed pages of inspiration. The law of the Lord again became his meat and drink, on which he feasted by day and by night; a new life was infused into his soul, which enabled him to bear his sufferings with true Christian heroism.

"In this condition I found him in the old Academy Hospital in Winchester, lying on the dirty floor, with a blanket for his bed and a wisp of straw to pillow up his wounded limb. While sitting by his side, trying to minister to his soul and body, I received from him this narrative substantially as I have given it to you. After much severe suffering, when our army fell back, he was sent to Staunton and thence to Richmond, where I again met him just in time to witness his last triumphant conflict with suffering and death. He was in a hospital, reclining on a clean, comfortable bed, his head resting on a soft, white pillow, on which the familiar name of a distinguished lady of Georgia was marked—she having contributed it from her own bed for the benefit of the suffering soldiers. Near him sat the matron of the hospital, rendering every possible comfort that the sympathy of a woman could suggest, intensely sharpened by the recent loss of a promising son, who fell in a late battle. Reduced by a secondary hemorrhage and amputation, Albert, with a calm, steady faith, came down to the cold waters of Jordan, where he lingered for a short time and dictated a letter to his mother, which I wrote for him, in which he gave an appropriate word to each one of the family, not even forgetting Maum Patty, his old nurse, and reserving a postscript, the last and best, for Jennie. I would like very much to give my readers a copy of this letter, but it is the exclusive treasure of the bereaved and afflicted ones, whose grief is too sacred for the intermeddling of any save the most intimate friends.

"After pausing a few moments at the close of the letter, he seemed self-absorbed, and soliloquized thus: 'I die for my country and the cause of humanity, and, with many others, have thrown my bleeding body into the horrid chasm of revolution to bridge the way for the triumphal car of Liberty which will roll over me, bearing in its long train the happy millions of future generations, rejoicing in all the grandeur of peace and prosperity. I wonder if they will ever pause as they pass to think of the poor soldiers whose bones lie at the foundation of their security and happiness? Or will the soul be permitted from some Pisgah summit to take a look at the future glory of the country I died to reclaim from fanatical thraldom? Will the soul ever visit at evening twilight the scenes of my childhood, and listen to the sweet hymn of praise that goes up from the paternal altar at which I was consecrated to God? Though unseen, may it not be the guardian angel of my loved ones?' Checking himself, he said: 'These are earthly desires, which I feel gradually giving way to a purer, heavenly sympathy.' Then, in a low, sweet voice, he repeated—

> 'Give joy or grief, give ease or pain,
> Take life or friends away,
> I come to find them all again
> In that eternal day.'

"He repeated the last line with an emphasis that threw a beauty and force into it which I never saw or felt before. Seeing that he was communing with his own soul, and that spiritual things in the opening light of eternity were rising in bold relief before his vision of faith, I withdrew a short space from him, feeling it was holy ground, 'where the good man meets his fate, quite on the verge of heaven.' He then gently laid his hand on his Bible and the daguerreotype that lay near his side, and amid this profound stillness, surrounded by a halo of more than earthly glory, gently as the evening shadows the curtain dropped, leaving nothing visible to us but the cold and lifeless clay, on which a sweet smile rested, as though it had seen the happy soul enter the pearly gates of the New Jerusalem. Thus, far from home and friends, this noble youth fell asleep in Jesus, swelling the long list of the honored dead; but, 'though dead, he yet speaketh.' The precious treasure, '*The Soldier's Bible*,' has been returned to the family, and is now one of those valued relics that bind many sad hearts with links of gold to bygone days."

CHAPTER XIV.

AUTUMN OF 1862.

Let us now turn to the Army of the West and gather up a few of the precious relics that lie scattered over that wide field.

After his masterly evacuation of Corinth, and the concentration of the army at Tupelo, General Beauregard, worn down by excessive toil, asked to be relieved from duty in order to recruit his shattered health, and General Bragg was placed in chief command.

In the month of October, the Confederates, under General Van Dorn, made an attempt to retake the town of Corinth, which was held by the Federals with a heavy force. The attack was very determined, and for a time promised to be successful; our forces fought their way to the very centre of the town, but the strong works and terrific fire of the enemy forced them to retire at the very moment when victory seemed within their grasp. Our men, especially the Missourians, under Gen. Price, fought with unsurpassed bravery, and the blood of hundreds of the noblest and best enriches the ground on which Corinth stands. The Federals attempted to cut off the retreat of our army by throwing a heavy column to the south of Corinth, but the genius and experience of Gen. Price completely foiled their plans, and brought the shattered battalions of the South to a position where they could make a successful stand.

The march of General Bragg from Mississippi into Tennessee, and the events that followed, are so well known that we need not do more than make such reference to them as may be essential in keeping up the thread of our narrative.

The marching and manœuvering of both armies, Confederate and Federal, ended in the battle of Perryville on the 8th of October. The desperate valor of the Southern troops bore down all opposition on this bloody field, and after driving the enemy before them and camping for the night on the field of battle, General Bragg, deeming it hazardous with his wearied men to renew the conflict with the heavily reinforced army of the Federals, withdrew in good order to Harrodsburg, and thence to Bryantsville. In his official report, General Bragg says of this battle: "For the time engaged, it was the severest and most desperately contested engagement within my knowledge. Fearfully outnumbered, our troops did not hesitate to engage at any odds, and though checked at times, they eventually carried every position and drove the enemy about two miles."

Many a Christian hero fell in this sanguinary battle, but among them all none offered a purer life on the altar of his country than Thomas Jefferson Koger, of Alabama. He was a pious, zealous, eminently useful minister of the Methodist Episcopal Church, South, and for nearly twenty years had been a member of the Alabama Conference. At the close of his term as Presiding Elder on the Columbus District, he entered the army of the South as a private in the ranks, but was afterwards appointed chaplain. In reference to his entrance upon a military life, exchanging the quiet round of ministerial duties for the bustle and toil of a soldier's life, we must let him speak in his own vindication, if any be needed.

In a letter to his dear friend, Rev. O. R. Blue, he says:

"I go from a deliberate conviction that it is my duty to go. It is under these feelings alone I leave my family. I go, trusting in God to bless and prosper me in the just cause. Pray for me." To his wife, writing from Bowling Green, he says: "As to the cause of my absence, I think there need be no apprehension. There is as much need of preachers and preaching here as in any place I have ever been yet; and I try to maintain my place as a Christian minister as earnestly and heartily as I ever did. It is a mistake to suppose that men in arms are beyond the reach and influence of the gospel. They are not; and the gospel is the only refining and elevating influence operating on them. Wife, children, home and its endearments, are only sweet memories here—not actual restraints, as they are when present. And then, the sick are always open to religious impressions."

At the expiration of the term of service of the regiment which he served as chaplain, he returned home, and at once set to work to raise a company for the war. It was his wish to return to the army as chaplain, but the person who was expected to take command of the new company having declined only the day before the election, he was the unanimous choice of the men for captain. Having been mainly instrumental in raising the company, he did not feel at liberty to decline, and thus unexpectedly he found himself regularly enrolled as a soldier. He carried the spirit of his Master with him into the camp; he prayed with his men every night, and preached to them on Sabbath whenever circumstances permitted. He maintained his integrity, and never compromised on any occasion his character as a minister of Christ. His men loved him devotedly, and always showed him the highest respect. The thoughts of this good man have a melancholy interest now after the storm of war is hushed, and we look back on the past as on a horrible dream. From the camp he wrote:

"No man leaves wife and children more reluctantly than myself. But I have made up my mind to do it, and must bear it. I am trying to lead a godly life, and do good as best I can in my place as an officer and minister of the gospel. I feel that I am in the way of duty, and can ask God's best blessing on my work. I am a soldier for conscience' sake. I am here because duty calls me, and for no other reason. If it were not the path of duty, I should utterly loath the interminable, never-ceasing confusion of camp life."

Again referring to his position as a soldier:

"I could not be a soldier unless conscience approved. It is only when my own land is invaded, my wife and children endangered, that I dare bear arms; and then, when interests so vital, so personal, are at stake, it is only by effort I could remain at home."

With a cheerful and buoyant spirit he endured the privations and fatigues of military life, sustained by such a noble and chivalric sense of duty. His march to Perryville was his last. After his regiment was drawn up in line of battle, his Colonel, passing along the line, observed him writing, and asked what he was doing. He replied, "Writing to my wife." This hurried note, written on the edge of battle, was the last message of love to his family. It was cut short by the order "Forward," and at the head of his men he plunged into the fight. His sword was shattered in his hand by a ball, and the next moment another pierced his body. He fell and died on the field. After the battle, two of his faithful soldiers, at their own request, were detailed to bury him, and while performing this sad duty were captured by the enemy. One who knew him well and loved him (Rev. J. B. Cottrell, of Alabama), draws his character in a few meaning lines:

"T. J. Koger will not again meet in Conference with us. Few of our number would be more missed. A very peculiar man in appearance, and a peculiarly true and earnest soul, he was most highly esteemed by us all. Few men ever loved the Church better, or were more at home in her councils or at her altars. He was popular among his brethren, and popular among the people. Perfectly fearless, he avoided no duty or responsibility. In every respect he was *reliable*. On the battle-field of Perryville he fell, attesting his devotion to his native

South. He was one of the few men who could have gone on to any position in the service in which he fell, and afterwards have come back to the work of a Methodist preacher. One bright, sunny spirit less—we'll miss and lament him."

On this hard-fought field the private soldiers, unknown to fame, fought and died like heroes. An eye-witness writes:

"A Christian soldier was pierced by a minie-ball in the left breast during the first charge of our troops at Perryville, and, in reply to a friend who proffered him assistance, said: 'No, I die. Tell my parents I die happy. On, on to victory. Jesus is with me, and can give me all the help I need.' A gasp, a shudder, and all was over—all of this world's pain and sorrow."

The constant movements of the armies in the West, after the battles of Corinth and Perryville, were unfavorable to the cause of religion among the soldiers. But in all the camps there were devout men who maintained their Christian character unsullied, and who, by example and precept, strove to lead their comrades to Christ.

One of the hindrances to the work of God was found in the passion for speculation and extortion that possessed the souls of thousands in the army and out of it. A writer in one of the religious papers, speaking of the condition of society in Western Georgia, said in November, 1862:

"Speculators and extortioners are, true to their instincts, ravaging this country, monopolizing every article of prime necessity as soon as it begins to get a little scarce. They seem to have forgotten the awful denunciations of God's word against all such characters and proceedings."

Against this base desire of gain at home, the South had to fight as hard as against her avowed enemies on the battle-field.

The spirit of prayer that prevailed among our soldiers

impressed even the minds of our opponents. In an interview with a committee sent by a convention at Chicago, comprising Christians of all denominations, to urge the abolition of slavery, President Lincoln said:

"The rebel soldiers are praying with a great deal more earnestness, I fear, than our own troops, and expecting God to favor their side; for one of our soldiers, who had been taken prisoner, told Senator Wilson, a few days since, that he met with nothing so discouraging as the evident sincerity of those he was among in their prayers."

In the midst of the grief that wrung the hearts of our people, they did not forget to call upon God for the restoration of peace to their unhappy country. A lady, one of those noble specimens of humanity that hovered like angels of mercy around the sick and wounded soldiers in the hospitals, or toiled for them in the silent and forsaken homes of the South, appealed to her sisters to devote one day, the 1st of December, 1862, to prayer for the restoration of peace. From Chapel Hill, N. C., she sent forth her appeal: "On that day, at 12 o'clock, let every woman's heart be lifted in prayer for her country. Let the sick woman on her bed remember the day and hour; let the busy forego her business; and, I was going to say, let the gay suspend her gaiety, but I trust there are no gay women in the South now; but let the young, beautiful, and hopeful, equally with those who can lay no claim to such titles, think of the dead, and the dying, and the mangled, think of the brokenhearted, the destitute, the homeless, think of the widows, the fatherless, the childless, of this awful war, and let every true-hearted woman be stirred to pray as with one voice on that day to God for help and for PEACE—an honorable PEACE."

To this appeal of the soldiers' truest friend, a soldier added his appeal from "the edge of battle:"

"We hope that no wife or mother or sister in the Confederate States will permit the call to go by unheeded. It is becoming that they, whose hands have not been imbrued with blood, should present this great petition to the throne of our Heavenly Father. Soldiers and countrymen, of whatever rank or station, let me suggest that we also unite with those mothers, wives, and sisters, on that day, and in that hour, to pray that the hand of the Destroying Angel may be stayed before we all are sunk in hopeless ruin. Let the workman close his shop; the merchant his store. Let all the trade and business of every description be deserted. Let the soldier retire to the silent grove, or unite in prayer with his pious comrades in the tent. Let the sentinel plead for it in his silent tread, and the sick soldier upon his lonely couch. Let Heaven be emphatically besieged on that day by the entreaties and supplications of earnest souls, for peace—an honorable peace. Oh! my countrymen, remember, only one hour of that time which is not yours, but God's, is all that is asked for, in which to unite with those whom we love (and who have shown in a thousand ways their love to us), to plead with the throne of Jehovah, for the inestimable blessings of peace and independence upon us and our posterity. God has told us that where even two or three of his children unite in asking a blessing he will give it to them in a special manner. Oh! my countrymen, will he shut those ears which are ever so ready to catch the first breathing of a penitent soul? will he, I say, shut them against the earnest cry of a penitent nation? On one remarkable occasion, when our Saviour was in great trouble, as we are now, he asked his disciples to watch and pray with him one hour. Shall he have to upbraid us, as he did them, with those sorrowful but tender words, 'What, could ye not watch and pray one hour?' Oh! blessed Saviour! help us so to watch and pray, in *that hour*, as that we may prevail with thee, and secure the blessings of a speedy peace to our tempest-tossed and war-worn people. Speak the word only, thou Son of God, to this great tempest. 'Peace, be still.' and there will be a great calm."

The approach of winter caused a cessation of military operations on a large scale.. General Bragg lay with his army in Middle Tennessee, covering several important strategic points; General Kirby Smith was in East Tennessee; General Pemberton was in the vicinity of Holly Springs, Miss.; while smaller bodies of troops were scattered over the country for the defence of the vast lines of communication with the East and the South. In all these camps, the chaplains and colporteurs were at work preaching the word, circulating religious papers, tracts, and portions of the Holy Scriptures, and thus sowing the seeds of that great revival which, later in the war, swept through the armies of the West like fire in dry stubble.

It has been often said that the Southern people rushed into the war without reflection, and without pausing to think of the awful calamities it would bring with it. This may have been so with many, but it was not so with all. The great minds of the South knew well what was involved in war, war in its worst type—civil war. In the autumn of this year (1862), Bishop James O. Andrew, of the M. E. Church, South, in an address to his Church, urging a full and cordial maintenance of the Christian ministry in time of war, uttered this prophecy, which the venerable man lived to see fulfilled: "We have as yet scarcely seen the half of the evils which this war is bringing on us. To be sure, there is sorrow enough, and poverty and lack of bread enough; in many, very many instances we have extortion and bankruptcy enough, and sufficient manifestations of heartlessness to make us sick of earth and most of its associations; yet these are not all, nor even a tithe of the evils which we suffer from the war."

The Bishop laments that "the tendency of a state of things in which war is the chief subject of thought and glorification is to exalt military studies and pursuits above everything else, and thus leave but little room for the cultivation of meekness, humility, gentleness, and faith and love, which constitutes the religion of the blessed Jesus; and, as these do not thrive well in a warlike atmosphere, there is great danger of losing, or, at least, very greatly abating, the spirituality and the power of the religion of the Church, and subtracting very materially from the respect which many professed Christians in the Confederacy have for all the institutions in the Church, and especially for the ministers of religion."

All previous wars, with hardly an exception, afforded ground for such a conclusion; but the great anomaly of our war was, that while religion may have languished at home, in the armies it flamed out with a power and brilliancy unheard of before in the annals of civil strife and bloodshed. This great fact came to view more clearly as the conflict deepened, and no man rejoiced in it more than did the eminent and venerable Bishop Andrew. At this day there are ministers of Christ of high talents and great usefulness, who were born of God amidst the smoke and flame of battle, and who heard the call of the Spirit to a nobler warfare above the rattle of musketry and the roar of cannon. And with these there stand now in the ranks of the laity, filling honorable and useful offices in the Church of God, their comrades, who, in the midst of like scenes, "tasted of the good word of God and the powers of the world to come." Mingled with sad remembrances of the great struggle, they have a joyous recollection of the time and the place when peace was planted in the soul on the field of blood.

> "The gladness of that happy day,
> Oh, may it ever, ever stay!"

CHAPTER XV.

WINTER OF 1862-'63.

THE battle of Sharpsburg was followed by a series of movements which brought both armies face to face again on the soil of Virginia. The unfortunate General McClellan fell under the ban of his government, and was superseded by General Burnside. The Federal army moved slowly southward from the Potomac to the Rappahannock, while the Confederates made a corresponding march through the Valley of Virginia, crossed the Blue Ridge, and placed themselves on the south side of the last named river. We quote from the "notes" of Rev. J. W. Mills, who fully participated in all the hardships of the army:

"October 29th.—Orders just received from headquarters to cook two days' rations, and be in readiness to march in the morning at an early hour. All is anxiety— no one knows whither we are to move. Are we to cross the Potomac and attack the Yankees? Or are we to go southwards to some point of railroad communication with home and friends? These are questions of importance to us. I hear men saying: 'Well, I will go anywhere I am ordered.'"

In this long march many of the soldiers suffered greatly for want of shoes and clothing. "Each regiment," says Mr. Mills, "has its barefooted squad, who are permitted to pick their way through the rocks as best they can." The feelings of our people in the Valley, as they saw the troops move on with the head of the column filing off towards the mountains, were very sad. "As we marched through Winchester the band played 'Old Folks at Home.' We saw ladies, young and old, looking on with sad faces, many of them weeping. Could we have spoken to these sorrowing ones, we would have said, 'Be not alarmed, Stonewall Jackson is *somewhere.*'"

"Friday, October 31st.—In lines and off at 7 o'clock. Many are limping with blistered feet and swollen joints. The barefooted stood the march better than those whose shoes were not a good fit. Many are carrying their shoes in their hands to-day. The Shenandoah river is to wade this morning, and we are anxious to get to it, hoping that the water will be some relief to scalded and burning feet. Some stripped their feet and legs, others plunged in with shoes and socks on. The water was almost freezing cold, and was, as we thought, a great benefit to our sore feet.

"On Sunday the army reached Culpeper, and each regiment gave a shout of joy as it went into camp within hearing of the whistle of the engine bringing news from home and friends. Three months before the army had left Gordonsville to drive the enemy out of Virginia. We have fought many hard battles, suffered hunger and weariness to an incredible degree; and done all this without a change of clothing, and many without shoes or blankets."

In this campaign many thousands of our wounded soldiers were necessarily left within the Federal lines; and, while many of them suffered and died in hospitals and prisons, it is pleasing to record instances of kindness shown to such as were more fortunate by good men and good women at the North. The case of the Rev. George G. Smith, of the Georgia Conference, chaplain of Phillips' Georgia brigade, affords a pleasing episode. He received a dreadful wound in the battle of Boonsboro; the ball struck him in the neck, passed through the body, and came out near the spine, cutting some of the nerves of the brachial plexus and paralyzing the left arm. In this condition he was captured, and for many weeks remained a prisoner in Maryland. With many other wounded Confederates, he had good reason to remember the kindness of sympathizing friends. Of his own case, he says:

"My personal obligations to these people can never be met. Literally, 'I was hungry, and they gave me meat; naked, and they clothed me; and sick and in prison, and they visited me.' A good woman took me to her house in Boonsboro and nursed me as her child, and a gentleman in Baltimore sent for me when he learned my condition, and did what he could to get me to his house—furnished me with money—and when at last he got me to his home, he furnished me with all he could conceive I needed. To his good wife and himself I owe more than I can ever repay."

Mr. Smith finally recovered of his wound, but partial paralysis of his system remains, which, however, does not prevent his continuing in the ministerial work. He is now an active and useful member of the Georgia Conference of the M. E. Church, South.

In the same battle (Boonsboro) a son of Bishop James O. Andrew was severely wounded and left upon the field. The venerable Bishop records his gratitude to those who befriended his boy. He says:

"The battle was fought on Sunday morning, and he lay on the field till next day; and during that night, he thinks, he must have died with cold but that two kind Federal soldiers took him to the fire, gave him some hot coffee, and covered him with a couple of overcoats and a blanket. He was moved to the hospital, but his wounds were not dressed until Wednesday. Shortly after, Mr. H. called, had him paroled, and took him to his home and treated him as if he were his own son. He speaks in glowing terms of the kindness of the people of Maryland, and especially of the great kindness shown to the Confederate prisoners by the ladies of Baltimore. I feel grateful to God for his care of my boy, especially in raising him up friends in a land of strangers. May God bless them all."

A singular phase of the war, on the part of the Federals, was the summary manner in which ministers were treated who fell under suspicion of disloyalty. Many were ejected from their pulpits, hurried away to the North, and, in some instances, confined in prison like common felons. In Nashville several prominent clergymen of the different Churches were for several weeks confined in the Penitentiary. The scene described in the following extract occurred in the same city:

"Rev. C. D. Elliot, though a Northern-born man, has been raised and educated in the South, and for over twenty years has been principal of the famous Nashville Female Academy. From the beginning of the war, and even of the issues that led to the war, he has been uncompromisingly Southern. No trimming in Elliot. Well, the Yankees took his Academy for a hospital. One day a stout fellow of the 35th Ohio regiment called at his door, wallet in hand. 'My name is ———; I came from the neighborhood of your brothers, and have messages from them to you. I feel a little unwell, anyhow, and thought I would call and stay with you.' 'Sir,' said Elliot, looking waspishly through his spectacles, 'when a man in *that* uniform calls on me on business I treat him civilly, but I decline all *visits* from such.' 'But I have messages from your brothers to you; they are my neighbors and—' 'Don't care. Don't want to hear any messages from them if they are on your side,' and the door slammed in Buckeye's face. A few days afterward this Buckeye and a Major, on horseback, passed by Elliot's premises. 'Changed your sentiments yet, sir?' said the Ohio soldier. 'Not at all,' was the reply; whereupon he struck Elliot (a small and feeble man) twice over the head and shoulders with a stick, and then kicked him. Turning to his Major—'Major, have I beat him enough?' The Major, putting his hand to his pistol, replied, 'Beat him just as long as you please!' 'Well, I guess that'll do for this time,' was the remark of the moderate member of the 35th Ohio regiment. A regiment was passing at the time. One of the sick soldiers, to whom Elliot had been kind, on witnessing this treatment, told him if he would lay the case before Gen. Buell he would get redress. Elliot answered, 'I look for my redress to the Southern army.'"

In New Orleans, where General B. F. Butler exercised authority, the services of the churches were interrupted by the arrest and deportation of ministers. The following appeared in a Northern paper as an item of news:

"The three disloyal Episcopal clergymen, Rev. Dr. Goodrich, Rev. Mr. Fulton, and Rev. Dr. Leacock, who have been forwarded to this city from New Orleans by Gen. Butler, staid at the Astor House until yesterday afternoon, when they were turned over to the custody of the United States Marshal, who will consign them to Fort Lafayette."

The offence of these ministers was that in the Sunday service they had omitted the prayer for the President of the United States. The following scene is a specimen of what occurred in many parts of the South under Federal rule:

"As the Rev. H. R. Smith, of Leesburg, Va., came from the pulpit, after the usual Sabbath services, Capt. McCabe, one of Mr. Lincoln's officials, arrested him for disloyalty, objecting to his sermon, his prayer, and chapter read from the Bible. The sermon was written, and, on examination, they were constrained to withdraw their charge against it. 'But you did not pray for the President of the United States?' Mr. Smith replied, 'No, sir, I prayed, as the Bible directs, 'for all in authority,' and if you consider Mr. Lincoln your President you could join in that prayer.' Well, the captain found that he must waive that item of the charge. 'But your chapter—I do not believe the words read are in the Bible.'

'Yes, sir, they are'—(Isaiah xliii: 5, 6.) 'But you should not have read them.' Mr. Smith said in reply: 'They have no reference to political questions—and do you intend to limit the reading of God's word?' 'Yes, sir!' 'You will then have your hands full before you get to the Gulf of Mexico.' The captain then said: 'Take the oath, sir, and you may go.' 'No, sir,' Mr. Smith replied, 'I will not.' 'Then we will send you to Washington.' 'Very well, sir.' 'Appear before me to-morrow morning prepared to go.' Mr. Smith appeared; but the captain and his counsellors, it appears, had thought better of the matter."

The winter of 1862 was ushered by the repulse of the Federals at Fredericksburg, and the year was closed by the battle of Murfreesboro and the frightful slaughter at Stone river. The movement against Fredericksburg was the fourth attempt to reach Richmond. Generals McDowell, McClellan, and Pope had failed, and now Burnside was hurled back across the Rappahannock with his shattered and beaten army. The leaders and the men who successively defeated four great armies of the North were worthy of the eulogies bestowed by impartial spectators of the war. Mr. Lawley, an English gentleman, who was in the South at this time, wrote to the London *Times:*

"It is a strange thing to look at these men, so ragged, slovenly, sleeveless, without a superfluous ounce of flesh upon their bones, with wild, matted hair, in mendicants' rags, and to think when the battle flag goes to the front how they can and do fight. 'There is only one attitude in which I never should be ashamed of your seeing my men, and that is when they are fighting.' These were General Lee's words to me the first time I ever saw him. They have been confirmed by every other distinguished officer in the Confederacy. There are triumphs of daring which these poor, ragged men have attempted, and attempted successfully, in this war, which have never been attempted by their Sybarite opponents. Again and again they have stormed batteries formidably defended, at the point of the bayonet; nothing of the kind has ever been attempted by the Federals."

The repulse at Fredericksburg was a staggering blow to the North. Their leading journals bewailed it as a great calamity. The New York *World* spoke of it as "the most terrible defeat of the war," and placed the loss of the Federal army at more than fifteen thousand men. Meagher's brigade of Irishmen went into the fight twelve hundred strong, and but two hundred and fifty could be found next morning. The *World* said editorially:

"Heaven help us—there seems to be no help in man. The cause is perishing. Hope after hope has vanished, and now the only prospect is the very blackness of despair. Here we are, reeling back from the third campaign upon Richmond, fifteen thousand of the Grand Army sacrificed at one sweep, and the rest escaping only by a hair's breadth."

The Louisville *Journal* said of this battle: "It is painful and absolutely sickening to read of the horrible slaughter of our troops at Fredericksburg. The war cannot be carried on much longer as it has been. Gen. French went into battle with seven thousand men, and two days after the battle only twelve hundred reported to him. The total loss in his brigade alone was thirteen hundred and fifty-five."

Concerning this disastrous battle General Burnside sent to Washington city this delicate dispatch:

"The army was withdrawn to this side of the river because I felt the position in front could not be carried. It was a military necessity, either to retreat or attack. A repulse would have been disastrous to us. The army was withdrawn at night without the knowledge of the enemy, and without loss either of property or men."

This victory was not gained without a vast sacrifice

of noble lives on the part of the Confederates. Gen. Lee was supported by some of his ablest Lieutenants, and never did they more gallantly execute the orders of their great chieftain. The following extract from Gen. Lee's official report will give the reader a correct view of the field and the disposition of our forces:

"The morning of the 13th, his arrangements for attack being completed about nine o'clock, the movement veiled by a fog, he advanced boldly in large force against our right wing. Gen. Jackson's corps occupied the right of our line, which rested on the railroad; Gen. Longstreet's the left, extending along the heights to the Rappahannock, above Fredericksburg. Gen. Stuart, with two brigades of cavalry, was posted on the extensive plain on our extreme right.

"As soon as the advance of the enemy was discovered through the fog, Gen. Stuart, with his accustomed promptness, moved up a section of his horse artillery, which opened with effect upon his flank, and drew upon the gallant Pelham a heavy fire, which he sustained unflinchingly for about two hours. In the meantime the enemy was fiercely encountered by Gen. A. P. Hill's division, forming Gen. Jackson's right, and, after an obstinate combat, repulsed. During this attack, which was protracted and hotly contested, two of Gen. Hill's brigades were driven back upon our second line.

"Gen. Early, with part of his division, being ordered to his support, drove the enemy back from a point of woods he had seized, and pursued him into the plain until arrested by his artillery. The right of the enemy's column extending beyond Hill's front, encountered the right of Gen. Hood, of Longstreet's corps. The enemy took possession of a small copse in front of Hood, but were quickly dispossessed, and repulsed with loss.

"During the attack on our right the enemy was crossing troops over his bridges at Fredericksburg, and massing them in front of Longstreet's line. Soon after his repulse on our right, he commenced a series of attacks on our left, with a view of obtaining possession of the heights immediately overlooking the town. These repeated attacks were repulsed in gallant style by the Washington Artillery, under Col. Walton, and a portion of McLaw's Division, which occupied those heights.

"The last assault was made after dark, when Col. Alexander's battalion had relieved the Washington Artillery (whose ammunition had been exhausted), and ended the contest for the day. The enemy was supported in his attack by the fire of strong batteries of artillery on the right bank of the river, as well as by the numerous heavy batteries on the Stafford Heights.

"Our loss, during the operations, since the movements of the enemy began, amounts to about eighteen hundred killed and wounded. Among the former I regret to report the death of the patriotic soldier and statesman, Brigadier-General Thomas R. R. Cobb, who fell upon our left; and among the latter that brave soldier and accomplished gentleman, Brigadier-General Maxcy Gregg, who was very seriously, and, it is feared, mortally wounded during the attack on our right."

Among the Southern soldiers who offered up their lives in this battle there was no nobler sacrifice than Gen. Thomas R. R. Cobb, of Georgia. His ability as a lawyer and statesman, and his pure Christian character, gave him great influence in the South, and particularly in his native State. He gave up all the bright prospects which opened before him in the civil service of his country, and cast his lot among the patriots of the army. His death was mourned with a sincere sorrow throughout the South. In the death of Gen. Maxcy Gregg, of South Carolina, the country lost one of its ablest and bravest soldiers. He had been in the struggle from the first note of war at Sumter, and gave his labors and his life to a cause which he regarded as one of the holiest for which a man could die.

The following incident is related of this heroic officer. During the retreat of the Confederate army from Maryland, after the battle of Sharpsburg, Gen. Gregg commanded the rear-guard, Gen. T. T. Munford, of Virginia, commanding the cavalry covering the rear-guard:

"When Gen. Munford reached the ford, Gen. Gregg and his men were just entering the water to cross to the Virginia side of the Potomac. Near by was an ambulance filled with gallant Confederates (many of them terribly wounded and torn in the battle of the previous day), entreating their comrades to carry them back to old Virginia. Gen. Munford seeing that the frightened driver had abandoned them, taking his harness and team with him, and that they were unable to ride behind his men, called Gen. Gregg's attention to the fact, whereupon the generous old Roman, uncovering his head, said to his men: 'Boys, see yonder your comrades who have been abandoned by a cowardly driver! They appeal to us for help! You who have escaped unhurt will not leave these poor fellows to their fate in sight of old Virginia.' In an instant they were transferring their arms and knapsacks. One generous lad, supposed to belong to the 14th South Carolina volunteers, catching hold of the singletrees of the ambulance, exclaimed, 'We will carry them back to old Virginia.' In less time than it takes to tell it, thirty of South Carolina's bravest sons were up to their waists in the water, bearing their comrades safely over the river, ambulance and all—the sad and gloomy countenances of the unfortunates seeming almost to forget their wounds as they caught up the strain, 'Oh, carry me back to old Virginia, to old Virginia shore.' Those who were too weak to sing waved their hats and handkerchiefs, and all were safely placed out of harm's way. As soon as this had been accomplished, Gen. Gregg replaced his hat and rode away to see that they were cared for."

The victory of Fredericksburg was achieved with a

small loss in point of numbers on the part of the Confederates; but among the honored dead there were many who yielded up their lives in joyful hope of a better life. Gen. Lee congratulated the army in the following general order, which, like all the utterances of that unequalled soldier and humble Christian, breathes the spirit of a true faith in God:

HEADQUARTERS ARMY OF NORTHERN VA.,
December 31, 1862.

General Orders, No. 138:

"1. The General Commanding takes this occasion to express to the officers and soldiers of the army his high appreciation of the fortitude, valor, and devotion displayed by them, which, under the blessing of Almighty God, have added the victory of Fredericksburg to the long lists of triumphs.

"An arduous march, performed with celerity under many disadvantges, exhibited the discipline and spirit of the troops, and their eagerness to confront the foe.

"The immense army of the enemy completed its preparation for the attack without interruption, and gave battle in its own time and on the ground of its own selection.

"It was encountered by less than twenty thousand of this brave army, and its columns, crushed and broken, hurled back at every point with such fearful slaughter, that escape from entire destruction became the boast of those who had advanced in full confidence of victory.

"That this great result was achieved with a loss small in point of numbers only augments the admiration with which the Commanding General regards the prowess of the troops, and increases his gratitude to Him who hath given us the victory.

"The war is not yet ended. The enemy is still numerous and strong, and the country demands of the army a renewal of its heroic efforts in her behalf. Nobly has it responded to her call in the past, and she will never appeal in vain to its courage and patriotism.

"The signal manifestations of Divine mercy that have distinguished the eventful and glorious campaign of the year just closing, give assurance of hope that the guidance of the same Almighty hand, the coming year, will be no less fruitful of events that will insure the safety, peace, and happiness of our beloved country, and add new lustre to the already imperishable name of the Army of Northern Virginia.

"R. E. LEE, General."

Of the battle of Murfreesboro, which closed this eventful year, General Bragg wrote on the night of December 31: "The bloodiest day of the war has closed." At seven in the morning the Confederates attacked the Federal lines and, after ten hours' hard fighting, took them at every point except on the **extreme left**, where they were successfully resisted. The vast numbers and resources of the Federals prevented us from seizing the fruits of this victory, and General Bragg in his dispatch said: "Unable to dislodge the enemy from his entrenchments, and hearing of reinforcements to him, I withdrew from his front." Such was often the sequel to a hard-fought battle during the war. Just when **we** expected to enjoy all the fruits of a victory, they were snatched from our grasp.

On that field of blood death showed himself in most hideous forms. Rev. Dr. Joseph Cross, who was with General Bragg's army, thus describes the battle-field after the fight:

"Ah! how many expired with the year. Here they lie, friend and foe, in every possible position, a vast promiscuous ruin.

"'They sleep their last sleep, they have fought their last battle;
  No sound can awake them to glory again.'

"After a pretty thorough inspection of the ground in

the rear of our lines, from Stone river to the extreme left, I rode to the front, where the dead lie thick among the cedars, in proportion of five Yankees to one Southron. Here are sights to sicken the bravest hearts—sad lessons for human passion and oppression. Here is a foot, shot off at the ankle—a fine model for a sculptor. Here is an officer's hand, severed from the wrist, the glove still upon it, and the sword in its grasp. Here is an entire brain, perfectly isolated, showing no sign of violence, as if carefully taken from the skull that enclosed it by the hands of a skillful surgeon. Here is a corpse, sitting upon the ground, with its back against a tree, in the most natural position of life, holding before its face the photograph likeness of a good-looking old lady, probably the dead man's mother. Here is a poor fellow, who has crawled into the corner of a fence to read his sister's letter, and expired in the act of its perusal, the precious document still open before him full of affectionate counsel. Here is a handsome young man, with a placid countenance, lying upon his back, his Bible upon his bosom, and his hands folded over it, as if he had gone to sleep saying his evening prayer. Many others present the melancholy contrast of scattered cards, obscene pictures, and filthy ballad books—"miserable comforters" for a dying hour. One lies upon his face literally biting the ground, his rigid fingers fastened firmly into the gory sod; and another, with upturned face, open eyes, knit brow, compressed lips, and clenched fists, displays all the desperation of vengeance imprinted on his clay. Dissevered heads, arms, legs, are scattered everywhere; and the coagulated pools of blood gleam ghastly in the morning sun. It is a fearful sight for Christian eyes!"

The scenes on the battle-fields and in hospitals are full of incidents showing the power of Divine grace to cheer and support the soul in the dark hour of death. "Tell my mother," said a dying soldier, "that I am lying without hope of recovery. I have stood before the enemy fighting in a great and glorious cause, and have fallen. My hope is in Christ, for whose sake I hope to be saved. Tell her that she and my brother cannot see me again on earth, but they can meet me in heaven." A little before bed-time of his last night he called to his surgeon (Mr. Leverett), and said: "Write to mother, and tell her she must meet me in heaven. I know I am going there." Thus died T. S. Chandler, of the 6th South Carolina regiment.

When Captain John F. Vinson, of Crawford county, Ga., came to die, he exclaimed: "All is well—my way is clear—not a cloud intervenes." As Lieut. Ezekiel Pickens Miller, of the 17th Mississippi regiment, fell mortally wounded on the field of Fredericksburg, he exclaimed: "Tell my father and mother not to grieve for me, for I am going to a better world than this." In this battle the gallant General Hanson, of Kentucky, fell while leading his men in Breckenridge's desperate charge at Stone river. Being outnumbered two to one, and his men being utterly exhausted by six days' exposure to cold and rain and four days' incessant fighting, with a loss of one-fourth of their number in killed, wounded, and missing, Gen. Bragg wisely determined to fall back behind Duck river, and rest his wearied army. The headquarters of the army were subsequently established at Tullahoma, thirty-eight miles from the fatal field of Murfreesboro.

It was now that the signs of that wonderful revival in the army of the West began to appear. "I shall never forget," says Rev. W. H. Browning, "the look of astonishment in the Association of Chaplains in January, 1863, when Bro. Winchester, a chaplain and a minister in the Cumberland Presbyterian Church, announced a conversion in his command, and stated that he believed we were on the eve of one of the most glorious revivals ever witnessed on the American continent! His countenance glowed with an unearthly radiance, and while he spoke 'our hearts burned within us.' He urged us to look for it—pray for it—preach for it. A revival in the army! The thing was incredible. And yet, while we listened to this man of faith, we could almost hear the shouts of redeemed souls that were being born to God. We could but catch the zeal of this good man, and went away resolved to work for a revival."

This pious man was not permitted to participate in the revival which he so feelingly predicted. He was soon called to the spirit world, and from his home among the blessed looked down upon the glorious scenes of salvation among the soldiers whom he loved so ardently, and for whom he prayed with a faith strong and unfaltering.

A General Association of Chaplains and Missionaries had been formed in this army in August of this year (1863), but the subsequent movements interfered greatly with its complete organization, and it was not until November following that it was properly reorganized and made really efficient. Rev. Dr. McDonald, President of Lebanon University, was the President, and Rev. Welborn Mooney, of the Tennessee Conference, Methodist Episcopal Church, South, was the Secretary. The proceedings of this Association Mr. Browning supposes were lost in the subsequent reverses of the army, and hence we are cut off from most reliable information concerning the progress of the revival.

The seeds of truth were sown by such faithful laborers as Rev. M. B. DeWitt, chaplain of the 8th Tennessee, Rev. Mr. Weaver, of the 28th Tennessee, Rev. Tilmon Page, of the 52d Tennessee, and Rev. W. H. Browning, chaplain of Gen. Marcus Wright's brigade. In other portions of the army, under the preaching of Rev. S. M. Cherry, Rev. Messrs. Petway, Taylor, Henderson, and scores of other devoted and self-sacrificing ministers, the revival influence became deep and powerful.

Rev. L. R. Redding, Methodist, of the Georgia Conference, M. E. Church, South, who labored as a missionary in this army, has furnished us an account of the work in his own and other corps during the winter and spring of 1863-'64. Beginning his work in Gen. Gist's brigade, and aided by Rev. F. Auld, Rev. A. J. P. De Pass, and other zealous chaplains, he soon witnessed scenes that filled him with the highest joy. The congregations increased daily, and soon a permanent place of worship was established in the rear of the brigade. The soldiers, eager to hear the Word of Life, soon fell to work and built a rude but commodious chapel, and furnished it with pulpit, seats, and lights. It was dedicated in the presence of the General and his staff by Rev. Dr. J. B. McFerrin, who, with his well-known zeal, had devoted himself to the work of an army missionary. An immense congregation attended, and the "Word ran and was glorified." From this time until the army marched away in the spring the revival progressed with increasing power. A Christian Association was formed, which met daily at half-past eight in the morning, for the purpose of uniting the members of the various Churches, as well as the new converts, in the work of saving souls, of gathering the results of the night meetings, and of hearing the recitals of religious experience. These meetings were marked by great fervor and power. The young believers were organized into private prayer-meetings, which met at seven o'clock in the morning. "Sometimes," says Mr. Redding, "I would quietly unpeg the door and walk in while the young men were engaged in their delightful meetings, and would find the young convert of the previous night leading in prayer, and earnestly invoking God's blessing upon his impenitent comrades." In the evening, at the close of dress-parade, the drums would beat *the Church call* on Chapel Hill. It was a glorious sight, just as the setting sun bathed the mountain tops in his ruddy light, to see those toil-worn veterans gathering in companies and marching to the house of the Lord. From all directions, down from the hills, out of the woods, across the valleys, they came, while the gallant Colonel McCullough, of the 16th South Carolina, himself a godly man, leads his men to the place of worship. Then the 24th South Carolina falls into line, led by their chaplain, Mr. Auld, and their brave Colonel Capers, son of the deceased Bishop Capers, of the Southern Methodist Church. The benches and the pulpit have to be removed from the house, and a dense multitude of hearers crown the chapel hill. A clear, strong voice starts a familiar old hymn, soon thousands of voices chime in, and the evening air is burdened with a great song of praise. The preacher now enters the stand, a thousand voices are hushed, a thousand hearts are stilled, to hear the word of the Lord. "Perhaps the speaker is Rev. William Burr, of Tennessee. As he rises with his theme, his silvery, trumpet-like voice, clear as a bugle note, rings far out over the mass of men, and hundreds sob with emotion as he reasons with them of righteousness, of temperance, and a judgment to come. At the close of the sermon, hundreds bow in penitence and prayer, many are converted, tattoo beats—the men disperse to their cabins, not to sleep, but to pray and sing with their sorrowing comrades; and far into the night the camps are vocal with the songs of Zion and the rejoicings of new-born souls." In this revival, described by an eye-witness, one hundred and forty were converted in two weeks, among them Colonel Dunlap, of the 46th Georgia, who united with the Presbyterian Church. Among the private soldiers that contributed to the success of this work, we are glad to place on record the name of W. J. Brown, of Company I, 46th Georgia. His influence with his regiment was very great, and he threw it all in favor of religion.

But soon came the order to march; the chapel and the snug cabins were exchanged for the drenched and dreary bivouac, and the sound of the gospel of peace for the notes of whistling minnies and bursting shells. In the battle, and in the hospital, the genuineness of those army conversions was fully tested. In the terrible campaign that followed, whenever the smoke of battle cleared away, and the weary men had a little rest, they gathered their shattered but undaunted cohorts, and, with renewed zeal, and with love tested in the fire of war, repledged their faith to each other and charged again and again the strongholds of Satan. Lying behind the strong barrier of the Chattahoochee river for a few days, these Christian soldiers built a brush arbor, and beneath it many souls were born of God. Dying, those noble men of the South gave testimony to the power of divine grace. "Can I do anything for you?" said the missionary, kneeling by the side of a private shot through the neck. "Yes, write to my poor wife." "What shall I write?" "Say to my dear wife, it's all right." This was written. "What else shall I write?" "Nothing else, all's right"—and thus he died. He was a convert of the camp.

"Passing through a large stable where the wounded lay," says Mr. Redding, "I noticed a man whose head was frosted with age. After giving him wine and food, I said, 'My friend, you are an old man. Do you enjoy the comforts of religion?' 'Oh, yes,' he exclaimed, 'I have been a member of the Church for twenty-five years. Often in our little church at home our minister told us that religion was good under all circumstances, and now I have found it true; for even here in this old stable, with my leg amputated, and surrounded by the dead and dying, I am just as happy as I can be. It is good even here. I want you to tell the people so when you preach to them.' I left him rejoicing."

Among the pious officers who worked faithfully in this revival, we have already mentioned Colonel Capers and Colonel Dunlap. We believe the former, since the war, has entered the Protestant Episcopal Church, and, if we are not misinformed, is now in the ministry. Colonel Dunlap, converted in camp, became an earnest Christian, and labored with zeal and success to bring his men to Christ. He was five times wounded, but survived the war, and is now an honored citizen of Georgia.

General C. A. Evans was a Methodist, and a class-leader before the war. He entered as a private in the 31st Georgia volunteers, was elected Major at its organization, and Colonel at its reorganization six months afterward. He greatly distinguished himself at the battles around Richmond, at Manassas, and at Fredericksburg. He was promoted and put in command of Gen. Gordon's celebrated brigade. The last year of the war he commanded Gordon's old division. He was an earnest, working Christian, and in the midst of war the call came to him to preach the gospel, but he wore his sword until the fatal day of Appomattox, when, with his noble comrades, he laid down the weapons of war, returned to his home, and was soon afterward licensed to preach and received into the Georgia Conference, M. E. Church, South. It is a singular incident that his first Circuit was called Manassas, and that his junior preacher was one of his old army couriers. He is still actively engaged in the ministerial work.

The revival was hardly less powerful in those regiments and brigades which were favored with the regular services of chaplains than in those that had none. The 2d Arkansas, of Liddell's brigade, Cleburn's division, had no chaplain at the time of which we write, but they were led by pious officers who strove to stem the tide of irreligion. "Lieutenant-Colonel Harvey, Captain H. D. Gregg, Lieutenant Wilfong, and others, being profoundly impressed with the great need of religious services, formed themselves into a band of Christian soldiers and began a moral warfare against the powers of darkness. They fought gallantly and well. They became really zealous and watchful pastors over their men. Mingling with the group around the crackling camp-fires, they seasoned conversation with religion. Profanity and vulgarity were rebuked, and cowered before the mild, living words of truth; many outbreaking sinners pledged themselves to pure lives, and by hundreds joined the band. They promised solemnly not to swear, nor gamble, nor to break the Sabbath, to use no spirituous liquors as a beverage, to indulge in no vicious habits, to cease to do evil and learn to do well. They held regular prayer-meetings, searched the Scriptures, exhorted one another daily, met and reported progress, and with fresh zeal returned again to their good work. When the harvest was so ripe for the sickle, who can wonder that when the Word was preached with power and unction among such men, thousands were gathered into the garner of the Lord?" Many of these brave soldiers afterward fell in battle; "but who can doubt," asks Rev. A. L. Davis, from whom we quote, "that their works shall live after them?" They sleep, indeed, in unknown graves along the line of that sad retreat from Dalton to Atlanta, but they live forever honored in the annals of their country, and forever enshrined in the hearts of their countrymen.

CHAPTER XVI.

SPRING OF 1863.

AFTER the terrible repulse at Fredericksburg, the Federal army lay along the north side of the Rappahannock, engaged as usual, after the failure of an "on to Richmond," in refilling its thinned ranks and mapping out a new route to the coveted city.

General Burnside, who had not conciliated his government by the rose-colored dispatch given in the last chapter, was set aside, and General Joseph Hooker placed in command of the Northern army. Our forces occupied the town of Fredericksburg, and extended their lines for some miles above and below. The fighting in the early part of the season was confined to cavalry skirmishes near the different fords of the river. The main body of the Confederate army remained in winter quarters, and here began one of the most powerful revivals witnessed during the war. Fredericksburg was the centre of the work, and the minister who contributed more to its success in the town than any other was the Rev. William Benton Owen, connected with General Barksdale's Mississippi brigade. Mr. Owen was earnest in calling to his help the ministers of all the different Churches, and, among others, he was favored at this time with the aid of Rev. Dr. J. C. Stiles, an eminent and eloquent minister of the Presbyterian Church. In the latter part of February he reached the town and entered into the work with his well-known ardor. He says:

"After my arrival we held three meetings a day—a morning and afternoon prayer-meeting, and a preaching service at night. We could scarcely ask of delightful religious interest more than we received. Our sanctuary has been crowded—lower floor and gallery. Loud, animated singing always hailed our approach to the house of God; and a closely packed audience of men, amongst whom you might have searched in vain for one white hair, were leaning upon the voice of the preacher, as if God himself had called them together to hear of life and death eternal. At every call for the anxious, the the entire altar, the front six seats of the five blocks of pews surrounding the pulpit, and all the spaces thereabouts ever so closely packed, could scarcely accommodate the supplicants; while daily public conversions gave peculiar interest to the sanctuary services. Of this class we have numbered during the week say some forty or fifty souls. Officers are beginning to bow for prayer, and our house to be too strait for worshippers. The audience, the interest, the converted, the fidelity of the Church, and the expectations of the ministry, are all steadily and most hopefully increasing."

But not only among the soldiers in the town did the gracious work go forward. In the camp, on the open fields, was the revival deep and powerful. In Gen. Anderson's brigade, of Hood's division, a Christian Association was formed, with J. C. Burnham, of Heard county, Ga., as President, J. F. Chambliss, of Talbot county, Ga., as Vice-President, and A. W. Watkins, of Baltimore, Md., as Secretary.

In their pamphlet, giving the reasons for this organization, they say, that for many months prayer-meetings largely attended had been held in the brigade, in which Christians had been built up in spirit, confirmed in faith, and many sinners converted to Christ. Feeling a necessity for an institution similar to the Churches at home, they "determined to form an Association which would supply this want and be acceptable to all orthodox denominations." They sent forth to their brethren at home this truly Christian message:

"We, soldiers, surrounded as we are by many temptations, and subjected daily to manifold trials, desire to publish to the Christian world the existence, the Constitution, and By-Laws, of our Christian Association, that the Church may be encouraged by the knowledge of the fact that Christian spirit and Christian efforts are not entirely unknown in the armies of our country, and that Christ has kept a few, as we trust, faithful followers, even where wickedness abounds. Nay! brethren, God has done much more than this for us, unworthy as we are; he has caused our hearts to rejoice in witnessing the turning of sinners from their sins. The angels have rejoiced more than once when they have looked down into our camps and seen new-born babes in Christ rejoicing in the love of a reconciled Father.

"Our reason for bringing our Association to public notice is because we believe that a knowledge of what we are trying to do for God will rejoice the souls of Christ's followers everywhere, and be encouragement to Christians who may be situated as we are."

The Creed subscribed by these noble men was simple, but apostolic:

"I believe in God, the Father Almighty, Maker of heaven and earth; and in Jesus Christ, his only Son, our Lord, who was conceived by the Holy Ghost, born of the Virgin Mary, suffered under Pontius Pilate, was crucified, dead and buried; the third day he arose again from the dead; he ascended into heaven and sitteth on the right hand of God the Father Almighty; from thence he shall come to judge the quick and the dead. I believe in the Holy Ghost; the Church of Christ; the communion of saints; the forgiveness of sins; the resurrection of the body; and the life everlasting. Amen."

Their Discipline was such as fitted earnest, straightforward soldiers of the Cross:

"All members of the Association are required to conform themselves to the rules of faith and Christian conduct, as laid down in the revealed word of God; and when any brother is charged with being in disorder, his case shall be referred to the brethren of the same faith and order with himself, who shall determine on his case and report at the next meeting, and their decision in the same shall be final and conclusive: Provided nevertheless, That the cardinal vices set forth in that portion of Scripture known as The Ten Commandments, together with gambling and drunkennesss, are expressly forbidden, and shall be cause for expulsion of a member by vote of the body. The offender to be tried according to the rule set forth in the 18th chapter of Matthew, 15th, 16th, and 17th verses.

"All members are required to attend meetings of the Association, whether called or regular; and when they fail to do so are expected to state the reasons at the next meeting.

"In case of the death of or disaster to any member of this Association, the same shall be held under obligations, by the love which its members owe to their God and brethren, to communicate the fact to his relatives or friends at home."

This was the whole of it, and under it was fostreed as noble a band of Christian patriots as ever fought or died for liberty and home.

Rev. W. C. Dunlap, chaplain of the noble 8th Georgia regiment, wrote in reference to this work:

"God has wonderfully blessed us of late. We have had going on in our midst a revival of religion, with more or less interest, since the battles in front of Richmond. Recently, however, it has grown greatly in interest; and before breaking up camps near Fredericksburg, the Lord was doing a mighty work in our midst. I have held prayer-meetings in my own regiment until ten o'clock many a night, and, after closing, the brethren would all retire to the woods, frequently accompanied by half-dozen mourners, and there, with no other covering save the open canopy of heaven, pour out their souls in humble supplication at a throne of grace, often remaining until after midnight; and, what is remarkable, I never have known the meeting to close without the witnessing influences of the Holy Spirit.

"I have often thought, could our people at home see us on such occasions, the stern warrior melted down into the tameness of a child by the sweet influences of the blessed Master, they would cheer up and take courage; for the prayers of the people of God shall never go unanswered, but shall be like bread cast upon the waters."

Rev. Samuel H. Smith, chaplain of the 60th Georgia regiment, of Lawton's brigade, camped near Port Royal, Va., referring to the growing revival in that portion of the army, gives a description of the services of a delightful Sabbath:

"At 11 o'clock A. M., I preached to a large audience from Malachi iii: 8, 'Will a man rob God?' At half-past two o'clock P. M., Col. Wm. C. Stiles, of the 60th Georgia, read to a very large and interested congregation Bishop Elliott's sermon, delivered in Christ church, Savannah, Ga., on the public thanksgiving day, September 18, 1862. The sermon produced a fine state of feeling throughout the audience. At candle-lighting we met for prayer. Rev. Mr. Chandler, of the 88th Georgia, delivered an exhortation, at the close of which six penitents knelt for prayer."

Thus was the Sabbath spent in camp by thousands of Southern soldiers.

In the great hospitals, where thousands of sick and wounded lay, the work was as great as in the camps. At Chimborazo, Richmond, there were at this time from three to five thousand sick men, and the religious influence pervaded all the wards. No sight could be more touching than to stand near the chapel and see the wounded and the pale convalescents hobbling and creeping to the place of worship at the sound of the bell. Fifty or more kneeling for prayer at the close of a sermon or exhortation was no uncommon sight. At Camp Winder, another large hospital near the city, there was a happy and saving religious influence, though the revival was not so general as at Chimborazo. It was the privilege of the writer to conduct a sacramental meeting in this hospital, at which devout soldiers, forgetful of all differences in creeds, knelt side by side in commemorating the Saviour's death. It was an inspiring and melting scene. The simple and earnest words of the sick soldiers as they lay on their hard, narrow beds, or gathered in groups at the sunny corners of their quarters, could not fail to touch the heart, and not seldom the hearer and narrator mingled their tears and rejoiced together in Christ.

Said a poor fellow, who was suffering greatly from two painful wounds, "When I was at home, I was wild and wicked, but since I have been in the army, I have tried to change my life, and since I have been wounded I have been able to trust my soul in the hands of God, and I feel that if he should call me to die, all will be well." He spoke with deep feeling, and the big tears filled his eyes and rolled down his pale face. Another from Georgia, who was dying of his wounds far away from home and friends, gave a like testimony, and, with tears of joy, praised God in full hope of heaven. Whether dying in hospital or on the battle-field, the testimony of the Christian soldier was the same. When Lieutenant E. P. Miller, of company K, 17th Mississippi regiment, lay dying on the field of Fredericksburg, the message he sent home was, "Tell my father and mother not to grieve for me, for I am going to a better world than this." When Capt. John F. Vinson, of Georgia, fell in the service of his country, his last words were, "All is well—my way is clear—not a cloud intervenes." Francis M. Bobo, of Spartanburg, S. C., exclaimed when dying, "I would not take ten thousand worlds for my prospect of heaven." "If I die in the hospital or fall in battle," said a young Georgia soldier, "weep not for me—all will be well." These are a few testimonies out of hundreds that might be recorded. They show the deep and joyous piety of thousands of the Southern soldiery.

The revival at Fredericksburg, already noticed, continued through the greater part of the spring with the greatest power. The labors of Dr. Stiles were blessed and honored in the salvation of many souls; but he was compelled to leave for other scenes of labor. Rev. Jas. D. Couiling and other ministers went to the help of Mr. Owen, and, by their earnest and pointed preaching, greatly promoted the work. An eye-witness, writing at this time from the scene, says:

"Last evening there were fully one hundred penitents at the altar. So great is the work, and so interested are the soldiers, that the M. E. church, South, has been found inadequate for the accommodation of the congregations, and the Episcopal church having been kindly tendered by its pastor, Rev. Mr. Randolph, who is now here, the services have been removed to that edifice, where devotions are held as often as three times a day. This work is widening and deepening, and, ere it closes, it may permeate the whole army of Northern Virginia, and bring forth fruits in the building up and strengthening, in a pure faith and a true Christianity, the best army the world ever saw."

In the churches, scarred and torn by the balls and shells from Federal batteries, the meetings were held night after night for many weeks, and the scenes were such as thrill the angelic hosts in heaven. In the space of six weeks one hundred and sixty professed religion in Barksdale's brigade, while scores of others were earnestly seeking salvation. Rev. W. C. Dunlap, in thanking the editor of the *Southern Christian Advocate* for reading matter furnished the soldiers, says of the general fast day:

"Last Friday will never be forgotten by this brigade

(Anderson's). The day before had been cold and raining, and, lest the next day should be as bad, many prayers were offered for a good day, which were answered, for we had one of remarkable brightness and beauty. The chaplains of our brigade had invited Bro. Crumley—a man universally beloved—to preach for us. Generals Hood and Anderson, with their staffs, were present. The music was helped out by the band, and Bro. C. preached a most appropriate sermon to a large and very attentive congregation. After the service, many retired to the woods and held prayer-meetings. There were like services on this day elsewhere. Rev. W. H. Simmons preached to General Toombs' brigade, and had an interesting meeting. Our meetings are still carried on with profit."

This day, March 27th, appointed by the President, Jefferson Davis, for fasting, humiliation, and prayer, was observed in the armies with unusual solemnity. A member of Barksdale's brigade tells how the day was spent by the devout soldiers:

"At half-past eight A. M. my mess, with those adjoining, met in my room for prayers, most of them being young converts; eight or nine prayers were offered aloud, the young men officiating by turns, though with most of them it was their first effort in public. At ten I went to another room in our company and conducted a similar meeting. It filled my heart with joy to see many of my comrades, so recently from the paths of vice and folly, now bending their knees to God, asking him to favor the land they had so often perilled their lives to defend. At 11 we assembled at the Episcopal church. On this occasion, perhaps, 1,500 were in attendance, mostly soldiers. Every grade, from private to Major-General, was represented. Rev. W. B. Owen, chaplain of the 12th Mississippi regiment, conducted the services; his theme was prayer; his text, 'Men ought always to pray and not to faint.' After services I visited some sick soldiers. At 3 P. M. we had a national prayer-meeting, conducted by Rev. W. H. Carroll, of Selma, Ala., a missionary and colporteur in the army. The service over, I retired to my quarters and took some refreshment for my body; my soul was much comforted. Calmly I looked back upon the labors of the day, and felt that I was seeing a day that had done more for my country than any other that had ever shone upon it."

Could a fast day have been more devoutly and profitably kept in the quiet days of peace than this was in the midst of the confusion and rush of war?

There was hardly a regiment of the army where the revival influence was not felt. Rev. W. A. Hemmingway rejoiced in a gracious revival in the 21st South Carolina regiment, which lasted for months. Rev. L. S. West, of the 13th Mississippi, conducted a meeting for six weeks, in which many were happily converted. Rev. S. H. Smith, of the 60th Georgia, Lawton's brigade, collected from the soldiers and officers $850 to purchase Bibles, Testaments, and Hymn-Books, and saw the men daily anxious "about the salvation of their souls.". Rev. F. Milton Kennedy, chaplain of the 28th North Carolina regiment, of Jackson's corps, found "the men generally interested in their spiritual welfare." A Chaplains' Association was formed, and weekly meetings held to consult upon the best method of prosecuting our work, and to pray for success. The chaplains of this corps issued an earnest appeal for more laborers. The fields were white to the harvest, but the laborers were few, while thousands of the noblest of the land, having left home and friends, were calling loudly and earnestly for the bread of life. To this and other calls the Churches responded by sending some of their ablest ministers into the army-work, who, by their earnest labors, greatly extended the area of the revival.

Captain Richard H. Powell, of the 3d Alabama regiment, gives an interesting account of the work: "For two months we have held prayer-meetings regularly, when military duties have not prevented, three times a week, which have constantly grown in interest. Last night twenty-six of these hardy soldiers presented themselves for prayer. They give the most earnest attention to all religious exercises, and gather in crowds to hear the gospel. They are reflecting most seriously upon eternal interests. *In the absence of a chaplain*, we are doing what we can in the interesting work of instructing them in the way of salvation, and pointing them to Jesus, the friend of sinners."

Deploring the want of ministers to break the bread of life to the starving thousands, Captain Powell says:

"Surely if the hundreds of ministers, who have comparatively little to do at home, knew how many thousands in the army languish and pine for the bread of life, they would certainly hasten to break that bread to them, that they might not perish. I have never seen such a field for doing good, and extending the Redeemer's kingdom on earth, as the army of Northern Virginia presents this day. The fields are already white unto the harvest, but the laborers, who must gather this rich harvest into the Master's granary, where, oh, where are they? It is astonishing to know what destitution of chaplains prevails. In this corps—General Jackson's—where an especial effort has been made to secure their services, *not one-half* of the regiments are supplied. Can you not, my dear sir, raise, in our behalf, the Macedonian cry, and urge zealous, laborious ministers of the gospel to come and help us? They will be received by the army everywhere with open, wide-stretched arms. Cannot Bishop Pierce devote a few months to missionary labors in the army of Northern Virginia this summer? Liberal souls at home will, doubtless, gladly devise the ways and means, while thousands of hungry, starving souls here will eagerly receive the message of life from his eloquent lips. Around our camp-fires we often think of him, and anxiously wish we could have the benefit of his ministrations.

"Yesterday I attended a Conference of the chaplains of Jackson's corps. It was a most interesting meeting, and a precious season of grace. Our hearts burned within us as they talked of God's dealings with their various regiments. They represent the different denominations, and are working harmoniously and successfully in this vast field. Occasional services will be held by them in our regiment, and we hope for good results."

In this regiment, a Christian Association was formed, with Colonel C. C. Battle, President; Captain R. H. Powell, Vice-President; Lieutenant W. H. Gardner, Secretary; Sergeant E. H. Hart, Assistant Secretary; Lieutenant W. T. Bilbro, Treasurer. These soldiers and their comrades expressed their sense of the need of mutual religious help in noble words: "In religion, as in everything else connected with the affairs of this world, there is strength in union. * * * Being engaged in a constant warfare with 'spiritual wickedness in high places,' beset on every side, and most sorely tempted, man needs the advice and encouragement of a brother who, similarly tempted and tried, by a word fitly spoken, or a consistent, upright walk and godly conversation, may strengthen him in his determination to serve God. Oh! how greatly we, here in camp, deprived of the sacred influence of home and all its hallowing associations, need the kindly offices of Christian brotherhood! How keenly we have felt the lack of fellowship and communion of hearts, has been shown—to our confusion be it said—by the crooked paths we have made for our feet, and the shame and reproach we have too often brought upon the name of our blessed Jesus. The leanness of our souls, the lukewarmness of our hearts, the delinquencies of our lives, barren of good works to the glory of God, all call for the genial, soul-cheering, heart-comforting influence of the communion of saints."

They gathered into their Association the members of all the different Churches, and mutually bound themselves to promote the welfare of the members, to exert a salutary and wholesome religious influence in the regiment, and by a life of holy living to constrain others to glorify their Father in heaven. Can we wonder that men of such character should fight well and die well?

The revival was greatly promoted by the free circulation of religious reading among the soldiers. Being almost wholly cut off by the strict blockade of all the Southern ports from foreign supplies of Bibles and Testaments, as a substitute select portions of the Scriptures, chiefly from the Psalms and the New Testament, were printed under the title of "Bible Readings," and sent by thousands to the various departments of the army. Small Hymn-Books were also printed in great quantities, and these, with tracts and religious newspapers, made up the religious literature of the camps. The arrival of these helps to the revival were hailed with delight by the soldiers, and eager crowds would surround the fortunate chaplain who had received a supply, and happy was the soldier who succeeded in securing even the smallest tract. Rev. William Hauser, chaplain of the 48th Georgia, and a diligent colporteur, says:

"The precious leaves from the tree of life are healing our sin-diseased soldiers. Swearing, and all other crimes incident to an army, are evidently diminishing, and deep piety is on the increase. Every night the holy songs of Zion go up on this balmy spring air, a sweet incense, I think, to the throne of the Eternal. Prayer-meetings are held every night in several of our companies, and a great desire is manifested to get Hymn-Books. Bless the Lord! He is working among us, and giving us, I do not doubt, a silent yet precious revival of religion, the effects of which are seen more and more plainly every day. It would do you some good to see how eagerly these gallant, weather-beaten warriors crowd around me to get tracts every time I have a new supply; but they want and much need something fresh every Sunday to engage their minds and keep them from resorting to ball-plays and cards. Our Colonel is not religious, but he has the greatest respect for Christianity, and seems to take great delight in affording me every facility for my work."

The religious influence now pervading the army was so powerful that the active movements of the spring campaign could not divert the minds of the soldiers from the great question, What must I do to be saved? Early in the season the attitude of military affairs in Virginia and North Carolina was this: Lieutenant-General Longstreet was in command of Southern Virginia, including the defences of Richmond, Petersburg, and portions of North Carolina. Major-General Elzy commanded the Department of Richmond; Major-General French, that of Petersburg and lower Virginia; and Major-General D. H. Hill, that of North Carolina. About the first of April Major-General Hood's division left Petersburg and marched towards Suffolk. On the 13th General Hood drew up in line of battle before the town, while his skirmishers boldly drove in the Federal pickets. Here for a week or more he remained, the enemy constantly expecting an assault; but besides heavy skirmishing, mutual shelling, and two or three gallant fights with the gun-boats in Nansemond river, the Confederates made no serious demonstrations against the place. The movement was not for the purpose of capturing Suffolk, but to divert the attention of the Federals while vast stores of provisions were being removed from the lower counties of North Carolina. This accomplished, our forces withdrew for more decisive operations in other quarters.

It would hardly be expected that on the lines near Suffolk much could be done in promoting the revival. But even there the work went on. Rev. W. A. Simmons, of Georgia, one of the most devoted and efficient chaplains in the army, says of the scenes he here witnessed:

"In the midst of all these changes and fighting, we manage to keep up our religious services. We preached on Sabbath at the time our batteries were assaulted, amid the most hideous thundering of artillery and in constant hearing of the picket-firing. The congregations were large, attentive, and serious. One young man came to me, late at night, to inquire the way of salvation. While passing the road I heard singing and prayer. It was a company of Christians, who had met in the darkness to hold a secret meeting. We received eight members on Sabbath evening into our Christian Association. Thus the work goes on. The moral tone of our brigade is rapidly changing. Card-playing is fast playing out, swearing is not heard so much as formerly, and attendance on preaching increases. May God bless the army."

On the main line of defence on the Rappahannock, General Lee lay with the main body of his army watching the movements of the vast array of Federals marshalled on the opposite side of that river, under command of General Hooker. The Federals had found the fords of Fredericksburg too bloody; they were now manœuvering for the fatal field of Chancellorsville.

CHAPTER XVII.

SPRING OF 1863.

LET us turn again to the armies of the West and Southwest.

On the coast the Federal fleets closely blockaded all the ports, and made demonstrations at the most important points. On the Mississippi, Port Hudson and Vicksburg were fiercely assailed, with serious damage to the Federals and with little loss to the Confederates. In Tennessee, Gen. Van Dorn greatly annoyed the Northern Generals by his swift and sudden movements against their forces in the neighborhood of Columbia, Franklin, and other places. The main army lay encamped at various points between Chattanooga and Murfreesboro, ready for any movement that might be necessary to checkmate the Federals. General J. E. Johnston assumed personal command of all our forces in that quarter, and established his headquarters at Tullahoma.

Rev. S. M. Cherry, one of the most devoted chaplains in the army, gives an account of the revival at this period in McCown's division, to which he was attached as chaplain of the 2d Georgia battalion. For ten weeks they encamped on the same spot freed from all the toil of war except guard duty. In the midst of their ease, the *long roll* late one afternoon called them to arms. In a few moments the whole command was pressing to the front. "While riding on," says Mr. Cherry, "I met with Rev. Dr. Bunting, chaplain of the Texas Rangers, who kindly consented to preach for us. We found General Ector's Texas brigade, and Colonel Vance's brigade, of North Carolina and Georgia troops, concentrated in a glade of rough rocks and gloomy cedars. Both commanders are official Church-members, and never object to preaching even on the outpost. Soon one thousand of our soldiers were grouped about the spot selected for Sabbath morning service. It was a grand sight to behold such a vast assemblage, seated upon the rugged rocks, to listen eagerly to the words of life. These were the heroic soldiers, once led in the far West by the ill-fated Ben. McCullough, in the battles of Missouri, and they have since distinguished themselves at Farmington, near Corinth, Richmond, Ky., and Murfreesboro, Tenn. Gallant sons of the Lone Star State are seated with the soldiers from the Empire and Old North States, who fought bravely beside them in the late bloody conflict of Murfreesboro. While all listened so attentively, I could but contrast the scene with the bloody charge made by the same men when the gallant General Rains fell upon a spot very similar to our preaching place. The theme of the preacher was: 'Whatsoever a man soweth, that shall he also reap,' and strong were his arguments and earnest his appeals to impress indelibly upon their hearts the truths of his sermon."

The great want of missionaries and chaplains was earnestly deplored by the godly officers and men, and a call was sent from nearly every division in the army for more laborers. At the regular meeting of the chaplains in General Polk's corps the self-denying ministers, who shared the rough life of the camp with the gallant men, resolved to make up what they lacked in numbers by increased devotion to their work and a deeper earnestness of soul in their lives and labors. "We must have a revival in our hearts if we would have it spread among the soldiers." These were right words, and the revival that followed told that they had not been spoken in vain.

In response to the "Macedonian cry" from the army measures were adopted by the Churches for supplying them with preachers. At the meeting of the Bishops and Board of Missions of the M. E. Church, South, held in April at Macon, Ga., the wants of the army were seriously considered. After the presentation and advocacy of the plan of Army Missions by Rev. Dr. A. L. P. Green, Dr. J. B. McFerrin, and Dr. E. W. Sehon, the meeting appointed a committee to take into consideration the spiritual wants of the army of the Confederate States, and to report a plan by which the M. E. Church, South, through the agency of its Missionary Board, might, in some measure, supply those wants. The President, Bishop Early, appointed the following ministers as the committee: Bishop Pierce, Drs. McFerrin, Summers, Sehon, Green, L. M. Lee, Myers, and Revs. R. J. Harp and W. W. Bennett. In response to the report of the committee the Mission Board adopted the following plan:

"Whereas information has reached this Board with regard to the destitution of ministerial service in the army of the Confederate States, and believing it to be the duty of the Church to supply as far as possible this deficiency: Therefore,

"1. Resolved, That the Board of Managers of the Missionary Society of the M. E. Church, South, establish a branch of its operations in the army of the Confederate States of America, to be called the Army Mission.

"2. Resolved, That the Bishops be and are hereby authorized and requested to appoint such general missionaries to the various departments of the army as in their judgment the demand requires and the funds of the Society may justify: Provided that they shall not appoint more than one general missionary to each army corps.

"3. Resolved, That each general missionary appointed by the Bishops shall travel through the department assigned him, preach to the soldiers, visit those of them who are sick and wounded, and report to the Bishop having charge of his department the condition and wants of the army, and suggest proper persons to be engaged as laborers in the field.

"4. Resolved, That the general missionaries shall co-operate with the Confederate States Bible Society, the various organizations in the several Annual Conferences, and the editors and publishers of religious journals in the Confederate States, in the circulation of the Holy Scriptures and a general religious literature through the army."

The other denominations adopted similar measures, and soon many of the leading ministers of the South entered upon the missionary work in the armies with a zeal truly apostolic, and with a success that cannot be fully known until the last day.

The news that they were to have more preachers in the army was hailed with joy by the soldiers. A writer from Kershaw's brigade wrote: "We are having good times in our brigade now—preaching twice a week and three times on Sunday. We have only two preachers, a Baptist and a Presbyterian—both good—but if we had *more* preachers, I think we would have a great revival. I never saw men so anxious to hear preaching. They crowd around the preaching place two or three hours before the preacher gets there." When the missionaries entered the army they found the fields white already to the harvest.

Perhaps the most unlikely place for a revival at this period was Vicksburg and its vicinity; and yet, even there, while closely pressed by heavy Federal forces, our soldiers were deeply pondering the question of salvation. The Rev. P. A. Johnston, chaplain of the 38th Mississippi Volunteers, wrote of a revival at Snyder's Bluff:

"The Lord is at work among us. His stately steppings are often heard and his presence felt to the comfort of our souls. We have had for the past week very interesting prayer-meetings. They were well-attended and the very highest interest manifested. Souls are hungry for the 'bread of life.'

"Often in these prayer-meetings there are from twelve to twenty mourners. There have already been two or three conversions, and four have joined the Church. Sinners are being awakened, mourners comforted, and the Christian established in the faith. The camp is a rough, hard life. But, sir, I feel fully compensated for every privation and hardship I have been subjected to.

"And now, one word to state a very important fact. The partitions are well-nigh broken down that have heretofore kept Christians so far apart. We know each other here only as Christian brethren travelling to a better world. Our meeting is still progressing. Pray for us."

There was scarcely a command in any part of the field that did not call for the gospel. Rev. J. W. Turner, writing from Savannah, Georgia, says: "'Our people seem to have deserted us,' was the language of a sick soldier in one of the hospitals in this city. He was a member of the 25th Georgia regiment, which has been encamped near this place for nearly eighteen months." The Baptists had given fruitful attention to this part of the field, as they did indeed with self-sacrificing zeal to every portion of the army. "There are three Baptist ministers," says Mr. Johnston, "acting as general chaplains, colporteurs, &c., within and around this city. They are giving their whole time to the distribution of Testaments, tracts, and Baptist periodicals, and to the preaching of the word." But few of any other denomination were laboring at this time in this portion of the army.

Of the forces stationed at Cumberland Gap, Rev. A. M. Jones, chaplain of the 55th Georgia, writes: "Having no house of worship, and the weather being very inclement and unpleasant, I have done very little preaching, but am endeavoring to do all the good I can by visiting the sick and procuring religious reading for the soldiers. Yesterday morning the mail brought us one hundred copies of the *Southern Christian Advocate*, which gives about ten to each company. With joy they were received, and with pleasure distributed among the soldiers. Walking through the regiment five minutes after this time, you might have seen, in almost every cabin and street, men deeply interested, poring over this silent messenger of intelligence and truth." Many a nail was fastened in a sure place by these messengers of truth sent by multiplied thousands into all the camps.

Some of the sermons preached by the leading ministers of the Churches were so memorable as never to be forgotten by those who heard or read them. The Rev. Dr. J. C. Stiles, of the Presbyterian Church, delivered a sermon on "National Rectitude," which was replete with the noblest sentiments and delivered with all the force and fire of his patriotic heart. Speaking of the vices which stood in the pathway of the Confederacy to a free nationality, he seized those who fattened upon their country's grief, and held them up to the gaze of the world. Of the speculator he exclaimed:

"Miserable man! How could he escape the all-pervading, generous patriotism of the day, and incarcerate his soul in such a cell of enormous degradation! The process is simple. His avaricious heart discovered that in our country the regular supply of merchantable commodities, which always keeps down the price, was cut off by the war, while the consumption of the same was as steady and undiminished as ever. Consequently, a steadily-increasing demand must as steadily augment the price. Let him then monopolize a large portion of necessary goods at their present value and hold over; ere long he must receive one, two, five, ten hundred per cent. upon his money, and ultimately make his fortune. Just there the man anchored his heart, his whole heart. This crisis of his country! What a nick of time for accumulation! How soon he must become a man of fortune, of enormous fortune! And, oh, the luxuries, and the power, and the pride, and the fame, and the rest of magnificent possessions! Over and over again he turns the absorbing subject in his thoughts in ever new and more enchanting lights—until he has churned up an egregious yearning of the bowels after filthy lucre. Nothing else does he see, or feel, or live for.

"Behold that great, hungry shark of the ocean! In the wake of the great ship he has scented the flesh and blood of the bait, and have it he will. He reaches the bullock's head, but teeth, bones, and horns are in his way. What cares he? Unchecked for an instant, he opens his prodigious jaws, and down go teeth, bones, horns, and all. So exactly with our great land-shark. The shining bait before him he will seize and nothing, nothing shall prevent him. But see! Self-respect and social standing and decency—they all lie in his way. If either of them survives, that fortune is not his. Nay! he cannot commence his hoarding. Mark the speculator! He halts not an instant, but forthwith extends his voracious mouth and crushes and devours them all, and drives on his fell pursuit.

"Wretched man! his fearful work of crushing human weal and heaven's law magnifies upon him at every move. Nothing now short of the most audacious and inhuman spirit can nerve him to another step. For if the fraternity which he leads is still determined to press on their scheme of unprincipled, heartless, reckless, acquisition—ever rising prices, and ever falling and failing currency, must, ere long, embarrass every fiscal measure of the legislator, cripple every wheel of the government, cut off supplies from every national agent, enfeeble every movement of the army, convulse the masses with dread anxiety about their daily bread, crowd the mansions of the rich with the cries of the famishing poor, and wake up the darkest apprehensions touching the ultimate issues of the country's struggle. But what of all this? It is nothing, nothing to the speculator. His whole heart is immovably fixed.

"There is no deed of darkness which the soul of the accomplished speculator is not primed and charged to accomplish. That miserable man! At such a time as this! Yes, at such a time as this, he can feed and fatten upon the tasked sinews of the government, upon the struggling liberties of the people, upon the scanty wages of the soldier, upon the failing morsels of the poor, upon the last solace of the sick, the wounded, and the bereaved, and *feel nothing*. He can ponder all the brutal, crushing cruelties of Northern subjugation, and dwell upon all the swelling, bursting, maddening endurances, endurances of the Southern captive, and yet *feel nothing*. The spirit of the South; that most beautiful, genial, admirable element of our national heritage—that Southern spirit, so brave, generous, proud, and independent—he can look forth into the future and see that spirit, that noble spirit, by most unholy persecution, crushed out of the people and lying a cold corpse over all these hills and valleys where once it lived so vigorous and happy an existence; *yes, and feel nothing*. Oh, yes! That fellow-man! He can gaze upon all this heart-rending spectacle and feel nothing, nothing but the splendors of that fortune he sucks out of the last drop of his country's blood. The love of money—oh, the love of money! Well saith Scripture, It is the root of all evil. Look out, speculator! Yet a little while, and that love of money shall pierce thee through with many sorrows and drown thy soul in perdition and destruction!"

The venerable Bishop James O. Andrew, of the M. E. Church, South, in an address to the ministers and members of his denomintion, said:

"These should be days of self-denial. Who can think of making parties and feasting on rich dainties, when thousands of gallant men, away from all their loved ones, are scarcely able to get the plainest food, and are enduring it all patiently, that we may be defended in the enjoyment of home and liberty; and when thousands of the loved ones, whom they have left at home, have scarcely bread to eat and clothes to wear? Is there not something heartless in the music of ball-rooms and theatres and in wine and brandy parties, when hostile fleets and armies are hovering around our cities and our whole sea-coast, threatening to carry devastation into all the land? Verily, the voice of confession and prayer would suit us better.

"I see that our President has again issued a proclamation calling on all the people to repair to the house of God, to fast, and humble and afflict our souls before him, beseeching him to forgive our individual and national sins, and to send us deliverance from the mighty fleets and armies which are marshalled against us and threaten to destroy us and devour our inheritance. I trust that all the people will obey the summons, and that on that day the confessions, thanksgivings, and supplications, of the whole people will go up with acceptance to the throne of the divine grace."

Charleston, S. C., was a point of great interest during the whole period of the war, and the fiery temper of the men who opened the fearful drama might be supposed to be unfavorable to the progress of the revival. But it was not so. Among the soldiers that lay for many weary months on the bare sands of the barren islands, and on the borders of the lagoons around that city, the work of grace went steadily forward. Christian Associations were formed, religious books, tracts, and papers were distributed, and earnest sermons preached, which resulted in most blessed scenes. In the 46th Georgia such an organization was formed, and the soldiers who united in it said: "Our object is to make it a despository for the names of members of the Church, that they may be known as such, and that thereby we may be the better enabled to watch over each other for good; that each may feel that *he* has something to do in teaching sinners the way of life; and that by a godly walk and pious conversation he ought to honor his profession and glorify the God of his salvation." One hundred and eighty-four Christian soldiers gave their names to the Association. Of this regiment, Rev. T. C. Stanley was then the chaplain, Lieutenant N. B. Binion was President of the Association, and W. J. Brown Secretary. These men came out not only to fight, to suffer, to die for their country, but to work for God and the truth in the midst of all the evils and corruptions of the camp.

The signs from other portions of the army in the West and Southwest were equally cheering. Along the lines in East Tennessee the revival began to spread with great power. Rev. W. B. Norris, writing from Loudon, Tenn., says:

"During the month (April) there has been a deep religious interest among the soldiers here. We have had a series of meetings for about two weeks, which, we hope, resulted in much good.

"The church in which we met was always crowded to the utmost, and there were always many seekers for the way of eternal life."

In the 59th Tennessee regiment there was a glorious work. Rev. S. Strick, the chaplain, says:

"God is at work among our men. Many are earnestly seeking the pardon of their sins—some have been converted. Our nightly prayer-meetings are well-attended by anxious listeners, and my tent is crowded daily by deeply penitent souls. Never have I known such a state of religious feeling in our army as at this time. God's Spirit is moving the hearts of our soldiers."

From the 38th Alabama volunteers Rev. A. D. McVoy sent good tidings:

"We have held nightly meetings almost uninterruptedly, whenever the weather permitted, ever since last October, with large attendance, much interest, and good results. Some conversions and accessions to the Church have gladdened our hearts. While stationed in Mobile we had every convenience for religious worship—a large arbor with seats and stands for fire. Since we have been transferred to Tennessee we have resumed our nightly meetings, either in quarters or upon some neighboring hill, where the shade is good, and where with logs we could construct our rude altar to God. Such a place as this has truly become a little Bethel to our souls. I never saw men more concerned about their soul's salvation. In a little gathering last night, which was greatly interrupted by rain, we had thirty to rise for prayers. The feeling seems to be deep and earnest. The members of the different Churches, who number over two hundred in my regiment, are greatly revived and aroused to duty. I have never found men listen with more profound attention to the word of God. We seem to be upon the eve of a gracious revival and outpouring of the Holy Spirit, for which we are praying, watching, and struggling."

Rev. F. Milton Kennedy rejoiced in a great revival in the 28th North Carolina regiment:

"I am having a delightful meeting in my regiment. Yesterday I administered the sacrament of the Lord's Supper to about one hundred communicants, and many, who have repeatedly met the shock of battle with unquailing hearts, were melted to tenderness and tears by the power of grace. Last night there were between thirty and forty penitents. Up to this time, as far as I have been able to ascertain, about fifteen have professed conversion, and upon the first invitation given to candidates for Church-membership (at the close of the communion service on yesterday), sixteen came forward. I trust the Church at home will remember the army in their prayers. There is a powerful and growing religious interest prevalent throughout large portions of this army, which only needs the impulse of a prayerful Church at home to sweep through the entire command and transform her heroic soldiery into a sacramental host."

Rev. W. T. Bennett, chaplain of the 12th Tennessee regiment, Polk's corps, wrote:

"Our regiment is being greatly blessed. We meet from night to night for exhortation, instruction, and prayer. Already there have been upwards of thirty conversions. Most of them have joined the Church. There are yet a large number of inquirers. The moral tone of the regiment seems rapidly changing for the better."

Rev. T. C. Stanley, to whom we have already referred, reported favorably from the 46th Georgia regiment. More than two hundred were enrolled in the Association, and the movement was heartily seconded by the field, staff, and line officers. Colonel Colquitt, Major Spears, Quartermaster Leonard, and others, gave aid and counsel to the chaplain.

Among the troops at Columbus, Miss., a work of much interest began, which was interrupted in its progress by their removal to Jackson. The chaplain laboring there, Rev. W. H. Smith, sent forth an earnest call to the home Churches for help. "Brethren! ministers! are you asleep? Do you not hear the cries of your countrymen calling to you from every part of the land? The soldiers feel their need of salvation, and are crying for the gospel! And will you withhold it from them? Awake! arise! gird yourselves with the whole armor of God, and come forth 'to the help of the Lord, to the help of the Lord against the mighty.'"

An officer of the 5th Georgia regiment, stationed at Bridgeport, Tenn., sent back home his appeal:

"Our regiment now numbers about 650, and these men have not heard a sermon in *five months*. What a thought! Who is to blame? The men? I think not. The officers? No. Who then? The ministry or the Christians at home. I have done all in my power to secure the services of some minister to preach for us, but have, so far, entirely failed. Our regiment is composed mostly of young men, many of them, at home, members of the Church—Christians; and shall it be said that any of these have backslidden or have died, and are forever lost, for the want of proper counsel? God forbid."

Rev. S. M. Cherry made a call from the army of Tennessee:

"There is much interest manifested in our corps now. The cry, 'Come over and help us,' is heard from the serious soldiers in several commands. The harvest truly is great and the laborers few. Revivals are reported in several brigades. Chaplains still scarce."

Rev. C. T. Quintard, of the Protestant Episcopal Church, chaplain for Polk's corps, and J. H. Bryson, of the Presbyterian Church, chaplain of Hardee's corps, in appealing to the public for aid in supplying Bibles, Testaments, and Hymn-Books to the soldiers, said:

"We feel that we need only mention the fact that our brave soldiers are asking for the Word of Life in order to secure from a generous public the most liberal contributions. Who can withhold, when the sick and wounded who fill our hospitals ask for the word of God to cheer and sustain them during their days of affliction, their nights of weariness and suffering? We feel confident that there are many who will give neither grudgingly nor of necessity, but with cheerful hearts and liberal hands. The religious interests of our soldiers demand and must receive prompt attention from every lover of good order, civil liberty, and piety towards God."

These and thousands of similar appeals stirred up the home Churches to redoubled efforts on behalf of their fellow-citizens in the field. The Bishops of the M. E. Church, South, in their appeal for means for the Army Mission, said:

"The moral character of the army is dear to all the people, and demands that prompt provision be made to preserve and promote it. The Church has precious interests at stake, in that many of her members are found in the ranks, and need ministerial instruction, and sympathy, and influence, to counteract surrounding temptations and keep up in vigorous action their personal piety. Moreover, the exposure of our fellow-citizens, kindred, and friends, to disease and death, in a thousand forms, makes an earnest effort for their salvation a duty which admits of no delay, and calls upon us all to do what we can to meet the emergency with loving hearts and liberal hands. The Great Head of the Church has manifested his gracious will by sending his Holy Spirit in a remarkable manner to the aid of those who are laboring in this important field.

"Men and brethren, help. Your country calls. Your Church implores your aid. Patriotism urges, by all the ties of citizenship and the claims of your imperilled countrymen. Piety pleads with you by the love of Christ and of souls, the sanctified hopes and affections of our immortal nature, the present duty and future glory of the Redeemer's kingdom upon earth. Let us be up and doing. Give freely, largely. Deny yourselves. Magnify the grace of God in you and toward you. Fill the treasury of the Lord, that we, your servants, for Christ's sake, may send the gospel of peace to every army of the Confederacy."

Rev. Dr. E. W. Sehon, the Missionary Secretary of this Church, travelled at large appealing to the people and collecting thousands of dollars for the Army Mission. "But one heart of patriotism," he said, "beats in the land. All are united in a struggle for justice and right, and all are laboring to sustain our noble army. We call for the same attention to be manifested by the Churches to their spiritual wants. With all the wise provisions of the Government in the appointment of chaplains, there is still a loud call for ministerial help. Other faithful preachers should be sent to aid in the great work of those already gone. On the march, in the hospital, and on the tented field—at all times and in every place—these men of God should be with our brave soldiers."

The action of other Churches was equally prompt and efficient. The Baptist Board of Domestic Missions set the sister Churches a noble example. At the General Convention, twenty-six missionaries were reported as laborers in the army—one in Florida; two in Alabama and North Carolina, respectively; three in South Carolina; four in Mississippi, Georgia, and Virginia, respectively; and six in Tennessee—and the Board determined to increase the number to the extent of men and means offering. These missionaries moved from camp to camp, and sometimes accompanied the troops on long marches, conversing with the men, distributing tracts, Testaments, religious papers, holding meetings for prayer and exhortation, and preaching as they found it convenient.

One feature of this army work deserves special notice. The aim of the laborers seemed to be to lead the soldiers to Christ, not to make them sectarians. It was alleged that the Baptist Tract Society was circulating tracts in the army teaching the peculiar tenets of that Church on the subject of baptism. This charge the *Religious Herald*, of Richmond, Va., one of the leading papers of that denomination, unqualifiedly denied, and declared that since the war opened their Board had not published a line bearing directly or indirectly on the question of baptism. A similar rumor prevailed concerning the Methodists issuing tracts teaching their views *contra* on the same question, but this was found to be untrue. Over-zealous men of both Churches might, on their own responsibility, have circulated old tracts bearing on these mooted subjects, but the publications of this class printed during the war avoided disputed points and taught the great cardinal doctrines and duties of religion.

The great concern of the people at home for the salvation of their fellow-countrymen in the armies soon bore fruit. In the army of Tennessee there was a glorious work, which embraced hundreds and thousands in its influence. The Rev. F. S. Petway, chaplain of the 44th Tennessee regiment, Johnson's brigade, Cleburn's division, in connection with other ministers, reported a wonderful revival in that celebrated command:

"In the latter part of March," he says, "Chaplain Taylor, of the 23d Tennessee regiment, commenced a series of meetings at Tullahoma, assisted by Rev. A. W. Smith, of the 25th, and myself, which continued for several weeks, until temporarily interrupted by military movements. These meetings have resulted in much spiritual benefit to professed Christians, while about one hundred and five souls have embraced Christ as their Saviour.

"In General Wood's brigade a meeting of great interest has for several weeks been under the supervision of Rev. F. A. Kimball, chaplain of the 16th Alabama, assisted mainly by Colonel Reed, Chief of Provost Marshal Department, in Hardee's corps, and Col. Lowery, of the 45th and 32d Mississippi, the result of which has been one hundred conversions. In the same brigade, Chaplain Otkin, of Col. Lowery's regiment, has been conducting religious services, which, from the best information received, has been productive of great good in restoring many wanderers to their former enjoyments and inducting about forty-five souls into the kingdom of Christ.

"In General Polk's brigade, Bro. Davis, of the 1st Arkansas, and Quarles, of the 45th Tennessee, have been laboring with commendable zeal and success in their respective commands, with occasional assistance from Chaplains Smith and Taylor, and as the fruit of their labors God has converted about seventy souls.

"In General Lidell's Arkansas brigade, which is destitute of a chaplain, a meeting was commenced five weeks since by Bro. Anderson, preacher in charge of Bedford Circuit, but who, in consequence of affliction, was forced to retire in the very incipiency of an encouraging revival. The charge of the meeting devolved on me, and with the efficient aid of Bros. Taylor, Smith, and Stevenson (the latter of whom is a supernumerary member of the Tennessee Conference), it has continued up to the present time, without any abatement of the interest. Each night crowds of penitents throng the altar for prayer, averaging from eighty-five to one hundred, and the number of conversions, according to the most correct estimate, will not fall below one hundred and forty."

The whole number converted at these meetings was four hundred and seventy-eight, while hundreds more, who had yielded to the vices and temptations of the camp, found the joy of salvation restored to their souls. Under the preaching of Rev. S. M. Cherry, in McCown's division, the conversions in two regiments reached one hundred and forty. In the brigades of Gens. Stuart and Wright, the revival was powerful and many were converted. "In these revivals," says Mr. Petway, "two encouraging facts are made manifest. We see officers, from colonels of regiments down to captains, lieutenants, and sergeants, giving their counsels and mingling their tears, songs, and prayers, with those of the private soldier, and a good number of those who are thus engaged have recently been made partakers of God's converting grace. Another fact worthy of notice consists in the marked attention and deep solemnity of the vast crowds to whom we preach.

"The idea of disrespect among soldiers to the worship of God seems to have gained the ascendancy in the minds of those at home, than which nothing is more unfounded. While the army is composed of every variety of character, some of whom have no aspiration beyond that of card-playing and low, vulgar profanity, yet there are hundreds, who, in point of intellect and high-toned morals, rank with the first men in the Southern Confederacy, and who, like the evergreen among the blasted shrubbery, shed a healthful influence around them. Could many of our fashionable city crowds be present and witness the marked respect paid by these men to the service of God, they would not only be proud of our army, but some among the *elite* would, perhaps, be put to the blush and acknowledge an example worthy of their imitation. And in order to remove false impressions abroad, with regard to these noble men who are suffering and sacrificing so much for the good of our country, I affirm, that, during a ministry of seventeen years, I have rarely, even in the most enlightened communities, preached to as large crowds to whose deportment during divine service so little exception could be taken; and in the assertion I will be sustained by a large majority of the chaplains. It is due to the soldiers that this fact be made public, and thus disprove a slander, so often repeated, that card-playing, profane swearing, and low vulgarity, are not unusual within a few steps of where divine service is being conducted. I have preached nearly one hundred sermons within eight months in the army, and such things have not yet fallen under my observation; and, moreover, were men even inclined thus to insult God and the ministry, the restraints of military law would soon place them beyond the possibility of repeating the act. So the charge refutes itself."

To this work Rev. Dr. J. B. McFerrin, who had been recently appointed army missionary, contributed greatly by his able and fervent sermons. He was personally known to thousands in the army of Tennessee, and his coming was like the visit of a father to his children.

The Presbyterian Church sent forth many of her ablest ministers. Rev. Dr. Waddell, Chancellor of the University of Mississippi, was appointed Superintendent of Army Missions in the West and Southwest, and he was ably supported by such men as Dr. Palmer, of New Orleans. Dr. Rutherford, Dr. E. T. Baird, Rev. J. H. Bryson, and many other earnest preachers. In the army of Northern Virginia, they had Dr. B. T. Lacy, Dr. R. E. Dabney, and others, who gave a great impetus to the revival by their unwearied and successful labors. Besides the regular missionaries, the pastors of the home churches of all the denominations visited and preached to the various camps, on all occasions, when they could spare time from their charges.

The attention given to the word preached was an index to the state of mind in the army congregations. "Could you see," said a writer from Kershaw's brigade, "the crowd that collects nightly under the large arbor prepared for the purpose, perhaps you would be surprised that, in the large concourse, not one word is spoken, not even in the outskirts of the congregation; but every man is looking intently at the minister, catching every word that falls from his lips." Another writer from a different command: "I have never seen men listen with more profound attention to the word of God. We seem to be upon the eve of a gracious revival and outpouring of the Holy Spirit, for which our friends at home, I trust, are offering up supplications daily."

The men of this regiment gave $425 to enable their chaplain to supply them with Testaments, tracts, and religious papers.

Rev. T. C. Wier, referring to the religious habits of the soldiers, says: "They listen with a quiet, deferential respect to the Word, rarely witnessed in our congregations at home. In addition to preaching and prayer-meeting on the Sabbath or during the week, we have public prayers at the Sunday evening dress parade. This custom was introduced into our regiment at the suggestion of our first Colonel, Hon. Robert McLain, a New School Presbyterian preacher. There is something impressive in this Sabbath evening prayer. It is a calm evening, and the men are drawn up in the order for dress parade. At the commad, 'parade rest,' leaning gracefully upon their arms, they come to the position of 'rest.' Our good Colonel then gives the command, 'Attention to prayer by the chaplain—heads uncovered,' when the chaplain, facing the regiment a few feet in front of the Colonel, offers a short, appropriate prayer. Such a scene might often have been witnessed last summer, while we were pleasantly camped near Columbus, Miss. Since that time, we have marched many a weary mile, and seen much severe service in the camp and on the bloody field. Our good Colonel fell mortally wounded in the attempt to storm Corinth, and found a soldier's grave near the memorable field. His last message to absent friends was, 'Tell them I fell in defence of a just cause.' We have lost other men, brave and true, and passed through various changes, but we still keep up the custom of prayer at the Sabbath evening dress parade."

Leaving now for a time the armies of the West, let us return to those noble heroes, who, in the East, felt and rejoiced in the wonderful outpouring of the Holy Spirit, which, whether in the camp, on the march, in bivouac, or on the field of battle, marked the history of the army of Northern Virginia from this time until the close of the war.

CHAPTER XVIII.

SPRING OF 1863.

REVIVALS, deep and genuine, prevailed in nearly every brigade of the army for weeks before the battle of Chancellorsville. In Barksdale's brigade, just before the fight, the number of conversions had reached two hundred, and when the heavy columns of Hooker began their movements the revival was spreading in greatest power. From their religious services the soldiers went forth to meet the foe; they hurled him back with dreadful loss, and again returned to hear the gospel from their ministers, and to hold their prayer-meetings. The Rev. W. H. Potter, of Georgia, who spent several weeks in the army, including the week of marches and battles, reported the work of grace to be progressing in a wonderful manner. Even the week's fighting did not interrupt it, but on the next Sabbath the regular services were held, and the revival went on with power.

The movements of General Hooker were made with the hope of deceiving General Lee, but he was met and foiled at every point. On the 28th of April he crossed three army corps over the river, about twenty miles above Fredericksburg. His crossing was met and opposed. On the same night three corps were crossed several miles below that place under cover of a heavy fog. These were held at bay by our fortified positions, while General Lee repelled the attack on his left wing. Afterwards, General Hooker made pretence of withdrawing his forces below the town, and sending them to aid his right wing; and, while General Lee was fully engaged in the wilderness near Chancellorsville, he suddenly assaulted and carried Marye's Heights, the strongest Confederate position near the town. On the 2d and 3d of May, General Lee drove the enemy from all his positions on our left, and immediately returning to his own right, re-took our lost positions and drove the Federals to the shelter of heavy batteries on the north bank of the river. On returning again to the left, he found that General Hooker had abandoned his entrenchments and re-crossed the river.

The following are General Lee's official dispatches to President Davis:

"MILFORD, May 3, 1863.

"Yesterday, General Jackson penetrated to the rear of the enemy and drove him from all his positions, from the Wilderness to within one mile of Chancellorsville. He was engaged at the same time in front by two of Longstreet's divisions. This morning the battle was renewed. He was dislodged from his strong positions around Chancellorsville, and driven back towards the Rappahannock, over which he is now retreating. Many prisoners were taken, and the enemy's loss in killed and wounded is large. We have again to thank Almighty God for a great victory. I regret to state that General Paxton was killed; General Jackson severely, Generals Heth and A. P. Hill slightly, wounded.

"(Signed) R. E. LEE, General.

"MAY 5, 1863.

"At the close of the battle of Chancellorsville, on Sunday, the enemy was reported advancing from Fredericksburg in our rear.

"General McLaws was sent back to arrest his progress, and repulsed him handsomely that afternoon. Learning that this force consisted of two corps, under General Sedgwick, I determined to attack it, and marched back yesterday with General Anderson, and, uniting with Generals McLaws and Early in the afternoon, succeeded, by the blessing of Heaven, in driving

General Sedgwick over the river. We have re-occupied Fredericksburg, and no enemy remains south of the Rappahannock in its vicinity.

"CHANCELLORSVILLE, May 7, 1863.

"After driving General Sedgwick across the Rappahannock on the night of the 4th, I returned on the 5th to Chancellorsville. The march was delayed by a storm which continued the whole night following. In placing the troops in position on the morning of the 6th, to attack Hooker's army, I ascertained he had abandoned his fortified position. A line of skirmishers pressed forward until they came within range of the enemy's batteries, planted on the north of the Rappahannock, which, from the configuration of the ground, completely commanded this side. His army, therefore, escaped with the loss of a few additional prisoners.

"(Signed) R. E. LEE, General Commanding."

The dark cloud that overhung this "great victory" was the death of Gen. Jackson. The sad story is here given as it was reported immediately after the battle, and is, no doubt, in the main correct. By one of his rapid flank movements he had gained the rear of Hooker's army, impetuously assaulted his strong positions, driven him out of them, and, but for the approach of night, would have made the retreat an utter rout. Having placed his men in position ready for any movement that the critical occasion might require, he rode forward with several of his staff about 8 o'clock on Saturday evening, the 2d of May, to reconnoitre the Federal lines in front in the deep forest. Soon coming on the enemy's advancing line of skirmishers, they turned and rode rapidly back towards their own men, who, mistaking the party for Federal cavalry, stooped and delivered a deadly fire at the distance of twenty paces.

"So sudden and stunning was this volley," says Dr.

Dabney in his life of Jackson, "and so near at hand, that every horse which was not shot down recoiled from it in panic, and turned to rush back, bearing their riders toward the approaching enemy. Several fell dead upon the spot, among them the courageous Captain Boswell; and more wounded. Among the latter was Gen. Jackson. His right hand was penetrated by a ball, his left fore-arm lacerated by another, and the same limb broken a little below the shoulder by a third, which not only crushed the bone, but severed the main artery. His horse also dashed, panic-stricken, toward the enemy, carrying him beneath the boughs of a tree, which inflicted severe blows, lacerated his face, and almost dragged him from the saddle. His bridle hand was now powerless, but seizing the reins with the right hand, notwithstanding its wound, he arrested his career and brought the animal back toward his own lines. He was followed by his faithful attendant, Captain Wilbourne, and his faithful assistant, Wynn, who overtook him as he passed again in the turnpike near the spot where he had received the fatal shots. * * * Here General Jackson drew up his horse and sat for an instant gazing toward his own men, as if in astonishment at their cruel mistake, and in doubt whether he should again venture to approach them. To the anxious inquiries of Captain Wilbourne, he replied that he believed his arm was broken, and requested him to assist him from his horse and examine whether the wounds were bleeding dangerously. But before he could dismount he sunk fainting into their arms, so completely prostrate that they were compelled to disengage his feet from the stirrups.

"They now bore him aside a few yards into the woods north of the turnpike, to shield him from the expected advance of the Federalists; and while Wynn was sent for an ambulance and surgeon, Wilbourne proceeded, supporting his head upon his bosom, to strip his mangled arm and bind up his wound. The warm blood was flowing in a stream down his wrist; his clothing impeded all access to its source, and nothing was at hand more efficient than a pen-knife to remove the obstructions. But at this terrible moment he saw General Hill, with the remnant of his staff, approaching, and called to him for assistance. He, with his volunteer aide, Major Leigh, dismounted, and, taking the body of the General into his arms, succeeded in reaching the wound, and staunching the blood with a handkerchief. The swelling of the lacerated flesh had already performed this office in part. His two aides, Lieutenants Smith and Morrison, arrived at this moment, the former having been left at the rear to execute some orders, and the latter having just saved himself, at the expense of a stunning fall, by leaping from his horse as he was carrying him into the lines of the enemy. * * * It was at this moment that two Federal skirmishers approached within a few feet of the spot where he lay, with their muskets cocked. They little knew what a prize was within their grasp; and when, at the command of General Hill, two orderlies arose from the kneeling group and demanded their surrender, they seemed amazed at their nearness to their enemies, and yielded their arms without resistance. Lieutenant Morrison, suspecting from their approach that the Federalists must be near at hand, stepped out into the road to examine, and by the light of the moon saw a field-piece pointed toward him, apparently not more than a hundred yards distant. * * * Returning hurriedly, he announced that the enemy were planting artillery in the road, and that the General must be immediately removed. * * * No ambulance or litter was at hand, although Captain Wilbourne had also been sent to seek them; and the necessity of an immediate removal suggested that they should bear the General away in their arms. To this he replied that if they would assist him to rise he could walk to the rear; and he was accordingly raised to his feet, and, leaning upon the shoulders of Major Leigh and Lieutenant Smith, went slowly out into the highway and toward his troops. The party was now met by a litter, which some one had sent from the rear; and the General was placed upon it and borne along by two soldiers and Lieutenants Smith and Morrison. As they were placing him upon it, the enemy fired a volley of canister-shot up the road, which passed over their heads. But they had proceeded only a few steps before the discharge was repeated with a more accurate aim. One of the soldiers bearing the litter was struck down, severely wounded; and had not Major Leigh, who was walking beside it, broken his fall, the General would have been precipitated to the ground.

"He was placed again upon the earth; and the causeway was now swept by a hurricane of projectiles of every species, before which it seemed that no living thing could survive. The bearers of the litter, and all the attendants, excepting Major Leigh and the General's two aides, left him, and fled into the woods on either hand, to escape the fatal tempest; while the sufferer lay along the road, with his feet to the foe, exposed to all its fury. It was now that his three faithful attendants displayed a heroic fidelity which deserves to go down with the immortal name of Jackson to future ages. Disdaining to save their lives by deserting their chief, they lay down beside him in the causeway, and sought to protect him as far as possible with their bodies. On one side was Major Leigh, and on the other Lieutenant Smith. Gen. Jackson struggled violently to rise, as though to endeavor to leave the road; but Smith threw his arm over him, and with friendly force held him to the earth, saying, 'Sir, you must lie still; it will cost you your life to rise.' He speedily acquiesced, and lay quiet; but not one of the four hoped to escape alive. Yet, almost by miracle, they were unharmed; and, after a few moments, the Federalists, having cleared the road of all except this little party, ceased to fire along it, and directed their aim to another quarter."

They took advantage of the lull in the Federal fire, and, with their sad burden, moved carefully along the ditch at the margin of the road. Troops were hurrying to the front, and fearing that the wounded General would be recognized by his men, the party moved farther into the thicket. They soon met General Pender, who recognized Jackson, and expressed his deep sympathy for the sufferer, and added, "My men are thrown into such confusion by this fire that I fear I shall not be able to hold my ground." Jackson replied instantly in a feeble voice, but with his well-known decision, "General Pender, you *must* keep your men together, and hold your ground." This was the last order of Jackson.

The party made their way through the tangled brushwood and thickets as well as they could towards the rear. The fire of the enemy re-opened, and in hurrying on the clothes of the wounded man were torn, and even his face lacerated by the stiff twigs and branches. Unfortunately one of the litter-bearers fell, and the General was thrown upon the ground and painfully bruised. He lay upon his mangled arm, from which the blood began to flow freely. When his men lifted him up a groan broke from him—the only complaint in all the terrible scene. Lieutenant Smith, fearing he would die on the spot, said, "General, are you much hurt?" To which he replied, "No, Mr. Smith; don't trouble yourself about me." After bearing him half a mile farther, most of the way under a shower of shot and shell, they reached an ambulance, in which his chief of artillery, Col. Crutchfield, lay wounded. Dr. McGuire, Jackson's chief surgeon, soon joined them, and proceeded at once to examine the General's wounds. He found him almost pulseless, but the copious bleeding had ceased. Stimulants were freely used; under their influence he revived, and the party moved on to the field hospital near Wilderness Run. To the anxious questions of his surgeon, the General said that he now felt better, but that several times as they came out of the battle he had felt as though he were about to die.

The heroic calmness of Jackson was well displayed when he was struck down by the cruel volley from his own men. To the quick, anxious questions of his friends he replied with great composure, "I believe my arm is broken," and "It gives me severe pain." When asked to have his right hand bound up, he said, "No, never mind; it is a trifle." And yet this right hand that had so often pointed out the path of victory to his men was almost shattered to pieces—two bones of it were broken and a bullet had almost gone through the palm. Without a particle of passion, he said, "All my wounds are by my own men," and said they were all received at the same moment. He was extremely anxious that his soldiers should not know that he was wounded. He said, "Tell them simply that you have a wounded Confederate officer." He would have his own name concealed, but no untruth told. As he was led along many of the men asked, "Whom have you there?" and some tried to see his face; Captain Wilbourne kept them off; but one or two of his veterans caught a glimpse of his face, and exclaimed, "Great God! it is General Jackson." The sad news spread rapidly along the lines; but the men believed his wounds to be slight, and their sorrow only increased their courage.

At midnight, in the field hospital, a consultation of surgeons was held, composed of Drs. McGuire, Coleman, Black, and Wall. Long and anxiously they watched the pulse for evidences of reaction; at length it came, and with it hope. The examination showed the necessity for immediate amputation of the left arm. Dr. McGuire explained this to him, and the General replied, "Doctor, do for me whatever you think best; I am resigned to whatever is necessary." He was placed under the influence of chloroform, and the mangled arm cut off by Dr. McGuire, and the ball extracted from the right hand. The General seemed insensible to pain, and said dreamily, "Dr. McGuire, I am lying very comfortably." He then sunk into a quiet sleep, and in half an hour was awaked to receive nourishment. He awoke promptly when called, and took a cup of coffee with relish, saying it was good and refreshing. This was the first nourishment he had taken since Friday evening, and it was now Saturday midnight. When he fell, and his field-glass and haversack were removed, the latter contained no rations, but only a few official papers and *two gospel tracts*. After taking coffee he conversed freely with the friends around him, and asked particularly whether he had said anything when under the influence of chloroform, and added: "I have always thought it wrong to administer chloroform in cases where there is a probability of immediate death. But it was, I think, the most delightful physical sensation I ever enjoyed. I had enough consciousness to know what was doing; and at one time I thought I heard the most delightful music that ever greeted my ears. I believe it was the sawing of the bone. But I should dislike above all things to enter eternity in such a condition." His attendants now urged him to suspend conversation and to seek repose in sleep. He ceased talking, and soon fell into a deep and quiet sleep, which lasted until 9 o'clock in the morning.

The manner and language of General Lee when he received the news of the wounding of Jackson were characteristic of that great and good man. Captains Hotchkiss and Wilbourne were sent to inform him of the result of the brilliant flank movement and of the fall of Jackson. They found the General lying upon the ground under a thick pine tree. It was before daybreak, but he at once asked them for the news of the battle. They described the battle, and informed him that Jackson was seriously wounded. The General was greatly moved at this, and after a pause, in which he seemed to be struggling with his emotions, said: "Ah! any victory is dearly bought which deprives us of the services of Jackson, even for a short time." He then dictated the following note to Jackson:

"*General*,—I have just received your note, informing me that you are wounded. I cannot express my regret at the occurrence. Could I have directed events, I should have chosen, for the good of the country, to have been disabled in your stead.

"I congratulate you upon the victory which is due to your skill and energy.

"Most truly yours,
"(Signed) R. E. LEE, General."

Our readers know the result of the great battle of Chancellorsville—so nobly begun by Jackson, and so bravely won by the Confederate army. Leaving the field of blood, let us go to the bedside of the wounded General. When he awoke from his long and quiet sleep on Sabbath morning, the sounds of a furious cannonade assured him that the battle was raging, but his pulse did not quicken nor his soul grow restless. When Rev. Mr. Lacy, his chaplain, entered the tent where he lay, he exclaimed: "Oh, General! what a calamity!" Jackson thanked him with his usual courtesy, and added, with an unusual freedom: "You see me severely wounded, but not depressed; not unhappy. I believe it has been done according to God's holy will, and I acquiesce entirely in it. You may think it strange, but you never saw me more perfectly contented than I am to-day; for I am sure that my Heavenly Father designs this affliction for my good. I am perfectly satisfied, that either in this life, or in that which is to come, I shall discover that what is now regarded as a calamity is a blessing. And if it appears a great calamity (as it surely will be a great inconvenience to be deprived of my arm), it will

result in a great blessing. I can wait until God, in his
own time, shall make known to me the object he has in
thus afflicting me. But why should I not rather rejoice
in it as a blessing, and not look on it as a calamity at
all? If it were in my power to replace my arm, I would
not dare to do it unless I could know it was the will of
my Heavenly Father." He referred to his feelings at
the time of his fall, and said he was in possession of
perfect peace while expecting death. "It has been," he
said, "a precious experience to me that I was brought
face to face with death and found all was well. I then
learned an important lesson, that one who has been the
subject of converting grace, and is the child of God,
can, in the midst of the severest sufferings, fix the
thoughts upon God and heavenly things, and derive
great comfort and peace; but, that one who had never
made his peace with God would be unable to control his
mind, under such sufferings, so as to understand properly
the way of salvation and repent and believe on Christ.
I felt that if I had neglected the salvation of my soul
before, it would have been too late then." Dr. Dabney
says these are nearly the exact words used by General
Jackson. They made a deep impression on the mind of
the minister to whom they were addressed, and he
speedily committed them to writing. After this conversation, the General, at the request of his physician, remained quiet for several hours. About midday Captain
Douglass came from the field with news of the victory.
He communicated to Lieutenant Smith such facts as he
thought would interest the General. To the narrative,
as repeated to him by Lieutenant Smith, Jackson listened with fixed attention. The part taken in the fight
by his old Stonewall Brigade deeply affected him. In
the very crisis of the battle General Stuart rode up to
them, and, pointing to the work he wished them to do,
gave the order: "*Charge, and remember Jackson!*" They
sprang forward at the word, drove before them three

times their own number, and decided the day. The General listened eagerly, and, trying to repress his tears, said: "It was just like them to do so; just like them. They are a noble body of men." Smith said: "They have indeed behaved splendidly; but you can easily suppose, General, that it was not without a loss of many valuable men." Jackson asked quickly: "Have you heard of any one that is killed?" "Yes, sir," said Smith; "I am very sorry to say they have lost their commander." He exclaimed: "Paxton? Paxton?" Smith—"Yes, sir; he has fallen." He said no more; but turned his face to the wall, and seemed to be laboring to suppress his emotion. Some moments after this, Smith remarked that Rev. Mr. Lacy had talked with General Paxton about his religious interests, and believed him to be a converted man. To this Jackson replied: "That's good; that's good." It is stated by Dr. Dabney, from whose Life of Jackson we are indebted for most of the facts connected with these sad scenes, that after Paxton had placed his brigade in position he spent the few moments that were left him in reading his New Testament, and when ordered forward, he replaced the book in his pocket and exhorted his men to do their duty and to entrust their safety into the hands of the Almighty.

The General now directed Lieutenant Smith to write a note which he dictated to General Lee, giving an account of his wounds and congratulating the Commander-in-Chief on the great victory which God had given to his army. To this note General Lee sent the noble reply already given. When the note was read to him he said: "General Lee is very kind; but he should give the glory to God." In speaking some time after this of the battle, he said: "Our movement yesterday was a great success; I think, the most successful military movement of my life. But I expect to receive far more credit for it than I deserve. Most men will think that I had planned it all from the first; but it was not so—I simply took advantage of circumstances as they were presented to me in the providence of God. I feel that his hand led me. Let us give him all the glory."

General Lee, thinking the Wilderness exposed to the incursions of the Federal cavalry, sent word that Jackson should be removed as soon as possible to Guinea's Station. On Monday he seemed so much better that Dr. McGuire determined to begin the journey. The road was cleared of obstructions by engineers so as to avoid jolting of the ambulance. The General was bright and cheerful during the twenty-five miles' travel, and just at nightfall the party reached the house of Mr. Chandler, near the station. He was placed in bed, and, after taking supper, spent a quiet night. During the journey he spoke freely of the war, and made kind and special reference to the Stonewall Brigade. In reference to a purpose of that noble band to petition the Government to allow them to assume this title as their own, he said: "They are a noble body of patriots; when this war is ended, the survivors will be proud to say, 'I was a member of the old Stonewall Brigade.' The Government ought certainly to accede to their request, and authorize them to assume this title; for it was fairly earned." He then added that "the name Stonewall ought to be attached wholly to the men of the brigade, and not to him; for it was their steadfast heroism which had earned it at first Manassas." In reply to a question as to the wisdom of General Hooker's plan of battle, he said: "It was, in the main, a good conception, an excellent plan; but he should not have sent away his cavalry; that was his great blunder. It was that which enabled me to turn him, without his being aware of it, and to take him by his rear."

After a day or two the bright hopes of his recovery began to fade. His pain and restlessness increased. Opiates were administered to quiet his nerves and to induce sleep. Under their influence his sleep was disturbed by dreams. He was told on Tuesday that Hooker was entrenched near Chancellorsville. He exclaimed: "That is bad—very bad." Falling asleep soon after, he called out: "Major Pendleton, send in and see if there is not higher ground back of Chancellorsville." He was again in the smoke and shock of battle. On Thursday Mrs. Jackson reached him, from Richmond. She was deterred from coming earlier by the Federal cavalry which infested the line of the railroad. When she arrived the General was worse, and the physicians were doing all in their power to arrest pneumonia, which had been developed the day before in an alarming form. Rev. Mr. Lacy went to the army to bring the General's family physician, Dr. Morrison. and, while seeking, called on General Lee and informed him of the dangerous condition of his great Lieutenant. The great commander expressed his hope that God would not take Jackson from him at such a time, and added: "Give him my affectionate regards, and tell him to make haste and get well, and come back to me as soon as he can. He has lost his left arm—but I have lost my right arm."

When Jackson was informed that his wife and infant child had arrived, he expressed great pleasure. As Mrs. Jackson came in she saw a sad change in her noble husband. "His features," says Dr. Dabney, "were shrunken by the prostration of his energies, and were marked by two or three angry scars, where they had been torn as his horse rushed through the brushwood. His cheeks burned with a swarthy and almost livid flush. Yet his face beamed with joy when, awakening from his disturbed slumber, he saw her near him. When he noted the shade of woful apprehension which passed over her face, he said tenderly: 'Now, Anna, cheer up, and don't wear a long face; you know I love a bright face in a sick room.' With a spirit as truly courageous as that of her warrior husband she commanded her grief, and addressed herself cheerfully to the ministry of love. Many a tear was poured out over her unconscious suckling; yet she returned to his sick-room always with a serene countenance; and continued to be, until the clouds of death descended upon his vision, what he had delighted to call her in the hours of prosperity, his 'Sunshine.' He now added, with reference to his impaired hearing, that he wished her to speak distinctly while in his room, because he wanted to hear every word she said."

From this time he began to grow rapidly worse, and it became apparent to all that the life of the hero was near its close. When he was spoken to by any one he knew, he roused himself; but generally he lay with closed eyes engaged in silent prayer. On Thursday night Dr. Morrison aroused him to take some medicine, saying: "Will you take this, General?" He looked at him steadily, and said: "Do your duty," and again repeated: "Do your duty." His thoughts in delirium wandered off to the field of battle, and he fancied his legions following him to victory. At one time he said, with his quick, sharp battle-tone: "A. P. Hill, prepare for action!" and, with the welfare of his soldiers still in mind, he said several times: "Tell Major Hawks to send forward provisions for the troops."

Friday morning Dr. Morrison expressed to him his fear of a fatal issue of his case. He dissented, and said in these precise words, as Dr. Dabney tells us: "I am not afraid to die; I am willing to abide by the will of my Heavenly Father. But I do not believe that I shall die at this time; I am persuaded the Almighty has yet a work for me to perform." He asked that Dr. McGuire should be called in, and his case be referred to him. He agreed with Dr. Morrison in opinion. But Jackson was still steadfast in the belief that he would recover. As late as Saturday night, when Dr. Morrison again expressed his fears, he dissented, saying: "I don't think so; I think I shall be better by morning."

In the midst of his severe sufferings his wife proposed to interest him, and, if possible, to soothe his pains, by reading from the Psalms; he at first said he was in too much pain to attend to them, but a moment after added: "Yes, we must never refuse that; get the Bible and read them."

On Saturday evening he desired to see his chaplain, and inquired of him whether he was engaged in efforts to secure the proper observance of Sabbath in camp—a subject in which he had long been deeply interested. On being assured that he was, he seemed pleased, and conversed at some length on the proper observance of the holy day. As the night came on and deepened, he suffered more intense pain, and called upon his wife to sing some Psalms. She, with the assistance of his friends grouped around his bed, sung several of his favorite pieces. He spent a restless night, tossing in pain upon his bed, and all the relief he felt was from sponging his brow with cold water.

Sunday, May 10th, was ushered in—the last day of Jackson's earthly life. He had often said he would prefer to die on the Sabbath. His wish was to be fulfilled. His end seemed so near that Dr. Morrison felt it due to inform Mrs. Jackson of his condition. Mrs. Jackson, knowing that he had often said he would wish to be notified of his approaching end, determined to break the sad tidings to him. He was lying almost in a state of stupor; and, when aroused by his wife, seemed scarcely to comprehend the nature of her announcement. She said several times: "Do you know the doctors say you must very soon be in heaven? Do you not feel willing to acquiesce in God's allotment if he wills you to go today?" He looked up into her face and said: "I prefer it." Then he repeated, with emphasis: "*I prefer it.*" She said: "Well, before this day closes you will be with the blessed Saviour in his glory." He replied distinctly and deliberately: "I will be an infinite gainer to be translated."

When Colonel Pendleton entered the room the dying General greeted him with his usual courtesy, and asked who was preaching at headquarters. When told that the chaplain was performing that duty he seemed pleased. Mrs. Jackson asked him if he felt the Saviour present with him. To this he answered, "Yes." She asked him if it was his wish that she and her little daughter should live with her father, Dr. Morrison. He said, "Yes, you have a kind and good father; but no one is so kind and good as your Heavenly Father." She then asked him where he would prefer to be buried. To this he gave no reply, but when she suggested Lexington he said, "Yes, in Lexington." His little infant girl was now brought into the room; as soon as he saw her he smiled, and, motioning toward her, said, "Little darling!" She was placed on the bed near him, and he tried to caress her with his wounded hand. He continued to toy with her until he sunk into unconsciousness and the cloud of death settled down upon him. He fell into an unquiet sleep, in which the attendants noticed his efforts to speak; at length he said, "Let us pass over the river and rest under the shade of the trees." These were the last words of Jackson.

His wife, now overcome with grief, bowed down over him; her tears fell fast on his face, and, kissing the cold lips, she exclaimed, "Oh, Doctor, cannot you do something more?" Her voice recalled him to consciousness once more. He opened his eyes, gazed upon her with a look of intelligence and love, and then closed them forever. A few more labored breathings, and the hero was dead.

Dr. Dabney relates a touching tribute to Jackson. A little daughter of Mrs. Chandler, whose heart the General had won in former visits to the family, had followed her mother about the house and noticed that she often wiped the tears from her eyes. At length she asked, "Mamma, will General Jackson die?" She was told that the doctors said they could not save him, and he was going to die. Fixing her eyes on her mother with a most earnest look, she said, "Oh, I wish God would let me die for him, for if I did you would cry for me; but if he dies all the people in the country will cry."

On this Sabbath, while the life of the hero was closing, the usual services were held at the quarters of the staff of his corps. A great congregation assembled. General Lee, and a brilliant array of his most famous officers, came to join in public worship. As the Commander-in-Chief saw General Jackson's chaplain approaching, he met him and anxiously inquired after his wounded friend. He was told there was little or no hope. With great feeling General Lee replied, "Surely General Jackson must recover. God will not take him from us, now that we need him so much. Surely he will be spared to us, in answer to the many prayers which are offered for him." He added afterwards, "When you return I trust you will find him better. When a suitable occasion offers give him my love, and tell him I wrestled in prayer for him last night as I never prayed, I believe, for myself." The great man then turned away to hide his emotion. The most fervent prayers were offered by the vast congregation for the recovery of the beloved General, but when Rev. Mr. Lacy returned he found he had passed over the river.

The sad event was flashed all over the country, and strong men wept like children as they read the mournful tidings. The body of the hero was borne to Richmond, and placed in the hall of the lower house of Congress in the State Capitol, where thousands gazed on the placid features of the warrior. On Thursday after his death the funeral cortege reached Lexington, and all that was mortal of Jackson was laid to rest in the beautiful valley in which he had gained so many victories.

Our space will not allow us to dwell on the peculiar traits of this singularly great man. One or two illustrative incidents we will give. The following anecdote was given by Rev. Dr. Lacy, in his lecture before the old command of the hero, on the *Reminiscences of Jackson:*

"*   *   *   I had often heard of that indescribable change of manner and appearance which came over Jackson when the war-bugle summoned him. I therefore watched him well. Soon couriers were seen dashing in every direction to summons out the army. That usual stooping, meek, thoughtful man was no longer before me, but a warrior, his eyes flashing, and through them his great military genius beaming; his form appeared to dilate, he appeared to comprehend all, and soon he was ready; the servant led his horse to the tent, the General went inside. I thought I would speak to him before he went forth. As I approached, the faithful old servant motioned me to stop, be silent—the General was at prayer. I waited sometime; at length the tent was drawn aside, and Jackson stepped forth. Never shall I forget the serene brightness that glowed upon his face. He only remarked, as he bade me good-bye, that 'all appears well.' He had held communion with his God, and went forth to victory. This was but an index to his every-day life. During our stay in winter-quarters, from my own tent I could look directly upon his. The table upon which he set his candle was on the opposite side from me, and each night, at his usual bedtime, if I looked, I could see the shadow of that truly great and good man cast upon the wall of the tent as he was bowed in prayer."

In a funeral discourse commemorative of Jackson by Rev. Dr. Dabney, the following incident is given:

"On the momentous morning of Friday, June 27th, 1862, as the different corps of the patriot army were moving to their respective posts, to fill parts in the mighty combination of their chief, after Jackson had held his final interview with him, and resumed his march for his position at Cold Harbor, his command was misled, by a misconception of his guides, and seemed about to mingle with and confuse another part of our forces. More than an hour of seemingly precious time was expended in rectifying this mistake; while the booming of cannon in the front told us that the struggle had begun, and made our breasts thrill with an agony of suspense, lest the irreparable hour should be lost by our delay; for we had still many miles to march. When this anxious fear was suggested privately to Jackson, he answered, with a calm and assured countenance, 'No; let us trust that the providence of our God will so overrule it that no mischief shall result.' And, verily, no mischief did result. Providence brought us precisely into conjunction with the bodies with which we were to co-operate; the battle was joined at the right juncture; and by the time the stars appeared, the right wing of the enemy, with which he was appointed to deal, was hurled in utter rout across the river. More than once, when sent to bring one of his old fighting brigades into action, I had noticed him sitting motionless upon his horse, with his right hand uplifted, while the war-worn column poured on in stern silence close by his side. At first it did not appear whether it was mere abstraction of thought or a posture to relieve his fatigue. But at Port Republic, I saw it again; and watching him more narrowly, was convinced by his closed eyes and moving lips that he was wrestling in silent prayer. I thought that I could surmise what was then passing through his fervent soul; the sovereignty of that Providence which worketh all things after the counsel of his own will, and giveth the battle not to the strong nor the race to the swift; his own fearful responsibility, and need of that counsel and sound wisdom which God alone can give; the crisis of his beloved country, and the balance trembling between defeat and victory; the precious lives of his veterans, which the inexorable necessities of war compelled him to jeopardize; the immortal souls passing to their account, perhaps unprepared; the widowhood and orphanage which might result from the orders he had just been compelled to issue. And as his beloved men swept by him to the front, into the storm of shot, doubtless his great heart, as tender as it was resolute, yearned over them in unutterable longings and intercessions, that "the Almighty would cover them with his feathers, and that his truth might be their shield and buckler.

"Surely, the moral grandeur of this scene was akin to that when Moses stood upon the Mount of God and lifted up his hands while Israel prevailed against Amelek! And what soldier would not desire to have the shield of such prayers under which to fight? Were they not a more powerful element of success than the artillery or the bayonets of the Stonewall Brigade?"

The following beautiful tribute to General Jackson was published in the New York *Citizen*, and is said to be from the pen of a distinguished officer of the United States Navy:

STONEWALL JACKSON.

He sleeps all quietly and cold,
    Beneath the soil that gave him birth;
Then break his battle-brand in twain,
    And lay it with him in the earth.

No more at midnight shall be urged
    His toilsome march among the pines;
Nor heard upon the morning air
    The war-shout of his charging lines.

Cold is the eye whose meteor-gleam
    Flashed hope on all within its light·
And still the voice that, trumpet-toned,
    Rang through the serried ranks of **fight**.

No more for him shall cannons park,
    Or tents gleam white upon the plain;
And where his camp-fires blazed of yore,
    Brown reapers laugh amid the grain!

No more above his narrow bed
    Shall sound the tread of marching feet,
The rifle volley, and the clash
    Of sabres when the foemen meet.

And, though the winds of autumn rave,
    And winter-snows fall thick and deep
About his breast—they cannot move
    The quiet of his dreamless sleep.

We may not raise a marble shaft
    Above the heart that now is dust;
But nature, like a mother fond,
    Will ne'er forget her sacred trust.

Young April, o'er his lowly mound,
    Shall shake the violets from her hair;
And glorious June, with fervid kiss,
    Shall bid the roses blossom there.

And round about the droning bee,
    With drowsy hum, shall come and go;
While west winds, all the live-long day,
    Shall murmur dirges soft and low.

The warrior's stormy fate is o'er,
    The midnight gloom hath passed away;
And, like a glory from the East,
    Breaks the first light of Freedom's day!

And white-winged Peace o'er all the land,
    Broods like a dove upon her nest;
While iron War, with slaughter gorged,
    At length hath laid him down to rest.

And where we won our onward way
    With fire and steel—through yonder wood—
The blackbird whistles, and the quail
    Gives answer to her timid brood.

 Yet oft in dreams his fierce brigade
  Shall see the form they followed far,
 Still leading in the furthest van—
  A landmark in the clouds of war!

 And oft, when white-haired grandsires tell
  Of bloody struggles past and gone,
 The children at their knees will hear
  How Jackson led his columns on!

 The announcement to the army of the death of Jackson by General Lee contains a fitting tribute by one who, beyond all others, knew his value as a soldier. In tears the veterans read these words from their great leader:

"With deep grief the Commanding General announces to the army the death of General Jackson. He expired on Sunday, the 10th, at 3¼ P. M. The daring, skill, and energy of this great and good soldier are, by the decree of an All-wise Providence, now lost to us; but while we mourn his death, we feel that his spirit still lives, and will inspire our whole army with his indomitable courage, unshaken confidence in God, our hope and our strength. Let his name be a watchword to his corps, who have followed him and victory on many fields. Let officers and soldiers emulate his invincible determination to do everything in defence of their beloved country.

 "(Signed)   R. E. LEE, General."

CHAPTER XIX.

SUMMER OF 1863.

AFTER the great victory of Chancellorsville, the Confederate army lay along the south side of the Rappahannock, watching the movements of the Federals, who held the opposite side of that river.

But few military movements of importance were undertaken for some weeks, and this period of repose and re-organization was well-improved by the zealous Christian workers in the army.

The fervor of the revival was even greater after the battle than before; in almost every regiment the reports of chaplains and colporteurs were most encouraging.

Rev. W. E. Jones, chaplain of the 22d Georgia regiment, wrote:

"The Lord is in our midst. Ever since the last great victory God has been pouring out upon this regiment his Spirit, almost without measure, and many have been converted, and forty-five have joined different branches of the Church, and there is a host of mourning souls. They rush to the altar by scores. The work is prospering throughout our entire army. I earnestly call upon all God's people, and especially upon parents, wives, and sisters, to pray for the salvation of these precious souls."

A private soldier, lamenting that there was no chaplain to his battalion, said:

"We have prayer-meetings every night, and God never fails to meet with us. Now, I know we are not dependent upon instruments of power for carrying on a work of this kind. On the contrary, very often the weakest are chosen."

In the 52d North Carolina regiment the work was glorious. Rev. J. M. Cline, the chaplain, said:

"God has blessed our regiment with a most glorious revival of religion. God has indeed been with us. During the last ten days fifty-six have joined the Church, and thirty-three have been soundly converted. The Lord has done great things for us. Lions have been changed to lambs. I never witnessed such a glorious revival before. The Church is greatly revived, and built up in the most holy faith. On last Sabbath I administered the sacrament of the Lord's Supper to one hundred and fifteen communicants. God was with us, and we had a refreshing season from the presence of the Lord. The revival is still progressing."

Upon the earnest labors of Rev. J. O. A. Cook, chaplain of the 2d Georgia battalion, God sent his blessing. A young convert of that command, writing to a comrade, said:

"Last Saturday night I commenced the work in good earnest, with the determination to pursue the object in view until I found the 'peace that passeth understanding.' On Sunday morning I was wholly convinced that my heart had been changed. Now I would not exchange my condition with that of the mightiest monarch. I would not sway the sceptre, in sin, in preference to being a subject of religion. The revival spreads. The Spirit of God is truly at work in the hearts of nearly all of the members of our little battalion. Soon I hope we will have the reputation of being a battalion of soldiers of Christ. We have a bright prospect ahead. Our prayer-meetings are larger, and a deeper interest pervades the minds of all."

Another earnest worker wrote: "It would rejoice your heart if you could visit the Pine Grove near our camp, and listen to the many voices here and there as they supplicate for the forgiveness of sin, for the regenerating blood of Jesus Christ to wash and purge their hearts from all guilt; and perhaps as you walked farther on you would stumble on a party of three or four, who had sought some secluded spot to converse upon the all-engrossing subject. The attendance upon our meeting, both at the Grove and at the camp, is increasing. Those at the Grove have become regular class meetings, and remind me so much of our little class-room as I listen to the experience of those who have lately found pardon for all their sins. Since the day of fasting and prayer, for the purpose of entreating God to carry on the good work, there has been a visible increase in the number of penitents at the altar. To-night there could not have been less than fifty. J. A. was gloriously converted this morning. A few had assembled at the Grove merely for conversation on religious subjects and an exchange of views. He was among the number, and while thus engaged he suddenly left and went into the woods. In a short time he came back with outstretched arms and beaming countenance, threw himself in O.'s arms, with the expression, 'I am so happy.' You can imagine what a holy influence it had upon those who were there. Since I have been writing G. has come in and told me that three glorious conversions have taken place in the Spaulding Grays, and a few moments ago C. also told me that F. B. was powerfully converted in the woods since the meeting. Is not this glorious news? Oh! how thankful we ought to be to our Heavenly Father for his great 'loving kindness and mercy to the children of men.' I never saw more zealous workers in the cause of Christ than C. and J. C. They are full of the Spirit, and can talk and think of nothing else."

The work went on not only in the camps and along the rear lines, but even in the trenches on the very edge of battle. "On Sunday evening," writes a soldier from near Fredericksburg, "we had a very interesting little meeting in the trenches. It began with some of the battalion singing. One by one the different regiments collected around and joined in. Soon it was turned into a prayer-meeting, and it proved to be one of the most interesting scenes I had witnessed for a long time."

In the 14th South Carolina regiment a Christian Association was formed for the purpose, as the Constitution declared, of being "helpers of each other's joy" in Christ, and "laborers together with God" in the promotion of his cause. We covenant together with each other and with Christ to strive to grow in grace ourselves, to use all means in our power to promote the growth of grace in each other, and to be instrumental in bringing others to a saving knowledge of the truth as it is in Jesus; in short, to realize and act out in our lives the truth that "we are not our own," but "are bought with a price," and are therefore bound "to glorify God in our bodies and in our spirits, which are God's." Of this Association Lieutenant-Colonel Joseph N. Brown was President; Lieutenant R. B. Watson and Adjutant W. P. Ready, Vice-Presidents; and Captain H. P. Griffith, Secretary and Treasurer.

The soldiers in the West were as fully blessed with the spirit of revival as their comrades in the East. Vicksburg and other points on the Mississippi were sorely pressed by the Federals, and there was much marching, countermarching, and fighting on the field and in trenches, but still the work of God went on with unusual power.

In response to the urgent demand for more laborers in this great field, the different Churches sent forth all earnest workers that could be spared from the home work.

Rev. Messrs. McFerrin, Petway, and Ransom, of the M. E. Church, South, went to the help of Gen. Bragg's army; Messrs. Thweat and Harrington, of the same Church, to the army in Mississippi; while Bishop Pierce, Dr. A. L. P. Green, and Rev. J. E. Evans, went to Gen. Lee's army in Virginia. Rev. Dr. Kavanaugh was sent to the army of General Price, and Rev. Mr. Marvin (now Bishop) was directed by Bishop Pierce to take position as missionary with any army corps west of the Mississippi. The work of these ministers, with that of other zealous men from sister Churches, gave a great impulse to the revival. In Colonel Colquitt's 46th Georgia regiment, camped near Vernon, Miss., the work was powerful, and great numbers were converted. "Last night," says Rev. T. C. Stanley, "there were about eighty presented themselves for prayer, kneeling upon the ground. The Christian heart could not but be touched while witnessing such a scene. We were under the tall spreading oaks of the forest, and the moon bathing all with its gentle beams, typical of the Spirit that was in mercy sent down from above, enveloping us as with a garment of love, cheering the heart of the Christian and comforting many a poor penitent."

In the ordeal through which Vicksburg passed before the siege closed, the feeling of dependence on God was very marked among the suffering soldiers. We take the following from a chaplain's journal, kept during the siege:

"Our case is desperate. I hope in God. There is much turning to Him now, to recount his promises, and to claim his protection. There is no difficulty now in having religious conversation. Everybody is ready for it. * * * * A bright Sabbath morning; but its stillness is broken by the harsh and startling detonations of the engines of destruction. I sigh for the sweet, undisturbed sanctuary. 'As the hart,' etc. Read a sermon to a small company of gentlemen to-day. Got on somewhat of a Sunday feeling. We sit up till a late hour every night, discussing the situation, etc. * * * * A furious fire was poured upon us this morning at 3 o'clock from the batteries beyond the trenches. One shot struck a hospital near me and killed one man; the others were frightened, and cried out most piteously.

Nothing that I have met is more harrowing to my feelings than scenes like this. Tried to observe to-day as the Sabbath by acts of piety and works of charity."

In the army of General Bragg the revival went on despite the sufferings of the troops in their retrograde movement to the vicinity of Chattanooga. Rev. W. H. Browning, writing to the *Southern Christian Advocate* of the work of grace, says:

"I am truly gratified to state to you that the religious interest in this army, though abated to some extent by the retrograde movement to this place, has again revived, and there is now a general spirit of revival manifest in every part of this army. In this brigade we have been holding meetings each night for more than two weeks. There are generally from thirty to fifty penitents at the altar each night, and about forty conversions. In most of the brigades in this division they are holding similar meetings. Indeed, the same may be said of the entire army.

"The most careless observer can but notice the marked change that has taken place in the regiments. Instead of oaths, jests, and blackguard songs, we now have the songs of Zion, prayers and praises to God. True, there are yet many profane, wicked, and rude, yet the preponderance is decidedly in favor of Christianity. I verily believe that the morals of the army are now far in advance of those of the country. And instead of the army being the school of vice, as was once supposed, and really was, it is now the place where God is adored, and where many learn to revere the name of Jesus. Many backsliders have recently been reclaimed—the lukewarm have been aroused, and sinners have been converted. Will not our families and friends at home awake to the importance of a deeper work among themselves? This is a time that calls for universal humiliation and prayer."

In addition to these extracts we can only give brief,

but expressive, records from other parts of the army. Rev. R. G. Porter, chaplain of the 10th Mississippi regiment, Bragg's army, says:

"It makes my very soul happy to witness the manifestations of God's saving power as seen here in the army—from ten to forty at the altar of prayer—have preaching every day when not hindered by the men being called off."

The Rev. Dr. Palmer, of New Orleans, preached with power and love, and under his word the revival deepened. Rev. C. W. Miller, army missionary, writes of the work in Georgia, Gen. D. H. Hill's corps:

"Since I arrived here as missionary I have been engaged every night in religious services with the soldiers. A revival and extensive awakening have been in progress in General Bate's brigade for four weeks. Every night the altar is crowded with weeping penitents. Several have been happily converted. To me it is the most interesting sight of my life. You cannot look upon these penitent, weeping men at the altar of prayer without thinking of the bloody fields of Perryville and Murfreesboro, and the victorious veterans rolling up to heaven the shouts of triumph. Here they are. Some sending up the note of a more glorious victory—others charging through the columns of the foe to 'take the kingdom of heaven by force.'"

From James' Island, near Charleston, a pious captain of a Georgia regiment writes:

"Since our chaplain came we have had a gracious revival. Many souls have been converted, and many added to the Church. And many of those who had grown cold have been revived, and we now have a warm-hearted, worshiping congregation."

Even under the fire of the Federal batteries the work went on. Rev. Mr. Browning, from Chattanooga, says:

"Yesterday evening, about 5 o'clock, the enemy began to throw shells across the river again, firing slowly for about an hour; notwithstanding this, at the usual hour (twilight) we had a very large crowd of anxious listeners at the rude arbor the men had erected for the worship of God. A short discourse was delivered, when the penitents were invited to the altar. Fifty or sixty came forward, earnestly enquiring the way of salvation. Ten of this number were converted and enabled to 'testify of a truth' that Christ was their Saviour. The work is still extending. Each night increases the attendance, the interest, and the number of penitents.

"During a ministry of a fourth of a century I have never witnessed a work so deep, so general, and so successful. It pervades all classes of the army (in this brigade), and elicits the co-operation of all denominations. We know no distinction here. Baptists, Cumberlands, Old Presbyterians, Episcopalians, and Methodists, work together, and rejoice together at the success of our cause."

Mr. B. writes again from the same place: "The glorious work of God is still progressing in this brigade. About one hundred and thirty conversions up to this time. The interest is unabated. From sixty to seventy-five penitents at the altar each night. It is wonderful that for nearly five weeks we have been enabled to continue this work, with but one night's interference from rain and one on picket. Surely the Lord has been good to us. We have been too closely confined to ascertain the state of the work in other brigades, further than that a good work is in progress in some of them, perhaps all. The chaplains of this corps have not met for several weeks. To-morrow is the regular time, but as the enemy shell the town every few days it is doubtful whether we will have a quorum."

The spreading revival called for all the workers that could be supplied from the home work. Bishop Early, of the M. E. Church, South, appointed Rev. J. N. Andrews, of the North Carolina Conference, a missionary to the soldiers in North Carolina, and the Rev. Leonidas Rosser, D. D., of the Virginia Conference, to take the place of Rev. Dr. James E. Evans, whose health had failed, in General Ewell's corps in the Army of Northern Virginia.

In midsummer of this year (1863) the people of the South were again called by the President of the Confederacy to observe a day of fasting and prayer. He issued the following proclamation:

"Again do I call upon the people of the Confederacy—a people who believe that the Lord reigneth, and that his overruling Providence ordereth all things—to unite in prayer and humble submission under his chastening hand, and to beseech his favor on our suffering country.

"It is meet that when trials and reverses befall us we should seek to take home to our hearts and consciences the lessons which they teach, and profit by the self-examination for which they prepare us. Had not our successes on land and sea made us self-confident and forgetful of our reliance on him; had not love of lucre eaten like a gangrene into the very heart of the land, converting too many among us into worshippers of gain and rendering them unmindful of their duty to their country, to their fellow-men, and to their God—who then will presume to complain that we have been chastened, or to despair of our just cause and the protection of our Heavenly Father?

"Let us rather receive in humble thankfulness the lesson which he has taught us in our recent reverses, devoutly acknowledging that to him, and not to our own feeble arms, are due the honor and the glory of victory; that from him, in his paternal providence, come the anguish and sufferings of defeat, and that, whether in victory or defeat, our humble supplications are due at his footstool.

"Now, therefore, I, Jefferson Davis, President of these Confederate States, do issue this, my proclamation, setting apart Friday, the 21st day of August ensuing, as a day of fasting, humiliation, and prayer; and I do hereby invite the people of the Confederate States to repair on that day to their respective places of public worship, and to unite in supplication for the favor and protection of that God who has hitherto conducted us safely through all the dangers that environed us.

"In faith whereof I have hereunto set my hand and the seal of the Confederate States, at Richmond, this twenty-fifth day of July, in the year of our Lord one thousand eight hundred and sixty-three.   JEFFERSON DAVIS.

{SEAL}

"By the President:
   "J. P. BENJAMIN, Secretary of State."

The field of conflict was now full of startling events. General Lee made his grand movement into Pennsylvania, which culminated in the terrible battle of Gettysburg. From East Tennessee to Texas the different armies on both sides displayed unusual activity.

There was but little time for religious services, but on every suitable occasion they were held, and much fruit was gathered even from fields soaking in blood.

The following scene will show with what true heroism our Christian soldiers met death:

"In the retreat of our army from Middle Tennessee one of the soldiers," says Dr. W. A. Mulkey, a surgeon in the army, "was struck by an unexploded shell, the ponderous mass sweeping away his right arm and leaving open the abdominal cavity, its contents falling upon his saddle. In a moment he sank from his horse to the ground, but soon revived, and for two hours talked with as much calmness and sagacity as though he were engaged in a business transaction.

"Soon several of his weeping friends gathered around him expressing their sympathy and sorrow. He thanked them for their manifestations of kindness, but told them that instead of weeping for him they ought to weep over their own condition; for, sad to say, if, even among the professors of his company, there was one who lived fully up to the discharge of his Christian duties, he was not aware of it.

"He said, 'I know that my wound is mortal, and that in a very short time I shall be in eternity; but I die as has been my aim for years—prepared to meet my God.' After exhorting those who stood around him to live the life of Christians, he said, 'Tell my wife to educate my two children and train them up in such a way as to meet me in a better world. Before she hears of my death I shall be with our little Mary in heaven.'

"He then observed that in entering the army he was influenced alone by a sense of duty; that he did not regret the step he had taken; and that while dying he felt he had tried to discharge his duties both as a soldier and Christian.

"Thus died an humble private in the ranks of our cavalry, in whose life were most harmoniously blended the characters of patriot, soldier, and Christian."

We are glad to record this glorious death of an humble private. It is but one out of many thousands. Those who are in high places have their words recorded, but it is rare that the humble toilers can be heard in the rush and roar of life's battle.

The untoward events of this summer's campaign served to depress the minds of soldiers and people. After a heroic resistance Vicksburg fell.

The bloody battle of Gettysburg was followed by Gen. Lee's backward movement to Virginia. Charleston was closely invested and was shelled most vigorously. A deep gloom hung over the South. But there was no despair. The pulpit and the press spoke words of cheer to the people.

Rev. Dr. E. H. Myers, of the *Southern Christian Advocate*, urged all to lift their hearts to God.

"There is great necessity," he said, "for us to cultivate our intercourse with Heaven. Our temporal condition looks none the brightest. God is trying us in a fiery furnace of war; and for the present, the battle seems to go against us. The high hopes for our country and of a speedy peace, which we entertained a few weeks since, have been in a measure disappointed, and we may be doomed to yet greater disappointment. But there is a refuge for the soul in every storm. God's peace and love, the joys and hopes of salvation, the sanctifying and comforting influences of the Holy Ghost, are not subject to human circumstances; and they may be ours amid every variety of calamity. But these are the fruits of the cultivation of personal religion; and, independent of every other consideration, the uncertainty of all other sources of comfort alone should be an inducement to us to betake ourselves to that refuge, to watch closely, pray much, believe with all our heart, and to cleave the closer to God, the louder the storm swells, and the more furiously the billows dash upon the wreck of earthly hopes.

"He who, in the dark hour, feels that he grows in grace and maintains soul-communion with God, stands upon a rock. He shall never be moved."

The same writer who has told us of the scenes in Vicksburg furnishes the following sad picture of the last day of the siege:

"July 4th.—When I awoke this morning an unusual stillness prevailed. No firing anywhere. Before very long hear that Vicksburg is surrendered. Went out to the field, and, with the most painful emotions, saw our brave boys stack their arms and march away. The terms are said to be favorable, paroling men and officers. Returned to town and witnessed the grand entry. Ere long the flag is raised upon the Courthouse; the guns fire a salute, and a band plays a triumphant air. My heart sank with such a 'Fourth of July Celebration.' I observe the conduct of the enemy to be respectful and considerate. No insolence of manner, and but little offensive taunting. They are pressing negroes, however, for their regiments, etc.

"July 5th.—Awoke this morning at 3 o'clock, hurting and sore from the hardness of my bed. Remained awake thinking! thinking! thinking! Arose and got a cup of *bona fide* coffee. Rations are short, though we will draw to-morrow from the Federals. They are swarming like Egyptian locusts. Last night they amused themselves all around with a grand pyrotechnic exhibition. I watched their rockets of different colors and spangles, but did not enjoy the fun. Preached to the regiment this morning. We were in a sequestered cove, with many recent graves around us to remind us of our bereavement; with our spirits beclouded by the gloom of our present situation, and our hearts *laboring* with gratitude for our preservation through the fiery ordeal just passed; and the worship of the hour was solemn and impressive. It will mark an era doubtless in the experience of many—this 'siege of Vicksburg.'"

CHAPTER XX.

AUTUMN OF 1863.

THE close of summer and the opening of autumn were marked by great religious power in all the armies of the Confederacy.

Rev. Dr. John C. Granbery, whose labors among the soldiers will ever be remembered by the surviving veterans of the war, in September wrote of his work to the *Richmond Christian Advocate:*

"I have been employed one month in my new position as a missionary to the army. Bro. Evans having been compelled by ill health to resign his appointment, Bishop Early transferred me, at my request, from Ewell's to Longstreet's corps. I naturally felt a preference to remain with those troops among whom I had labored as a chaplain from almost the commencement of the war. The last four weeks I have been preaching daily, and sometimes twice a day, in the brigades of Pickett's division. I have never before witnessed such a wide-spread and powerful religious interest among the soldiers. They crowd eagerly to hear the gospel, and listen with profound attention. Many hearts have been opened to receive the word of the Lord in every brigade. It would delight your heart to mark the seriousness, order, and deep feeling, which characterize all our meetings. In Armistead's brigade, where I have been most constantly working in co-operation with Bro. Cridlin, a Baptist, and chaplain of the 38th Virginia, and with other ministers, there have been some seventy professions of conversion, and the altar is filled morning and night with penitents. The change is manifest in the whole camp. Men have put away their cards; instead of blasphemy, the voice of prayer and the sweet songs of Zion are heard at all hours. There is little gambling, but all seem contented and interested. We have many proofs that it is a genuine and mighty work of grace. Yesterday reminded me of Sabbath at camp-meeting. There reigned here a deeper quiet. Divine services began at an early hour of the morning, and continued into the night with brief intervals. At 9 A. M. Sabbath School was held under the auspices of the Christian Association. At 10 A. M., 4 and 7 P. M., the congregation met for preaching and other exercises. It was a happy day—a season of refreshing from the presence of the Lord. Bro. August is conducting an excellent meeting in his regiment. Already there have been forty-two professions of faith, and the work deepens and widens. I have enjoyed the privilege of being with him frequently, and have never seen a revival progress in a more satisfactory and promising manner. The Christian Associations which have recently been organized in the different brigades will, I doubt not, accomplish great good. They furnish an opportunity for the public confession of Christ and the enjoyment of the friendship of saints. They are a nucleus for lay co-operation with the chaplains, or lay labors in the absence of chaplains. In Kemper's brigade the revival, which began last spring, still goes on, chiefly under the ministry of Rev. Dr. Pryor, of the Presbyterian Church. He is a most laborious and efficient workman."

In a circular sent out to the Churches and people by the Chaplains' Association of the first and second corps of General Lee's army, urging hearty co-operation in the work of saving souls, most cheering accounts of the revival were given:

"The Lord is doing wonderful things for Zion in the ranks of our army. Christians are daily growing in grace and fidelity. Sinners are turning by hundreds to the King of Righteousness and finding that peace which comes by faith; while many are yet seeking the Prince of Life. We believe that, under God's direction, much of this work has been done by the fraternal intercourse secured by our organization. May the Lord bless you with his Spirit and give his Word prosperity through your instrumentality."

The religious, and even the secular papers, often filled columns with the news of God's work among the soldiers. The *Richmond Christian Advocate*, published in the coveted capital of the Confederacy, said:

"Not for years has such a revival prevailed in the Confederate States. Its records gladden the columns of every religious journal. Its progress in the army is a spectacle of moral sublimity over which men and angels can rejoice. Such *camp-meetings* were never seen before in America. The bivouac of the soldier never witnessed such nights of glory and days of splendor. The Pentecostal fire lights the camp, and the hosts of armed men sleep beneath the wings of angels rejoicing over many sinners that have repented.

"The people at home are beginning to feel the kindling of the same grace in their hearts. It is inspiring to read the correspondence, now, between converts in camp and friends at home, and to hear parents praise God for tidings from their absent sons who have lately given their hearts to the Lord.

"'Father is converted,' says a bright-faced child of twelve years, 'Mamma got a letter to-day, and father says that there is a great revival in his regiment.' The child is too happy to keep her joy to herself. What glorious news from the army is this! This is victory—triumph—peace! This is the token of good which the great King gives to cheer his people. It is the best evidence that prayer is heard, and that the Lord is with us. Let us show ourselves grateful for such grace and 'walk worthy of God who has called us to his kingdom and glory.' Let fervent prayer continue and patient faith wait on God, 'who is able to do exceeding abundantly above all that we ask or think.'"

The letters from the converted soldiers were often the means, under God, of awakening an interest in the Churches at home. And back to the army went letters telling how hearts were touched and made truly penitent by reason of the tidings sent from the boys in the tents and trenches.

From Gen. Bragg's army that veteran soldier of the Cross, Dr. J. B. McFerrin, wrote:

"I have the pleasure of saying that notwithstanding the recent numerous movements of the army of Tennessee the work of God still progresses. Many have been brought to Christ in various brigades, and wherever the troops remain long enough in one place religious services are observed with great effect. The chaplains and missionaries work with zeal, and have much good fruit. Let our friends at home thank God and take courage. Hundreds of soldiers are coming to Jesus. My health is good, though I feel weak with jaundice. We now have at work in this army as missionaries from our Church: Revs. R. P. Ransom, C. W. Miller, Wellborn Mooney, W. Burr, Bro. Allen, and your humble servant. We expect Bro. Petway."

Soldiers were converted by thousands every week. From Virginia Rev. G. R. Talley wrote:

"God is wonderfully reviving his work here, and throughout the army. Congregations large — interest almost universal. In our Chaplains' meeting it was thought with imperfect statistics that about five hundred are converted every week. We greatly need chaplains — men of experience and ministerial influence. Our Regimental Christian Association, as a kind of substitute for a church, and our Bible-classes, are doing well."

Under the powerful stimulus of such a revival the Churches at home redoubled their efforts to supply preachers.

The Executive Committee of Domestic Missions of the Presbyterian Church sent *fifty-three* ministers to the armies. The other Churches also called on their best men for this work, and gladly they went out into the harvest. Oh, what scenes they witnessed! what meetings they held! At noon or night, in sunshine or in storm, in the huts of the soldiers, in the fields and woods, in the crowded hospitals, the men of God lifted up their voices and the men of war wept, and bowed, and prayed before the Lord of Hosts.

But even when there was no minister to lead, devout laymen were used by the Lord to carry on his work. A Lieutenant in Buford's brigade, army of Mississippi, wrote:

"A glorious revival of religion has just closed in our brigade for want of more laborers. The fruits of the meeting are a large number of conversions, and a still larger number of earnest penitents. I believe all the mourners are in earnest and fully determined to accomplish their salvation. We have in our regiment a very prosperous Christian Association, which meets every Wednesday night, and a prayer-meeting every night, which is always largely attended by an attentive audience. Having no chaplain or preacher in the regiment, we feel that the work of the Lord devolves upon the lay members; and quite a number of them take a lively interest in the great work—stand up boldly before the people as advocates for the cause of Christ; and oh! how beautiful it is to see the young beginner, boldly, yet tremblingly, pleading with God in behalf of his fellow-soldiers! Pray for us, that the Lord may prosper our efforts to advance his kingdom."

The venerable Bishop Andrew, of the M. E. Church, South, went among the soldiers like a father among his children, and rejoiced in the privilege of preaching to them the Word of Life.

Of a visit to the soldiers at Demopolis, Ala., most of

whom were paroled prisoners from Vicksburg, and among whom were many of the gallant men who came from Missouri with Gen. Price, he says in a letter to the *Southern Christian Advocate:*

"On last Sabbath I visited Demopolis, where there are a good many soldiers, mostly paroled prisoners who were captured at Vicksburg. Most of these have been recently exchanged, and will, I suppose, soon be in the field again. On Sunday afternoon I preached in the camp of Gen. Cockerell's Missouri brigade to quite a large and attentive congregation. At the close I was requested by the chaplain, Rev. Bro. Howard, of the Cumberland Presbyterian Church, to preach for them again on Monday morning at 9 o'clock, to which I consented, and the next morning was in my place and tried to give them a plain, affectionate talk, to which they listened with apparent interest. At the beginning of the services I baptized a young man who had been converted at one of the soldiers' prayer-meetings; for the young men of the brigade have kept up a regular prayer-meeting for many months.

"I was glad to find among the young men of the army a good many sons of the preachers and of others, my old friends in Missouri. It did me good to hear from them, and to know that many of these young men worthily represent and recommend the religion of their fathers. May God bless and keep them faithful to the end."

The Bishop pays a well-merited tribute to the men of Gen. Price's corps, and gives us the impressions of his great and clear mind during the conflict:

"I think, from what I saw and heard, that these Missourians are good soldiers and very orderly in their general deportment in camp. They belong to the class who came South with Gen. Price, and have been in the army ever since; and, best of all, not a few of them are decidedly pious. Gen. Cockerell is a Cumberland Presbyterian, and Col. McCown is a Methodist. Both of them have a good reputation for piety. If we had all such officers and men we could not fail to be victorious. May God help us, for we have but little to hope for from man. Well, God reigns. He has important results to accomplish; and when they shall be accomplished, we shall have peace on some terms. I believe we shall ultimately triumph; but I fear our people have yet a bitter cup to drink. I have, from the beginning, believed that the institution of slavery was to be either destroyed or established on a firmer basis. This is still my opinion. My impression is, that, let the struggle terminate as it may, the value of that class of property is to be very greatly affected."

On Sunday, the 20th of September, the fierce battle of Chickamauga was fought. The little stream bears an Indian name, which means the River of Death. We know not whether, in bygone days, any bloody fight between Indian tribes secured to it this name, but if so, in this dreadful contest it was rebaptized in blood. The flower of our Western army, with some of the best Lieutenants and soldiers of Gen. Lee's invincible army of Northern Virginia, met the Federals. It was here that Gen. Hood lost his leg; it was here that Gen. Preston Smith and Gen. Deishler were killed; it was here that thousands of the sons of the South poured out their blood to swell the "river of death."

After a most obstinate resistance, the Federal army was driven from the field and forced to take refuge behind entrenchments near Chattanooga.

Rev. S. M. Cherry, one of the most faithful laborers among the soldiers of the Western army, gives an account of the blessed scenes that were witnessed among the wounded and dying men. Of the work of the chaplains he says:

"Dr. McFerrin was at Cleburne's Division hospital, where his son was, slightly wounded, and his nephew, Rev. John P. McFerrin, severely wounded, working with the sufferers. Dr. Cross, chaplain on Gen. Buckner's staff, was on the field and at the hospital. Bros. Mooney and Miller were at Stewart's Division hospital, active and industrious in attending to the wounded and dying. Dr. Petway came in good time to render efficient aid in the double capacity of surgeon and minister. I saw Brothers Burr and Browning on the field; also Brothers Quarles, Harris, A. W. Smith, Fitzgerald, Daniel, and others, looking after their wounded and suffering soldiers. Chaplain Willoughby was with the dying and superintended the burial of the dead of our division. Bro. McVoy came in time to minister to the wants of his men at the hospital, and many others were at the post of duty if not of danger."

"It was encouraging," he says, "to the Christian heart to see the soldier of the Cross die so heroically. Said Mr. Pool, a member of the Methodist Church in Columbus, Ga., whose shoulder was shattered, 'Parson, write my wife a calm letter and tell her how I died; for I will never be able to write her again. Tell her I was ready and willing to die.' Mr. Turner, of Elbert county, Ga., was horribly mangled by a shell, and while on the gory litter said to me, 'I want to die; all is well.'

"Sam Robins, of Spring Place, Ga., amid the flying, falling, and exploding shells, handed me his hymn-book and his wife's ambrotype, having the night previous talked long with me about his religious enjoyments, pious mother, and praying father, sending messages of love to his youthful wife, and declaring that he felt no fear or dread of the coming conflict, though he seemed to be impressed with the idea that he would not survive the battle. He fell the first day without speaking a word. Others died full of faith and hope. Several of the slain were devoted Christians. I miss them much at our religious services now. On last Sabbath, at the close of the sermon, about twenty-five arose or knelt, declaring their resolution to lead new lives—several officers among the number. Most of our commands being engaged in constructing fortifications on Sabbath evening, I had the privilege of preaching to Liddell's Arkansas brigade, which is encamped at Missionary Ridge. From the preaching place we had a fine view of Chattanooga and the Federal defences. The attendance and attention of the audience were very good. They have enjoyed a gracious revival of religion the past summer, and need chaplains very much.

"At twilight I preached to a Kentucky brigade, commanded of late by the ill-fated Gen. Helm. There are many Christian gentlemen in that command. I preached for them again at 6½ o'clock last evening. They meet every evening for religious service just after 'retreat' is sounded. Brother Mooney preached for our brigade last night. It is stationed in reach of the enemy's guns."

Mr. Cherry gives us an account of one of the saddest scenes that can be witnessed in an army, the shooting of a deserter. He called to see the poor young man and found him deeply penitent for his sins:

"I attended him in his last moments. When he reached the place of execution he knelt beside his coffin and grave, and in the presence of the entire division offered an audible, earnest prayer, making confession of his great sin and praying for God to pardon him, and touchingly alluded to his only sister, and wife, to whom he had been married but one year, and commended his departing spirit to God. He was calm while the sentence was read, listened attentively to the lesson read of the dying Saviour and penitent thief, and responded fervently during the recital of the hymn, 'There is a fountain filled with blood,' etc. His feet and hands were bound and eyes hoodwinked. The command was given, aim, ready, fire, and he fell, pierced by five balls through the head and body. Thus perished the young deserter."

There was scarcely a spot where soldiers were gathered where the revival did not manifest its saving power.

Think of a revival within the limits of battered Fort Sumter.

Near the close of September, Rev. A. B. Stephens, chaplain of the 11th South Carolina regiment, wrote:

"We now constitute the garrison at Fort Sumter. On the last fast-day I began a meeting which has been going on and increasing in interest all the while till now. God has honored us with a gracious revival of religion among the soldiery of this command. A few months ago but two officers in the regiment were members of the Church. Now but few more than that number are not professors of religion. About 200 have joined the Church, and a larger number have been converted and are now happy in the love of God. It would do your soul good to visit the old Fort, battered and scarred as it is, and hear the soldiers make the battered walls ring with the high praises of the living God. No camp-meeting that I have ever attended can come near it."

In Gen. G. T. Anderson's Georgia brigade, composed of the 7th, 8th, 9th, 11th, and 59th regiments, the influence of a Soldiers' Christian Association was most powerful for good.

"It has drawn out and developed," says a soldier of the brigade, "all the religious element among us. It has created a very pleasant, social feeling among the regiments, and has blended them into one congregation. The three chaplains of the brigade work together, and thus lighten the burdens of each other, and also extend help to the two regiments that are without chaplains. The Association now numbers over 400 members. We recently broke up a camp, where, for four weeks, we have enjoyed an unbroken rest; and it has been one long 'camp-meeting,'—a great revival season,—during which we held divine services daily. It has been a time of great joy with us, reviving pure, evangelical religion, and converting many souls. Above 80 members have been added to the Association as the fruit of our meeting. A great revolution has been wrought in the moral tone of the brigade. During a part of this time we were assisted by Rev. Mr. Gwin, of Rome, Ga., of the Baptist Church, and by Rev. Dr. Baird, of Mississippi, of the Presbyterian Church. Their labors were highly appreciated, and were very valuable. The 8th, 9th, and 11th regiments, each have Sabbath Schools, which are a new and interesting feature in the religious teachings of the army. Much interest is taken in it. Full one-third of my regiment are members of my school."

In Law's brigade the work was equally deep and powerful.

"Last March," says a soldier, "I was quite sick, and was sent to the hospital in Richmond, Va. At that time my regiment (the gallant 4th Alabama) was extremely wicked. You could scarcely meet with any one who did not use God's name in vain. You could see groups assembled almost in every direction gambling. I obtained a furlough and returned home to my dear wife and children, who live not far from your city. I returned to my command some two weeks since, and to my surprise and delight I found at least three-fourths of my company not only members of the Church of the living God, but professors of religion. This state of affairs is not limited to my company, but it extends throughout the entire regiment, and I might say the whole brigade (Law's brigade). God grant that this good work may continue to flourish throughout the entire army."

In the cause of the South the greatest and the humblest of her sons yielded up their lives freely to secure her freedom. Among those who died this year the name of Gen. John Buchanan Floyd stands prominent. Before the war he had filled various offices as a statesman. In 1849 he was chosen by the General Assembly of Virginia Governor of the State, and served for the legal term. In 1857, on the accession of James Buchanan to the Presidency of the United States, he was called to the post of Secretary of War. When the war broke out in 1861 he entered the Confederate army as Brigadier-General, and for a time commanded a part of the forces in Western Virginia. He was afterwards transferred to the army of the West, and was at Fort Donelson, where he participated in the terrible battle that preceded the loss of that stronghold. With Gen. Pillow and several thousand men he withdrew from the Fort before it was surrendered to Gen. Grant. Failing health disqualified him for the arduous duties of a soldier, and he retired to his home in Virginia. In little more than a year and a half after the Fort Donelson affair he was in his grave. It is pleasing to know that in his last illness he turned with a penitent heart to Christ Jesus as his only hope of salvation. Rev. E. E. Wexler, of the Holston Conference, M. E. Church, South, was called to see him in his last hours, and gives a description of the scene:

"I was summoned by telegraph," he says, "to attend the bedside of Gen. Floyd, and reached him four days before his death. I found him calm and peaceful—his mind as clear and his judgment as sound as ever in his life. He took me by the hand, telling me he could not survive more than a few days. He spoke of his religious feelings and prospects in the most beautiful and satisfactory manner. I wish I could recall his language, but can do so only very imperfectly. He said he was not afraid to die; that he had the strongest assurance of his acceptance with his Maker. He felt that he was a sinner, and that his only hope was in the infinite mercy of God through the Lord Jesus Christ. As he spoke of the goodness of God, his heart seemed to glow with gratitude and love; and as I repeated the promises of the Bible suited to his case, his eyes kindled with interest and the large tear-drops flowed copiously over the manly face of the battle-scarred warrior.

"He said that in public life he had many enemies; that he had been wronged—deeply wronged—yet he fully and freely forgave it all; that before that God in whose presence he expected very soon to stand he could say that he had no malice nor aught in his heart against any man. He had been impressed with the importance of connecting himself with the Church, but had been hindered from doing so by various causes, but now he wished to be received into its communion and to receive the holy sacrament, and I saw no good reasons why his wishes should not be granted; accordingly, he was received into the Church and the sacrament administered. These solemn and impressive services being performed, much to the gratification of himself and friends, he now felt that his work was done. After this he conversed but little, being very weak, and much of the time suffering severe pain; yet he retained full possession of his faculties to the last, and the same calm, peaceful state of mind. Much of the time he was engaged in prayer, and often seemed anxious that his departure should be hastened."

In the army of General Lee, while it lay on the upper Rappahannock, the revival flame swept through every corps, division, brigade, and regiment. Of the work which came under his eye in Ewell's corps Dr. Rosser wrote:

"My plan is, to visit and preach to this corps, division by division, and brigade by brigade—stopping longest where I can do most good, noticing vacancies in the chaplaincy, circulating religious reading as it reaches me, and sympathizing with the sick and wounded soldiers. A nobler work cannot engage the heart of the preacher, or the attention of the Church and nation. I can but glance at the work at this time.

"The whole army is a vast field, ready and ripe to the harvest, and all the reapers have to do is to go in and reap from end to end. The susceptibility of the soldiery to the gospel is wonderful, and, doubtful as the remark may appear, the military camp is most favorable to the work of revival. The soldiers, with the simplicity of little children, listen to and embrace the truth. Already over two thousand have professed conversion, and over two thousand more are penitent. The hope of the Church and the country is in our armies, and religion in the army should be a subject of the most serious concern to the Church. That Church that does most for religion during the war will do most for religion when the war is over. Let our Church have an eye to this, and with a holy faith and zeal grasp both the present and the future. Oh, let the shepherds come and gather the lambs in the wilderness!

"We want our best men here—men of courage, faith, experience—holy men—hard working men—sympathizing men—self-denying men—men baptized afresh every day by the Holy Ghost for the work. No place here for slow men, mere reasoners and expositors, however learned or eloquent; war has no time to wait for such men—the soldier has no time to wait for such men—he may die to-morrow. The few men now with us in this corps—and noble men they are—can do but a tithe of the work required—some of them have the work of a brigade. We want more and the best. Let our Churches be content to spare them.

"We want vastly more religious reading. Oh, it is affecting to see the soldiers crowd and press about the preacher for what of tracts, etc., he has to distribute, and it is sad to see hundreds retiring without being supplied! One wishes to give himself away to meet the want. While the country is expending hundreds of millions of dollars, and pouring out its blood like water on the altar of patriotism, let the Church be as prominent in devotion and zeal to religion in the army. Let religion rival patriotism in activity. Light up the great camp of war with celestial fire."

The sufferings of the soldiers were very great, exposed as they were, with poor rations and clothing, to inclement weather, and often sleeping on the bare, muddy ground. Rev. A. D. McVoy, writing to the *Southern Christian Advocate* from Chattanooga, says:

"In the trenches the dull days are passed without improvement. It is true we have splendid scenery, and these huge mountains enclose a magnificent theatre of war. We can climb the rugged sides of Lookout or Missionary Ridge and look down upon two armies watching each other, hesitating to attack each other in their present positions. But for the past two weeks the clouds have gathered thick and low over us and drenched the country with superabundance of rain. The cold, mud, and rain, have produced great suffering and sickness among the troops; for we have been entirely without shelter in very exposed positions. Up to the present very few flies have been furnished—no tents. In our field hospital we have over three hundred and fifty sick from our brigade (Clayton's)."

But in the midst of these hardships the work of salvation steadily progressed.

"I never saw," says Mr. McVoy, "men who were better prepared to receive religious instruction and advice. In fact, they earnestly desired and greatly appreciated the attention of the chaplains and missionaries in this respect. The dying begged for our prayers and our songs. Every evening we would gather around the wounded and sing and pray with them. Many wounded, who had hitherto led wicked lives, became entirely changed, and by their vows and determinations evinced their purpose to devote themselves to God. Most of those who died in a conscious state gave gratifying and satisfactory testimony of the efficacy of the religion of the Lord Jesus Christ in a dying hour. I witnessed some triumphant deaths—prayer and praise from dying lips. One young Tennesseean, James Scott, of the 32d Tennessee, I think, attracted the attention of all. He continually begged us to sing for him and to pray with him. He earnestly desired to see his mother before he died, which was not permitted, as she was in the enemy's lines, and he died rejoicing in the grace of God. We will long remember Jimmie Scott. An attractive countenance, pleasing manners, he endured his intense sufferings with great fortitude; not a murmur or complaint was heard from him, and his strong religious faith sustained him to his dying moment.

"I might go on and describe many scenes like the above to show how our wounded boys die. They know how to fight, and many of them know how to die."

The devotion of the ladies of the South to the sick and wounded soldiers was so earnest, unselfish, and untiring, that it will stand forever as an example of true heroism.

The hospital at which Mr. McVoy served was established at the house of a lady who, with a bleeding heart, gave herself to Christian ministrations with sincere love.

"With one son killed and the other severely wounded, and the care of a large family upon her, her place devastated and ruined, her stock killed up, she ceased not to minister to the wants of our wounded and comfort the suffering, distributing all the milk and eggs she could procure. Many a wounded soldier will long remember Mrs. Thedford, for she was truly a mother to them in their hours of distress and pain. The entire family were untiring in providing for the wounded. Mrs. Durrett, from Tuscaloosa, although she arrived some time after the battle, when most of the wounded had been sent off, contributed greatly by her motherly nursing and attention to relieve and comfort. Not much can be done in the army at present by the chaplains and missionaries until the rainy season shall pass. I was glad to meet the Rev. Mr. Miller, from Kentucky Conference, who has just arrived to commence his operations as a missionary. He was mounted on a beautiful Kentucky horse, fully equipped for the contest."

Some, nay, many of our readers will recall the sad scenes witnessed by Rev. C. W. Miller in a trip through a portion of the South. "Along the railroads," he says, "the 'tax in kind' is being deposited in such quantities that we imagine if an old Egyptian could raise his head after a sleep of 3,500 years and look upon the corn, etc., in this land, he would think that it was the seventh year of plenty in the days of Joseph.

"And yet, hundreds of homes are saddened by hunger and want. The grasp of extortion's mailed hand and marble heart is upon all this abundance; and hungry orphans and penniless mothers starve in a land of plenty! 'I speak that I do know, and testify that I have seen.' 'If the clouds be full of rain they empty themselves upon the earth,' thus teaching men to pour forth the blessings which Heaven has deposited with them for the poor; but they heed not the lesson, and challenge the ascending cries of orphans, widows, and helpless age, to bring down God's vengeance.

* * * * * * * * * *

"On my return I visited the memorable field of Chickamauga. Everywhere may be seen the marks of an awful struggle. Trees are scarred and perforated by balls of all sizes. Solid oaks and pines, in many instances of enormous size, are shivered by cannon-balls. But the saddest sight there is the long array of Confederate graves. All over that bloody field sleep, in their narrow beds, the deathless heroes of the 19th and 20th of September. No hand of affection plants a rose or trains the evergreen over their grave. Side by side they repose upon the field their valor won. The grand old forest above them stands sentinel at their graves, whilst turbid Chickamauga sings their requiem along its banks.

"We are preaching and laboring for the spiritual good of the soldiers as much as the situation will allow. The troops are in line of battle, and we assemble a regiment or two around their camp-fires at night and speak to them the Word of Life. The soldiers receive gladly the truth, and are always anxious to hear preaching. Never was there an ampler field for ministerial labor. May God give success to the efforts of his servants with these brave men."

We have already stated that the Presbyterian Church sent over fifty laborers into the army. At the session of the Synod of Virginia Dr. J. Leighton Wilson, Secretary of Missions, gave a sketch of the army revival and urged that his Church prosecute its Army Mission work with increased zeal. Dr. Wilson said:

"There is a state of religion in the army of Tennessee quite as interesting as that in the army of Northern Virginia. The Rev. Dr. Palmer says he has never before seen so great a movement. Go where you will, and only let it be known that you are to preach—it hardly makes a difference who the preacher is—and crowds will attend to hear. Dr. W. thought it doubtful whether there had been anything since the days of Pentecost equal to this wonderful work of the Holy Spirit of God in our army. If ever there was a mighty, an imperative call upon us, it is now. If we do not rise to the occasion, our Church will degrade herself before the world and before other denominations."

Of his work after the battle of Chickamauga Dr. J. B. McFerrin wrote:

"The revival in the army progressed up to the time of the Chickamauga fight; and even since, notwithstanding the condition of the troops moving to and fro, or engaged in erecting fortifications, the good work in some regiments still goes on. The good accomplished by the ministry of the Word will never be appreciated by the Church till the light of eternity shall reveal it. Some of the fruits have already ripened; souls converted in the army have gone to the rest that remains to the people of God. The chaplains and missionaries will have many seals to their ministry. Oh! how joyful to think of being the honored instruments of bringing brave souls in the tented field to enlist under the banner of the Captain of our salvation.

"Since I last wrote to you I have witnessed much suffering in the army. The terrible fight at Chickamauga sent many to their long homes, and made cripples for life of hundreds who were not mortally wounded; but, my dear brother, to witness the dying triumph of a Christian soldier gives one a more exalted appreciation of our holy Christianity."

Near the close of autumn (November 24-25) the battle of Missionary Ridge, so disastrous to the Confederates, was fought. The army of Gen. Bragg had been greatly reduced in numbers by sickness and by the withdrawal of Longstreet's corps to East Tennessee. Gen. Wheeler was also absent with nearly all our cavalry. The army was left with little more than one-third the strength it had at Chickamauga. The Federals first assaulted and carried the strong position on Lookout mountain. They next massed heavy columns against Missionary Ridge, and after a desperate resistance the Confederates gave way and the whole army began to retreat.

The Rev. C. W. Miller gives a vivid description of the battle on the Ridge:

"Wednesday morning, November 25, dawned brightly, and at 7 o'clock the decisive struggle commenced for the possession of Missionary Ridge. The bleeding remnant of Walthall's and Moor's brigades had reached the shelter of our last defensive position; Breckinridge's corps was placed on the left, and Hardee's on the right, along the summit of the Ridge; a breastwork of logs and earth had been hastily constructed Tuesday night on the top. The work of death began. The battle rolled refluent tides along the rocky summit until it seemed to quake beneath the tread of the god of war. Victory everywhere spread her wings over our banners, and a mutilated foe staggered beneath the death-dealing volleys until about half-past three P. M. At that time the enemy, rendered bestial by intoxicating drink, charged up the steeps of Missionary Ridge, and gained a position on its summit from which they could not be dislodged. This disaster was incurred in the following manner: The regiments occupying the fortifications along the tops of the Ridge were divided, and one-half of each one placed at the base of the mountain, next the valley of Chattanooga. When the abolitionists advanced, those at the base, according to orders, delivered their fire and retreated up the mountain. The enemy, as could easly have been foreseen, charged up immediately in the rear of these retreating forces, thereby placing our own men as a sure protection between themselves and our guns in the entrenchment above. In this way they reached the summit of the Ridge held by a brigade, which did not wait to discharge their pieces, but fled, leaving the foe in undisputed possession of a large portion of that part of the Ridge occupied by our left. Thus Cobb's famous battery was lost, not however until their ammunition was expended.

"Night now put an end to the struggle, and soon the rush of wagons, the long line of retreating infantry, and squads sf panic-stricken stragglers, told too plainly to be misunderstood the sad truth that the whole army was retreating from the strongest natural position in the Confederacy.

"Lewis' brigade of brave Kentuckians was ordered to cover the retreat, and nobly did they discharge their duty. About one corps of the foe pursued us as far as Ringgold, where, being infatuated by his fancied success, and supposing that we were routed and demoralized, they fell into a seemingly planned ambuscade, which uncovered itself upon their flanks and front. Their entire first line of battle was subjected to an enfilading and cross fire which sent whole companies reeling and staggering in death. We captured 500 of them, and so completely crushed the head of their advancing column as to effectually end the pursuit."

After reaching a safe position, General Bragg, at his own request, was relieved of the chief command, and General Hardee placed at the head of the Army of Tennessee. Winter quarters were fixed at Dalton, Ga., and the most vigorous measures were adopted to refit and reorganize the shattered forces of the South.

It is difficult for any one who was not in the army to conceive of the circumstances under which our devout soldiers often worshiped God. During a seven-days' bombardment of Jackson, Miss., a scene occurred that shows with what a calm faith men worship God in the midst of danger and death. All day long a storm of shot and shell had rained upon the city. "As the night shades were covering the wounded, dying, and dead," writes an officer of the 26th South Carolina, General Evans' brigade, "our zealous and beloved chaplain, Rev. W. S. Black, of the South Carolina Conference, gave notice to the different commanders of companies that he would like to have a word of prayer with and for them, indicating the centre of the line as the most suitable place. It would have made your heart glad to see those brave and half-starved soldiers (who had had but one meal a day for several days, and at this time were breaking their fast for the first time that day,) throwing down their victuals and flocking to the indicated spot. The Chaplain gave out his hymn, and then officers and men united in singing the praises of God. Oh! how we felt to praise and adore Him who had been our preserver through the storms of the day; and when it was said 'Let us pray,' I imagine that I (with many others) had never more cheerfully humbled ourselves in the dust, and lifted our hearts to God in believing prayer. It seemed to be (of all others) the time to pray! The missiles of death, the music of the distant cannon, and the sharp, cracking sound of the sharpshooters' guns, were in striking contrast with the hallelujahs and praises of that devoted band of Christian soldiers. At such a sight angels might gaze with astonishment and admiration. Our blessed Saviour, whose ear is always open to the plaintive cry, drew near and comforted our hearts. Some of us felt that all would be well both in life and death."

CHAPTER XXI.

WINTER OF 1863-'64.

The armies in the field on both sides used the interval of winter to repair their wasted energies for the spring campaign.

The towns held by the Federals, and those besieged by them, continued to feel the heavy hand of war. Charleston had a terrible bombardment on Christmas day, 1863, which makes it a red-letter day in the history of that city. No person who was there can ever forget the scenes.

"For hours before the eastern sky was streaked with the first gray tints of morning the cold night air was rent by other sounds than the joyous peals from the belfry and the exploding crackers of exhilarated boys. At one o'clock A. M. the enemy opened fire upon the city. Fast and furiously were the shells rained upon the city from five guns—three at Battery Gregg, one at Cummings' Point, and one at the Mortar Battery. The shelling was more severe than upon any former occasion, the enemy generally throwing from three to five shells almost simultaneously. Our batteries promptly and vigorously replied to the fire, but without their usual effect in checking the bombardment, which was steadily maintained by the Yankees during the remainder of the night and all the following morning until about half-past twelve o'clock. Up to that hour no less than 134 shells had been hurled against the city. There was no more firing until about five o'clock in the afternoon, when one more shell was fired. On Sunday morning about three o'clock four shells were thrown in quick succession. There had been no further firing up to a late hour that night.

The damage, we are glad to say, bore no proportion to the severity of the bombardment. Several houses were struck, but in most instances the tremendous missiles buried themselves harmlessly in the earth. There were but two casualties: Mr. Wm. McKnighton, aged 83, while standing by his fireside, had his right leg taken off by a shell, another fragment of which crushed the foot of his sister-in-law, Miss Plane. While this heavy bombardment was going on two fires broke out that burned several buildings on Broad and Church streets, the loss being about $150,000."

The work of the chaplains in winter quarters went on earnestly, and prepared the way for the extraordinary work of grace which blessed the armies in the last year of the war.

From the army at Dalton, Ga., now under command of General Joseph E. Johnston, there came an earnest call for Testaments and Bibles. "A soldier showed me." says Rev. S. M. Cherry, "a Testament a few days ago that he had brought from his home in Tennessee, and had carried in his side-pocket for over two years. Another solicited a Bible, saying that just before he left Missionary Ridge he found part of an old Bible and read it, and was now desirous of getting the entire volume of inspiration. Often I am approached by the soldiers, who inquire, 'Parson, is there no chance to get a Bible. I am very anxious to procure a copy, and am willing to pay any price for a pocket-Bible.' We are unable to supply one-fourth of the demand for the Scriptures; and yet we know there are thousands of Bibles all over the South—that are rarely read by the possessors. Almost every library contains a small pocket-edition that perhaps has not been opened for six months, and many families could collect several that are perhaps lying away, dusty and mildewing, upon the shelves."

Under calls like this from every portion of the armies the families of the South sent thousands of copies of the word of God to the soldiers. Some of these had a few lines written on the blank pages, saying that "this precious book belonged to a son who had fallen in his country's cause; and, though prized as a dear relic from the battle-field on which he died, it is sent back to give comfort and light to his comrades who still struggle for liberty and right."

Of his work at Dalton Dr. McFerrin says in a letter to the *Southern Christian Advocate:*

"Since I last wrote to you I have visited some of the hospitals, and preached in several places to citizens and soldiers; to the well and to the sick and wounded. The sermons of the ministers of Christ are greatly appreciated by many, whilst others 'care for none of these things.' There is need for a great work of God in the army as well as at home. Soldiers and citizens alike need the revival of God's work.

"Now is the time specially for the distribution of religious reading matter in the army. When the soldiers are cut off in a measure from the preaching of the Word, they need books, tracts, and papers. Let them come as freely as possible.

"Well, I suppose the Yankee papers have announced my *death*, and, perhaps, accompanied the announcement with remarks not very friendly. Thank God, Mr. Editor, your humble brother still lives, and is trying to grow wiser and better in these times of war and cruelty. He lives, he trusts, to preach the gospel to the soldier and the citizen, and to minister comfort to the sick, wounded, and dying, Yes, he has had the privilege, and felt it to be his pleasure and duty, to pray for wounded prisoners taken from the enemy's lines. Yankees, wounded and in prospect of death, have thanked him for his pleadings with God in their behalf, and for pointing them to Jesus, the Friend of sinners. Let my enemies North revile, yet, from 'my heart of hearts,' I can pray God to have mercy on them and lead them to repentance and salvation. 'Bless them which persecute you; bless and curse not.'"

We have already referred to the gallant band that General Price led from Missouri, and their deeds of valor at Corinth, Miss., and other places, are well-known to those who can recall the scenes in the Southwest. One of the most faithful laborers in this corps of our army was Rev. Dr. B. T. Kavanaugh, who has kindly sent us the following account of the revival which prevailed in General Price's corps on this side and beyond the Mississippi:

"Among those who came out of Missouri with Gen. Price's army were Jno. R. Bennett (your brother), W. M. Patterson, Nathaniel M. Talbott, and myself, besides Bros. Minchell, Harris, Dryden, and McCary. Subsequently we were joined by brother E. M. Marvin (now Bishop) and others.

"But little visible effect followed our preaching for the first year or two, while the soldier's life was a novelty; but, after two years' hard service, the romance of the soldier's life wore off, and a more sober and serious mood seemed to prevail in our camps.

"The first decided revival that occurred under my observation and ministry was in the State of Mississippi, to which State I had followed General Price's army, while we were encamped near Tupelo. Here we kept up nightly meetings for several weeks in our camp, and there were some forty conversions or more. Bros. Bennett, Harris, and myself, held a profitable meeting near Granada, Miss., where we had some conversions; but for a length of time the army was kept in motion so constantly that we had but little opportunity for religious services.

"When the army retreated from Big Black into Vicksburg Bros. Bennett, Patterson, and myself, rode together into that devoted city. The regiment to which I was then chaplain had been captured at Big Black, and as I had no duties to perform. I told those brethren that I should make my escape from the city before the enemy's lines were thrown around us, and requested them to join me. Bro. B. refused, saying he should stick to his men; and P. refused to leave B. alone.

"I obtained leave of absence and made my escape by riding all night alone, and found myself outside of Grant's lines the next morning, and went into Selma, Ala., where I spent the summer. I requested Bishop Paine to give me a commission as a missionary to Gen. Price's army, which was then in Arkansas. I obtained it, and left the house of Robert A. Baker, my cousin, in Alabama, on the 15th of September, 1863. I succeeded in making the trip, crossing the Mississippi, just below Bolivar, swimming my horse, and arrived in Gen. Price's camp early in October.

"My first work was to organize all the chaplains and missionaries into an Association for mutual aid and cooperation. When we went into camp at Camp Bragg, 30 miles west of Camden, we there commenced our work in earnest. Through the winter of 1863–'64 we kept up our meetings in camp, had seats and pulpit prepared, and were successful in having more than one hundred conversions.

"After the battles of Mansfield and Pleasant Hill, in Louisiana, our armies returned to Arkansas and made an encampment at a place called Three-Creeks, on the southern line of the State of Arkansas. Here I commenced preaching on the 10th of June, 1864, and continued our meetings until the 10th of September. An extensive revival commenced within a few days after our meeting commenced, and grew in interest and power to the close. We had preaching, beginning at early candle-light—or rather pine-knot fires on stands around the preaching-place. After about ten o'clock at night, the preaching and other exercises at the stand closed; but this was but the beginning of the night's work.

"As soon as dismissed, the young converts gathered in groups of tens and twenties, and went off in companies into the adjoining woods; and taking their friends, penitents seeking religion, with them, they spent the whole night in singing, praying, and praising God. I had lodgings close by the camp at Mrs. Tooke's, a sister of Gen. Buckner, from which, night after night, at all hours, until morning, I could hear the shouts of the new-born souls and the rejoicing of those who were laboring with them for their salvation.

"This meeting continued, after this manner, until a large majority of the two brigades were happily converted. Before we had progressed very far, an effort was made by some of the officers to interrupt us by having 'roll-call' observed at nine o'clock. I went to Gen. Parsons, who was the Division commander, and requested him to suspend roll-call at night altogether. He said, 'Doctor, I will do anything in my power to promote this great reformation; for I assure you that since your meetings commenced I have not had a complaint entered against a single man in my army, and the people in the country have not been disturbed by a single soldier.' Roll-call was suspended.

"The people in the country around us became interested in our meetings, and attended them. The remark had been made by many, before our revival meetings commenced, that it was very difficult for a man to be religious in the army; but now it was far more common to hear it said that no one could be very religious unless he belonged to the army.

"Like meetings were held in other camps of the same army at some ten, twenty, and thirty miles from us. Bros. Jewell and Winfield, of Camden, were zealously and constantly engaged in the great work in the encampment near their homes, and were very successful.

"At Three-Creeks I had the efficient aid of Bros. Talbott, Minchell, and Dryden, from Missouri, and a Baptist chaplain from Arkansas, whose name I do not remember.

"To sum up the results of these gracious revivals in the army, we may safely say that at Three-Creeks there were 500 conversions. Under Bros. Winfield and Jewell there were 300. At Camden and Camp Bragg there were 200. Making in all in Arkansas 1,000 souls.

"To show the genuineness of this work of grace upon the lives of these converts, we have to remark that after our camp was broken up, and the army was put upon the march to distant fields, wherever we went into camp but for a night our boys held prayer-meetings every night, greatly to the astonishment of the people in the country who were witnesses of their devotion.

"After the army was disbanded, in riding through the country in Arkansas and Texas, I met with some of our converts, who had returned to their families and parents, and they were still true to their profession and evinced a decidedly firm Christian character.

"The parents of some of those young men have since told me that in place of having the characters and habits of their sons ruined by being in the army they had returned to them as happy Christian men."

We also give the testimony of one of the most pious and devoted chaplains in the Army of Northern Virginia. Rev. P. F. August, who served with the gallant Fifteenth Virginia regiment, Corse's brigade, writes to us:

"The 15th Virginia regiment, Corse's brigade, Pickett's division, shared in the blessings of the great revival in the Confederate army. I have the names of about fifty of that regiment who were converted while in the field of service. One of these, J. R. Eddleton, a very young man from Hanover county, was mortally wounded in a skirmish. When borne off the field on a litter he said to his comrades: 'Boys, tell my mother how I went'—meaning, Tell her that I fell discharging my duty with my face to the enemy. For twenty-four hours he suffered very much, but met death, not only calmly, but triumphantly. He left an assurance that he was accepted with God, and felt that the blessed Saviour would save him forever. His dying request was that his mother should be written to and informed that he died in the faith. Many who belonged to the 15th regiment are now living, and are active and useful in the Church, who were converted in the army. One particularly I would mention—Captain M. W. Hazlewood—well-known in Richmond as an active, zealous Methodist. He continued in the army to the close of the war, but for more than two years he was very wicked. In 1863 he gave his heart to God, and went to work at once for the great Captain of his salvation. He was instrumental in the army in leading a number of precious souls to Jesus. Since the close of the war he has been a very active member of the Church in Richmond, where as a layman he has been remarkably successful in persuading sinners to seek the Lord.

"A large number of the men of that regiment were pious when they entered the army. Their perseverance in serving the Lord proved that they had on the gospel-armor. Many of them lived through the war, and came out of it strong in the faith of God. Others fell on the field of battle instantly killed. They departed covered with the honors of war and with the glory of a saving faith in Christ. Their record below was one of Christian fidelity—on high, no doubt, it was acceptable to God. Among those who deserve to be specially mentioned are the names of Major John Stewart Walker, an upright, conscientious Christian, and one of the purest men I believe that ever died or lived—also Lieutenants Melville C. Willis and Jones Daniels. The last named two were bosom friends, who likewise fell instantly killed. On the same field and about the same time their lives were yielded a sacrifice to the Southern cause.

They were lovely and pleasant in their lives, and in death they were not separated.

"Besides those of the 15th, I have quite a large number of names of soldiers belonging to other regiments in Corse's brigade, who were converted in the army; some of whom I have met since the close of the war, and who assured me that they were still striving to get to heaven. When Christ's jewels gathered from earth shall be displayed to an admiring universe, I doubt not many thousands of precious souls converted in the late Confederate army will shine as stars forever and ever in the firmament of glory."

The earnest purpose of the home Churches to promote the army revival was manifested by the number of ministers sent among the soldiers. We give a list of those who were sent by the Mission Board of the M. E. Church, South:

Revs. Leo. Rosser and J. C. Granbery in the Army of Northern Virginia; J. B. McFerrin, C. W. Miller, W. Mooney, R. P. Ransom, and W. Burr in the Army of Tennessee; J. S. Lane and E. B. Duncan in the Department of Florida; J. J. Wheat and H. J. Harris in Mississippi; W. C. Johnson to General S. D. Lee's corps, North Mississippi; J. J. Hutchinson to army about Mobile; and beyond the Mississippi river, J. C. Keener to Louisiana troops, and B. T. Kavanaugh and E. M. Marvin to Missouri and Arkansas troops.

Besides these, and others probably whose names have escaped us, the Conferences of the M. E. Church, South, emulated other Churches in sending forth laborers into the great harvest.

Rev. Dr. Myers, of the *Southern Christian Advocate*, in noticing these facts, says:

"The Mississippi Conference appointed one missionary and two chaplains to the army; Memphis, one missionary and six chaplains; Alabama, four missionaries and twelve chaplains; Florida, one missionary and two chaplains; Georgia, eight missionaries and eight chaplains; South Carolina, thirteen chaplains; North Carolina, two missionaries and eight chaplains; Virginia, two missionaries and twenty chaplains. Here are nineteen missionaries and seventy-one chaplains from these eight Conferences. Of course, the Conferences beyond our lines furnish a number also; but except in the case of the General Missionaries, sent out by the Parent Board, we can give no guess even as to their numbers."

The Georgia Conference determined, if possible, to furnish one missionary to each Georgia brigade, and at the session of 1863 the work was begun by sending seven ministers:

"R. B. Lester to Jackson's brigade, Army of Tennessee; A. M. Thigpen to Colquitt's brigade, near Charleston; J. W. Turner to the troops in and around Savannah, and on the coast below there; G. W. Yarbrough to Wofford's brigade, Gen. Longstreet's army; T. H. Stewart to Thomas' brigade, and P. O. Harper to Gordon's brigade, Army of Virginia; and L. B. Payne temporarily to visit the hospitals between Atlanta and Guyton C. R. R. until a brigade is selected for him. Another, T. F. Pierce, is now in the State military service, and will receive his appointment to a brigade when his term expires."

That a faithful minister had his hands full of work in the army may be seen by the following sample report of a missionary:

"Dec. 17, 18, and 19.—Services consisted of exhortation, singing, and prayer.

"20.—Sunday—Made appointments to preach with three Georgia regiments. Went to them. The weather too cold for service. Visited and prayed with sick.

"21.—Very cold day. Visited and prayed with sick men.

"22.—Regimental prayer—also visited sick men.

"23.—Wednesday—Assisted in religious services at

Chaplains' meeting; in the afternoon preached in —— Georgia, at night in —— Georgia regiment.

"24.—Exhortation, singing and prayer with regiment.

"25.—Visited sick soldiers.

"26.—Exhortation, singing, and prayer, with regiment.

"27.—Sunday, 10 o'clock—Preached in —— Georgia; 3 o'clock held prayer-meeting; and at night closed services for —— Georgia, with exhortation.

"28.—Went to appointment to preach, but rain prevented meeting. Afterwards held a meeting for exhortation and prayer. Then visited Brigade hospital; talked and prayed with the sick.

"29.—Had regimental prayers.

"30.—Went to preach for a regiment, but was prevented by its going off on picket duty. Had prayer with —— Georgia regiment.

"31.—An unfavorable, rainy day. Not likely to have service to-day.

"I fear you will consider the number of sermons as too small. The cold weather and rain together have prevented the congregations from assembling on several occasions when I had made appointments for preaching. You will notice I report prayer and exhortation with regiments. I have assembled the troops together for service, and when the weather has been unfavorable to remaining in the open air I have given a short exhortation and have concluded with singing and prayer."

The experiences of soldiers are so full of child-like simplicity that one never tires of reading them.

A soldier converted on the march was met by his chaplain, who knew that he was under conviction, and asked by him if he had given himself to Christ:

"Yes," said the stalwart warrior with a glowing countenance, "I have found him. Why, sir, when we set off on that march I felt such a weight upon my soul that I could scarcely drag myself along, but after a while God heard my prayers, and then the burden was gone and I felt as if marching was no trouble at all."

Good men that work for God faithfully die well even in war, on the field or in the hospital. Captain Thos. O. Byrd, of the Fourth Mississippi regiment, was a zealous Christian among his comrades. He says, writing to his friends at home:

"I have prayers in my tent every night with the boys, and assist others to take up the Cross. I have just had prayers with some wild young men, who are now engaged in singing with much zest and feeling. Oh, what a field is open here! Fare is rough, but gladly would I live thus for life for Christ's sake and the good of man. I have gained a great victory to-day. I believe God will bless this work. I feel his love burn in my heart while I write. I know God will bless my labors if you and Sister ———— and the children will pray for me."

Again: "I find I lack courage to speak out for the cause of our holy religion more than ever, and you know full well that I have always been more or less lacking in this particular; yet I trust through faith and prayer to come out safe at last, though it may be as through fire."

He sickened and died in the army. A kind lady approached him as he was nearing the verge of eternity. Said he:

"God bless you, sister; this is the way Jesus went"— meaning perhaps alone among enemies. "Tell my wife Farewell—all is right—to meet me in heaven."

Another Christian, dying in the hospital, wrote to his wife:

"I don't want you to be uneasy about me, but do not forget to pray for me. I still have strong confidence in the Lord, and endeavor to put my trust in him in all cases. I hope the Lord may take care of you; and if we should not meet again on earth, may we meet in heaven, where wars and sorrows are forever gone. God helping, we'll meet you there."

The death of Col. Peyton H. Colquitt was that of a true Christian hero. He had served at Norfolk, Va., and as Colonel of the 46th Georgia at Charleston and in Mississippi. On the field of Chickamauga he was in command of a brigade. It was ordered to charge a battery; and while riding up and down the line in front of his men, speaking to them words of encouragement, he was struck in the breast by a ball and fell from his horse.

His friend, Hon. W. F. Samford, wrote a touching memorial of the gallant soldier, from which we extract the following account of his last moments:

"He was carried to a shade, and there the chaplain of his regiment, Rev. Thos. Stanley, attended him. I give the account of the closing scene in his words: 'When I found the Colonel he thought his wound was mortal, and though he had not recovered from the shock he seemed calm and collected. I talked with him very freely on the subject of religion. He constantly expressed a spirit of resignation to the providence of God, and that he had no apprehensions whatever in regard to the future; that he had tried to do his duty, and felt in the last hour that he was accepted of his Saviour. In this hour his faith never wavered—he said he was 'going to the land of light and peace, where he should meet his many loved ones who had gone before;' and again, 'Tell my dear wife I go to meet our angel child, and to come to us.' At one time he said: 'The providence of God is inscrutable, but I submit in hope.' He died without a struggle. It is comfortable to know that all his wants were supplied during his sufferings. He experienced no pain, and was conscious to the last moment. As soon as he was wounded Gen. Forrest sent his surgeon to him; the poor people, who had been bereft of all their worldly substance, went to see him from miles around.'"

While the work of grace went on among the soldiers at home, there were thousands of prisoners confined at different points in the Northern States, who felt and rejoiced in the power of God to comfort and save in their helpless and suffering condition. A young wife and mother, whose husband was in prison, wrote to one of the leading papers urging prayer for our captive soldiers, that they might have strength to bear up under their trials, and that God would remove the obstacles to a speedy exchange of prisoners.

Never did men need more the consolations of religion than those who on both sides were held as prisoners of war.

The winter of 1864 was extremely severe. At Cairo, Ill., the mercury, near the last of January, stood at 15 degrees below zero. At St. Louis it was at 25 below zero, and the river was crossed by heavy wagons on the solid ice. At Chicago the guards at Camp Douglass had to be changed every 30 minutes to prevent freezing, but were all frost-bitten in this short time

The *Times* of that city said of the condition of the prisoners:

"The suffering and tortures endured by the prisoners was beyond the power of pen to portray. Unaccustomed to the Northern climate and cold lake and prairie winds, their light Southern garb was a poor protection against the ordinary temperature of the elements. But with the winds maddened into fury, the air filled with freezing snow, they suffered as no people ever suffered before. Through the crevices of their thin board barracks the wind whistled as if in very mockery, bringing the snow in such quantities as to cover the floor and the beds upon which they had to sleep. So desperate was their condition that they were compelled to sleep by reliefs. Dividing off into squads of four, two would retire to their cold berths, covering with the blankets of the four, while the others kept up the fire. Thus in turns of four hours each did these poor mortals attempt to brave the raging of the storm. In many cases the snow had frequently to be shaken from the blankets of the sleepers. With all their ingenuity they could not keep warm, and numbers of them will suffer from the exposure of this dreadful storm for all time to come. To add to the horrors of their situation many of them were sick, and the wailing wind and searching cold added fresh terrors to their sufferings."

This is but a sample of what was endured in all the Northern prisons. Can any calamity upon a nation be worse than war?

But let us turn from these sad scenes to a more cheerful picture opening in the far Southwest. Beyond the Mississippi, as Dr. Kavanaugh has already related, his work and that of his co-laborers was greatly blessed of God. In a letter to Bishop Paine, of the M. E. Church, South, he gave a report of the revival and its results in two months:

"Gen. Fagan's Arkansas Brigade—Members received into Army church, 209; conversions, 85. Gen. Churchill's Arkansas Brigade—Joined the Army church, 112; converted, 35. Gen. Tappan's Arkansas Brigade—Joined, 245; converted, 40. Gen. Parson's Mississippi Brigade—Joined, 85; converted, 35. Total members Army church, 651; conversions, 195.

"The Army church was organized before my arrival; gotten up by Bro. Marvin, (now Bishop M. E. Church, South,) aided by others. It has worked well. In Tappan's brigade, the devoted chaplains have built a large log church, 60 by 30 feet, and are determined to keep up their meetings. I dedicate it next Sunday.

"I am greatly delighted with my work on this side of the river. I have gone into it with all my energy, and indeed over-did my strength the first round; but as the weather is not so favorable for out-door work this round I shall not be able to preach so often. It is truly delightful to see the work prosper in our hands as it has done for the past two months.

"The army here has gone into winter quarters. Every brigade is well-provided with log-huts, and with all that is necessary for their comfort while in camp."

"The following is the Constitution of the Army church organized by Bro. Marvin:

"ARTICLES OF FAITH AND CONSTITUTION OF THE CHURCH OF THE ARMY, TRANS-MISSISSIPPI.

"The Christian men in the army, believing that the habitation of God by his Spirit constitutes the Church, agree, for their edification and for the conversion of their fellow-men, to organize the Church of the Army, with the following articles of faith and constitution:

I. We believe the Scriptures of the Old and New Testament to be the Word of God, the only rule of faith and obedience.

II. We believe in one God, the Father, the Son, and the Holy Ghost; the same in substance; equal in power and glory.

III. We believe in the fall in Adam, the redemption by Christ, and the renewing of the Holy Spirit.

IV. We believe in justification by faith alone, and therefore receive and rest upon Christ as our only hope.

V. We believe in the communion of saints, and in the doctrine of eternal rewards and punishments.

The Christian men who have been baptized, adopting these articles of faith and constitution, in each regiment, shall constitute one church; who shall choose ten officers to take the spiritual oversight of the same.

Of the officers so elected the chaplain, or one chosen by themselves for that purpose, shall act as Moderator.

The officers will meet once a month, and oftener if necessary; and in the exercise of discipline will be guided by the direction of Christ. They will keep a record of the names of all the members and the manner in which their ecclesiastical connection with this church is dissolved."

From the Trans-Mississippi let us return to the banks of the Rappahannock and note the revival scenes as we come.

Writing from Kingston, Ga., Feb. 4, Dr. J. B. McFerrin says:

"We have a good meeting in progress. It has been going forward since Sunday last. Large crowds, mostly soldiers, are in attendance. Many penitents, some conversions, and a few backsliders reclaimed. Last night five asked for membership in the Church of God. We give the applicants choice of Churches and receive them into various Christian organizations—different divisions, but one *grand army*."

From Dalton, Feb. 3, Rev. A. D. McVoy sent good tidings:

"We have a large Brigade church built, in which we have been holding services for two weeks. About ten days ago we commenced a series of nightly meetings; at first more on the order of prayer-meetings, but the interest began to increase so rapidly that in three nights we found a revival springing up in our midst. Great crowds gather nightly. We find our church too small. Large numbers are seeking the Lord—forty to fifty every night. The word of God and religious services seem to be better appreciated at present than ever before in this brigade. Men's minds appear to dwell more on religion and the soldiers more concerned about their soul's eternal welfare. The meeting is progressing with increasing interest. Eight joined the different Churches—one, the Presbyterian; two, the Baptist; and five, the Methodist Church. Missionary C. W. Miller is preaching for us at present with great success. A number of ladies from the neighborhood attend, making the scene very homelike.

"The prospect before us is very encouraging. Wickedness and vice seem restrained. Members of the Churches are becoming revived. The Spirit of the Holy

One is present and felt. Good resolutions are being formed by many in every regiment. A number are endeavoring to fulfill their promises made to God upon the eve of and during the late battles. We are expecting and praying for great things."

The work of Rev. L. B. Payne in hospitals in Georgia for one month was 27 sermons, distributed 300 papers, 18,000 pages of tracts, and about 32,000 pages of reading matter in books, which he had procured by soliciting donations. Some have been awakened, others professed conversion.

Rev. J. W. Turner, in and near Savannah, Ga.:

"He preached in January 16 sermons, travelled about 400 miles, distributed 177 books, conversed privately with several soldiers on religion, and prayed with 102 soldiers who professed to be seeking Christ."

Rev. A. M. Thigpen labored in Colquitt's brigade near Charleston. In the 23d Georgia, 60 conversions. The meeting was conducted in harmony by Presbyterians, Baptists, and Methodists.

Rev. Geo. W. Yarbrough reported from General Longstreet's army near Russellville, Tenn:

"At Petersburg I entered upon my missionary work, having been thrown with a large number of troops on their way to this army; and, having been supplied by the Evangelical Tract Society there with a variety of very interesting religious papers. Dr. Miller, the agent, promised me an abundant supply as soon as transportation could be furnished.

"I went through the cars on Saturday, furnished all the troops by way of preparing them for the Sabbath, and was glad to find them not only willing, but eager to read them.

"I find that Dr. Stiles' pamphlet on 'National Rectitude' is very popular. That army evangelist may look for an abundant harvest when the resurrection trumpet rolls its notes along the battle-fields of this revolution.

The faces of these war-worn veterans often brighten at the mention of his name. We hope to see him in our camps again. Heaven bless him in his high employ."

From Gen. Lee's army Rev. J. M. Stokes, chaplain 3d Georgia, reported to the *Southern Christian Advocate*.

"Zion is flourishing again in this army. There are as many as twenty chapels. We have had a meeting in progress two weeks, and the interest is increasing daily. We have had several conversions, and there were, I reckon, fifty mourners at the altar for prayer last evening. Our chapel seats between 300 and 400, and is full every night unless the weather is very inclement.

"Bro. B. T. Lacy, chaplain to Gen. Ewell's corps, visited and preached for us about a week ago. He preached us a most excellent sermon, and gave us much advice and encouragement privately. His visits to the different brigades can but have the most gratifying effect both upon the chaplains and their congregations. I wish we had just such a man to every division to superintend its spiritual matters.

"There is a great harvest here, which ought to be reaped at once, and if it should pass this season we fear that much of it will be gathered by the enemy of souls."

Rev. J. O. A. Cook, chaplain 2d Georgia battalion, Wright's brigade, wrote most cheeringly of the work in the same army:

"It would do your heart good to witness our camp-services, to see the immense throng that crowd our rude chapels, to listen to the soul-stirring music as with one voice and one heart they unite in singing the sweet songs of Zion, and to note the deep interest and solemn earnestness with which they listen to the preaching of the Word. I have never seen anything like it. I can but believe that the blessing of God is upon us, and that he is preparing us for a speedy and glorious peace.

"Bible-classes and Sabbath Schools have been organized in many of the brigades. The soldiers are taking great interest in them. We organized our Sabbath School a few evenings since, beginning with seventy members. There is, however, a want of Bibles. If every family would furnish one of the several Bibles lying about the house the army would be very well supplied.

The great chieftain Lee looked with the eye of a tender father upon his noble soldiers engaged in this work, and to promote it issued the following order on the observance of the Sabbath:

HEADQUARTERS A. N. V., Feb. 7, 1864.
General Order, No. 15:

I. The attention of the army has already been called to the obligation of a proper observance of the Sabbath, but a sense of its importance, not only as a moral and religious duty, but as contributing to the personal health and well-being of troops, induces the Commanding General to repeat the orders on that subject. He has learned with great pleasure that in many brigades convenient houses of worship have been erected, and earnestly desires that every facility consistent with the requirements of discipline shall be afforded the men to assemble themselves together for the purpose of devotion.

II. To this end he directs that none but duties strictly necessary shall be required to be performed on Sunday, and that all labor, both of men and animals, which it is practicable to postpone, or the immediate performance of which is not essential to the safety, health, or comfort of the army, shall be suspended on that day.

III. Commanding officers will require the usual inspections on Sunday to be held at such times as not to interfere with the attendance of the men on divine service at the customary hour in the morning.

They will also give their attention to the maintenance of order and quiet around the place of worship, and prohibit anything that may tend to disturb or interrupt religious exercises. R. E. LEE, General.

CHAPTER XXII.

SPRING OF 1864.

THE preparations on both sides in the early spring of 1864 gave promise of a year of great battles. After the repeated failures of six successive Federal Generals to take Richmond, General Grant was appointed to the command of all the Federal armies, and he fixed his headquarters with the Army of the Potomac. General Lee confronted him with the Army of Northern Virginia. At Dalton, Ga., was General Johnston with an admirably equipped army, and opposed to him were the gathering thousands of Federals led against him by Gen. Sherman in the memorable campaign that ended with the capture of Atlanta.

At other places the opposing powers brought smaller armies to confront each other. There were few in the South that did not feel that this year's work must decide the great questions at issue. The Confederate government made another call for men, embracing those between seventeen and eighteen and forty-five and fifty. The strictest measures were adopted for the purpose of securing the service of every available man. All absentees were recalled to the ranks, and the different armies brought up to the last degree of strength. The year 1864 was to witness the battles of the giants.

But in the midst of all this preparation for the hideous work of blood the revival rather increased than decreased in power. The deep and solemn conviction that great events were impending turned the thoughts of the people to God. From the Confederate Congress came a call to humiliation, fasting, and prayer. The people in the armies and at home were urged to call upon God,

"That he would so inspire our armies and their leaders with wisdom, courage, and perseverance, and so manifest himself in the greatness of his goodness and the majesty of his power, that we may be safely and successfully led through the war to which we are being subjected, to the attainment of an honorable peace; so that while we enjoy the blessings of a free and happy government we may ascribe to him the honor and the glory of our prosperity and independence."

The Southern people strove to maintain a calm trust in God in the presence of their great danger. Even in beleaguered Charleston, while shells were screaming in the air and falling in the streets and houses, the people met in the churches and devoutly worshiped. They had encouragement to pray. For it really seemed that the shield of God's protection was over the city. An eye-witness says:

"Probably five thousand howling missiles of death have fallen with dreadful crash in and near the city, and all that at a cost immediately of about five lives. And amid it all the people of God, Sabbath after Sabbath, have assembled at their places of worship, and thus, rising above all the commotion of war, hold communion with Him who rides on the whirlwind, who tempers the winds to the shorn lamb, the infinite God reconciled through Christ to a sinful world."

From the armies that knew how each passing day brought them nearer to death the reports were most cheering.

"It does one's heart good," writes a chaplain, "to be at some of our Chaplain and Missionary Associations and hear the reports come up from the various regiments and brigades of the wonderful revival in the army."

Another says: "The awakening has been very extensive. Strong men bow themselves, and the man hardened by three years of war and the corrupting influences of the camps comes to the altar of prayer and 'mourns his follies past,' praying God for pardon."

"We have," says another, "two hundred volumes of religious books which are let out to the regiment upon rules adopted by our Sunday Schools."

Among the most touching scenes were the sacramental occasions in the army. At such times all denominational lines were forgotten, and Christians of all the Churches knelt together and received the emblems of a Saviour's love.

Rev. A. G. Haygood describes such a scene in the Army of Tennessee:

"We invited all of God's children to join with us in this holy feast. As hundreds joined in that oft-used hymn—

"That doleful night before his death,
    The Lamb for sinners slain,
Did, almost with his dying breath,
    This solemn feast ordain,"

many Christians wept, and sinners looked seriously and wonderingly on. It was so unlike the rude scenes of war. I shall never forget, and I shall always feel it, when I remember how these rough-bearded, war-worn, and battle-scarred veterans of three years' fierce conflict crowded around the log—the rude altar improvised for the occasion—to celebrate the death of their gracious and adorable Redeemer. Three-fourths of the communicants—and they were from the various denominations represented in the command—were in tears."

The religion of the soldier was of the best type. Rev. C. W. Miller says:

"My observation is that the religion of the army approximates more nearly that of the primitive days of Christianity than anything which I have witnessed in the halcyon days of peace. The soldier's situation is peculiarly favorable to the growth of a benevolent, unselfish, and primitive piety. Political storms disturb not the calm of his soul. His musket is his platform. The 'love of gain' finds no fostering facilities. Necessity has taught him to be 'content with his wages'—eleven dollars per month. Sectarian strife and pulpit gladiators no longer warp and embitter the great current of his heart. And thus, freed from these former hindrances, he cultivates that religion which teaches the heart to love God with all the mind, soul, and body, and his neigbor as himself."

The work at Dalton while the army lay there was almost without a parallel. In the coldest and darkest nights of winter the rude chapels were crowded, and at the call for penitents hundreds would bow down in sorrow and tears.

Dr. McFerrin was a tower of strength. He won his way to the hearts of the soldiers by his candor and kindness, and had the blessed privilege of leading thousands to Christ. He was ably supported by other missionaries and by the chaplains, and under their combined efforts such a revival flame was kindled as is seldom seen in this sinful world. Dalton was the spiritual birthplace of thousands. Many are in heaven. Some still rejoice and labor on the earth. "Come to the army," shouted a missionary to his brethren, "for the harvest truly is great, but the laborers are few."

The religious enthusiasm of our soldiers did not fail to impress the more sober-minded and reflecting among our opponents.

A Southern chaplain, who remained with our wounded men after the battle of Gettysburg, wrote to a paper at home an account of a sermon he heard from a Federal chaplain, in which he contrasted the religious spirit of the two armies.

"One Sabbath afternoon," he says, "soon after the battle it became necessary for me to go to Gettysburg, and, passing through one of the principal streets, I saw a little group of people in one corner of an open square engaged in public worship. Approaching the spot, I soon found myself in the midst of an assemblage of thirty or forty persons, mostly women and soldiers, engaged in divine worship, while around them was a throng in busy conversation about the events of the day as unconcerned in their manner as if no religious services were being held. The minister had commenced his sermon, and I did not learn the text; but the subject was the recognition of God's providence, and the sense of dependence upon him essential to national success. He had already spoken of the utter want in the mind of the Northern people of this feeling of dependence upon God, and of their constant failure to take any steps to secure his favor. He was speaking, as I approached, of the gross irreligion and unblushing wickedness of the Northern army; and, in order to make the impression deeper, he drew an eloquent contrast between the spirit of the Northern army and that which he supposed to actuate the army of the South.

"The Southern army, said he, is one which, from its commanding Generals to its lowest privates, is pervaded with the sense of dependence upon God. The highest councils of its military leaders are opened with prayer for His divine guidance and benediction. Every battle is planned and every campaign conducted in the spirit of prayer. More than this: Every soldier is taught to feel that the cause in which he contends is one that God approves, that if he is faithful to God his Almighty arm will protect, and his infinite strength ensure success. Thus believing that God's eye of approval is upon him, that God's arm of protection is thrown around him, and that God's banner of love is over him, the Southern soldier enters the field of battle nerved with a power of endurance and a fearlessness of death which nothing else can give.

"You may call this, said the speaker, fanaticism, en-

thusiasm, or what you will; but remember, you are fighting an enemy that comes from the closet to the battle-
field, that comes from its knees in prayer to engage in
deadly strife, that comes in the belief that its battles are
the battles of Jehovah, that his smile is resting upon its
banners and will ensure success. With what indomitable strength, said he, does such a conviction, whether
true or false, endue men? What power it has to make
every man a hero, and every hero if need be a martyr!
How can we hope for success, contending against such
an army, even though our cause is just, while we ignore
our dependence upon God, deny ourselves communion
with him, and thus lose our great source of strength?

"I do not care to follow the speaker further. It was
with mingled emotions of sorrow and gratitude that I
listened to him—sorrow to think that our army should
fall so far short of the ideal presented by the speaker—
gratitude because I felt that in many respects the picture
was true."

The influence of many leading officers of the Confederate army was fully in favor of the revival. In a letter
from Gen. Johnston's army, Rev. J. J. Hutchinson describes a most pleasing scene. He says:

"Ten days ago Gen. Pendleton, a hero of Manassas
memory, preached to the soldiers at Dalton. General
Johnston and very many other officers were present. On
the same day Major-General Stewart, who is an Elder in
the Presbyterian Church, assisted in this brigade in the
administration of the sacrament of the Lord's supper.
On the same day I preached to Gen. Finley's brigade,
where the General and his staff were present, and where
he united audibly with our prayers. Gen. Cleburne, the
hero of many battle-fields, treated me with much attention and kindness—had a place prepared for preaching
in the centre of his division, where himself and most of
his officers were present, and where I was assisted by
Brigadier-General Lowry, who sat in the pulpit with me

and closed the services of the hour with prayer. I partook of the hospitality of Gen. L. at dinner, and spent several delightful hours in profitable religious conversation. The General is a Baptist preacher, and, like the commander of the division, is a hero of many well-fought battle-fields. He takes great interest in the soldiers' religious welfare, often preaches to them, and feels that the ministry is still his high and holy calling. I wish I had the space to give you more of his interesting life's history, and to speak of this noble and pious officer as he deserves."

The same missionary says: "Never have I seen such a field for preaching the gospel and inculcating religious truth as the Confederate army now presents; 'the fields are white unto the harvest.'"

In many of the hospitals the revival was deep and powerful. The conversion of the sick soldiers and the happy deaths often witnessed made a deep impression on the minds of unbelievers. At one of the large hospitals in Tennessee the following scene was witnessed. At the close of a sermon a call was made for penitents. Among others that came forward and bowed in prayer was a surgeon. At the close of the service he took the chaplain by the hand and said:

"I am a great sinner! I have a pious mother—was brought up in the lap of the Church—studied my profession in N———, travelled and studied in Europe—came home and entered the army a skeptic and scoffer of religion."

"But," said he, "I see such a difference between the death of the believer and the unbeliever, the question has forced itself upon my mind, *What makes the difference?* I took from my trunk the Bible my mother gave me five years ago, making me promise to read it, which, in the excitement of worldly pleasures, I had wholly neglected. The sight of that heavenly book, just as it was when she gave it to me, with the remembrance of her parting kiss, her parting tear, her parting prayer, brought a little fountain of tears from my eyes and a prayer from my swelling heart.

"I read it and found the answer to the question, *What makes the difference?* in that beautiful text, 'Precious in the sight of the Lord is the death *of his saints.*' I came here to-night resolved to accept, publicly, the invitation of the gospel which, for two days and nights, you have so earnestly urged upon this congregation. Oh, that I had submitted my stubborn heart to God years ago! I thank God that I am spared to bear testimony here to-night that Christ is able and willing to save the chief of sinners." "Oh," said he, as his eyes filled with tears of joy, "that my dear mother knew that her prodigal son had returned to his Saviour! But she shall know as soon as a letter can reach her. Oh, that I could have told the congregation to-night what a great sinner I am and what a great Saviour I have found."

"Well," said the chaplain, "with your permission I will give a statement of the cause of your awakening, and the state of your feelings of joy and gratitude to-night."

The history of his case was given with thrilling effect.

There are gleams of light amidst the dark scenes of war. The devotion of the Southern people generally to the cause for which we battled for four years, and their cheerfulness in dividing almost the last loaf with the soldiers, are worthy of permanent record. Rev. Wm. H. Stewart, of Thomas' (Georgia) brigade, pays a well-merited tribute to the people of the Valley of Virginia who felt the heavy hand of war:

"Let me say something about the affectionate liberality of these Valley Virginians toward our dear soldiers. They have had Jackson's army quartered here, and Shields' and Fremont's. They have had sheep, hogs, cows, horses, and negroes, stolen, and their timber destroyed; and yet their love of country and care for soldiers is unabated. Still they give their milk and butter and lodging, and even board in some instances, to the soldiers free of charge. Some of them are known to practice self-denial that they may have more to spare to the soldiers. The dear brother and sister Peel, with whom I board, give freely at all times of the day, and often at night prepare supper for hungry soldiers. And now I'm about to leave, they say that they have not charged a Confederate soldier for anything to eat since the war began, and they are sure they will not begin with me."

The general fast on the 8th of April was observed with great solemnity by the people at home and in the army. General Lee issued the following order in his army:

HEADQUARTERS A. N. V., March 30, 1864.
General Order, No. 21:

In compliance with the recommendation of the Senate and House of Representatives, his excellency, the President, has issued his proclamation calling upon the people to set apart Friday, the 8th of April, as a day of fasting, humiliation, and prayer.

The Commanding General invites the army to join in the observance of the day. He directs due preparation to be made in all departments to anticipate the wants of the several commands, so that it may be strictly observed. All military duties, except such as are absolutely necessary, will be suspended. The chaplains are desired to hold services in their regiments and brigades. The officers and men are requested to attend.

Soldiers, let us humble ourselves before the Lord our God, asking through Christ the fogiveness of our sins, beseeching the aid of the God of our forefathers in the defence of our homes and our liberties, thanking him for his past blessings and imploring their continuance upon our cause and our people. R. E. LEE.

Rev. S. H. Smith, writing of the observance of the day in Gordon's brigade, says:

"I have no idea that ever before was there such a day realized by the present generation. Old professors of religion expressed a degree of confidence in God, of an early deliverance from this bloody revolution, that astonished themselves. Who can tell but that yesterday was the birth-day of Southern independence? Oh! if we could have ascended above the earth and looked down upon a nation upon their knees before God, confessing their sins and suing for mercy, I imagine we could have heard the shouts of the redeemed and the songs of the angels as they exclaimed, 'Peace on earth and good will to men.'"

In Gen. Johnston's army, by general orders, all military operations were suspended that all officers and men might have an opportunity of properly observing the day. "The great stillness of the men," says an eyewitness, "exceeded anything ever seen." The devout officers joined heartily in these services, and some of them delivered stirring exhortations to their soldiers.

"Gen. Gordon," says Rev. P. O. Harper, missionary, "takes an active interest in religious exercises and in the spiritual welfare of those under his charge, which, I am sorry to say, is not the case with all the officers in the brigade. On yesterday (fast-day) morning his brigade, or all who chose to attend, were called together by his order at sunrise for prayer in the open air. He addressed the assemblage in a sensible and feeling discourse. The scene was most affecting and impressive. The morning was clear and brilliant, and, apparently, God smiled upon the sight. The assembly, to the number of eight hundred or a thousand, bowed their knees (and I trust their hearts) before the Omnipresent and Omnipotent God. The occasion, the circumstances, and the brilliancy of the lovely spring morning, rejoicing in the God of nature and declaring his glory and goodness, was well-calculated to stir to their deepest depths the souls of devout worshippers."

This day of fasting and prayer was observed with the deeper solemnity, inasmuch as the people felt that they were on the verge of tremendous battles.

"Most of us," said a chaplain in General Lee's army, "have made up our minds that the spring campaign here will open with the most desperate clash of arms that freedom ever cost on this continent."

The chaplain's words were true. In front of General Lee the Federals were gathering in immense strength. At Dalton, Ga., they massed their finest Western army against Gen. Johnston. In the far Southwest General Banks had a heavy force, but he was met and driven back by the Confederates under General Kirby Smith. And now from the soldiers standing in the very front of death there came a solemn warning against the frivolities in which many engaged in our afflicted land. From the Christian Association of the First regiment of Virginia artillery an appeal was sent forth against "the gayety and pleasure-seeking" of the times. These faithful soldiers of Christ and of their country said:

"We believe this war which is now desolating our land is a righteous judgment and chastisement from the hand of a just God for those various sins of which we have been and are still guilty; and we cannot believe, either from God's revealed word or from the dictates of our consciences, or from the teachings of those principles of right and justice and morality which have been implanted in our breast in the wise and merciful providence of God, that it is right or proper thus to answer God's call upon us for mourning by sounds of joy and rejoicing."

They urged their friends at home to join them "in seeking to do what we can to avoid receiving the afflictions of God's hand with an improper spirit, or engaging in any frivolities or pleasures, even though some of them may be innocent in ordinary times, which may in any way serve to turn our hearts from a proper spirit of humility before God, or from a proper sympathy for the mourning ones of the land, or from that proper feeling of sorrow and gravity which belongs to a people so deeply afflicted."

And to this end," said they, "we ask all professed followers of Christ, and all who pray to the God of nations, whether they have engaged, or may engage or not, in these things which we condemn, that they join us in special prayers, both public and private, to our Lord and Redeemer, that he will so incline our hearts to see his will that we may be of one mind and spirit in this matter, and that he will so direct and guide us that we may do the things which are right in his holy sight."

These were noble words from the Christian men of our army who stood at the very hour they were written on the borders of that dreary Wilderness over which the storm of battle soon burst in all its power.

In the lovely month of May General Grant began his movement towards Richmond. He crossed the Rappahannock at Ely's and Germana fords. Gen. Lee sent two corps of his army under Ewell and Hill to oppose him. The Federals assaulted these with desperate valor, but were repulsed. The battle was renewed the next day, May 6th, and for a while the Federals had the advantage, but the lost ground was soon recovered by the Confederates and the original lines restored. "Every advance," said General Lee in his report of this day's bloody work, "thanks to a merciful God, has been repulsed."

In these fights Gen. John M. Jones and Gen. Jenkins were killed, and Generals Longstreet, Stafford, and Pegram were wounded, besides many other officers of lower grade and a vast number of private soldiers. Among the leading officers lost by the Federals was Gen. Wadsworth.

At the same time that this bloody work was going on in Virginia the like scenes were enacted in Georgia. Here the movement was towards Richmond, there towards Atlanta. General Sherman made a determined effort to flank Gen. Johnston by a movement on Resaca; but the sagacious Confederate silently moved the mass of his army, and the Federals found more work on hand than they were able to do.

To aid Grant in his movement from the line of the Rappahannock a heavy Federal force was concentrated on James river between Richmond and Petersburg, which was held in check by Gen. Beauregard, who had come up from Charleston, S. C.

Gen. Banks was at the head of a large Federal army in Louisiana, but he was almost as unfortunate there as he had been in the Valley of Virginia earlier in the war.

The battles between Lee and Grant in the Wilderness and at Spottsylvania Courthouse, between the 4th and 13th of May, were the fiercest ever seen on this continent. The battle of the 12th was the most terrible of all. The Federals began the attack before daybreak, and overwhelmed and captured a large portion of Gen. Edward Johnson's division. But this gain only aroused the Confederates to greater efforts. Nine hours the battle raged. The fire of the artillery was an unbroken roar; and, to add to the awful scene, a thunder-storm burst over the field and flashed its lightnings through the sulphurous clouds that hung over the combatants. At some points along the lines the men fought each other at musket-length across the breastworks. The Federals in line, from six to ten deep, would come boldly up to our works only to be swept down by the iron hail poured into their very breasts. From daybreak until two o'clock this work of death went on. The limit of endurance had been reached. The Federals, exhausted and shattered, withdrew beyond the reach of Confederate bullets. It is said that many prisoners taken, both officers and men. were drunk. We know not if this be true, but if it be, how awful the responsibility of those who dealt out ardent spirits to these soldiers, and then marched them like beeves to the shambles.

After this battle Gen. Lee issued a general order in which, after enumerating the success that had attended our arms at different places, he said of the men who had fought under his own eye:

"The heroic valor of this army, with the blessing of Almighty God, has thus far checked the advance of the principal army of the enemy and inflicted upon it heavy loss. The eyes and hearts of your countrymen are turned to you with confidence and their prayers attend you in your gallant struggle.

"Encouraged by the success that has been vouchsafed to us, and stimulated by the great interests that depend upon the issue, let every man resolve to endure all and brave all until, by the assistance of a just and merciful God, the enemy shall be driven back and peace secured to our country.

"Continue to emulate the valor of your comrades who have fallen, and remember that it depends upon you whether they have died in vain.

"It is in your power, under God, to defeat the last great effort of the enemy, establish the independence of your native land, and earn the lasting love and gratitude of your countrymen and the admiration of mankind."

In all their dangers and privations our soldiers did not lose sight of their duties to God, and on every occasion they renewed the blessed revival scenes of more quiet days. One of the most intelligent army correspondents thus described the hardy veterans during a brief period of rest:

"I rode along the lines to-day and found the men resting after their many marches and hard battles. Some were reading their well-thumbed Bibles; some were indicting letters to the loved ones at home to assure them of their safety; some were sleeping—perchance dreaming of the bloody work still remaining to be done; others were enjoying the music of the Brigade bands, as they rehearsed those solemn and touching airs which the grand old masters of the art divine, in their most holy and impassioned moods, have given to the world; and others again were sitting under the trees, with their arms stacked near at hand, listening to the word of life, as preached by those faithful servants of God, the hardy, zealous, self-denying chaplains of the army. As the army thus rested—its great heart quiet, its huge arms unstrung, its fleet-feet still—I could but reflect, and wonder as I reflected, that this vast machine, this mighty giant, this great unmeasured and immeasurable power, should be so terrible in battle and yet so calm and gentle and devout in the hour of peace."

And of that noble army led by General Johnston in Georgia another writer said:

"It is wonderful to see with what patience our soldiers bear up under trials and hardships. I attribute this in part to the great religious change in our army. Twelve months after this revolution commenced a more ungodly set of men could scarcely be found than the Confederate army. Now the utterance of oaths is seldom, and religious songs and expressions of gratitude to God are heard from every quarter. Our army seems to be impressed with a high sense of an overruling Providence. They have become Christian patriots and have a sacred object to accomplish—an object dearer to them than life. They have also perfect confidence in their commanders. Such an army may be temporarily overpowered by vastly superior numbers, but they never can be conquered."

In the battles of this season thousands of godly men cheerfully gave up their lives for the cause of the South. The death of Maj. James M. Campbell, of the 47th Alabama, and a minister of the Alabama Conference, M. E. Church, South, was very sad.

Rev. Frank Brandon, missionary in Law's brigade, gives the account of his death:

"On the morning of the 14th of May, when all was comparatively quiet around, while seated in conversation with Maj. Cary, of the 44th Alabama regiment, a sharpshooter spied his head, which was not entirely concealed by our breastworks, and fired the fatal shot that pierced his hat-band, passing through the head and killing him instantly. The shot was among the last fired by the enemy before abandoning their breastworks in front of our division.

"He was a gallant officer, never shrinking from danger when duty called—cool and fearless upon the field, leading the veterans of the heroic 47th, in the hottest of the fight. Owing to the pressure of military duty, he was unable to preach as often as we wished or as he desired; but I can say, after having been intimately associated with him ever since he has been in service—messing with him most of the time—that he maintained his Christian integrity and ministerial character."

An officer of the 18th Virginia cavalry thus describes a scene in Gen. Imboden's brigade just on the eve of a fight:

"Before the charge, and while we were in line, the command to dismount was given, when our noble old chaplain sang a hymn and then prayed, the whole regiment kneeling. It was a solemn and impressive sight just on the eve of battle. And God blessed our arms with victory. The chaplain prayed that if it should please God we might scatter our enemies, but oh! preserve the lives of these dear ones and prolong them for thy glory. Truly did God answer the prayer of the devout old man—they were scattered to the four winds, and we lost not a man."

Rev. L. B. Payne says of the work in General Johnston's army:

"Since my last report, which was for April, we have

been in line of battle or on the march nearly every day. Notwithstanding we have had prayer-meetings in the breastworks several times, and I have preached some six or seven times; and, thank God! the revival still goes on. Souls have been converted every time I have had meetings during our fights. Some twenty-five have joined the Church, and thirty or more have been converted in the last month. Several have professed conversion after they were wounded and come to the infirmary."

CHAPTER XXIII.

SUMMER OF 1864.

The boast of General Grant while the movements described in the preceding chapter were going on, was, that he would "fight it out on that line if it took all summer;" but after the bloody repulses in the Wilderness and at Spottsylvania Courthouse, he thought better of the matter, and edged his way down towards Richmond until he found himself in the position formerly occupied by Gen. McClellan. This position he might have taken without the loss of a man by simply moving his army by water from the Rappahannock to the James or the York, and making his base of operations on either of those rivers. But with a strange pertinacity he fought his way down, losing, it is estimated, not less than 75,000 men.

On Friday, the 3d of June, Grant appeared on the Chickahominy and attempted to cross that stream at the Grape Vine bridge. General Lee drew up his army to oppose him, and here was fought one of the bloodiest battles of the war. The attack began at daybreak. The Federals came on in columns of ten deep, and threw themselves recklessly upon the Confederate works only to be slaughtered in heaps. Standing behind their breastworks, the Confederate soldiers received each assault with the utmost coolness, and suffered but little loss.

At one o'clock the attack ceased and the Federals withdrew, leaving on the field thousands of dead and wounded men. It is asserted that here, as on the 12th of May, many of the Federal soldiers tumbled drunk over the breastworks and were made prisoners, while others, after firing their guns, were too much intoxicated to reload them. General Lee, in riding over the field, declared that the slaughter exceeded that of the 12th of May. The loss of the Confederates was only a few hundreds.

The number of Christian men who freely offered their lives in the battles in all parts of the South can never be fully known until the last day. Before the writer now lies a letter in which are the names of seven ministers of the different Churches, who fell killed or wounded in the battles in Georgia on the line of General Johnston's movement from Dalton to Atlanta. The writer of this letter, Rev. S. M. Cherry, says in reference to the mortality among the ministers who fought in our armies:

"A very large proportion of our ministers who have gone into the army as officers or soldiers have been killed or wounded. Is it merely accidental or an intimation that the proper sphere of the preacher is to minister to the spiritual wants of the soldiers, and not voluntarily to shed human blood? Jesus said to a disciple who wielded a sword for the defence of his Saviour, 'All they that take the sword shall perish with the sword.' Should not the minister of peace be 'pure from the blood of all men,' and not simply of the soul but also of the body?"

Among the most eminent men who buckled on the sword was Bishop Polk, of the Protestant Episcopal Church. He had received a military training at West Point, and felt it to be his duty to offer his services to the cause of the South. He commanded a corps in the Army of Tennessee. On the 14th of June he fell instantly killed by a cannon-ball on Pine Mountain, near Marietta, Ga. In company with General Johnston and several other Generals, he rode out to reconnoitre the Federal lines. Reaching the top of the mountain about eleven o'clock "the party dismounted, and all their horses were left below the crown of the knoll. Some one had suggested that so large a group of officers at so exposed a point might attract the fire of the enemy. The suggestion had scarcely been offered before a shell from one of the enemy's batteries, recently planted, about nine hundred yards distant, passed very near them. The group then began to disperse in different directions. General Johnston and Lieutenant-General Polk moved off a few paces together and separated—the former selecting a path lower down the hill, and General Polk proceeded along the cone of the knoll. General Johnston had scarcely parted from General Polk before a second shell from the same battery struck the latter in the chest, and he fell without a groan.

"Colonel Gale, of his staff, who observed his fall, ran immediately back to the spot, but before he had reached it the great soul of his loved General had sped beyond the clouds. There was a slight tremor of the lower jaw, but the eyes were fixed and the pulse had ceased. A three-inch rifle-ball or shell had taken effect in the left arm, above the elbow, crushing it and passing through the body, and also through the right arm just below the shoulder-joint, leaving it in the same mutilated condition as the left, portions of the integuments serving to secure the arms still to the frame. The opening through the chest was indeed a frightful one and, in all probability, from the direction of the missile, involved the heart and lungs in its course. The position of the General, on the slope of Pine Mountain, at the moment of the sad occurrence, accounts for the upward tendency of the shot, as indicated in the course traced on his person.

"The enemy's battery by this time began to fire with great rapidity, and the body was borne back on a litter under a heavy fire. Upon examination of the pockets of his coat were found, in that of the left side, his Book of Common Prayer for the service of the P. E. Church, and in the right pocket four copies of the Rev. Dr. Quintard's little work, entitled 'Balm for the Weary and the Wounded.' Upon the fly-leaves of each of these little volumes, indicating for whom they were intended, was inscribed the names respectively of General Joseph E. Johnston, Lieutenant-General Hardee, and Lieutenant-General Hood, 'with the compliments of Lieutenant-General Leonidas Polk—June 12th, 1864.' Within the fourth volume was inscribed his own name. All were saturated with the blood which flowed from the wound."

Of many Christians who fell and died on the field of battle no record of their dying testimony for Christ remains; but from others, who survived their wounds a short time, we have assurance that God can make the death of the soldier not only peaceful, but triumphant. Maj. Pickens B. Bird, of Florida, was wounded, and died in a hospital near Richmond. When ordered to Virginia he said: "I never expect to see home again." In the first fight he engaged in after reaching the lines near Richmond he fell mortally wounded. When told that he must die, he said: "But for leaving my wife and children, I should not feel sad at the prospect of dying. There is no cloud," he said, "between me and God now." A little while before he died he tried to sing, "Jesus can make a dying bed," &c., but his strength failed him. Resting a few moments, he said: "Jesus *can* make a dying bed feel soft as downy pillows are."

The constant movements of the armies in all sections of the South at this period of the war greatly interfered with the work of the revival; but still the fire burned, and often on the outer lines the most delightful meetings were held in which many gave their hearts to God. A writer from the Army of Tennessee said:

"There will be more Christians under the leadership of General Johnston in the next great battle than have ever faced the foe in this army." And he adds: "Some of the happiest men I have ever seen were in the battle of Resaca."

A devoted captain said, when advancing to meet the enemy:

"'I believe God will take care of me; but should he

see fit to take me I am prepared.' Another: 'If I am killed write to my wife, I am prepared—to raise my children 'in the nurture and admonition of the Lord,' and to meet me in heaven.' One, while suffering greatly of a wound, said: 'I am ready to die.' A noble Tennessean died shouting the praises of God on the gory battle-field. It is thus that many of our devoted soldiers feel and die. May the mantles of these Christian warriors fall upon their companions in arms."

Along the lines in front of Petersburg, after General Grant had crossed the James and taken position on the south side, the meetings were resumed with great interest and success. "I held a prayer-meeting," says Rev. G. W. Yarbrough, "in our brigade (Wofford's Georgia) the night after my arrival here, and preached to the same command last Sabbath. It affords me pleasure to report that the revival fire kindled a few months ago in our camps has burned along the march of our victorious troops. Some who shook hands with me at our last sacramental meeting, two night before the second Wilderness battle, have left the shouts of their conquering comrades to join in celebrating a grander triumph. Others remain with their armor buckled about them more tightly than ever to illustrate, amid the increasing hardships and trials of this struggle, the power of our holy religion."

Rev. A. W. Smith, of the 25th Tennessee regiment, wrote from the lines below Richmond:

"We have in progress one of the best revivals I ever saw. Twenty-four have already professed religion and joined the Church, and fifty and sixty mourners are at the altar at every hour's service, and great interest is manifested by all. Brothers Taylor, Godby, and White, of Lexington, Va., Carter's battery, have labored with with great zeal and effect."

Rev. L. R. Redding reported from the lines near Atlanta: "A most gracious revival is in progress in Gist's bri gade. We have built a bush-arbor in rear of our line of battle, where we have services twice a day. Up to the present writing (July 18th) twenty-five have joined the Church, and penitents by the score are found nightly at the altar. In other portions of the army chaplains and missionaries report sweeping revivals in progress. Thus, notwithstanding the booming of cannon and bursting of shell, the good work goes bravely on."

Rev. J. B. McFerrin wrote from Atlanta to the *Southern Christian Advocate:*

"The other day I rode to the line of battle to see the soldiers as they were resting in a shady wood. To my great joy, a young captain whom I had baptized in his infancy approached me and said: 'I wish to join the Church, and I wish you to give me a certificate; the Lord has converted me.' I gave him the document with a glad heart. 'Now,' said he, 'if I fall in battle, let my mother know of this transaction. It will afford her great joy.' Oh, it was good to be there and feel that God was in that place.

"Yesterday I baptized Col. T., of Tennessee. He is a lawyer and a statesman, and has been in the army from the beginning of the struggle. He became interested on the subject of religion months ago, sought Christ, found the pearl of great price, united with the Church, was baptized in the name of the Holy Trinity, and now sends home his letter to have his name recorded with his wife's on the Church Register, and I trust it is inscribed in the book of life."

Rev. Neil Gillis, writing to the same paper, from camp on the Chattahoochee, said:

"I never heard or read of anything like the revival at this place. The conversions were powerful, and some of them very remarkable. One man told me that he was converted at the very hour in which his sister was writing him a letter on her knees praying that he might be saved at that moment. Another, who was a backslider, said to me at the altar that his case was hopeless. I tried to encourage him; discovered hope spring up in his countenance; then commenced to repeat such promises in the Scriptures as I could remember, and while I repeated: 'Believe on the Lord Jesus Christ, and thou shalt be saved,' he bounded to his feet and began to point others to the Cross with most remarkable success."

Not only in the army at home did our soldiers manifest the deepest interest in religion, but even in the dreary prisons of the North they prayed for and received the Divine blessing. An officer at Johnson's Island writes to the *Southern Presbyterian:*

"This is the last quarter of a long, long twelve-months' confinement. I try to pass my time as profitably as I can. We have preaching regularly every Sabbath, prayer-meetings two or three times a week, and worship in my room every night. We also have a Young Men's Christian Association, Masonic meetings, etc. I attend all of these and fill out the rest of my time by reading the Bible. We have had some precious religious times. There have been about one hundred conversions; colonels, majors, captains, and lieutenants, being among the number."

A lieutenant writes thus: "I am glad to state that I am a better man than when you saw me last. There are about two thousand officers here, and I never have seen so great a change in the morals of any set of men as has been here in the last four months."

The incidents of the campaign for this season are rich in spiritual fruits. In hospital and on the open field the Christian soldiers met death bravely. Said a young Kentuckian to a minister who asked him, "Do you think you will recover?" "No," said he, "tell my brother that I died in a holy cause, and am ready to meet God." It is now, in times of great peace, a matter of wonder how men could calmly worship under the fire of formidable batteries. "Late one afternoon," says Rev. C. W.

Miller, writing of the scenes on the retreat from Dalton, "the firing along the line had lulled, and the writer called the brigade together for worship. A chapter from the Holy Book had been read, a song sung, and several fervent prayers offered. Presently, while a soldier was praying, and all were devoutly kneeling before God, a distant report as of the discharge of artillery was heard; then in an instant *whirr, whirr, whirr—boom!* went a 32-pound shell just above our heads, and buried its fragments in the hillside a little beyond us. But the 'devout soldier' prayed on. Another and another shell *shrieked* above us, but the prayer was regularly finished, the preacher pronounced the benediction, and the men went to their *casemates*, as they called their holes in the ground. I have related this incident to show you how indifferent men become to danger under the indurating influence of war."

It is a pleasing fact to remember that the Federal prisoners were not neglected by our faithful ministers.

"We have seen," says an eye witness, "a group of wounded Federal soldiers, with broken arms, shattered legs, and bleeding sides, solemnly engaged in prayer, the missionary leading their devotions; and while he invoked God's mercy the big tear would glisten in the eye or roll down the bronzed cheek. Then we exclaimed,— 'It is a faithful saying, and worthy of all acceptation, that Christ Jesus came into the world to save sinners: and that God is no respecter of persons.' Thank God for a gospel that offers salvation to every son of Adam."

It is even now a source of pleasure to recall the scenes in war-days when the eager men gathered to hear the Word. A chaplain thus describes a scene in which he was the chief actor:

"Under the shadow of one of those beautiful forests of oak (alas! they have all been destroyed) that surrounded the little village, in silence and solemnity the soldiers gathered together. Generally, they waited until I had chosen my position; and then, without any formality, but without the slightest levity, they took their seats on their oil-cloths or blankets, against the trees, on projecting roots or rude stools, or on anything that would be a protection from the damp earth—some even taking off their coats or hats to sit on. Nor did they sit as in churches at home (for surely that was a church and a fit temple likewise), only in front of the speaker; but crowding near him and all around him, and near one another, they seemed to think that there was influence and warmth in contact, and that the words of the speaker would become cold were they at any distance. My gravity was very nearly upset, my lips twitched, when a kind-hearted brother (I hope he will excuse this) spoke quite authoritatively to his comrades, 'Stand back, boys, give the young man *walking* room; he can't *shout*.' Not being one of the 'shouting' sort, I didn't need perhaps as much space; but I was always obliged for 'walking room.'"

Let not the skeptical reader think that the religion of such worshippers was without depth and power. Many of them were, it is true, plain, unlettered men, but in sincerity and faith they have hardly ever been surpassed. "Can I do anything for you?" said a missionary, kneeling by a dying soldier. "Yes; write to my wife," was the feeble reply. "What shall I write?" In a whisper he replied, "Say to my dear wife it's all right." The words were written down. "What more shall I write?" said the minister. "Nothing else—all's right," and then he died. He was converted in the army.

Out in an old stable lay a number of wounded men. Among them was a man whose head was frosted with years. The minister approached him and said, "My friend, you are an old man. Do you enjoy the comforts of religion?" "O yes," replied the poor fellow, "I have been a member of the Church for 25 years. Often in our little church at home the minister told us that religion was good under all circumstances, and now I have found his words true, for even here in this old stable, with my leg amputated and surrounded by the dead and dying, I am just as happy as I can be—religion is good even here, and I want you to tell the people so when you preach to them."

The following touching scene is described by Rev. J. A. Parker, who labored as an army chaplain. He was conveying a number of wounded soldiers by water to the hospitals at Mobile :

"At two o'clock in the morning we started in a skiff for the city. The wind was high and the water rough. Poor wounded men, how they suffered the pangs of thirst, with no water save that from the bay. A young soldier, whom I had promised to convey to the city, lay senseless the most of the morning. About midday he roused up and asked, 'How far?' 'In sight of the city,' said I. After lying quiet awhile, he asked why it was so dark. I told him it was not dark—that it was light and I could see the city, and that we would soon relieve him of the rough sailing and make him comfortable. I then left him and went to the other end of the boat to use an oar, for we were drifting. He soon asked for the preacher, and I returned to him. He called for water, which I dipped in a tin-cup from the bay and gave him. After drinking, he asked to be sheltered from the sun. This we could not do, but we encouraged him by our approach to the city. 'Yes,' he replied, 'shut my eyes and let me go to the city. I am going home—almost there.' He closed his eyes and died."

A writer in the *Christian Sun* gives a touching scene in which a Christian soldier met his death :

"On the lines near Petersburg, Va., on a beautiful morning in the last days of summer, a young soldier, connected with a Georgia regiment, might have been seen seated in a ravine, and at the mouth of a bomb-proof, which had been made in the side of the hill, reading carefully the word of God. This young man had come to be regarded the model man of the regiment for morality and devout piety. He entered the army at the commencement of the war a Christian, and maintained his reputation untarnished through all the immoralities of camp-life, daily becoming more devout and more Christ-like in his spirit and conversation. He was, in person, well formed, yet not very robust, his hair rather dark, and his eyes a deep blue, with a very light beard. In manners he was as gentle as a woman, yet his comrades assured me that in battle he was as bold as a lion and as brave as the bravest. The Bible from which he was reading on the morning referred to was the gift of a pious mother on entering the service. He had carefully preserved it through all the weary marches and hard-fought battles in which his regiment had participated, and a mother's prayers had followed with it wherever he went. While intently reading, and so absorbed as not even to hear for the moment the bursting mortar-shells around him, a comrade came running to tell him that a special friend of his own company had been killed in the trenches by the bursting of a shell among them. He closed his Bible, and clenching it in his hand, ran to the place where his friend lay dead. Just as he arrived at the spot, and his eyes rested on the mangled form, a parrot-shell came whizzing, and exploding in the immediate vicinity, he was struck on the head and instantly killed. He fell on the body of his lifeless comrade, still clasping his Bible, even in death holding on to the Word of Life."

The amazing labor of the armies in Virginia and Georgia, the two most important points of military operations at this period, did not abate the religious ardor of the soldiers. In a letter from the lines in front of Atlanta the Rev. S. M. Cherry gives an account of the scenes he witnessed on a Sabbath day:

"At 9 A. M. I reached the Missouri brigade of Gen.

French's division, and found the soldiers gathering for prayer-meeting. At 11 o'clock brother Bounds was to preach the funeral sermon of Rev. Mr. Manning, a pious young minister of the Cumberland Presbyterian Church, recently appointed chaplain of a Missouri regiment, but before he received his commission he was killed in battle while in the discharge of his duties as an officer of the line. As I approached Sears' Mississippi brigade I saw a group of soldiers, with uncovered heads, bowing beside a row of new-made graves, two of which contained the forms of comrades now being consigned to the cold clay. Chaplain Lattimore was engaged in prayer. I joined in the solemn burial services of the soldiers slain in the strife of Saturday."

Next he came to the brigades of Ector, McNair, and Gholson:

"I looked around for a suitable place for preaching. A central point to the three commands was selected, but not a single tree or shrub was to be found to screen us from the intense heat of an August sun. Soon the singing collected a large congregation of attentive soldiers. A caisson served for a pulpit, while the cannon, open-mouthed, stood in front of the foe. We were in full range and in open view of the enemy, but not a single shell or minnie-ball was heard hissing or hurtling near during the hour's service. The soldiers sat on the ground, beneath the burning sun, listening seriously to the words of life. At the close of the sermon they crowded up to get Testaments and papers. I regretted much that I could only furnish five of the former to a regiment."

"On Friday an intellectual young officer came forward and joined the Church. The day following he was killed in a skirmish with the enemy. During the service in Sears' brigade there was a sharp skirmish in the front of that command, and the pickets were so closely pressed that the officer in command of the brigade sent a reinforcement to their support immediately after he returned from church. A continuous cannonade to the left did not interrupt the service. Strange to see soldiers in the line of trenches, with a sharp fire in their front, and a rapid roar of artillery on their flank, and a shower over head, yet quietly sitting or patiently standing to hear the preaching of the gospel!"

Amidst the scenes Mr. Cherry passed a wounded soldier who called him and said with joy, "I am all right, sir; I thank God for it. For two years I have not seen a dark day. *I cannot doubt now.* I will meet my old mother in heaven. I am mortally wounded." "One ball had broken his arm and passed through his lungs—another had passed through his thigh—and yet he lay without uttering a groan, and talked pleasantly with his friends, and was happy in prospect of death."

On this Sabbath, in one division, eight sermons were preached in full sight of the Federal lines, and even within range of small arms. Among the Missourians who held an exposed position the revival went on with power, and sixty joined the Church during the week.

Let us now for a moment leave these noble Christian soldiers, in their happy meetings under the fire of musketry and cannon, and look in upon their comrades who languished in Northern prisons. We have before us a letter, written from Fort Delaware to the *Christian Observer*, giving an account of a revival among the Confederate officers there confined. They had in the morning at half-past nine an "inquirer's prayer-meeting;" at 12 M. "the professor's prayer-meeting, where the Church-members pray for each other, leading the meeting in turn."

"It was a new business to me," says the writer, "when my turn came, but you must know I am preparing for the work and must learn. God's help enabled me to get along tolerably well. He always fits the instrument for his work.

"We get a mail daily, morning papers at noon, and

boxes of nic-nacks come promptly when our friends start them. All the officers here (and there are about 600) seem to be in good health and spirits. The general health of all on the Island is good, considering the number of privates (6,000) confined here. All seem to enjoy themselves; and, altogether, there are worse prisons than Fort Delaware. We have a large lot to play in. We have here in our barracks three ministers—Rev. Dr. Handy, of the Presbyterian Church of Portsmouth, Va.; and Capt. Harris of Georgia and Capt. Samford of Texas, local Methodist preachers. A revival of religion has been in progress for two weeks—17 converts, many backsliders reclaimed, and a refreshing season to old professors, numbering 150 reported names. These are among the results of the revival."

We have looked into Fort Delaware and other Northern prisons, where thousands of Confederates suffered, languished, and died. Let us look into Andersonville, where Federal prisoners felt the horrors of confinement. A writer, who had visited this prison, says:

"There were, at the time I left, 28,000 to 30,000 prisoners in the stockade, and, I presume by this time, they have had many added from the front at Atlanta.

"The mortality amongst them was very great. I visited the cemetery on Sunday week and they had buried thirty-five on that day, and on Friday before they buried seventy. Up to the time I left I think they had buried near 4,500—at least, so the burial party told me.

"I have heard much said about the condition of the prisoners there, and much commiseration expressed for them; but, I failed to see any brutality exhibited towards them. They have the same rations that our brave troops receive; and, as for their being exposed, they are not more so than our own brave men in Northern Georgia and Virginia. The only difference is, that they are confined to a limited space and are restrained in their movements. The whole space of 24 acres is covered by huts they have built—some of blankets, others of old tents, oil-cloths, pine-straw, earth, etc., and some of boards. There is also a sutler appointed by the government, who sells them vegetables, fruits, eggs, or anything else he can procure, except munitions of war and liquor."

The same writer states a remarkable fact connected with the history of this prison, which we do not remember having seen before, and the correctness of which we have no means of confirming:

"The Federals," he says, "have established in the interior of the prison a court of justice, where all criminal offences are tried. The Friday before I arrived there they hanged six of their number, who were tried, found guilty, and condemned by the court to suffer death for their crimes against their fellow-prisoners. They sent to the commandant of the prison for tools and materials to build the scaffold, and the rope to hang them with; and they then proceeded to execute the sentence of the court with all the decorum and solemnity that would have been observed by our own people."

It is certainly strange that the officers in charge of this prison should have allowed such a court to be established by the prisoners; but in war, which is a dreadful trade, we are met on all sides by scenes that would shock us terribly in times of peace.

In the far Southwest the great revival influence, already noticed by Dr. Kavanaugh, was felt among the soldiers with great power. In two brigades there were over five hundred conversions. The scenes were much like those witnessed sixty or seventy years ago. Dr. K. says in his report:

"Wicked men come into the congregation, or into the outskirts of it, and are suddenly stricken down and fall to the earth, and remain for hours speechless and apparently unconscious. Some of their friends became alarmed for them and spoke of running for the doctor. But old Bro. Talbott happened to be experienced enough to know something about such cases, and told the bystanders to give themselves no uneasiness, for it would all come out right in the end. Generally they would lie about two hours, and then rise shouting the praises of God their Saviour. There have been several cases of this kind.

"All the conversions are sound, clear, and powerful. There is no such thing as urging the mourner to believe he "has received the blessing;" but each is able to tell, for himself, what great things God has done for him. Conversions take place at all hours through the day and night. Many are converted in the woods—sometimes alone, and sometimes with a friend or two. There is no abatement in the work as yet, but our meetings are kept up to a late hour every night. Off at a little distance you can hear singing, praising, and praying, all going on at various points throughout the two brigades, very much resembling a very large camp-meeting in olden times, when there was much more zeal and power manifested than is now known in like meetings."

At Atlanta the Confederates, now commanded by Gen. Hood, held that city against the heavy battalions of Gen. Sherman. The fights along the lines were frequent and deadly, but the religious enthusiasm of the soldiers was undiminished.

"They are not afraid of death," writes a devoted chaplain, A. D. McVoy, "and are ready to die when God calls them."

Among those brought in wounded from the front lines there were many Christians whose deaths were morally grand.

"I witnessed," says Mr. McVoy, "the passing away of a Louisianian of Gibson's brigade, 4th La., the other day. Seldom have I seen a stronger Christian faith, a firmer reliance on God, and a clearer assurance of salvation in a dying hour. He was cruelly lacerated by a piece of shell that had ploughed deeply across his right side, and his sufferings were intense and unremitted. Still his mind was fixed upon God. 'Chaplain,' said he to me, 'I am dying. I have done my duty. I wish I could be spared to see victory secured to my brave comrades, but it is the will of God, and I cheerfully submit. I am suffering a thousand deaths, but when I think upon the sufferings of my Saviour, that he endured ten thousands more than I for the salvation of my soul, my sufferings are nothing.' Then he would fervently pray, and besought me to pray with him, which I did. This comforted him greatly, so that he almost shouted for joy. 'Chaplain,' said he, 'I have three motherless children in Louisiana, and could I only gaze once more upon them, could I but fold them to my breast, could I but kiss them good-bye, I would die contented; but God's will be done. I commit them into the hands of my Heavenly Father. I want them instructed to know and serve God that they may meet me in heaven.'

"One of his companions, who had brought him out of the trenches, was kneeling over him and weeping bitterly. 'Chaplain,' said the dying soldier, 'this is the best friend I have in the army; pray for him that he may meet me in heaven.'

"When asked what word he desired to leave with his company, he said, 'Tell them to be better boys. Some of them are reckless and wicked. Tell them to repent, serve God, be good soldiers, and meet me in heaven.'

"When asked how he felt in view of death, he said, 'I have no fears; all is clear. Jesus died for me; I know he will save me. Blessed be the Lord.' His Colonel passing by, came to his side and said, 'Is this you, Dawson? I am sorry to find you so dreadfully wounded?' 'Yes, Colonel, I am dying, but I am going home to heaven. I have tried to do my duty. It is God's will, and I cheerfully give myself up a sacrifice on the altar of my country.'

"He then committed himself to God and lingered for

some hours, continually praying and praising God, when he died the glorious death of a brave Christian soldier."

Writing further of the glorious work the same faithful laborer says:

"Many are joining the Church. While exhorting a large group of soldiers a few nights since to come to Christ a young man rushed forward and threw his arms around my neck, crying out, 'I have found Jesus, I have found Jesus! Oh, how good my Saviour is! Bless the Lord, O my soul!' This was a very affecting scene, and induced many to think seriously concerning their souls.

"Thus the work of God is going on amid the cannon's roar, the fatiguing monotony of the trenches, and the heroic movements of the picket line. Religion is infusing a spirit of fortitude, endurance, and determination, into the hearts of the soldiers that no hardship, no suffering, can undermine or break down."

Bishop Lay, of the P. E. Church, in a letter to a relative in Charleston, S. C., describes a scene of the deepest interest in the same army. The Bishop was earnestly laboring as a missionary in the Georgia army. He says:

"Yesterday, in Strahl's brigade, I preached and confirmed nine persons. Last night we had a very solemn service in Gen. Hood's room, some forty persons, chiefly Generals and Staff Officers, being present. I confirmed Gen. Hood and one of his Aids, Capt. Gordon of Savannah, and a young Lieutenant from Arkansas. The service was animated, the praying good. Shells exploded near by all the time. Gen. Hood, unable to kneel, supported himself on his crutch and staff, and with bowed head received the benediction. Next Sunday I am to administer the communion at headquarters. To-night ten or twelve are to be confirmed in Clayton's division. The enemy there are within two hundred and fifty yards of our line, and the firing is very constant. I fear it may be hard to get the men together. I wish that you could have been present last night, and have seen that company down, all upon bended knee. The reverence was so marked that one could not fail to thank God that he has put such a spirit into the hearts of our leaders."

In the Virginia army now collected in its main strength on the long lines of defence around Richmond and Petersburg, the work of grace was not less powerful than in Georgia and beyond the Mississippi. But near the close of July the usual course of the soldier's life on these lines was broken suddenly by an event terrible even in the midst of war.

For many days the Confederates were impressed with the belief that the Federals were engaged in mining towards their works at certain points, but the exact location of the main operations could not be ascertained. All doubts on the subject were soon put to flight. On Saturday, July 30, about 4 o'clock in the morning, a dull, heavy sound was heard, followed by several others similar, and at the same moment the Federal batteries opened a furious cannonade. It was soon found that a mine had been sprung under one of the salients on our lines and not far from the centre of the defences.

Orders were sent to Gen. Mahone to cover the threatened point, and that officer moved promptly with his own Virginia brigade, and instructed Saunders' Alabama and Wright's Georgia brigades to follow. On reaching the ground twelve Federal flags were seen waving from that part of our line which had been carried in the explosion, and the whole place swarmed with Federal troops, white and black. As the Confederates formed into line, and were about to move forward, the Federals rushed out for a charge. Our men held their fire until they came quite near, and then poured in such a storm of bullets that the whole mass fell back in disorder. Then the Confederates charged in turn, and, rushing forward, drove the Federals up to and over the breastworks, from the top of which they delivered a plunging fire that completed the confusion of the enemy.

But the bloody work was not done. Only a part of the lost line had been recovered. Saunders' brigade was ordered up to retake the remaining lines; and, after a splendid charge, every inch of lost ground was regained.

"The enemy," says a writer from the scene, "made but slight resistance to this charge. The chasm caused by the enemy's explosion appears to be about 40 feet in depth, and some 200 feet in circumference, and resembles what one would imagine to have been the effects of a terrible earthquake. Immense boulders of earth were piled up rudely one above the other, and great fragments of bomb-proofs, gun-carriages, limbers, etc., were lying promiscuously in every direction. One man was caught between two boulders near the surface of the ground and literally crushed between them. He still remained in this painful position, with only his head and neck visible, our men not having had the time to extricate him. Life had long been extinct."

The crater made by the explosion of the mine presented a ghastly spectacle. It was lined with mangled bodies that lay in every conceivable position. The sudden and terrible explosion produced a temporary confusion in the Confederate ranks, and if a heavy column had been pushed through the chasm the result might have been most disastrous; but the prompt and gallant resistance of the Confederates changed the whole aspect of the affair.

The loss of the South was heavy in this battle, and Virginia mourned the death of some of her bravest children. Petersburg sustained a severe loss, as numbers of her best young men were in Mahone's troops; and many a household mourned a hero son who nobly died for his country.

The Federals opened a heavy fire from their siege-guns on the city immediately after the explosion of the mine, and for two hours the shells rained down upon the streets and houses; but in the mercy of God no one was killed. One citizen lost a finger, which was cut off by the fragment of a shell.

This day's work is known in the history of the war as "The Battle of the Crater."

CHAPTER XXIV.

AUTUMN AND WINTER OF 1864–'65.

THE condition of the armies in the East and South west was not specially favorable to the revival at the close of the summer.

At Petersburg the Federals made desperate efforts to cut Gen. Lee's lines of communication with the South, but were foiled by the activity of the Confederates. In Georgia Gen. Hood was forced to abandon the city of Atlanta, and Gen. Sherman entered and made it the starting point of his famous "March to the Sea." In East Tennessee, at Greenville, the gallant cavalry-leader, Gen. Morgan, met his death under most painful circumstances. Finding the house in which he slept was surrounded by Federal troops, he sprang from his bed exclaiming to his staff, "We must not be captured!" He escaped to another dwelling-house, but the person living in it called to the Federals that Gen. Morgan was in the house. He ran out, and in passing through a vineyard was shot down and killed. His body was delivered to his staff, and a permit given to send it into the Confederate lines. Thus died a noble and heroic soldier.

The constant activity in the army in Georgia hindered to some degree the progress of the revival, but every lull in the storm of battle was made use of by the chaplains and missionaries.

Dr. McFerrin says:

"Meetings have been frequently held when the soldiers were in line of battle. The religious interest I think has not at all abated since our great revival in the winter and spring. Hundreds in many parts of the army are seeking the fellowship of Christians by uniting with the Church of the Lord Jesus Christ."

A writer from the 13th Mississippi regiment, stationed in the Valley of Virginia, says:

"The spiritual condition of the brigade is truly encouraging. We had an excellent prayer-meeting last night. The Spirit was in our midst. Some fifteen or twenty penitents presented themselves for prayer. We have religious services of some kind almost every night. Sixteen have been received into the Church this month; yet we have been almost continually on the march, not having remained so long as three days at any one camp. As far as my observation goes, about the same state of religion exists in the other brigades of this army. A great work is surely going on. May it continue until the uttermost parts of earth feel the gracious influence. Dr. Stiles says, 'The way to convert a nation is to convert its army.' If our army is a body of Christians, when the clash of arms and the din of war shall have hushed in our borders, and they be scattered broadcast over the land, they will be to our country as the 'salt of the earth,' preserving it, giving us a moral and religious character that will make us a nation that can truly be called the people of God."

It is a fact over which we may rejoice that out of the Southern armies did come many earnest Christians who have been "the salt of the earth." In all the Churches there are now ministers who found the Lord in the midst of war, and when they laid down the sword of the flesh took up the sword of the Spirit, and are now valiant leaders in the hosts of King Immanuel. And there are thousands of zealous and useful laymen who, in the blessed scenes of the army revival, in the log church, or under the spreading trees on the bare ground, and in the hospital, gave themselves to God in a perpetual covenant. The Army Revival gave to the South multitudes of faithful men, and they are now in all the Churches the living proofs of its genuineness and power.

In this, as in the earlier years of the war, the dying testimony of Christian soldiers was of the greatest value in impressing the minds of their unconverted comrades.

A soldier on the lines near Petersburg wrote home to his wife, "Grieve not for me. I am all right. My trust is in God, and I know it is well-founded. If we meet no more on earth, let us meet in heaven." Not long after, while sitting in his tent answering a letter from his wife, he was killed by the bullet of a sharpshooter.

A gallant Georgia soldier, just before going into his last battle, said to his comrades, "I may fall, but I fear not death."

Lieut. Carpenter, of Gen. Morgan's command, when dying near Lexington, Ky., "prayed, sang, wept, and shouted glory! glory!"

These are but samples of the death-bed scenes of our war-times. Thousands upon thousands went up on high with the shout of victory on their dying lips.

In this connection we give the reader a view of what was called by our suffering prisoners at Johnson's Island "an exchange." "Asa Hartz," a Confederate officer confined there, in a letter to a friend gives this touching picture:

"We vary our monotony with an occasional exchange. May I tell you what I mean by that? Well, it is a simple ceremony. God help us! The 'exchanged' is placed on a small wagon drawn by one horse, his friends form a line in the rear, and the procession moves; then passing through the gate, it winds its way slowly round the prison-walls to a little grove north of the enclosure; the 'exchange' is taken out of the wagon and lowered into the earth—a prayer—an exhortation—a spade—a headboard—a mound of fresh sod—and the friends return to prison again—and that's all of it. Our friend is 'exchanged;' a grave attests the fact to mortal eyes, and one of God's angels has recorded the 'exchange' in the book above. Time and the elements will soon smooth down the little hillock which marks his lonely bed, but invisible friends will hover around it till the dawn of that great day when all the armies shall be marshalled into line again—when the wars of time shall cease and the great eternity of peace shall commence."

The Missions of the different Churches to the Southern armies was a work which, as we have seen, was attended by heaven's richest blessings.

In the report made by Bishop Pierce to the Conferences of the M. E. Church, South, of their part in this labor of love, he says:

"The importance of our missionary work in the army cannot well be exaggerated. Measurably shut out, as the Church is, from other fruitful missionary fields, the Providence and Spirit of God have opened to it here a field where the harvest is white, and where it only needs a wise disposition of laborers to insure an abundant ingathering of souls. We have considered how best we may make such a disposition of our means and labors in this field as to secure the advancement of God's kingdom and the promotion of his glory."

The men sent forth into this field were found in every part of the South where men stood in arms. Even in beleaguered Charleston, where shells rained down for many months in the streets and on the houses, the faithful missionaries called the suffering but heroic soldiers to the hopes and blessings of the Cross.

A writer from that city tells of the terrible bombardment and the merciful preservation of the people under the good hand of God:

"On Thursday evening three guns were opened simultaneously upon the devoted city, and in five hours one hundred and ten shots were made in rapid and awful succession. It was a tempest of whizzing, screaming bolts of destruction, agitating the air and reverberating in their earthquake explosions as though the infuriated demons of the bottomless pit had been turned loose upon us! For some days the bombardment continued most vehemently, but it gradually subsided in temper and in rage, until now we hear the explosions in the lower portions of the city among the deserted and inoffensive buildings, recalling the normal state of the siege. The shells fell all around me—one striking opposite, a little over one hundred yards, and another two doors from my residence. Sitting in my parlor, I could smell the 'villainous salt-petre' when the explosion occurred. The proximity was not pleasant, particularly at night when one was disposed, in a somewhat nervous condition, to yield to

"Tired Nature's sweet restorer, balmy sleep."

"These messengers of death have been passing thick and fast among the inhabitants of the city, tearing up the streets; cutting gas-pipes and plunging us into darkness; thundering against churches and dwellings, and creating generally a great tumult; but, how few of the citizens have been harmed in their persons! Yet, what hair-breadth escapes have been made!

"I saw, but a few days since, the interior of a gentleman's residence which a shell had entered; cutting the tester and passing through the pavilion of his bed, it penetrated the opposite wall and lodged in the adjoining room. Both himself and his wife were in the house at the time and he remains there still. In another instance a similar missile entered a chamber, and passing between the slabs and bed-clothes of a crib in which an infant was lying, left the little creature unhurt, but lost in the convolutions of its bedding!"

The desolation of this once beautiful city was painful to behold at this period of the war. The writer just quoted thus describes the scene:

"Passing through the lower wards of the city, you would be particularly struck with two things: First, the sad desolation. The elegant mansions and familiar thoroughfares, once rejoicing in wealth and refinement and the theatre of busy life—the well-known and fondly-cherished churches, some of them ancient landmarks, where large assemblies were wont to bow at holy altars, and spacious halls that once blazed with light and rang with festal songs, are all deserted, sombre and cheerless; and this is enhanced by the forbidding aspect of that vast district of the city which was laid in ashes three years ago, and which remains in unmolested ruins as the monument of Charleston's long and dreary pause in the grand march of improvement. Here you perceive her humiliation."

The movements of the army under Gen. Hood were so rapid at this season that there was but little opportunity to conduct religious services. While that army lay near Tuscumbia, Ala., Rev. J. B. McFerrin wrote to the *Southern Christian Advocate* giving a sad picture of the results of the war to a once rich and beautiful country:

"The beautiful Valley of Tennessee is almost a waste. From Decatur to Tuscumbia there are but few plantations near the main road which have not been desolated. Many beautiful mansions, with out-houses, cotton-gins, barns, stables, and negro cabins, have been burned. Churches have been committed to the flames, and old La Grange College is laid in ashes. You can scarcely imagine the ruin and devastation that everywhere meet the eye. Now the people, once rich and prosperous, have scarcely bread to eat.

"What our future movement will be I cannot foretell. There are various conjectures; some guess one point and some another; all are in good spirits and hope for some grand result from this extraordinary campaign of Gen. Hood. Time will prove the wisdom of the move; or, if a failure, no one doubts that it is a bold and extraordinary measure to check the enemy. Such has been the rapidity of our marches that we have had scarcely any opportunity for religious services. Many of the chaplains and missionaries accompany the troops and preach when circumstances justify it. At Jacksonville, Ala., we had an interesting season; we had preaching several nights in succession; several penitents at the altar, and four were added to the Church. Except a short detention there, we have been on the march almost constantly since the middle of September. When the army goes into winter quarters, if we can have convenient places for worship, we expect a rich harvest of souls."

The marches and privations of this army were really wonderful, and yet were endured with the greatest heroism. In one month the marching averaged twelve miles a day, and the whole distance traversed within thirty days was over four hundred miles. And yet these noble men were longing for the days of peace to come again. "I trust," says one writing from Hood's army, "that peace begins to dawn even from to-day. The Northern election is over, and God grant that it may bring peace to our distracted country."

Gen. Hood having moved his army from the vicinity of Atlanta, Gen. Sherman made preparations for his famous march from that city to the Atlantic Coast. In passing through Georgia, the country was laid waste in a track from twenty to thirty miles wide. All kinds of stock were killed, and a great deal left on the ground. Provisions of every kind for man and beast were taken; all means of transportation were destroyed; and many houses were burned, while in others the furniture was ruthlessly broken to pieces. Gen. Sherman in his march proved his own declaration that "war is cruelty."

The discipline of war was terrible to the people of the South, but in the end it was beneficial. In the midst of desolation and blood they turned their thoughts to Him who holds in his hands the destinies of nations, and out of great sufferings the patience and faith of the gospel shone forth in brightness and power.

The incidents of General Sherman's march were often painful to the last degree. From multitudes of people the last morsel of bread was taken, and in some instances delicate women were pushed to the verge of starvation.

A soldier writing to his father recites a peculiar case of suffering. While on detached service in South Carolina he, with several other soldiers, was hospitably entertained by an elegant young lady, who received them in the parlor and gave them a sumptuous meal. "One of the number passing the same road, after Sherman's hordes had passed over the country, found the same young lady in a hut living on parched corn. He gave her all the provisions his haversack contained. When she received them she burst into tears saying she never would breathe a prayer to heaven but what he should be remembered."

A writer from the scene of devastation in Georgia says:

"They spread desolation broadcast, taking everything in their way in the breadth of about twenty miles. Corn, fodder, meal, flour, horses, mules, hogs, cattle, sheep, poultry of every description, servants that could be enticed and forced off, and these in great numbers."

Strange as it may seem, in the midst of such visitations, the hearts of many were softened and turned to God.

An observant writer said at this period of the struggle:

"The privations, sufferings, and bereavements produced by the war have prepared the minds of thousands to read and understand the Holy Scriptures as they never understood them before. They are studying the sacred volume, the history of ancient wars, and the prophetical books of the Bible, with new interest, and learning that it is God who has 'made desolations in the earth,' and who also 'maketh wars to cease unto the end thereof.'"

We have referred to scenes in the prisons North and South where thousands languished and died. In Richmond was a prison noted over the whole country. We refer to "The Libby." Here were confined many hundreds of Northern soldiers; to them the gospel was preached by Southern ministers, and may we not hope that some at least found the peace of God in the midst of war? The writer himself had the privilege of offering spiritual consolation to Federal soldiers, sick, wounded, and dying, and he rejoices to believe that not a few rested their souls in the last trying hour upon the merits of Christ.

The following testimony comes from one who was personally engaged in the blessed work of leading soldiers on both sides to the fountain of life:

"In Richmond the Rev. Dr. Woodbridge, of the Protestant Episcopal Church, and family (and this was true of other clergymen), were found ready to furnish books, papers, etc., to abate the rigors of prison-life to Federal soldiers in the Libby. One of the chaplains relinquished his other work and devoted himself to visiting and preaching to the officers and soldiers and to ministering to their wants. This was followed up by frequent visits and ministrations of various kinds; and it is said that all the supplies sent from the North to the prisoners of war were brought about by a chaplain in a North Carolina regiment.

"I have witnessed a scene which I wish I could photograph upon the minds of the friends of soldiers in the North. It was at the Libby prison. Thousands of soldiers were confined there. The largest upper floor was selected for religious worship. The chaplain of the 6th North Carolina regiment, who had devoted himself to this work, had gathered around him a large throng of these men. They were arranged in semi-circles; the first rows sat upon the floor, the next were on their knees, the others stood in the rear, so that all could see and hear. In the midst was the chaplain. 'Should you ever be permitted to get back to your friends and homes I wish you to tell it there that we ministers of religion in the South came to you here, not to upbraid you with invading our homes, but to comfort and cheer you in your present uncomfortable condition; and it will be my study to avoid saying anything that can be so construed as to give you pain. I stand among you as but a poor representative of the Southern people. If others were here in my place they would win your hearts by their loving words, and your minds by the wisdom of their counsels; but as it falls to my lot to address you, let me tell you the plain and simple story of Him who once came a long way and suffered much in order to speak words of life and love and hope to those who were all their lifetime in bondage through fear of death, and to break their bonds asunder and set them free; yes, and to place them in a land of peace and plenty, where there shall be no more war.' It would be impossible to recall the words spoken; but the emotions of these men as they listened to words of life and love and home amid scenes of death and war, emotions that flashed in every feature of their countenances, and the wondrous earnestness and power of their song as they all joined in when the address was ended—

"Lo! what a cloud of witnesses encompass us around:
Men once like us with suffering tried, but now with glory crowned"—

these are still fresh in my recollection. I am the only one living that witnessed that scene; Lieutenant Sceva, Captain May, and all those officers and men, are now dead."

The life of a Christian, whether in peace or war, should be a life hid with Christ in God; the death of a Christian in peace or war is but a translation to a higher life in heaven. Let us look at the proof of the power of grace as given in this period by our dying soldiers. Lieut. J. P. Duncan fell at his post near Petersburg, Va. "His last noble act was to distribute a package of tracts to his men on the subject of heaven. He stepped on a log in rear of his guns to look at the enemy's movements, and was instantly killed." William Smith Patterson, of the Palmetto Sharpshooters, was a noble soldier of Christ and of his country. Colonel Walker, his commander, wrote to his mother:

"Your son was a gallant young man, and fell bravely doing his duty in the foremost ranks while engaging the enemy. He was never found lacking in his duty either as a soldier or Christian. He was shot through the body, and died almost instantly."

"When I told her," says Dr. Whitefoord Smith, "the sad tidings, her first words were, 'Glory! glory! glory! The Lord gave, and the Lord hath taken away; blessed be the name of the Lord. I know he is safe, and I would not have him back if I could by asking.'"

Such were the mothers whose sons upheld the banner of the South.

Sergeant Alfred L. Robertson, of the 12th Georgia regiment, fell in one of the battles in the Valley of Virginia. He was a Christian from childhood. "He told me," says a friend, "as he lay dying upon the battlefield, that he knew his time had come and he was willing to go, feeling that all was bright, desiring only something to alleviate his suffering until his spirit should wing its way to the realms of the blessed."

Captain Henry F. Parks and Captain Wesley F. Parks were sons of Rev. W. J. Parks, of Georgia. The former was converted at eight years, the latter at thirteen; both entered the Confederate army and fought gallantly. Wesley died of disease—Henry by the bullet.

"When he was stricken down upon the battle-field he begged his comrades to leave him and to take care of themselves, for he felt sure that he had received his 'last furlough.' Said he, 'Tell my father and friends that I died praying.'" They were buried on the same day.

Andrew J. Peed, of the 59th Georgia, received four wounds in a charge; he lived five hours, and then fell asleep in Jesus. "Just before his death he said, 'Farewell, boys;' and he requested a fellow-soldier to tell his wife that he was ready to die, and happily ended earth's toilsome journey."

We might largely multiply such scenes, but these are enough to show the faith of our believing soldiers in the dying hour. And their testimony was not given, be it remembered, in their peaceful homes, with kind friends and kindred ministering around them, but on the blood-stained battle-field, or in the close and cheerless hospital, far from the scenes of their childhood, and often in the midst of strangers. But the Friend that sticketh closer than a brother was near, and his words were sweeter to them than even the memories of home.

In the close of this year (1864) the revival power was as great, perhaps greater, among our soldiers than at any previous period. A writer from that part of the army stationed in East Tennessee says:

"Not a meeting is held by the chaplains of the different commands but what they have large assemblies of soldiers in attendance; and when the invitation is extended to those who desire an interest in the prayers of the Christians, many are seen pressing through the crowded throng and bowing humbly on the cold, damp ground, with but the broad, blue sky for a covering What scenes—resembling so strongly the great revival periods of the early pioneer settlements. The eloquent voice of the minister, the heavy sighing of the penitent, and the deep melancholy spirit of the soldier-audience, is a scene for the artist, and one of no small moment. Not an evening passes by but what there can be seen here and there gathered together small clumps of soldiers singing sacred songs, and occasionally sending up an humble prayer to heaven. The idle jester, and he who would make light of their romantic worship, stand in awe, and refrain from saying anything that would tend to mortify or molest their feelings. How often do we hear the expression, not alone from the young, but the aged soldier, as the crowded throng disperses and they go winding their way to their respective commands, that, 'I am determined to live a better life and move in conformity with the Christian Church,' etc."

Up to January, 1865, it was estimated that nearly *one hundred and fifty thousand* soldiers had been converted during the progress of the war, and it was believed that fully one-third of all the soldiers in the field were praying men and members of some branch of the Christian Church. A large proportion of the higher officers were men of faith and prayer, and many others, though not professedly religious, were moral and respectful to all the religious services and confessed the value of the revival in promoting the efficiency of the army.

As the cloud of war in mid-winter grew thicker and darker over the Confederacy the zeal and faith of the chaplains and missionaries increased. In Petersburg, in December, a meeting was held in which Rev. Dr. Armstrong, Rev. L. C. Vass, Rev. Dr. Pryor, Rev. J. Wm. Jones, and Rev. J. C. Granbery, with other faithful laborers, participated. The object was to form an Association of Chaplains and Missionaries for the purpose of conducting more systematically the work of grace among the war-worn veterans. Dr. Armstrong preached an appropriate sermon from the words, "The entrance of thy words giveth light; it giveth understanding to the simple." They agreed to hold regular monthly meetings, and at these reports of the work in each brigade and in the hospitals were to be presented and read—all necessary measures taken to promote the cause of religion throughout the army. Along these lines of defence in the last months of the war the work of grace was powerful, and many a noble soldier pressed into the kingdom.

A soldier gives a picture of the Church in the army:

"A stranger to pass along our lines here would conclude we were a very religious people. He would see commodious churches every six or eight hundred yards. They are made of logs, of course. To save labor and heat they are three or four feet below the surface. The congregation is well and comfortably seated. Prayer-meetings are held twice generally during the week, and preaching twice on Sabbath. Young Men's Christian Associations are organized. I understand that the Association near us attached to Corse's brigade have invited many distinguished gentlemen to lecture before it this winter, and that there is a prospect of success in the worthy enterprise. The great theme will be the twin duties—Piety and Patriotism. These are noble subjects. The world furnishes many splendid illustrations for the speakers, and they will use them with effect I doubt not. Thank God, in our own short history we can furnish noble examples of both these cardinal virtues. Our cause has been already baptized in the blood of Christian patriots."

CHAPTER XXV.

SPRING OF 1865.

WE are near the end of the tremendous struggle for Southern independence.

In the last month of winter the famous Hampton Roads' Conference was held between President Lincoln and the Southern Commissioners. The only terms offered were unconditional submission to the Federal authorities, and it proved an utter failure. In Richmond gloom and anxiety filled the minds of the people. The noble army of Gen. Lee, reduced to thirty thousand men, had a line forty miles long in front of Gen. Grant, with his splendidly equipped force of a hundred and fifty thousand men. Gen. Johnston, in command of the remnant of Hood's army and portions of other forces, could count only twenty-five thousand men to confront forty thousand, flushed with victory, moving from the South under Gen. Sherman.

In the midst of disasters, and under the thickening gloom of war clouds, the people of the South lifted up their voice to Him that ruleth the nations. The President, in accordance with a resolution of the Confederate Congress, appointed the 10th day of March as a day of fasting, humiliation, and prayer, with thanksgiving. In the spirit of a Christian patriot he addressed his proclamation to the suffering people of the Confederate States:

"It is our solemn duty, at all times, and more especially in a season of public trial and adversity, to acknowledge our dependence on His mercy, and to bow in humble submission before His footstool, confessing our manifold sins, supplicating His gracious pardon, imploring His divine help, and devoutly rendering thanks for the many and great blessings which he has vouchsafed to us.

"Let the hearts of our people turn contritely and trustfully unto God; let us recognize in his chastening hand the correction of a Father, and submissively pray that the trials and sufferings which have so long borne heavily upon us may be turned away by his merciful love; that his sustaining grace be given to our people, and his Divine wisdom imparted to our rulers; that the Lord of Hosts will be with our armies, and fight for us against our enemies; and that he will graciously take our cause into his own hand and mercifully establish for us a lasting, just, and honorable peace and independence.

"And let us not forget to render unto his holy name the thanks and praise which are so justly due for his great goodness, and for the many mercies which he has extended to us amid the trials and sufferings of protracted and bloody war."

To this earnest call there came a response from all parts of the South. In the churches, in the hospitals, in the camps and in the trenches, thousands bowed in humble prayer for the blessing and mercy of God.

And, as in earlier periods of the war, many of the brightest examples of endurance and faith were found in the army. The anchor of hope held more securely as the storm increased. The serene courage and perfect trust of Christian soldiers were the richest legacies of those gloomy days. The Rev. Thomas A. Ware, of the M. E. Church, South, who labored with untiring zeal as a Chaplain in the army of Northern Virginia, gives a vivid picture of a scene after a day of blood. In the midst of the surgeon's work, as he spoke to the sufferers stretched upon the ground, his ear caught the soft murmur of prayer.

"I turned," he says, "to catch the words. I saw one form bent over another, prostrate on the grass, until the lips of the suppliant nearly touched the pale face of the sufferer. 'Oh, precious Redeemer!' he said, 'we thank thee for thy *abounding grace*, which of late brought him from the ways of folly and sin to know and love thee, and that now makes this dark hour the brightest of his life. Be thou graciously with him to the end. Mercifully pour into the hearts of his dear ones at home the balm of thy love and, sweetly resigning them to thy will, bring them all at last to meet him in heaven.' The prayer was ended. 'Amen,' murmured the faded lips. The Chaplain recognized me, and gave me an introduction to the dying man. 'I trust you are a Christian, my friend,' said I, 'and that even now you are resigned and happy.' 'Oh, yes,' he said. 'I entered the army a wicked man, but I must tell you now of the influence of a good sister. Will you please unroll my knapsack, sir, and get me a letter lying on my clothes? I wish you to read it to me. I have often read it, but *you* will be so kind as to read it to me now.' I obeyed. The touching appeal for patriotism and piety, especially the *entreaties* for the latter, couched in all the tender sentiments of a sister's love, evoked frequent ejaculations of prayer that 'God would reward and bless her forever.' 'Oh, sir.' he said, 'her precious letters have proven my salvation. Thank God for such a sister.' Soon after the manly form lay cold and stiff on the ground, and the spirit, leaving the impress of its rapture on the up-turned face, went with the angels to heaven to await the coming of its best beloved."

Not only the veterans, but the boys, died in faith and glorious hope.

"As I walked over a battle-field," says a writer, "I found an interesting boy, who was rolled in his blanket, and resting his head against a stump. He had been fearfully wounded through the lungs; his breath came painfully; and his broken arm hung helplessly at his side. His lips were pallid from loss of blood, and it seemed as though such pain and exhaustion would quickly wear his life away. I said:

"'My dear boy, you are severely wounded.'

"'Yes; I am going to die.'

"'Wouldn't you like to have me write to your mother?'

"'O yes! I do,' he eagerly said; 'you will write to her, won't you? Tell my mother I have read my Testament and put all my trust in the Lord. Tell her to meet me in heaven, and my brother Charlie too. I am not afraid to die.'

"And then, exhausted by the effort, the head fell back and the eyes closed again. Several soldiers had gathered about, attracted by the patient heroism of the boy; and that sermon from those white lips was a swift witness to them of the power of the religion of Jesus. Strong men turned away to hide their tears as they saw that young soul, strengthened and cheered in its agony by the hopes of the gospel. It was not hard to assure him of Christ's love and remembrance, and lead him still closer to the Cross. At length the eyes opened again:

"'Tell my mother that I was brave, that I never flinched a bit.'"

We cannot forbear to record a rare instance of the devotion of a soldier to the spiritual welfare of his comrades in his last hours:

"W. E. Howard, of Douglass' Battery, a soldier from Texas," says Dr. J. B. McFerrin, "was converted in one of our revivals in the army and became an active, zealous Christian. During one of the fights last fall he was mortally wounded. Before his death he requested his effects converted into cash and applied to the cause of Christianity in the Army of Tennessee, especially in circulating religious reading among the soldiers. Lieutenant Harden thinks when all is realized there will be about eight hundred or one thousand dollars to dispose of in this way."

Of all who adhered most firmly to our cause in the

darkly closing days of the struggle, the women of the South have the noblest record. By their letters from homes, where they were pinched with want, they infused just courage into the hearts of fathers, husbands, and brothers, and held many a desponding soldier to the post of duty. The same writer, from whom we have quoted, says:

"'If I were to go home without leave,' said a Colonel to me yesterday, '*my wife*, though I am sure as anxious to see me as it is possible I should be to get home, would send me back.' You are right, sir, 'tis home influences that make us, under God, what we are. If a man falter, they at home are apt to be responsible. Depression is rather reflected from home on the army than from the army home.

"'You know the circumstances,' said an enraged soldier to me as to 'a father confessor,' asking my advice as to a rash act to which he felt he had justifiable provocation. 'Do you think my dear wife would think any the less of me if I did it?' 'She may not censure,' I replied, 'but she *must* regret. The *heart of your dear wife* would perhaps cling to you even in folly and crime, but you may *break* that heart.' The appeal was sufficient. 'Sir,' said he, 'I'll take your advice—I'll desist.'"

The women of the South were never happier than when serving the soldiers. On every great highway there were open houses for the weary, wounded, hungry, and footsore, where rest, and food to the very last quart of meal and pound of meat, were freely tendered. Speaking of what he saw at "Sunshine," the residence of Bishop George F. Pierce, near Sparta, Ga., Dr. E. H. Myers says:

"Bishop Pierce keeps the apostolic rule that a Bishop must be a 'lover of hospitality,' in which good work he is nobly seconded by a wife whose time seems almost wholly given to providing for the weary, wayfaring soldier. While I was at 'Sunshine,' the current of travel had somewhat slacked, yet, even then, the callers were at the rate of from twenty to thirty a day. Tired soldiers, wounded soldiers, want a shelter for the night; hungry soldiers want a lunch or a full meal; sick soldiers want a glass of milk, or some little delicacy; and these wants recur, not at regular meal-time, but at all hours of the day, and sometimes of the night. And the applicants are not denied. What though the cook is at work, with extra help, all day? The supply of prepared food must be kept up, and every needy case must receive attention. And thus has it been at 'Sunshine' since November, and thus must it be until another route for travel is opened." Such scenes were daily repeated in thousands of Southern homes.

The truly devout spirit that pervaded the armies of the South in the last days of the war could not be more fully shown than in the following resolutions adopted by Benning's, Bryan's, Wofford's, Anderson's, and Evans', brigades of Georgia troops:

"Resolved, 1st. That we hereby acknowledge the sinfulness of our past conduct as a just and sufficient ground for the displeasure of Almighty God; and that, earnestly repenting of our sins, we are determined, by his grace, to *amend* our lives for the future; and, in earnest supplication to God, through the mediation of his Son, Jesus Christ, we implore the forgiveness of our sins and seek the Divine favor and protection.

"Resolved, 2nd. That we earnestly and sincerely request our friends in Georgia to remember us in all their supplications at a throne of grace: praying that we may be enabled to continue steadfast in the foregoing resolve; that we may secure, through Divine grace, the salvation of our souls; that God may preserve our lives through the coming campaign, nerve our arms in freedom's contest, and crown our labors, privations, and toils, with Southern independence, peace, and prosperity."

"These resolutions," says Rev. T. B. Harden, ' were

unanimously adopted in every instance except one, and then there was but one vote in the negative."

The same spirit animated a large majority of the soldiers in other armies of the Confederacy, as they nobly stood with daily decreasing numbers in the darkly closing days of the war. Richmond, the centre of the struggle, was destined soon to hear the tramp of the last regiment of Southern soldiers as they departed southward across her burning bridges. A picture of the city at this period will not be out of place. As the capital of the Confederacy it was the point to which all eyes were turned. The various government offices added thousands to the population. Refugees crowded in from all parts of the State and from other States, until her population reached to nigh a hundred thousand. Nearly every dwelling-house was packed from cellar to garret. Beautiful women, refined and educated, and accustomed to all the luxuries of life, cleaned their own rooms, cooked their own meals, and endured all the privations of war with a patience, cheerfulness, and courage unsurpassed in the history of any people. A writer, from the midst of the scenes he describes, says:

"All the government departments are filled with fair workers. The most accomplished find employment in the War, Post Office, Commissary, and other departments requiring recording clerks, while others labor in the clothing and other inferior bureaus. Even the government telegraph office has its fair bevy of fair operators. Those who cannot obtain such positions as are mentioned betake themselves to the Confederate laboratory, or if no government employment can be had, turn a willing hand to any business which can earn them an honorable support. Not one of this vast crowd of refugee ladies is to be seen at the doors of the charitable institutions of Richmond. With a self-reliance which reaches sublimity, they depend wholly upon their own exertions in their hour of need.

"Many of these ladies are the descendants of the Masons, Henrys, Tylers, Tazewells, Randolphs, Wythes, Prestons, McDowells, Smythes, Paxtons, and other families of the Old Dominion, whose names are historic. Their ancestral homes are desolate or in ruins. Fire and sword, shot and shell, have made homes once blooming gardens of beauty, a blackened desolation. But there are no tears shed by the fair beings who are reduced to poverty. They think that from woman's lips should fall no murmur of complaint while soldiers brave all the hardships of war, in defence of the Old Commonwealth and her sister States of the Confederacy."

The condition of the Confederacy at this time cannot be conceived of by any one who did not live there as an actor in the bloody drama, now so near its close. The Federal armies drew nearer to the coveted Capital and to all the important lines of communication with the sister States of the South. They were daily growing stronger, while General Lee's army was daily growing weaker. The last desperate resolve was to ask the owners of slaves to send them to the camps of instruction to be drilled for soldiers. The proportion called for was twenty-five per cent. of all the male slaves between the ages of 18 and 45 in each State. General orders were issued relative to the treatment of these slave soldiers. The officers were ordered "to bestow humane attention to whatever concerned their health, comfort, and discipline—to a uniform observance of kindness and forbearance in their treatment, and to protect them from injustice and oppression." No slave was to be accepted as a recruit, unless with the owner's consent, by written instrument, confirming, as far as he might, the rights of freemen. But at the late period of the war when this scheme was adopted it was not possible to put it into execution, and it may be well doubted whether at an earlier date it would have been successful.

The evident purpose of General Grant to move his

left wing far enough to the south of Petersburg to cut General Lee's most valuable railroad line induced the Confederate leader to attack the Federals on their right, near the Appomattox river. The Confederates assaulted with their usual valor, and carried two lines of works and one or two heavy forts, but the Federals massed their artillery, and poured in so terrible an enfilading fire as to compel a speedy evacuation of the captured lines. Five Forks, fought on the first of April, compelled the evacuation of Petersburg and Richmond.

General Lee dispatched to President Davis that his lines had been hopelessly broken, and that the city should be immediately evacuated. This sad news was received by the President as he sat in his pew on Sunday morning in St. Paul's church. That night he left the city with the members of his Cabinet and the attaches of the several departments and retired to Danville. From that place he issued a stirring proclamation urging the Southern people to show that they were no less able to endure misfortune with fortitude than to encounter danger with courage. In a few hours after the departure of the government Richmond was in flames, and "all the hopes of the Southern Confederacy were consumed in one day, as a scroll in the fire." In the midst of the awful conflagration the Federal troops marched in and gazed upon the funeral pile of Southern hopes.

In the meanwhile General Lee, with the remnant of his army, was struggling through deep and miry roads towards Farmville.

He hoped to be able to reach Danville and establish a new defensive line along the Roanoke and Dan rivers, but the Federals, fresh and well-equipped, moving rapidly with heavy cavalry forces by parallel roads on his left, cut off that line of retreat, and the only alternative was to push directly to Lynchburg. The dispirited, weary and famished Confederates dropped out of ranks constantly as their lines straggled along the wretched roads, until less than ten thousand remained when they reached Appomattox Courthouse. But they stood ready in their pitiable condition to give battle at the signal of their Chief to the powerful army that was closing around them.

Those who were of that band of heroes know with what bitterness of grief they learned that their last line of retreat was cut off, and that the leader whom they loved as children love a father, rather than spill their blood in vain, had determined to surrender the fragment of the Army of Northern Virginia. Strong men sat down and cried like children; some, it is said, stuck their swords into the ground and snapped them asunder, while not a few made ready to escape through the closing lines of the Federals, for the purpose of joining the forces of Gen. Johnston in North Carolina.

The impression made upon the minds of the Federal officers and soldiers is given in the following extract from an oration before the Society of the Army of the Potomac, delivered by General Stewart L. Woodford, of New York:

"The morning crept slowly on—first into gray dawn, then into rosy flush. Still on! Still on! The mist crept upward and into line you wheeled, and on your musket lay down, each man in place, to get scant rest, which, even in terrible marching, you neither sought nor heeded. You were squarely across Lee's front, and had closed forever his last line of retreat.

"The enemy, reaching your cavalry advance, saw the serried line of Union troopers. Gordon gathered and massed his men for their last charge. Tattered and hungry, worn by ceaseless marching and fighting with no hope of victory, with little possible hope of escape, they closed their lines with fidelity of discipline and soldierly resolution, to which words can do little justice, but which each soldier's heart must recognize and honor.

"As the old guard closed around their Emperor at Waterloo, so those men closed around the flags of their lost cause. My heart abhors their treason. But it warms beyond restraint to their manhood so grandly brave, even in disloyalty. Slowly they advanced to their last attack. No battle yell, no crack of the skirmisher's rifle broke the strange stillness of that Sabbath morn. Steadily, silently they came when Sheridan drew back his horsemen, as parts some mighty curtain, and there stood the close formed battalions of infantry, the cannon gleaming in the openings, quietly awaiting the coming of Gordon's men.

"Instinctively your enemy halted. Meanwhile Lee has turned back to meet Grant and surrendered his command. Sheridan swung his cavalry around upon Gordon's left and was about to charge, when Custer reached Longstreet. Assurance of surrender was given, and the end had come.

"The Sabbath day, with tears and in sorrow, Southern men folded the banners of the 'Lost Cause,' and their bravest and best sought honorably to bury them from sight forever.

"How sad it is that poor ambitions, jealousies of race, the wretched greed of pelf and place, and the miserable hates of social rivalries should so often disturb the hearty reconciliation of that surrender, and for a time revive the bitterness which you then sought to bury in a common grave."

The interview between Generals Grant and Lee has often been described. We give the following from Gen. George II. Sharp, who was a member of General Grant's staff, and who witnessed the scene:

"They met in the parlor of a small brown house Gen. Grant sat in a rocking chair, not appearing to the best advantage, as he was without his sword, and his coat was buttoned up so carelessly that buttons and button-holes were in the wrong places. Lee sat proud and majestic, dressed in a new uniform that he probably then wore for the first time, every particle of his dress neat and soldier-like, down to the well-polished spurs. Grant apologized for not being equipped, having ridden out without his sword. Lee bore himself with composure, and betrayed his agitation only when the roar of 400 guns proclaimed the victory of the Union. Then General Lee glanced reproachfully toward Grant, as though to say, 'You might have spared me this.'"

The news of General Lee's surrender reached Mr. Davis at Danville on the 10th of April. He went thence to Greensboro, North Carolina, where he met Generals Johnston and Beauregard, both of whom assured him that in their judgment it was useless to continue the struggle. The surrender of General Johnston followed a few days after this interview, and all resistance to the Federal armies east of the Mississippi ceased. The army west of that river, under General Kirby Smith, soon after laid down its arms, and the great civil war was ended.

It is a noteworthy fact, and one that speaks well for the character of the American people, that the soldiers on both sides returned so quietly to the pursuits of a peaceful life after the disbanding of the armies. Throughout the South "almost every cross road," says an eminent writer, "witnessed the separation of comrades in arms, who had long shared the perils and privations of a terrible struggle, now seeking their homes to resume their pursuits as peaceful citizens. Endeared to each other by their ardent love for a common cause, their words of parting, few and brief, were words of warm, fraternal affection; pledges of endless regard, and mutual promises to meet again.

In closing our narrative the question arises, were the fruits of the army revivals enduring? To this question thousands can this day, more than twelve years after the banners of the South were furled, give an emphatic affirmative response. In all the churches of the South there are earnest, devout and active Christians, who date their spiritual birth from some revival in Virginia, in the West, or in the far South. And before them vividly rises the rude camp church, the gathering throngs from the various commands, the hearty singing, the simple and earnest prayers, the tender appeals of the loved chaplain, urging all who stand on the perilous edge of battle to fly for refuge to the Friend of sinners, the responsive approach to the place of prayer, the sobs, the groans, the tears of men who could look steadily into the cannon's mouth, the bright faces, the shouts and hand-shaking, and embraces of new-born souls—these are the bright spots to which memory returns and delights to dwell upon in that dark period that drenched the land in blood and put a load of grief upon every household.

Strange as it may seem to many readers, the call to preach the gospel of Christ came to the hearts of the men of war on the tented field; and no sooner were their carnal weapons laid aside than they buckled on the Divine armor, and, seizing the sword of the Spirit, entered the battle against the powers of darkness. In this we find one of the strongest proofs of the genuineness of the Army Revival. Truly, its fruits are still enduring. Thousands who were participants in that glorious and, to some, strange work, have passed the flood of death and are seen no more among men, but the seed they sowed in trench and camp and hospital, in the bivouac, and on the weary march, was watered from above and has borne a rich harvest. And may we not hope that the full fruition of this work is to be realized in that era of peace and good will which is even now descending upon our common country?

www.ingramcontent.com/pod-product-compliance
Lightning Source LLC
Chambersburg PA
CBHW020537300426
44111CB00008B/708